The Author in His Work

The Author in His Work

Essays on a Problem in Criticism

Edited by
Louis L. Martz and Aubrey Williams

Introduction by
Patricia Meyer Spacks

New Haven and London   Yale University Press
1978

Designed by Thos. Whitridge and set in Bembo type.
Printed in the United States of America by Vail-Ballou Press,
Binghamton, N. Y.

Published in Great Britain, Europe, Africa, and Asia (except
Japan) by Yale University Press, Ltd., London. Distributed in
Australia and New Zealand by Book & Film Services,
Artarmon, N.S.W., Australia; and in Japan by Harper & Row,
Publishers, Tokyo Office.

Library of Congress Cataloging in Publication Data
Main entry under title:

The Author in his work.

   "Bibliography of writings and editions by Maynard Mack":

   Includes index.
   1. English literature—History and criticism—Addresses,
essays, lectures.   2. Authors in literature—Addresses, essays,
lectures.   3. Mack, Maynard, 1909-   —Addresses, essays,
lectures.   I. Martz, Louis Lohr.   II. Williams, Aubrey L.
PR151.A95A9   820'.9   77-16309
ISBN 0-300-02179-8

To Maynard Mack
hominem agnoscis ex operibus eius

Contents

The Author in His Work: An Introduction   ix
PATRICIA MEYER SPACKS

Theme: The Poet in His Poem

"A Garden, and a Grave": The Poetry of Oliver Goldsmith   3
ROGER LONSDALE

Milton's Dialogue with Omniscience in *Paradise Lost*   31
GEORGE DE F. LORD

Creation and the Place of the Poet in *Paradise Lost*   51
JANET ADELMAN

Paradise Lost: The Solitary Way   71
LOUIS L. MARTZ

"The Counterfeit in Personation": Spenser's *Prosopopoia,
or Mother Hubberds Tale*   85
KENT T. VAN DEN BERG

Rochester: The Body Politic and the Body Private   103
RONALD PAULSON

"The Power of Prospect": Wordsworth's Visionary Poetry   123
R. A. FOAKES

"The Living World for Text": Life and Art in *The Wild Swans
at Coole*   143
DAVID YOUNG

Variations on the Theme

Conscience and Consciousness: Thomas More   163
RICHARD S. SYLVESTER

Shakespeare's Essays on Dramatic Poesy: The Nature and
Function of Theater within the Sonnets and the Plays   175
ALVIN KERNAN

"Give me your Hands": Reflections on the Author's
Agents in Comedy 197
EUGENE M. WAITH

Thomas Traherne: Revelations in Meditation 213
JAMES M. OSBORN

Rhetoric and Poems: The Example of Swift 229
WILLIAM K. WIMSATT

The Mystery of Personal Identity: Swift's Verses on
His Own Death 245
DAVID M. VIETH

Addison's Popular Aesthetic: The Rhetoric of the
Paradise Lost Papers 263
LILLIAN D. BLOOM

Allusion and the Definition of Themes in Congreve's
Love for Love 283
ARTHUR W. HOFFMAN

Allusion and Expression in Eighteenth-Century Literature 297
PETER HUGHES

Autobiography and the Eighteenth Century 319
GEORGES MAY

Johnson and Savage: Two Failed Tragedies and a Failed
Tragic Hero 337
FRANK H. ELLIS

The Significance of Biographical Context: Two Poems
by Lord Byron 347
JEROME J. MCGANN

Stendhal's Silken Prison 365
VICTOR BROMBERT

Spaces: *To the Lighthouse* 375
IAN GREGOR

Bibliography of Writings and Editions by Maynard Mack 391

Index 397

The Author in His Work

AN INTRODUCTION

The commentary assembled in this volume exemplifies the richness and some of the perplexities of criticism in our time. Maynard Mack's friends and admirers, as their statements inadvertently speak to and comment on one another, here honor a great critic in their practice of his craft. As they do so, they expose the difficulties and rewards of attending to the fact that novels, poems, meditations, plays, and periodicals issue from human minds while claiming reference to events and objects outside those minds. In *The Garden and the City* Professor Mack brilliantly analyzed the intricate connections between art and life in the case of Alexander Pope. Enlarging the scope of investigation to include literature by many authors in several genres and languages, the essays gathered here define further aspects of the convoluted link between works and writers. Like Pope, they show, other authors use their selves dramatically in their writing; as with Pope, to say so raises more questions than it immediately resolves.

The first group of essays, stating the theme as "The Poet in His Poem," implicitly and explicitly define three important issues emerging from consideration of six male poets writing in four centuries. One issue is the matter of literary vocation and how it functions as subject in various poetic modes. Writers as diverse as Rochester and Wordsworth reveal themselves quite specifically *as poets,* not as men, conveying their sense of the activity of poetry as symbolically all-inclusive. That activity has many ramifications, many relationships to other aspects of experience; the critic can describe its diverse patterns. But to focus on the poet's concern with himself as poet leads to a second problem: what do we mean, in these contexts, by "the poet"? We can hardly be so naïve as to assume a total identity between the historical figure who wrote *Paradise Lost*—whose nature, at any rate, must remain irrecoverable—and the figure of the poet evoked in *Paradise Lost;* to grant this implies a further range of dilemmas. A third issue emerges as one contemplates these two: how is the twentieth-century reader implicated in the interchange between poet-as-creator-of-the-poem and poet-as-imagined-presence-in-the-poem? Even perception of the necessary difference between these beings—both fictions, given the unknowability of the "real" poet—involves the reader in a covert drama of recognitions which generates part of the pleasure of the poetic experience. But the precise nature and source of that area of pleasure remain largely unexplored.

The critics represented in part one hint or investigate this group of problems. Roger Lonsdale establishes a context for his fellows as well as himself with his review of the critical history of Goldsmith's most famous poems. The shift from the nineteenth-century assumption that *The Traveller* and *The Deserted Village* acquire all their force from their autobiographical impact, to the more recent view that autobiography has no place in poems whose power derives from an interplay of rhetorical strategies, supplies material for an emblematic tale, reminding us how critical perception derives from critical fashion, what we see depending upon our position in time. From our present vantage point, Lonsdale suggests, we can glimpse more varied possibilities than our immediate predecessors perceived; we can thus avoid the simplifications of equating the experience recorded in a poem directly with that of its author, and also the opposed reductiveness of denying all connection between the internal and external happenings of a man's life and the events he chooses to set down. The special importance of "the poet" as subject for Goldsmith emerges by partial indirection, in his resolution of *The Deserted Village* through the unexpected image of Poetry departing from England's shores, an image which, as Lonsdale demonstrates, clarifies the emotional significance of other action in the poem.

For Milton, as three essays here make clear, his own role as poet becomes intimately involved with his epic theme. George Lord demonstrates how the steady dialogue, in *Paradise Lost,* between divine and mortal consciousness evokes the epic poet's double nature in the creative act. At once divine creator, summoning his own reality, and fallen man, he contains in himself much of the drama he reports as enacted by a more distant cast of characters. Janet Adelman, with a similar awareness of the poet's use of himself as character, emphasizes Milton's implicit perception of the danger for the poet of duplicating the sin of Satan (and of Eve) by making the self and a self-wrought creation the center of the universe. Only assurance of divine inspiration can protect the epic creator from the ultimate horror of solipsism. Louis Martz, inviting the reader's imaginative participation in his examination of *Paradise Lost* in the light of its ending, shows how the blind singer, "Adam's descendant," like Adam and Eve at the end and like Satan early in the poem, proceeds on a pilgrimage, his implicit goal, salvation, to be achieved only through sequential acts of loving remembrance; of such acts is *Paradise Lost* composed.

Spenser, Rochester, Wordsworth, and Yeats, the vastly different poets providing subjects for the remaining essays in this section, also share preoccupation with the meaning of acts of poetic creation. Kent van den Berg analyzes how levels of fiction making define the narrator's role in Spenser's *Prosopopoia,* the poet evoking the tension between a desire for masks and hatred of maskers; Ronald Paulson argues that the writing of poetry duplicated the symbolic outpourings of love and war for Rochester, who thought costiveness and looseness his only alternatives; R.A. Foakes reveals how a poet who made himself his primary subject struggled with the problem of self and object throughout his work; David Young demonstrates that Yeats in certain poems unites life and art as subject, enacting in the poems themselves the processes of discovery that produced them. The specific forms of poetic preoccupation, in other words, differ as much as one might expect. Yet at all levels of public performance—whether the poet claims, like Wordsworth and Yeats, to offer intimacies of self-revelation; or thunders in a God-gifted organ voice; or considers explicitly the problem of how public and private concerns relate to one another, as Rochester does; or presents himself, like Goldsmith, in postures which seem artificial through their very air of emphasis—these writers find ways to proclaim the high importance of their vocation.

To put the matter in this way, of course, evades the problems implicit in the notion of literary evocation of identity. The question of what one means by "the poet" demands lengthy exploration, but one can assume an area of general agreement about what is meant by the vocation of poetry writing. For all important poets between Spenser and Yeats, and for their critics, the act of creating poetry involves arrangements of language. Milton's procedures in arriving at linguistic patterns might differ from Wordsworth's, his sense of the meaning of the act would not entirely duplicate Rochester's, but all three men would concur in a belief that their occupation involved creating orders of words. The critics considering "the poet in his poem," accordingly, concentrate on what the poet does rather than who he is. When they touch on the latter issue, they often betray uneasiness. Van den Berg quotes Walter Ong on the necessary disguises of writing: "Masks are inevitable in all human communication." Adelman observes in a footnote that she uses the term "Milton" to designate both the narrator of *Paradise Lost* and the historical figure who created the poem "because these entities seem to me impossible to disentangle." Paulson acknowledges the practical problem confronting the critic ("we will never know what Rochester really was"), but points out the necessity of proceeding on the basis of educated guesses, attempting to discover the "fictions that derive from Rochester himself." Once one accepts the inevitability of masking, the direct proclamations of Wordsworth—this is how I feel, here is the way I once felt—become no less dubious than Rochester's assertions of physical impotence or, alternately, of extravagantly indulged lust. Wordsworth's statements actually mean something more like, "this is the way I want you to believe I feel." The kind and degree of belief we are willing to accord largely defines the nature of our response.

Thus the involvement of the reader becomes an issue directly implicit in any attempt to define the poet in his work. If poets create themselves as figures in their poems, readers choose, consciously or unconsciously, to accept such figures as more or less approximate to reality. Moreover, a poet's manipulations of his own presence in his work often involve the reader directly in the action and the problems of the poem. Thus, as Adelman points out, the pattern of imitation in *Paradise Lost,* with the figure of the poet duplicating on a lower level the divine act of creation, also implicates the reader, who faces in his / her own life necessities of choice comparable to those confronted by Adam and Eve, by Satan, and more immediately by the singer who relates their story. Spenser, van den Berg argues, likewise forces the reader into moral confrontations by his shifts in levels of discourse. Moving from simple to complex presentation of narrative, he challenges the reader to engage with the problems of interpretation which some characters in his story are themselves unwilling to face. Yeats, less challenging in approach, learns how to "allow the reader backstage," Young observes, in order to intensify the active process involved in vicarious participation in the poetic happening. The moral

and emotional drama involved in narrative and lyric poetry alike becomes part of the reader's direct experience, several of these critics
suggest, specifically through the ways that the poet emphasizes his
own role within his poem.

The modes of the reader's involvement and of the writer's manipulations of role become increasingly clear through the multiplication of
examples and of critical approaches in the second part of this volume,
"Variations on the Theme." Here, in fact, a new theme begins to
emerge: the importance and the range of artifice in literary creation.
The author presents himself in his work by a series of artifices; the
author in his work *is* in fact an artifice. The critic's awareness of artifice
leads, by a crucial and universal paradox, to revelation of a work's
conveyed authenticity. The dimensions of this paradox emerge most
distinctly in the first and the last essays in the second section, dealing
with a sixteenth-century man and a twentieth-century woman:
Richard Sylvester's piece on Thomas More and Ian Gregor's on Virginia Woolf. Sylvester, concerning himself largely with a relatively
"private" form of writing, More's letters to his daughter from the
Tower, demonstrates how, under sentence of death, More used role
playing as his crucial form of communication, the theatricality of his
self-presentation forcing his daughter, too, into a pre-established part.
To explain himself adequately was almost literally a life and death
matter—he could not hope to save himself from his fate, but only
adequate self-justification could give his death full public meaning.
His brilliant elucidation of the operations of his conscience (in the older
meaning of "consciousness" as well as in its modern sense) depended
on his deployment of artifice.

Virginia Woolf, by Gregor's account of her, began the writing of
To the Lighthouse from an almost diametrically opposed position. Unlike More, she ostensibly wished to create a fiction, its raw material
autobiography. Gregor shows how memory and fantasy were converted to art, and, more provocatively, he conveys how that conversion created new difficulties. The reader's perplexities about *To the
Lighthouse,* he suggests, may be epitomized in the discovery that
finally "there is nothing to separate the novelist from the novel": artifice has led back to life until the two inextricably merge.

The intricate relationships between artifice and actuality of course
bear directly on the issues established in the first section, although these
issues recur less insistently in the second part. The author's vocation as

subject has considerably less importance in the later essays. Alvin Kernan, writing about the Renaissance, points out that the high value of art
and of the artist became a new theme in the sixteenth century and
outlines Shakespeare's shifting examinations of and meditations about
drama's relation to reality, a relation which in its multiplicities helps
him to convey his sense of the ultimate power and significance of
art. James Osborn, considering the prose meditations of Thomas
Traherne, reminds us of the felt necessity that the writer subordinate
the importance of his creation to that of the spiritual ends it served. But
the related question, "Who *is* the writer?", takes on new complexity in
this part of the book, speci_ically in relation to the dominant issue of
artifice. Traherne's early readers, Osborn tells us, found his use of the
first person singular pronoun offensive in the context of religious
meditation. His insistence on using it implies recognition of the necessity of selfhood for experienced spiritual life, despite the fact that the
effort at self-transcendence supplies the center of that life. Traherne
represents one extreme of attempted authenticity; at the opposite extreme one finds the various versions of "Swift" in the lines on the death
of Dr. Swift. David Vieth defines them clearly—he who writes the
poem, the different he who composes the footnotes, the various Swifts
evoked in the text, both through the statements of others and through
those of the narrator. The mystery of the poem derives from the mystery of those divergent identities, poetic artifices which emphasize
human instability and the dubieties of perception. The fictionality of
the poet's character, thus acknowledged, focuses all responses to the
poem, although Vieth's summary of previous interpretations emphasizes the wide range of responses it makes possible. And that necessary ambiguity itself, it might be argued, contributes to the poem's
experienced import.

The ostentatious artifice of Swift's poem makes biographical interpretation, for a twentieth-century reader, obviously irrelevant to
understanding of artistic effect. Yet biography often demands attention as one tries to come to terms with the devices of authorial self-
presentation. Jerome McGann's account of the history of two Byron
poems comprises a lucid statement of the necessities of biography,
with implications beyond the specific texts he considers. Recognizing
the convenience of ignoring biography—a convenience of which critics have long availed themselves—McGann argues in relation to individual instances that to neglect the facts of a poem's composition may

distort, in large or small ways, the meaning of the work. To know the dates of Byron's poems, the women to whom they were addressed, the story of his relations with those women, necessarily affects one's comprehension of the texts. McGann does not, of course, argue that biography can substitute for criticism: the critical act begins with reaction to words on the page. But for adequate understanding of the nuances of those words, knowledge of biographical facts may be essential. Awareness of the human being who set pen to paper in the first place helps one to fathom a text which derives from human feelings. Conversely, as Victor Brombert demonstrates in the case of Stendhal, a text may lead back to the psychological matrices underlying it. The critic finds in the French novelist evidence of a persistent tension between yearning for lucidity and need to dissemble, a tension conveyed alike in works of fiction and of professed autobiography and in personal letters, a paradox which helps to account for characteristic patterns of imagery in Stendhal's work. Byron's artifices of poetic construction and poetic stance can be understood in relation to their historical origins; Stendhal's artifices of imagery reveal their creator's psychology. Writers before the nineteenth century, on the other hand, often insisted by implication on their *lack* of a psychology, defining themselves in relation to their audiences or in terms of a historical tradition rather than by personal reactions or feelings. Thus Addison, Lillian Bloom explains, in his *Spectator* essays on *Paradise Lost,* although he is using and exposing his own cherished aesthetic convictions, deliberately identifies himself from time to time with various critics of the past. Eugene Waith writes of the comic dramatist's devices for making actors into surrogates for himself—not to express his convictions from the stage, but to make specific claims on the audience, for approval and applause. The tradition originates in Roman comedy, but extends into the English Renaissance. Thus a form of writing in which the author is traditionally cut off from direct self-revelation evolves the artifices which allow him at least formalized self-expression.

One can know the author in his work, all these critics remind us, only through the study of his artifice. Yet artifice generates many sorts of knowledge: understanding of the writer as spiritual being (Traherne), awareness of the multiple possibilities of interpretation (Swift), alertness to biographical data (Byron) or to psychological nuance (Stendhal), to a critic's place in his tradition (Addison) or a playwright's in his (the comic dramatists treated by Waith). And it makes many kinds of demand on the reader. The reader belongs to the past as well as the present; authors have often defined themselves in relation to their original audiences in ways no longer central to our immediate experience of their work. The critic, however, can restore lost complexities. Thus Sylvester's account of More's letters stresses their relation to the specific reader to whom they were in the first instance addressed, the beloved daughter whom the letters involve anew in his drama. Waith reminds us of the dramatist's inevitable problem: how to manipulate his audience into the proper response. Early English playwrights, working with viewers more accustomed than we to classic stage conventions, employed those conventions to stress the importance of the audience, insisting that dramatic success depended on the affective response of those watching a play. Kernan's references to Shakespeare's audience apply alike to the original and the twentieth-century viewers of his work. Inasmuch as many plays deal with the power and the limitations of drama, the feelings and reactions of those watching, their sense of the meaning of what they see, must partly control the dramatic message. Thus the audience of *A Midsummer Night's Dream,* participating in the stage courtiers' mockery of a crude dramatic performance, becomes implicated in the question of whether even such crudities as Bottom's have some relation to a truth more profound than that of literal happening. Shakespeare both allows his viewers the pleasures of condescension and trains them to recognize its inadequacy as a total response.

Of course the audience of a stage performance has somewhat more reality—both literal and imaginable—than the reader of a text. More wrote to a specific person (granted, he also wrote for a larger, vaguer set of readers); he could therefore evade the problem of how to deal with an unknown audience. The reader, for most writers, is as much a fiction as "the author in his work" is for the individual reader. If the author makes himself known by his artifices, those artifices function primarily to affect, were presumably intended to affect, the unknown reader. Bloom suggests in some detail how carefully Addison worked to control the reactions of the original readers of *The Spectator,* a group whose nature and probable responses he believed himself to know. Closer in time to *Paradise Lost* than we, far more involved in debate about the epic, convinced of the importance of literary issues and more profoundly convinced of the high import of sacred subject matter, those readers nonetheless required, Addison believed, to be led by slow stages and clever devices toward the aesthetic convictions he wished to inculcate. This author can best be known in his work, Bloom argues by implication, through his mode of imagining his reader. Swift's relation to his readers, as evoked by Vieth, differs dramatically from that of his near-contemporary. If Addison tries to control each response, Swift aggressively asserts the impossibility of control, given the self-absorption of human beings. "Affective reading," Vieth maintains, must supply the clue to the meaning of the verses on the death of Dr. Swift; the diverse possibilities of such reading point backward to the painful wisdom of the poem's creator.

Any reader of this collection will recognize some obvious and important relationships among individual essays, often emphasized by their arrangement. William Wimsatt on Swift leads to Vieth on Swift; Arthur Hoffman on allusion in Congreve prepares for Peter Hughes on eighteenth-century allusiveness in general; Georges May on autobiography precedes Frank Ellis on a Johnson biography and McGann on the uses of biography. But subtler connections also operate. Most of the pieces just mentioned touch only indirectly on the critical categories thus far established—largely ignoring the significance of the artist's vocation, the perceived nature of the writer in his work, the relationship of the reader to writer and work—yet they generate possible conclusions about all three through their concentration on specific aspects of literary artifice. Frank Ellis writing of Dr. Johnson, for example, puts the *Life of Savage* into the context of Johnson's failed tragedy and Savage's and outlines the formal arrangement of the biography in relation to a model of tragic form. By implication, Johnson (or "Johnson") thus emerges in a fresh light; but Ellis makes no direct claim of the revelatory significance of his finding. Similarly, Hoffman on Congreve: he argues that the structure of allusion in *Love for Love* should be taken seriously, showing how literary references control the comedy's meanings in richer and more subtle ways than other commentators have perceived. The meaning of this allusiveness to our understanding of Congreve as a figure glimpsed behind and through his drama remains undefined but richly implicit.

The other three essays hitherto neglected in my summary—Wimsatt's on the poetry of Swift, Hughes's exploration of allusiveness in eighteenth-century literature, May's discussion of autobiography—bear in particularly suggestive ways on the themes that emerge through this collection. Hughes and May, dealing with large subjects, refer to many authors and many texts; Wimsatt confines himself to a narrow aspect of the work of a single poet. But all three critics illuminate the relationship between a mode of exegesis concentrating on formal aspects of a text and the desire implied by the title of this volume, that criticism should lead back to heightened awareness of human reality.

Wimsatt concerns himself mainly with technical aspects of Swift's poetry: his development of an "anti-sublime and anti-pathetic idiom" of tetrameter couplets. What does Swift's technical choice of the short rather than the long couplet mean and imply? For Swift, it meant "release and freedom"; Pope, on the other hand, found the short couplet "a hobble." As Wimsatt elaborates the freedom Swift found and made through his chosen form, he provides a dazzling demonstration of the implications of technique. Swift's interest in objects, in metamorphosis, in the commonplace, in the ironies of assumed or of barely imaginable relationship, his energy and exuberance—all, we are shown, express themselves through his poetic form. One can concentrate even on the inclusions and exclusions of a single rhyme, learning thus about its maker. Wimsatt's own choice of technique in this essay—his decision to focus on what seems simple and small—declares his own allegiances as he clarifies Swift's.

Georges May contemplates the literary genre (he argues, however, that it is *not* a genre) traditionally involved with self-revelation. Wimsatt shows the unexpected revelatory power of technical decisions; May reminds us of the complex motivations involved in documents which claim to expose the self. His approach historical, he asks why autobiography suddenly flourished in the eighteenth century, and in beginning to answer that question he demonstrates the ultimate impossibility of resolving historical issues. But his approach implies something about many authors in many works. What may be most important, in the context of this collection as a whole, is its reminder that the author in his work comprises a social as well as an individual phenomenon. Autobiography in the eighteenth century, as May explains, may be characterized partly by its new stress on individual self-exposure. Yet this stress itself reflects historical conditions. May considers the trend toward secularization, the intensifying belief that truth emerges through an accumulation of particulars, the gathering suspicion that truth might be subjective. The attitudes implied by such trends, beliefs, and suspicions affected virtually all thinkers; the proliferating documentation of individuality thus reveals the kind of internal experience that individuals in a given social climate share.

Hughes's sense of the meaning of history differs from May's. In his
essay on eighteenth-century allusion, he attempts to reconstruct verbal phenomena of the past in relation to a specific literary situation with
little reference to the social. Arguing that the importance of allusion in
the eighteenth century has been both neglected and misunderstood, he
claims that the constant references to an earlier tradition imply less the
burden of the past than that of the present, the effort of such writers as
Swift and Pope to escape from the heavy allusiveness and excessive
productivity of their contemporaries into a use of parody and imitation which conveyed relative respect for their ancestors, contempt for
their literary siblings. "The solution found by eighteenth-century
writers," Hughes believes, "had to lie in making of the way back a new
way forward." Through both referential and repetitive allusion, they
enriched their texts, generated meanings, and declared a relationship
with the past dependent not on any providential theory of history but
on a belief in the continual transformability of relevance.

Both Hughes and May suggest, then, that any effort to discover the
author in his work must involve awareness of the special language in
which he writes, a language individually defined in every instance but
belonging also to a period, a set of conventions, and behind the conventions, of convictions, and of communal hopes and anxieties. One can
start with the particular—a rhyme of Swift's—or with the general—
the new literary phenomenon of autobiography, or a period's characteristic emphasis on parody. In either case, form leads back to feeling:
the progress implicit in all the essays in this book. Pope declared as
critical essentials "A *Knowledge* both of *Books* and *Humankind*." The
essays collected here suggest how the one leads to the other.

Patricia Meyer Spacks

Theme: The Poet in His Poem

ROGER LONSDALE

"A Garden, and a Grave":
The Poetry of Oliver Goldsmith

I

Oliver Goldsmith remains notoriously the most elusive personality in the otherwise voluminously documented Johnson circle, no less a puzzle to the modern biographer than he appears to have been to his contemporaries. And if the appearance of Arthur Friedman's edition of the *Collected Works*[1] has imposed some order on what had been a confusingly miscellaneous literary output, Goldsmith's place in eighteenth-century literary history, whether as satirist or sentimentalist, as late neoclassicist or proto-Romantic, seems to be a subject which still offers plenty of scope for discussion.

In one area, however, that of his two most ambitious poems, agreement appears to have been reached during the last decade. Ricardo Quintana's essay on *The Deserted Village* in 1964,[2] a corrective to naïve interpretations of the poem as an emotional utterance by Goldsmith himself, stressed instead its rhetorical artistry, in which the "I" in the poem is a point of view manipulated by the poet like a character in a play, by no means to be confused with the "real" Goldsmith. "After all, Goldsmith was an Augustan," Quintana declares, and to the Augustans, who thought in terms only of general human experience, direct self-revelation was foreign. Later critics have elaborated this rhetorical emphasis. Richard Eversole[3] has argued that in *The Deserted Village* the "disposition of thought conforms to the structural rules of a classical oration" and, with the assistance of Cicero and Quintilian (and, some may think, Procrustes), has discovered a traditional seven-part rhetorical structure in the poem. We are to consider its apparently personal emotion, its sentimentalism, as no more than a device to persuade the poet's audience to agree with his political thesis.

Leo F. Storm has gone even further in detaching the poet from his poem.[4] Not merely is the sentimental aspect "a conscious rhetorical device for heightening the drama of the poem rather than . . . a revelation of Goldsmith's personal stress of feeling": even its ideas, the earnest condemnation of luxury and its attendant social evils, need not be thought of as convictions seriously held by Goldsmith himself, in a poem the basic concern of which was merely "to defend the conservative social order." Formally the poem blends aspects of the English georgic and of topographical poetry, and exploits the stock emotional and intellectual associations of these familiar genres for the rhetorical purpose of dramatizing a degenerating society. R.J. Jaarsma[5] has also argued that *The Deserted Village* must be understood as "a kind of poetry that exercises a deliberative control over its material." The view that the poem "is a kind of *cri de coeur* may safely be dismissed": Goldsmith is no "romantic, longing for a return to thoughtless innocence," nor is Auburn the recreation "of a lonely mind almost drowned by waves of sentimentalism." The essence of the poem is its protest against the destruction of humanistic social values and Auburn is merely a device to reveal the glaring impotency of modern social progress. The eviction of Goldsmith from his poetry was completed in 1969 by Robert H. Hopkins, in the course of an elaborate discussion of *The Traveller*.[6] On no account is the "I" in the poem to be equated with Goldsmith himself. Quotations from Aristotle's *Rhetoric* enable us to understand that the persona's appeals to our pity and sympathy are merely devices to condition us to the political argument of a poem which cannot "be legitimately read as autobiographical statement," but "must be viewed in the objective context of rhetoric."

Such unanimous disapproval of any tendency to an autobiographical reading of Goldsmith's poetry might be interpreted as an indirect tribute to the strength of the temptation to indulge in it. Nineteenth-century readers of Goldsmith, of course, surrendered enthusiastically to that temptation, for *The Traveller* and *The Deserted Village* seemed to lend themselves better than most Augustan poetry to a demand for a close and "sincere" relationship between the poem and the poet's personal life. Sir James Prior, Goldsmith's biographer, found in *The Deserted Village* "those personal allusions that always add to the interest of a poem." For Washington Irving, the poem was "truly . . . a mirror of the author's heart and of all the fond pictures of early friends and early life for ever present there." Thackeray described Goldsmith as "the most beloved of English writers," explaining that "Your love of him is half pity," pity for "the career, the sufferings, the genius, the gentle nature" of "this honest soul" as revealed directly in *The Deserted Village,* in which "the whole character of the man is told." Far from finding him elusive, the nineteenth-century reader was confident that Goldsmith spoke spontaneously and openly of his own life and sorrows in the poetry, the very absence of precise biographical information about the man only encouraging this belief. In 1900 Henry James summed up the attitude of the previous century to *The Vicar of Wakefield* in terms which apply equally well to the poetry:

> The books that live, apparently, are very personal. . . . The author of this one never, at any rate, lets go our hand; and we, on our side, keep hold with a kind of sense, which is one of the most touching things our literature gives us, of all that, by doing so, we make up to him for.[7]

Goldsmith's reputation was probably at its highest when he could inspire in his readers this response of mingled love and pity to a curious entanglement of himself and his writings. The corrective emphasis of modern criticism was desperately needed if greater eighteenth-century poets than Goldsmith, notably Pope, were to be appreciated. It is unnecessary to chart the process by which the poet has been separated from his poem, a process aided by influential theories of authorial impersonality, the distinction between "the man who suffers" and "the mind which creates," the weighting of tradition or sociology against the individual talent, and a renewed emphasis on rhetoric and the persona. In the crucial reappraisal of Pope, there has been no more influential essay than Maynard Mack's "The Muse of Satire,"[8] which insisted on the traditional aspects of his satiric voice, on the distinction between the historical and the dramatic Pope. More recently, in *The Garden and the City,* Mack has brilliantly analyzed the dramatic figure who speaks in Pope's later satires to demonstrate the blending of the personal experiences of the "real" Pope of Twickenham with features deriving from Roman models and seventeenth-century retirement literature.[9] Mack declares at once that he is offering literary history and biography rather than criticism, from which the former are "more or less separable." Yet the effect of his demonstration of the complexity of the poetic Pope should be a deterrent not merely to those who would make simple assumptions about poetry as self-expressive, but, implicitly at least, to those who would confine themselves at the other extreme to a strictly rhetorical approach.

The self-dramatization in Pope's later poetry, a fact hardly digested in our generalizations about his age, might be considered a unique case, since he could blend traditional and rhetorical elements with a level of personal experience which was verifiable, not merely retrospectively, but by his original audience. Pope's contemporaries did not and could not venture so far: the "I" in their poetry, if projected at all, speaks either as a virtually anonymous, judicious intelligence, who can count on the agreement of the reasonable members of his audience, or as a traditional poetic personality, adopting standard and recognizable genre guises, or as an ironically but unambiguously impersonated mask. When, as is evidently the case with Goldsmith, the poetic "I" seems to speak more idiosyncratically, especially when projecting a problematically suffering self, we can either decide that this is a different kind of poetry (the currently unfashionable resort to Pre-Romanticism), or seek some way of accommodating the phenomenon to the assumption that all eighteenth-century poetry is public, traditional, and formally contrived. If such "sentimentalism" cannot be identified as ironic (the preferred solution), the alternative is to categorize it as rhetorical. The rhetorical "I," as we have seen, remains essentially impersonal, an emotional self projected merely for persuasive purposes, its only function to alter the reader's opinion.

Apart from avoiding simpleminded reading of the poetry as autobiographical statement, the rhetorical approach has a further advantage. Sentimental or didactic aspects of the "I," which would be unattractive or unconvincing if attributed directly to the poet himself, are apparently acceptable if they can be thought of as part of a quasi-theatrical performance by a manipulated poetic self. The limitation of the approach, however, is simply the nature of the questions it begs, its sweeping identification, for example, of Goldsmith as securely "Augustan" in his poetic habits and intentions, and its assumptions about the static nature of eighteenth-century poetry. The evidence suggests that, on the contrary, by the mid-century a number of poets were fumbling in various ways to discover a personal voice which could not be reduced simply to the anonymous, traditional, or rhetorical. I have attempted elsewhere,[10] no doubt temerariously in the present climate, to trace some features of Thomas Gray's tentative search for acceptable poetic means of speaking of personal experience, in an age which officially doubted its interest or value. The case of Goldsmith might also deserve reconsideration, to discover whether the attraction of the rhetorical approach is also its limitation, its fastidious distaste for what is likely to be disconcertingly messy: the complex possibility that the increasingly obtrusive "I" in later eighteenth-century poetry is combining traditional features and rhetorical habits with genuinely self-expressive intentions.

The evidence must ultimately be the poetry itself, and the exercise proposed is not the traditional pursuit of literal parallels with Goldsmith's biography. Yet since the rhetorical approach rests on crucial if implicit assumptions about Goldsmith's intentions, evidence about his attitude to his own poetry might have clarified the situation. Most of what we know about the man, however, in the years in which he wrote *The Traveller* (1764) and *The Deserted Village* (1770), derives from Boswell's far from sympathetic depiction of him, from a few uninformative letters, and from a fund of usually farcical or dubious anecdotes. There is more striking and consistent evidence, about his personality at least, in the previous decade, the years following his departure from Ireland, in the letters he wrote to relatives and friends, whether they are read as directly confessional or as in themselves "rhetorical" attempts at persuasion (self-justification, appeals for money or sympathy). Throughout these early years in Edinburgh, Holland, and London, Goldsmith—often well aware of the "egotism" of his letters—is preoccupied with his loneliness, poverty, social inferiority, and unprepossessing appearance and manner. Melancholy, self-derisive, with a frustrated sense of his own talents, resentful of the contempt which he has habitually received—whether in Ireland, in spite of his nostalgia for it, or in his first years in London, because of those Irish origins themselves—the young Goldsmith is a strikingly self-conscious and self-absorbed figure, even, or perhaps especially, when indulging in humorous but intense fantasies about his future fame.[11] As early as 1753 there is a revealing echo of Gray's *Elegy,* published only two years earlier: "Poverty, hopeless poverty, was my lot, and Melancholy was beginning to make me her own." The echo betrays the attraction of the figure of Gray's isolated, melancholy, doomed poet in that conclusion to the *Elegy* which Goldsmith would later particularly praise as "pathetic and interesting."[12]

There is at times a curious and in some ways gratuitous transference of this awkwardly self-conscious self into the literary personality projected in Goldsmith's early miscellaneous prose, as in the anxious, blundering self which admits its own self-conscious pretense of ease and impudence in the introduction to his short-lived periodical *The Bee* in 1759.[13] (Goldsmith was fascinated by distinguished men— Samuel Butler, Berkeley, Boyle, Pope—whose genius was belied by an unattractive appearance or awkward manner.[14]) The self, when it obtrudes, is always problematic: "when we talk of ourselves, Vanity or Resentment have always too much to say," he commented cryptically at the very end of his series of "Chinese Letters" in *The Public Ledger*.[15] Yet when collecting these essays as *The Citizen of the World* in 1762, Goldsmith spoke openly, if anonymously, in his introduction about his isolation and frustration:

> But at present I belong to no particular class. I resemble one of those solitary animals, that has been forced from its forest to gratify human curiosity. My earliest wish was to escape unheeded through life; but I have been set up for half-pence, to fret and scamper at the end of my chain. Tho' none are injured by my rage, I am naturally too savage to court any friends by fawning. Too obstinate to be taught new tricks; and too improvident to mind what may happen, I am appeased, though not contented. Too indolent for intrigue, and too timid to push for favour, I am—But what signifies what am I.[16]

One of the essays in *The Citizen of the World* describes a poet reading to a club of authors an epic poem which, he explains, is "an heroical description of nature. . . . The poem begins with the description of an author's bed-chamber: the picture was sketched in my own apartment; for you must know, gentlemen, that I am myself the heroe." The enterprise is clearly preposterous, yet rather, one suspects, because of its incongruous heroic pretensions than because of its author's impulse to describe himself and his own humble circumstances. Goldsmith had in fact sent a version of these lines in 1759 to his brother Henry and, in spite of their ostensibly comic purpose, their resemblance to his own situation at that time has been noted. The complexity of his attitude to the poet's self-centered epic is suggested by the fact that he later adapted the lines as part of his depiction of the humble happiness of Auburn in *The Deserted Village*.[17]

There is little that is heroic about Goldsmith's own life. In spite of his later literary success, his financial incompetence meant that he was almost continuously dependent on the booksellers for a living. Even if his early distaste for the mere "compilations" of others—as opposed to true scholarship—necessarily modified as he himself attempted to justify the popularizing historical, literary, and scientific compilations of his later years, it is hard to believe that he viewed these profitable enterprises with any deep satisfaction.[18] Goldsmith was also sensitive enough to know very well that his contemporaries to the end of his life saw him, with attitudes ranging from the amicably patronizing to the contemptuous, as a somewhat ludicrous figure. Biographically, his two major poems, both written with painstaking care and with no immediate financial motive, almost certainly represent what he himself considered the only true manifestations of his literary integrity and talent. In that sense their function was that they should deserve his own respect and demand that of the literary world.

II

As we approach his poetry, it would simplify matters if it were clear that Goldsmith, the impersonal rhetorical strategist of the modern critics, had in practice any enthusiasm for the art. On the contrary, in reviews and essays Goldsmith repeatedly attacked the assumptions of formal rhetoric, especially as employed in instruction in oratory. The terms in which he does so, sometimes with the aid of the *Encyclopédie,* are clearly as relevant to writing as to oratory. In *The Bee* he mocks the "pedants" who

> have ranged under proper heads, and distinguished with long learned names, *some* of the strokes of nature, or of passion, which orators have used. I say only *some* for a folio volume could not contain all the figures which have been used by the truly eloquent, and scarce a good speaker or writer, but makes use of some that are peculiar or new.

In his subsequent discussion of the inadequacies of English preaching, he demands a greater appeal to the passions of a popular audience, "not by the labours of the head, but the honest spontaneous dictates of the heart." The fervor and spontaneity of the preaching of the Methodists, of whom Goldsmith has otherwise a low opinion, explain their greater effectiveness.[19] In another attack on rhetoric, he mentions the two ancients recently enlisted by critics to enable us to read his own poetry.

> These strong and vigorous emotions, therefore, can be no where taught, but they may be extinguished by rule; and this we find actually to have been the case: we find no Grecian orator truly sublime after the precepts of Aristotle, nor Roman after the lectures of Quintilian.[20]

Goldsmith's objections spring from a deeper source than dislike of rhetorical figures. They are directed against assumptions calculated to inhibit the speaker or writer, to obstruct communication between the natural emotions of the orator or poet and the hearts of the audience, and to falsify the true voice of feeling. Within the limits of the critical vocabulary available to him, his views on poetry are consistent with this position.

It might no doubt be argued that Goldsmith's own poetry merely displays a "rhetoric" of sincerity and spontaneous emotion and that he would still expect his reader to respond to the "I" in his poetry as to a dramatic performer manipulated by a real and unaccountable Goldsmith in the background. A neglected comment on Savage's *The Bastard* in 1767 makes clear that Goldsmith did not take for granted that poetry must be read in this way:

> Almost all things written from the heart, as this certainly was, have some merit. The poet here describes sorrows and misfortunes which were by no means imaginary; and, thus, there runs a truth of thinking through this poem, without which it would be of little value, as Savage is, in other respects, but an indifferent poet.[21]

Even if Goldsmith's response to the poem must have been reinforced by Johnson's moving *Life of Savage,* the attraction of the poetry of sincerity, grounded in real experience, is clear. The comment on Savage also clarifies Goldsmith's aims in the poem he had himself published three years earlier.

The dedications to his two major poems deserve particular attention, for they provide the best guidance we will obtain about the response Goldsmith hoped for. In the first state of the first edition of *The Traveller,* published in December 1764, the dedication consists of a single sentence, inscribing the poem to the Reverend Henry Goldsmith (a clergyman in Ireland) from "his most affectionate brother, Oliver Goldsmith." In the second state, which appeared shortly afterwards, Goldsmith's name was placed for the first time on the title page of one of his works, and the dedication was greatly expanded.

Goldsmith now explains the propriety of the affectionate dedication to his own brother by the fact that "a part of this Poem was formerly written to you from Switzerland." The subsequently verifiable fact that Goldsmith had indeed travelled in Switzerland some ten years earlier is less relevant than what he was choosing to emphasize to his original readers: that his poem had a genuine autobiographical basis. In other words, the poet within the poem, seated on a mountain in Switzerland and addressing his brother, is equated with the real Goldsmith who addresses his brother Henry in his dedication to the poem. Goldsmith emphasizes his brother's humble and pious life *because* of its relevance to his poem: "It will also throw a light upon many parts of it, when the reader understands that it is addressed to a man, who, despising Fame and Fortune, has retired early to Happiness and Obscurity, with an income of forty pounds a year." Henry's "sacred office," his humble but useful life as a clergyman, is contrasted with those who labor in "the field of Ambition," and of all kinds of ambition "that which pursues poetical fame, is the wildest." Goldsmith's own poem is thus deliberately characterized as a manifestation of such rash ambition, rash because of the factors which, as he goes on to explain, threaten true poetry: over-refinement in the arts, which has led "the powerful" to neglect poetry for painting and music; learned criticism, mistakenly seeking to "improve" poetry by emphasis on its self-conscious technical aspects; and partisan politics, which have made crude political satire (presumably that of Churchill) fashionable. Goldsmith's own aim is to moderate political hostility, by showing that equal happiness can exist under different forms of government and that any principle of happiness can be carried to excess. Such an aim, implicitly, is not merely for the good of the nation: Goldsmith has said enough to suggest that he is also concerned to create the conditions in which his own poetry would be appreciated.

It would be naïve to read *The Traveller* as a literal outpouring by the "real" Goldsmith, just as it would be rash to ignore conventional elements in the presentation of the "I" in the poem. Yet it is hard to see what more Goldsmith could have done to place his poem in an autobiographical context and to verify it as a genuine autobiographical utterance. Efforts to relate the poem to established genres usually relapse into gestures towards pastoral, georgic, and topographical poetry, ignoring the fact that it is a verse epistle addressed by Goldsmith to his own brother. Such verse epistles from abroad, as Dodsley's *Collection* indicates, form a recognizable subgenre in the period, and at times *The Traveller* echoes earlier poetic contrasts of European nations with each other or with Britain. What is impossible to ignore, both in the dedication and in the poem itself, is the enlarge-

ment of the decorously personal but non-self-revelatory element in
the traditional verse epistle, to the point where the reader could hardly
avoid feeling that, as Goldsmith would later say of Savage's poem,
"the poet here describes sorrows and misfortunes which were by no
means imaginary." The point may seem an elementary one: and yet
Hopkins's elaborate analysis of the poem neglects the dedication, repeatedly insists that the "I" in the poem is "not to be equated with
Goldsmith," that it cannot "legitimately be read as an autobiographical statement" but "must be viewed in the objective context of
rhetoric," ignores the presence of the brother within the poem, and
looks instead to Aristotle for guidance in responding to it.[22]

The proof sheets of the poem show that it was originally to have
been called *A Prospect of Society*.[23] When published, it was entitled *The
Traveller, or A Prospect of Society,* a sufficient indication that the narrator himself was to be as much the subject as its political content. The
expansion of the dedication continues the process to the extent of in-
forming the reader that the "I" in the poem *was* to be equated with
Goldsmith himself. A sentence in the dedication later omitted, no
doubt because of its slightly ludicrous implications, still indicates
Goldsmith's frustration at the difficulty of speaking directly to the
hearts of his readers, a situation oddly recreated by a rhetorical reading
of the poem: "Though the poet were as sure of his aim as the imperial
archer of antiquity, who boasted that he never missed the heart; yet
would many of his shafts now fly at random, for the heart is too often
in the wrong place."[24]

Yet examination of the poem itself may suggest that Goldsmith
had in fact underestimated the problems created by his personal presence in the poem and that he found it difficult to draw the poetic self and
its predicament into a coherent relationship with his philosophic and
political concerns. He was seeking a response from both the head and
the heart of his reader, and his success in unifying it is limited. The
opening of *The Traveller* draws at once on the situation established in
the dedication. No convention would seem to account for the emphatic portrayal in lines 1–10, with their suspended syntax and
weighty movement, of the poet as a melancholy, friendless wanderer
against a broad European background, a "houseless stranger" whose
heart turns "with ceaseless pain" to his brother. Indeed, this deeply
personal note will be convincing enough to call into question the authority of any other tones the poet may subsequently adopt. Lines

11–22 endow the dwelling of the poet's brother, his "earliest friend," with overtones of sanctity and blessedness. Yet from such humble happiness, benevolence, and hospitality, which he once shared, the poet is mysteriously but emphatically excluded (23–30). His predicament of lonely wandering, of exile from the "Blest . . . spot," is unexplained: he is passively "destin'd" and "impell'd" by "fortune" to wander and yet to "find no spot of all the world my own."

At line 31 the poet's utterance is fixed in time and place: "Even now, where Alpine solitudes ascend," he sits for "a pensive hour . . . / . . . above the storm's career," to look down upon the "hundred realms" visible below him. This elevated perspective, even if only a temporary respite, marks the moment of attempted conversion of the exiled wanderer's unhappy isolation into a traditional philosophical detachment. Yet Goldsmith finds it no easy matter to make sense of the poetic self's spiritual exhaustion, to construe such deprivation in acceptable terms (37–50). To "repine" amidst such "store"—"Creation's charms" as embodied in the prospect before him—would be "thankless pride" towards the beneficent Creator. Apparently it is the poet's "philosophical mind" which is in danger of arrogantly disdaining the satisfactions ordained by Providence for ordinary men. If the narrator's predicament is hardly elucidated, it is now possible that by leaving the "blest . . . spot," his brother's household, he himself disdained those "little things" which "are great to little men." The philosophical compensation ought to be, as the poet knows, that kind of cosmopolitan sympathy which "Exults in all the good of all mankind," as Lien Chi Altangi had earlier explained in *The Citizen of the World:* "The philosopher, who extends his regard to all mankind, must have still a smaller concern for what has already affected or may hereafter affect himself; the concerns of others make his whole study, and that study is his pleasure."[25] Lines 45–50 accordingly rehearse, in what is in effect a form of serious parody, the conviction that a proper sense of the blessings of Creation on all men is a sufficient compensation for the poet's private sorrows.

Yet the apostrophic style of these lines betrays the uneasiness of the effort to move from self-absorption into philosophic sympathy with the good of mankind, to accept that, even if there is "no spot of all the world my own" (30), it is consolation enough to find that "the world, the world is mine" (50). The following paragraph (51–62) admits as much. An apparently querulous voice in the harmony of man, nature and God regularly celebrated by his contemporaries, the poet compares himself to a "lone miser," who rejoices in heaven's blessings, but still sighs and yearns for more. At first the simile seems to characterize the poet's own lonely longing as unattractively selfish and even obsessive. Hopkins sees it only as an effective rhetorical anticipation of the poem's main concern, its "indictment of laissez faire political economy," and quotes at length from Malachy Postlethwayt, a contemporary economist, to illustrate the age's attitude to the evils of hoarding.[26] Goldsmith's own views on misers might seem more relevant. On at least three occasions in *The Bee* he had argued that misers, who "have been described as madmen, who, in the midst of abundance, banish every pleasure, and make, from imaginary wants, real necessities," have been misrepresented by "the vain and idle." They are usually "Men who, by frugality and labour, raise themselves above their equals, and contribute their share of industry to the common stock." Indeed, "it were well, had we more misers than we have among us. I know few characters more useful in society."[27]

Such passages should not merely correct facile assumptions about Goldsmith's economic views but emphasize the dangers of making all elements of a poem rhetorically subservient to some sweepingly defined purpose. And yet, whatever Goldsmith's own views, to choose to present the poetic self through the traditionally despised figure of the miser is an acknowledgment of the dubious respectability of self-absorbed introspection and betrays Goldsmith's difficulty in giving the narrator's private predicament, the lonely yearning of the miser, a more acceptable meaning. What is in fact offered is an unexpected version of Pope's "Self-love and Social [are] the same." Just as the misunderstood miser, according to *The Bee,* serves society, it turns out that the poet's sorrow is not after all self-absorbed:

> Yet oft a sigh prevails, and sorrows fall,
> To see the hoard of human bliss so small;
> And oft I wish, amidst the scene, to find
> Some spot to real happiness consign'd,
> Where my worn soul, each wand'ring hope at rest,
> May gather bliss to see my fellows blest.
>
> [57–62]

The poet's apparent ingratitude is on behalf of mankind. The "sympathetic mind" is unable to rejoice with conviction in the general good when mankind is still relatively so unblessed. We will be given no more adequate explanation of the poet's lonely wanderings and "worn soul" than this: that he is seeking, on behalf of mankind, the good society in which his own "real" happiness will be to recognize that of others.

What is puzzling about this explanation is that the poet had seemed in the opening lines to have identified just such a "blest . . . spot" in his brother's household: its unexplained inaccessibility makes its existence only the more obtrusive. Similarly, in the next two paragraphs (63–80), the cosmopolitan poet's mild irony against the narrowly "patriotic" instinct which leads all men to describe their own as "the happiest spot" is itself ironically qualified by his own original painful recognition that "His first best country ever is at home." Furthermore, the patriotic delusion, man's very ability to adapt to extremes of climate, is clearly in itself a kind of happiness, as Goldsmith's later discussion of different nations will show. The irony turns inadvertently back on the disabled poet-philosopher: to travel in search of happiness is only to equip oneself to assess the limitations of the happiness of others, and to lose one's own capacity for it.

Such ironies, springing from the poet's own conspicuous presence as melancholy seeker of happiness, seem to have been too complex or involuntary to sustain. Not surprisingly, Goldsmith starts to play down the subjective aspect. Suddenly it is "we," not "I," who "roam" and "compare" the blessings of different nations (73–75) and whose "wisdom" (77) will in due course arrive at judicious conclusions about them. Yet even as the poet begins to adopt the tone of a confident lecturer ("But let us try these truths with closer eyes," 99) addressing a larger and more representative audience than his brother, he must attempt to dispose of the problematic, suffering self:

Here for a while my proper cares resign'd,
Here let me sit in sorrow for mankind,
Like you neglected shrub, at random cast,
That shades the steep, and sighs at every blast.
[101–04]

Hopkins's comment that "rhetorically" the simile "reminds the reader again of the tone that the narrator holds toward the argument which he presents" seems curiously uninformative.[28] The lines make clear that the poet's idiosyncratic sorrows, his "proper cares," are after all

obstinately distinct from his generous "sorrow for mankind," revers-
ing the fusion attempted in lines 57–62; and we are reminded that they
will be ignorable only "for a while." To go on to describe that aspect of
the self which remains as a neglected, sighing shrub, cast at random on
the hillside, is almost ostentatiously to insist on the unhappy private
predicament of the judicious surveyor of nations who now takes over
the poem.

The following survey of Italy, Switzerland, France, and Holland
(105–316), in which Goldsmith reveals considerable descriptive
power and some epigrammatic talent, need not be followed in detail.
The assessment of the happiness of each country, and the argument
that each tends to concentrate dangerously on some favorite happiness
(as if by some national ruling passion), are, in tone at least, objective
and judicious. The symmetry of the balancing of the effects of Nature
and Art in each society, and of the contrast between the different nations, supports the authoritative tone. At line 313, however, the poet
begins once again to obtrude emotionally, his agitation proceeding
from his concern at the state of Britain, where, while the climate is
mild, the extremes lie in the proud, rational, freedom-loving, self-
venerating British themselves. The blessings of British freedom are
balanced by evils: proud self-dependence leads to neglect of natural
and social claims, even to conflict, ferment, and faction. The natural
"bonds" which should link men in harmony are replaced by enslaving
"bonds" of wealth and law (349–60). Unexpectedly, the first victims
of this dangerous situation in Britain are "talent" and "merit" (354).
The reference to poets who once, with reasonable expectations,
"wrote for fame" (358) recalls the contrast in the dedication between
the wild ambition of seeking poetical fame and Henry Goldsmith's
humble retirement from the world. The threats to poetry described in
the dedication, over-refinement and political faction, are apparently
identical with the evils which threaten the national well-being in the
poem itself.

If the emotional "I" who returns at line 361 is no longer the detached, judicious lecturer on European nations, he is still on the whole
distinct from the passive and mysterious sufferer of the opening of the
poem. His emotion is that of apparently justified indignation at identifiable evils. The exclusion of the more problematic self is enacted in a
revision Goldsmith made at this point. The poet denies (361–62) that,
by stressing the dangers of Freedom, he intends to flatter the monar-

chy or the aristocracy. In the first edition, he had gone on to exclaim, "Perish the wish; for, inly satisfy'd, / Above their pomps I hold my ragged pride." The poet's "ragged pride" too obtrusively detracted from the authority of the analyst of Britain's ills, awkwardly recalling the friendless wanderer of the poem's opening, who had seemed anything but "inly satisfy'd," and the couplet was removed. Otherwise, the mounting emotion at this stage of the poem recalls the fervent (and more embittered) indignation of Pope's later satires, as the poet's normally "Calm . . . soul" (379) is roused by such evils as aristocratic contention for power at the expense of the monarchy and control of the law by the rich.

At line 393 the poet once more addresses Henry Goldsmith ("Yes, brother, curse with me . . ."), as if seeking to establish some connection between the personal sorrow focused initially on his brother's dwelling and his present state of patriotic indignation, which has led him, somewhat self-consciously, to "Tear off reserve, and bare my swelling heart" (390). Hitherto his concern at the state of Britain has noticeably failed to embody itself in any single, expressive visual image. Now the poet deplores the triumph of wealth in Britain by defining it as the exchange of her "useful sons" as colonists for the "useless ore" of foreign luxuries (397–98). The following description of Opulence maintaining her grandeur by depopulating villages (401–12), as is well known, anticipates the elaborate treatment of the subject in *The Deserted Village*. The poet's anguished, sympathetic imagination visualizes the innocent villagers as passive exiles in a savage colonial America (413–22), "Even now" entangled in dangerous forests, threatened by savage beasts, murderous Indians, and violent storms, surrounded by "distressful yells":

> The pensive exile, bending with his woe,
> To stop too fearful, and too faint to go,
> Casts a long look where England's glories shine,
> And bids his bosom sympathize with mine.
>
> [419–22]

The last line is unexpected. Surely it is the poet's role to sympathize with the exiled villager? Obviously, the pensive exile may well share the poet's outraged conviction that "England's glories" are ill-purchased at the cost of such suffering. Yet the line seems to mean more: that the nature of the suffering of the poet and the exile is identi-

cal. The private predicament of the opening of the poem, consciously
set aside in its "philosophical" center, has reemerged, validated by
patriotic indignation, to project itself into the fate of the villagers, a
nightmare version of the poet's own exile. The equation of the "pensive exile" in America with the mysteriously deprived poet, who is
spending a "pensive hour" on a mountain to utter this meditation, is
even clearer in the earliest version of line 422, in which the villager
"gives his griefs to sympathize with mine." The inaccessibility of his
brother's happy dwelling to the poet, puzzling in the literally autobiographical terms invoked by Goldsmith himself, is half-explained
by its imaginative equation with the once happy but depopulated village later in the poem. But what also emerges is that, like the villager,
the poet's more immediate exile is caused by his rejection from a society increasingly dominated by wealth and political faction, a spiritual
alienation from a Britain inimical to poetry itself and the values on
which it depends. The threats to poetry, as outlined in the dedication,
are also those which depopulate villages.

Goldsmith may well have intended to conclude the poem with this
only half-articulated identification of poet and villager. The earliest
version of the poem, *A Prospect of Society,* ends at this point, and it is
likely that it was Samuel Johnson who insisted on a more lucid and
orthodox resolution and, indeed, wrote half of the final paragraph.[29]
Goldsmith, however, begins it: "Vain, very vain, my weary search to
find / That bliss which only centers in the mind . . ." (423–24). Di-
vergence between the problematic and judicious selves in the poem is
reflected in the two possible readings of this couplet, which presumably means that the search for anything other than inner happiness is
vain but half-admits that, in the poet's own case, the search for inner
happiness is itself futile. Under Johnson's influence any such wavering
is only momentary, and the poem concludes in a mood of resolute
Christian stoicism, Johnson himself contributing all but two of the last
ten lines. Although there may be terrors and tyrannies under any form
of government, they hardly affect the happiness, the "domestic joy,"
of the individual, "which no loud storms annoy." Perhaps echoing the
original search for "a spot" which the poet could call "my own" (30),
Johnson ends the poem by insisting that "reason, faith and conscience"
are "all our own" (438).

Hopkins, admitting the difficulty created by this anti-political
conclusion to a supposedly rhetorical political poem, concludes that

the poet has resolved to be "inner-directed": when "cohesive government fails" the individual must find happiness in his own virtue.[30] The effect of Johnson's conclusion is, however, emphatically different: that such matters as "cohesive government" are *irrelevant* to the individual. It is far from clear, indeed, what the poet himself resolves—in his own person he ends with a baffled question (425–26)—or, moreover, what inner or external resources are available to him. What "pleasure and repose" or "domestic joy" await the pensive poet, who is still after all a neglected sighing shrub on a foreign mountainside? If the message that "no loud storms" need annoy the individual will be of little comfort to the exiled villager, above whom "the giddy tempest flies," it will be hardly more consoling to the poet himself, elevated only temporarily "above the storm's career" on his mountain.

In effect Johnson's conclusion to the poem subverts all that has preceded, prescribing indifference not merely to the poet's own fate and "proper cares" (101), but to all that had enabled him to move sympathetically out of the self: the hope of greater happiness for mankind, sorrow at the dangers of corruption in man and society, anxiety at the specific evils threatening his own country. Goldsmith's only contribution in the last ten lines is a single couplet (435–36), which revealingly alludes to two examples of barbarous and excruciating punishment of those who dared to oppose the *status quo:* in the context of Johnson's dignified and reassuring conclusion, they obtrude as if to register the painful suppression of sympathetic imagination which has taken place.[31]

Ultimately, of course, as the dedication had made clear, the poet is a version of Oliver Goldsmith, who has after all made his way from his mountaintop to London, where he is now publishing his poem as an act of wild poetic ambition. Whatever problems the disturbed and disturbing poetic self had created within *The Traveller,* it would not seem unreasonable to conclude that one purpose of the poem was the self-dramatization of the poet; or, inverting the recent "rhetorical" approach, to assert that its philosophical and political content should be read as no more than a rhetorical device for winning respect and sympathy for the poet. Frederick M. Keener has recently described Pope as "a man who, with more dedication than any English poet before him, tried to speak out of his own quotidian life in an attempt to win the love of his readers, by being, as much as possible, convincingly himself."[32] If Goldsmith, less adequately equipped in most ways than Pope, was similarly seeking the love of his readers, his poem apparently won it for him. Hitherto an anonymous or laughable figure in the literary world, Goldsmith was suddenly respected and celebrated. According to Sir Joshua Reynolds, "His *Traveller* produced an eagerness unparalleled to see the author. He was sought after with greediness." Mrs. Cholmondeley, after hearing the poem read aloud by Johnson, graciously exclaimed, "I never more shall think Dr. Goldsmith ugly."[33]

III

The evidence of *The Traveller* suggests that Goldsmith's instinct was to move towards what Wordsworth would later praise in "that class of poets, the principal charm of whose writings depends upon the familiar knowledge which they convey of the personal feelings of their authors." Wordsworth was discussing Burns: "On the basis of his human character he has reared a poetic one, which with more or less distinctness presents itself to view in almost every part of . . . his most valuable verses"; and again, "Not less successfully does Burns avail himself of his own character and situation in society, to construct out of them a poetic self,—introduced as a dramatic personage. . . ."[34] Yet it is noticeable that, when he came to publish *The Deserted Village* in 1770, Goldsmith made no attempt to give the poem any literal autobiographical status. He may have become aware in *The Traveller* of the problems and restrictions entailed in such a procedure. There was, moreover, little in his actual circumstances which might encourage him to make them the basis of a dignified poetic self, as Pope had eventually done and as Cowper, for example, in a quite different way would do early in the following decade ("My delineations of the heart are from my own experience"[35]).

The rhetorical critics, refusing to treat *The Deserted Village* as literal nostalgia for his childhood on Goldsmith's part and concentrating on the poem itself, have undoubtedly illuminated certain aspects of its method and preoccupations. Their insistence on a total distinction between Goldsmith and the "I" of the poem would no doubt be more convincing if that poetic self were clearly differentiated from the "I" of *The Traveller*. Yet, as Johnson observed, the later poem was "sometimes too much the echo" of *The Traveller*,[36] and there is nothing to indicate that the "I" in *The Deserted Village* is not essentially the same self as had proved so appealing in the earlier poem, identified firmly as Oliver Goldsmith. The characteristics and preoccupations of the later "I" are strikingly similar to those of *The Traveller*. Indeed, if elements which had tended to remain discrete or even to conflict in *The Traveller* are now more adequately fused, it is through a more consistent and intimate presentation of the poetic self and its response to the ruined landscape in which the poet stands. The emphatic account of "my wanderings round this world of care" (83–96) and the search for happiness which has brought him back to Auburn seem explicitly to allude to the poet of *The Traveller* ("My prime of life in wand'ring spent and care," 24), as do the themes of dispossession and exile and the tones of patriotic indignation. If both poems could be described as topographical, the landscape of Auburn is, of course, surveyed in no judicious cosmopolitan spirit: what now concerns the poet is the landscape of memory, an internalized topography. As a result, the disparity between the problematic and judicious selves in *The Traveller* is replaced by a relatively unified poetic self, whose melancholy is explicable and justified, and whose personal emotional involvement is more sustained. What had remained at best a tentative recognition in *The Traveller* of the shared fate of poet and exiled villagers becomes in *The Deserted Village* the poem's central situation.

Recent critics of the poem would still consider such features of the poem as subservient to its primary aim of persuasion to a political viewpoint (however defined). In this situation the poem's dedication turns out once more to be relevant. *The Deserted Village* is addressed to a much more distinguished figure than Henry Goldsmith, but Goldsmith noticeably makes Sir Joshua Reynolds a fraternal substitute for the brother who had died in 1768: "The only dedication I ever made was to my brother, because I loved him better than most other men. He is since dead. Permit me to inscribe this Poem to you." Goldsmith then makes what must seem a remarkable admission about his poem. He acknowledges that Reynolds, like "several of our best and wisest friends," will object that the rural depopulation it deplores does not exist and that "the disorders it laments are only to be found in the poet's own imagination." To such a reaction Goldsmith can oppose only the sincerity of his convictions and his conscientious observations in the countryside. Yet the whole question of rural depopulation, implicitly admitted to be controversial and complex, would require more elaborate discussion than he wishes to offer. He prefers not to "tire the reader with a long preface," when he wants instead "his unfatigued attention to a long poem." Goldsmith's final paragraph relates his views on depopulation to the increasing "luxury," which politicians consider to be a national advantage. Allying himself with the ancients in the belief that luxury destroys kingdoms, he admits that "so much has been poured out of late on the other side of the question" that his own views are virtually isolated.

Goldsmith surely concedes a remarkable amount, not merely to economists, politicians, and the general tide of opinion, but to the views of his "best and wisest friends," such as Reynolds. It is more than an admission that his views are highly personal, since he acknowledges that those who know him best believe that the poem really embodies the "disorders" of the poet's own imagination. Nothing in the rest of the dedication is calculated to challenge this judgment. The effect of the dedication is not, as in the case of *The Traveller,* to identify the poem as literally autobiographical, but to emphasize its direct relationship to Oliver Goldsmith in another way, in its origins in his idiosyncratic imagination.

It is hard to believe that Goldsmith was unaware of the reaction he would obtain. Indeed, his dedication may even have encouraged it. The first reviewers of *The Deserted Village* all separated what they took to be its highly dubious politicoeconomic argument from its unusual imaginative appeal.[37] If, as we are now told, the poem's rhetorical purpose was political persuasion, it should at least be admitted that, as far as its immediate audience was concerned, the poem was a striking rhetorical failure. The first readers of *The Deserted Village* evidently thought it quite as reasonable to read the political content as an occasion for the exercise of the poet's sensibility and imagination, as to insist that these aspects of the poem were purely rhetorical in function. It is also an undeniable fact that within a generation admirers of *The Deserted Village* were assiduously exploring every possible autobiographical feature of the poem, and investigations of its literal origins in the poet's own childhood in Ireland had reached elaborate proportions by 1811.[38] No earlier English poem had excited—or invited?—such a response.

Goldsmith's emphasis on his "imagination" in the dedication, however, may have been an instinctive precaution against a too literal reading of the poem, either as autobiography or as an economic tract. It is worth emphasizing that *The Deserted Village* is only incidentally (305–08) concerned with the enclosure and redistribution of the land, which undoubtedly had a disturbing effect on the poorer rural classes, but which was an essential accompaniment to the major agricultural improvements which took place during the century. Goldsmith's concern is primarily with a different and tangential issue, the acquisition and improvement of pleasure parks by wealthy members of the aristocracy and middle class. In certain cases the improvement of such estates could involve the clearance of local communities,[39] although Goldsmith's friends and reviewers refused to believe that the practice was widespread. Yet out of this situation Goldsmith devised a simple formula for England's ruin, which his imagination found deeply compelling: wealth made in the colonies is being used in Britain to force the humbler rural classes to emigrate to the colonies. For this reason, Goldsmith's pessimistic vision, in a period proud of its agricultural achievements, is of a countryside in the process of devastation; and for the same reason that vision was from the first recognized as highly idiosyncratic. Even Goldsmith's own dedication concedes his friends' belief that he was reading his own problems into the landscape.

As for the poetic self within *The Deserted Village,* in spite of efforts to reduce it to pastoral, georgic, or loco-descriptive conventions, there is no precedent, except less elaborately in Gray's *Elegy,* for a poem in which the poet's own memory and imagination actively recreate its essential landscape. John Scott of Amwell, in the long discussion of the poem in his *Critical Essays* (1785), was puzzled by its "desultory structure" (apparently failing to recognize its artful rhetorical design as expounded by recent critics).[40] Yet Scott's desire for a more orderly contrast between Auburn in the past and in the present might in itself point to what Goldsmith was in fact attempting: a structure which went some way to embody the flux of personal emotion and memory, the coexistence of past and present in the reflecting mind.

To state as much is merely to make clear the obvious psychological and poetic limits to Goldsmith's ability or intention to render with "Romantic" fidelity the subtle movements of consciousness. *The Deserted Village* is very far from being mere emotional flux. The repeated contrasts of the once happy and now deserted village lead to indignant general conclusions about the reasons for this state of affairs. Goldsmith's manner is at times didactic and oratorical. "Sweet Au-

burn" *is* an idealized embodiment of health, innocence, and content-
ment, and of doomed rural virtues in general. The poet, although
affectionately remembering the "seats of my youth," tends to remain
an observer of the village's life even in his recollections, loitering and
pausing in the landscape, hearing Auburn's mingled sounds from a
hillside, ultimately detached as if in part the reader's sympathetic representative in his own memories, with touches of self-conscious condescension at times to the "honest rustics." On the other hand, his
account of his hopes of returning to Auburn to impress the villagers
with his knowledge of the world is disarmingly derisive of this very
role (89–90), and his personal response to Auburn is most convincing
when simplest and most specific, as in the description of its evening
sounds and in the central character sketches. John Scott's comments on
the diction of such passages can remind us of the original freshness of
what we now take for granted. Such passages seemed to Scott to "convey village ideas, in village language" and only just to escape being
"prosaick or mean": they are acceptable only "because we know that
they are the effect of choice, not of incapacity."[41]

Scott also drew attention, with some distaste, to another aspect of
the poem's diction, which may lead finally to preoccupations in the
poem ignored in recent discussions. As Scott pointed out, certain
words are repeated, especially in the opening description of Auburn, in
an almost obsessive manner: "sweet," "lovely," "smiling," "dear,"
"charms."[42] Goldsmith's aim seems not merely to have been to
achieve an almost incantatory lyrical effect at points (for example, 31–
36), but to insist by means of this diction on the sexual identity of
Auburn as an innocent girl, who will be betrayed, raped, or prosti-
tuted.[43] The "bashful virgin" (29) and "coy maid" (249), who help to
focus this aspect of the happy village before the outrageous activities of
the "tyrant" (37) (the exact nature of his desecration is left vague at
first), are survived in the ruined village only by the "wretched ma-
tron," "yon widowed, solitary thing" (129–136), who must labori-
ously eke out a pathetic living from the wasteland. She is not, of course,
quite the sole survivor, for she has been joined by the poet himself. In a
way that at first seems only incidentally curious, the poet and the
wretched old woman are equated by the description of her as "The sad
historian of the pensive plain" (136).

The sexual theme becomes explicit in lines 287–302, the repetitions of "charm" and "charms" linking the passage with the opening

description of Auburn. Goldsmith compares a declining nation, betrayed by luxury and resorting to surprising splendors while its peasants are scourged from the land, to a "fair female," who could afford to be "unadorned and plain" in her youthful beauty, owing nothing to art, but who must resort to "all the glaring impotence of dress" as her "frail" charms fade. Auburn itself had embodied the healthy and innocent condition of the nation, yet the "fair female['s]" vulnerability to the processes of time in Goldsmith's simile might seem to give the nation's decline an inevitability distinct from the specific causes he deplores. Underlying the passage is that familiar and virtually irresistible cycle from simplicity to refinement to decadence which animates so much of Goldsmith's writing about politics, history, and the arts.

Almost immediately the sexual theme recurs, as the poet sympathetically imagines the fate of villagers driven to the city. Such exiles include "the poor houseless shivering female," lying "Near her betrayer's door" (325–36). Yet unexpectedly, Goldsmith makes clear that it was this girl's own ambition, not the depredations of the "tyrant," which had led her to leave her innocent village for the town. Such an emphasis might suggest a vulnerability in Auburn itself (not merely to time or to the local "tyrant") hardly to Goldsmith's purpose, although the "frail" charms of the female in the earlier simile (291) might now retrospectively acquire a further sexual implication. Goldsmith, however, explicitly refuses to envisage a similar fate for the "fair tribes" of Auburn, who are obliged to emigrate instead (337–41). Yet the description of the ruined girl may have implications which go beyond incidental pathos. Within the poem only one other ambitious wanderer had voluntarily left the country for the town, the poet himself, and the possibility emerges that his fate, involving some loss of innocence or prostitution of his talents, has been similar.

Throughout the poem the obtrusion of the poet's own memories, hopes, and disappointments have entangled his experience inextricably with that of Auburn. Its innocence had been his, its destruction the ruin of his hopes, and the sympathy the villagers deserve is hardly to be distinguished from the sympathy to which the poet himself is entitled. In Gray's *Elegy* the escape from the predicament of the mournful poetic self is enacted by means of sympathy for others (villagers once more), which in turn entitles the poet to a sympathetic epitaph: the poet, inhibited from demanding sympathy directly on his own behalf, can arouse it for a projection of the deprived self. The same process is enacted in different terms and with less inhibition in *The Deserted Village*. As in *The Traveller*, the villagers are exiled to a strange and menacing environment. By now, they have become little more than personifications of the rural virtues whose supposed disappearance the poet deplores (363 ff.).

The effect of this disembodiment of the villagers is to allow a final emphatic obtrusion in the poem by the poet himself, which has perplexed some critics but which serves to bring to the surface a number of underlying preoccupations. The poet, pondering in the ruined landscape on the departure of the "rural virtues" from England, unexpectedly reveals in his long final apostrophe that "sweet Poetry" is also departing:

> And thou, sweet Poetry, thou loveliest maid,
> Still first to fly where sensual joys invade;
> Unfit in these degenerate times of shame,
> To catch the heart, or strike for honest fame;
> Dear charming nymph, neglected and decried,
> My shame in crowds, my solitary pride.
> Thou source of all my bliss, and all my woe,
> That found'st me poor at first, and keep'st me so.
>   [407–14]

This is no mere routine assertion of the link between Poetry and Liberty. It would appear that Poetry itself and the poet's renunciation of her—or, perhaps, Poetry's renunciation of the poet—rather than politics or economics is the true subject of the poem. The reappearance of the recurrent diction of its opening links "sweet Poetry," "loveliest maid," "Dear charming nymph" with sweet, lovely, dear, charming Auburn in its happiness; and Poetry can preserve her virtue from "sensual joys"—rape and prostitution—only by departure and exile. Auburn evidently represented not merely the rural virtues which avarice destroys, but the kind of poetry which is rooted in them and which is similarly vulnerable in a commercial society. Poetry's inability "To catch the heart, or strike for honest fame" recalls precisely Goldsmith's pessimism, in his dedication to *The Traveller*, about the folly of poetical ambition and the poet's inability to reach the heart. In a society where Poetry is "neglected and decried," it becomes a furtive, introspective pursuit, "My shame in crowds, my solitary pride." The poet's poverty, a favorite topic of Goldsmith, is only an outward manifestation of the indifference of society to his art. A less clearly articulated consequence of the female personification of Poetry is the suggestion in lines 411–14 of some inadequacy in the poet himself, as if Poetry were a beautiful woman whom the poet had compromised and could not honestly maintain. Having come close to a personal renunciation of his art (at least one reviewer reading the passage so[44]), Goldsmith depersonalizes the final lines, encouraging Poetry to resume her proper role elsewhere than in Britain, notably in remote and primitive parts of the world. Samuel Johnson once more stepped in to close down the poem, with four massively clinching lines (427–30).

Thus *The Deserted Village* itself enacts the collapse of the very poetic conventions in which it might have sought refuge: the pastoral and georgic modes are devastated within the poet's own imagination, the traditional celebration of retirement (97–112) is mocked by the ruined village to which the poet has "retired," the only topography worth describing is the landscape of memory, the tyrant's ravages are a hideous parody of the tradition of "country house" poetry still available to Pope, and the whole poem negates the familiar "Whig" panegyric of English commerce and liberty.

The closing lines of the poem finally (in more than one sense) invoke another poetic form, the "progress poem," in which Augustan poets had celebrated the westward migration of Poetry and Liberty from ancient Greece to Britain. It is possible, however, to overestimate the optimism implicit in the form. As Aubrey Williams has shown, *The Dunciad* is in one aspect a grotesque inversion of the process, describing instead the relentless progress of barbarism and darkness[45]; and even if such poets as Collins and Gray had continued to explore the form, an increasingly frustrated note of uncertainty about the actual "progress" of poetry and liberty in Britain is evident. Goldsmith's variation of the form is drastic in its implications. The closing lines of *The Deserted Village* apparently dramatize that precise moment in the "progress" of Poetry when she necessarily departs from Britain's shores in search of a more hospitable environment. As she does so, Goldsmith is driven to counter his own despair by uncharacteristically apostrophising the primitive visionary role of Poetry, its connections with liberty and prophecy, the functions it can no longer perform in England. He does so partly by echoing the lines in Gray's *The Progress of Poesy* which describe, in the words of Gray's note, the "Extensive influence of poetic Genius over the remotest and most uncivilised nations; its connection with liberty, and the virtues that naturally attend on it."[46] Unlike Collins and Gray, who had sought ways of availing themselves of it in their own poetry, Goldsmith could only acknowledge this power and then renounce it, envisaging no personal compensation or redemption in the visionary powers of the imagination. Left alone in a landscape which is at once "a garden, and a grave" (302), he has no role but the provision of appropriate epitaphs for those who survive only in his memory, and for his own art. His poem has enacted what, a decade earlier, he had dreaded: that "the muse shall seldom be heard, except in plaintive elegy, as if she wept her own decline."[47]

NOTES

1. *Collected Works of Oliver Goldsmith,* ed. Arthur Friedman, 5 vols. (Oxford, 1966), hereafter cited as *Works.* I have quoted Friedman's text of the poems throughout.

2. "*The Deserted Village:* Its Logical and Rhetorical Elements," *College English* 26 (1964):204–14.

3. "The Oratorical Design of *The Deserted Village,*" *English Language Notes* 4 (1966): 99–104.

4. "Literary Convention in Goldsmith's *Deserted Village,*" *Huntington Library Quarterly* 33 (1970): 243–56.

5. "Ethics in the Wasteland: Image and Structure in Goldsmith's *The Deserted Village,*" *Texas Studies in Literature and Language* 13 (1971): 447–59.

6. *The True Genius of Oliver Goldsmith* (Baltimore, 1969), pp. 66–95.

7. Quotations are from *Goldsmith: The Critical Heritage,* ed. G. S. Rousseau (London, 1974), pp. 69,268,296,339–41.

8. *Yale Review* 41 (1951): 80–92.

9. *The Garden and The City: Retirement and Politics in the Later Poetry of Pope* (Toronto, 1969).

10. *Versions of the Self: The Poetry of Thomas Gray* (Chatterton Lecture, British Academy), 1973. An important aspect of attitudes to this development has been usefully traced by Leon Guilhamet, *The Sincere Ideal: Studies on Sincerity in Eighteenth-Century English Literature* (Montreal, 1974), which does not, however, refer to Goldsmith's poetry.

11. *The Collected Letters of Oliver Goldsmith,* ed. Katharine C. Balderston (Cambridge, 1928), esp. pp. 5,12,14,16,27–28,31,38,57–58,66.

12. *Collected Letters,* p. 16; Gray, *Elegy,* 120; *Works,* 5:320.

13. *Works,* 1:353.

14. *Works,* 1:207–09, 3:34,45,253.

15. *Works,* 2:476 n.

16. *Works,* 2:15.

17. *Works*, 2:128; *Collected Letters*, pp. 63–65; *The Deserted Village*, 227–36.

18. For Goldsmith's varying attitude to "compilers" and "compilations" see *Works*, 1:136,161,234,306,356; 2:86;4:329; 5:296,314,317,330, 332–33,336,354. For a revealing passage on the theme "I must write, or I cannot live," see *Works*, 3:182–83.

19. *Works*, 1:476, 481.

20. *Works*, 1:169. For similar attacks on rhetoric see also 1:334–35 and 463–64.

21. This is Goldsmith's introductory comment on *The Bastard* in his anthology *The Beauties of English Poesy* (1767), *Works*, 5:326.

22. Hopkins, *The True Genius*, pp. 69,95.

23. *Works*, 4:238; and my edition of *The Poems of Gray, Collins and Goldsmith* (London, 1969), pp. 623–24.

24. *Works*, 4:246 n.

25. *Works*, 2:189.

26. Hopkins, *The True Genius*, pp. 76–77.

27. *Works*, 1:407,437,460–61.

28. Hopkins, *The True Genius*, p. 80.

29. For Johnson's part in the poem see my edition of *The Poems of Gray, Collins and Goldsmith*, pp. 623–25.

30. Hopkins, *The True Genius*, pp. 91–92.

31. See *Works*, 4:269 n. It may be added that Adam Smith's influential discussion of sympathy in *The Theory of Moral Sentiments* (1759) opens with a discussion of our response to the idea of a man tortured on a rack. But Goldsmith would also remember Voltaire's assertion of the irrelevance of the celebrated Damien case to normal civilized life (such as his own in Switzerland) in a letter translated by Goldsmith in *The Bee* in 1759 (*Works*, 1:392).

32. *An Essay on Pope* (New York, 1974), p. 142. Mr. Keener makes a vigorous case for a closer connection between the "real" Pope and his poetry as a whole than has recently been fashionable.

33. Sir Joshua Reynolds, *Portraits*, ed. F. W. Hilles (New York, 1952), p. 44; *Johnsonian Miscellanies*, ed. G. B. Hill (Oxford, 1897), 2:268.

34. *A Letter to a Friend of Robert Burns* (1816) in *The Prose Works of William Wordsworth*, ed. W. J. B. Owen and J. W. Smyser (Oxford, 1974), 3:123, 125.

35. Quoted by Guilhamet, *The Sincere Ideal*, p. 255.

36. Boswell, *Life of Johnson*, ed. G. B. Hill and L. F. Powell (Oxford, 1934–52), 2:236.

37. See *Works*, 4:279–80; my edition of *The Poems of Gray, Collins and Goldsmith*, p. 672; *Critical Heritage*, pp. 76–80,84–86.

38. See Edward Mangin, *An Essay on Light Reading* (1808), pp. 136–50 and especially R. H. Newell's edition of the *Poetical Works* (1811); but the autobiographical reaction had begun earlier.

39. See Paul Mantoux, *The Industrial Revolution in the Eighteenth Century* (London, 1928, rev. ed., 1961), pp. 171–72; A. J. Sambrook, "An Essay on

Eighteenth-century Pastoral, Pope to Wordsworth (II)," *Trivium* 6 (1971): 103.

40. *Critical Essays* (1785), p. 251.

41. *Critical Essays*, p. 267. In his "Life of Parnell," published three weeks after *The Deserted Village*, Goldsmith attacked the misguided innovations of contemporary poets, who imagine "that the more their writings are unlike prose, the more they resemble poetry" (*Works*, 3:423).

42. *Critical Essays*, pp. 253–59.

43. Morris Golden drew attention to female innocence as a symbol in the poem in "The Broken Dream of *The Deserted Village*," *Literature and Psychology* 10 (1959):41–44, although his purpose and conclusions are somewhat different from mine. That the childhood world of Auburn is innocently sexless is less clear than Golden suggests: the "bashful virgin" (29) permits herself "side-long looks of love" and the "coy maid" (249) is—ambiguously—"half willing to be prest."

44. John Hawkesworth in the *Monthly Review (Critical Heritage*, p. 86): "We hope that, for the honour of the Art, and the pleasure of the Public, Dr. Goldsmith will retract his farewel to poetry. . . ." The fact that Hawkesworth had earlier described Goldsmith as writing "in the character of a native of a country village" in the poem interestingly suggests the flexibility of the relationship of poet and persona in the minds of Goldsmith's first readers.

45. *Pope's Dunciad: A Study of Its Meaning* (London, 1955), pp. 42–48.

46. *The Progress of Poesy*, 54 n. John Scott (*Critical Essays*, pp. 293–94) commented on the echo, a resemblance which A.D. McKillop also noted but found puzzling in view of Goldsmith's dislike of Gray's *Odes* ("Local Attachment and Cosmopolitanism" in *From Sensibility to Romanticism*, ed. F. W. Hilles and H. Bloom [New York, 1965], p. 204). But Goldsmith had quoted the lines in question in his review of the *Odes* with an approving comment on their meter (*Works*, 1:114–15).

47. *Works*, 1:337.

GEORGE DE F. LORD

Milton's Dialogue with Omniscience in *Paradise Lost*

No poet in the great tradition of Western epic has projected himself more fully into his poem than Milton in *Paradise Lost*. Where Homer, Virgil, Tasso, and Spenser left relatively few autobiographical traces in epics which seem to have aspired to a condition of anonymity, Milton, especially in the invocations to books 1, 3, 7, and 9, emphasizes the emotional, psychological, and spiritual circumstances in which he was composing his poem. Far from concealing traces of personality, Milton employed the tradition of divine inspiration to explore his role as instrument and collaborator of the heavenly muse. As a result *Paradise Lost* conveys a sense of his ubiquitous presence and is everywhere marked by the impress of his personality. Not only has Milton outdone his progenitors in magnitude and range of subject; he has also established for himself a unique epic role as man and poet. In "soaring above th' Aonian Mount" to "write of things invisible to mortal sight" and venturing thereby "to justify the ways of God to men" he not only extended the range of epic from eternity to eternity but affirmed simultaneously his paramount achievement as a quasi-divine poet of omniscience.[1]

The boldness of Milton's venture is the more remarkable in light of his essential subject, the Original Sin of aspiring to divine knowledge. The dangers for the poet of reenacting the sin in singing of it are manifold and obvious. Milton was clearly aware of them, and his autobiographical invocations dramatize the struggle to reconcile the grandeur of his aspirations to his condition as an inheritor of Original Sin and to his obligations as a Christian. Not the least heroic aspect of Milton's venture is his identification with Satan. Far from being of the Devil's party without knowing it, he elaborated the analogies between Satan's proud lust for preeminence and his own unmatched ambition as a poet. The hazards of his enterprise are continually evoked by references to soaring, to heights and depths, to rising and falling which everyone recognizes as a dominant motif in the poem.

Milton's unabashed projection of himself into his epic is one reason for the continuing discussion about the hero of the poem. In addition to the Satanists, there are critics who champion Adam, Eve, Adam and Eve, the Son, and even Abdiel. There are those who feel the poem has no hero, or that the role of hero is distributed among several characters. It has even been suggested that the real hero is the ideal reader, one of that "fit audience though few" for whom Milton was writing. Without examining these conflicting claims I would like to explore the ways in which Milton qualifies as the representative Man whose achievements endow him with the status of hero.

But first let us consider what distinguishes Milton from his predecessors in the role of poet and narrator. In the Homeric epics there is scarcely a trace of the conscious artist at work reflecting on the process of composition or the experience of divine inspiration. There is not even an "I" or a "me" in the *Iliad*'s invocation to represent the poet as an entity separate from the muse. The anonymous voice simply tells her to sing the wrath of Achilles. The traces of the poet's personality are so faint and few that scholars have lept hungrily upon them, such as the diffident remark at the beginning of the catalogue of the ships (2.484) where the poet asks the muse to tell *him* the names of the captains of the Danaans and their lords, "for ye are goddesses and are at hand and know all things, whereas we hear but a rumor and know not anything" (485–86).[2] This distinction between the divine omniscience of the muses and the ignorance of the poet is important and will be considered further on. About the only other trace of Homer's personal involvement in the *Iliad* is his use of the vocative to address Patroclus just before his death.

Similar instances of this personal address in which for a moment the poet drops his customary anonymity to suggest his emotional involvement with a character occur in the repeated references in the *Odyssey* to Eumaeus, the first loyal person Odysseus encounters on his return to Ithaca. The repeated *o subote* I take to be an extraordinary tribute to a faithful servant whose fidelity to his long-absent lord is thus singled out for recognition.

The presence of Homer in the *Odyssey* is not substantially greater than in the *Iliad*. Instead of asking the muse to *sing* he asks her to *tell me,* and he permits himself to comment a little more frequently on characters and action: the sailors of Odysseus who ate the forbidden cattle of Apollo he calls *fools* and lays the blame for their destruction on their own "blind folly," a phrase which Zeus applies a few lines later to Aigisthus and Clytemnestra for the murder of Agamemnon. Thus even this exclamation of disapproval may be construed as coming via the muse rather than as the poet's personal comment on the action.

In his prominent use of *I sing* at the beginning of the *Aeneid* Virgil is a touch more self-assertive than Homer. It may be one significant indication of their spuriousness that four lines prefixed to the *Aeneid* in Suetonius but absent in all good MSS show an obtrusion of autobiographical detail unmatched by anything else in the poem:

> Ille ego, qui quondam gracili modulatus avena
> carmen, et egressus silvis vicina coegi
> ut quamvis avido parerent arva colono,
> gratum opus agricolis; at nunc horrentia Martis[.]

Even if spurious the passage is enormously influential. Spenser incorporated it into the beginning of *The Faerie Queene* and used it as license to project himself into the poem in the pastoral figure of Colin Clout, and Milton, in starting *Paradise Regain'd* with his own version of these lines, also emphasized the self-conscious artistry of the Virgilian progression from eclogue to epic. Not only do the lines point to the steadily increasing presence of the poet in the poem but they foreshadow the evolution of the epic tradition toward long autobiographical poems like *The Prelude* and quasi-epics like *Don Juan* in which the poet's personal reflections shoulder aside the exploits of the nominal hero. After Milton had exhausted the possibilities of true epic the genre inevitably transformed itself into such egocentric works or moved in the direction of the mock-heroic or the picaresque novel of ordinary life.

This brief survey suggests a steady increase in the poet's preoccupation with himself and with the process of poetic creation. With this tendency toward self-projection and self-analysis in the epic tradition we find a concomitant tendency to mingle the figure of the poet with the hero of the poem. Ultimately the disappearance of God from these Romantic avatars of the epic accelerates the process, which culminates in Wordsworth's egotistical sublime.

These contrary leanings—on the one hand toward the objective, formal, and impersonal and, on the other, toward the subjective, improvised, and autobiographical—are balanced in *Paradise Lost*. The theocentric force of Milton's myth is, of course, a primary factor in disciplining the egocentric tendencies of the poet's self-concern, but it is equally obvious from the vast number of failed religious epics that the religious myth cannot guarantee such a balance. Milton's astonishing achievement in reconciling and harmonizing the inward drive of self-conscious authorship with the outward drive toward supernatural authority is finally attributable to the extraordinary candor, subtlety, and insight with which he dramatizes the interior workings of religious doubt and faith, of despair and hope, of egotism and self-lessness, of pride and humility, in the meditative process of epic creation.

To achieve this harmony between the subjective and the objective Milton established a dialogue between the omniscient voice—in religious epic ipso facto divine or divinely inspired—and the voice of the limited, fallible, mortal poet. These voices correspond to and evolve from the omniscient, muse-inspired narrator of classical epic, whose purest example is found in the *Iliad,* and the delegated narrator whose knowledge of things, already limited by his being a mere man, may be further impaired by pride, fraud, self-ignorance, or various ulterior motives. Satan is a prime example of the second voice trying to sound like the first, as in the ludicrous account he gives to Abdiel of diabolical self-sufficiency:

> That we were form'd then say'st thou? and the work
> Of secondary hands, by task transferr'd
> From Father to his Son? strange point and new!
> Doctrine which we would know whence learnt: who saw
> When this creation was? remember'st thou
> Thy making, while the Maker gave thee being?
> We know no time when we were not as now;
> Know none before us, self-begot, self-rais'd
> By our own quick'ning power. . . .

$$[5.853-61]^3$$

The autogeneous myth of Satan marks the extremest form of the egocentric creator, in which ignorance (We know no time when we were not as now) claims omniscience.

In writing the epic of Everything Milton had to assume the omniscient voice. In writing the epic of Man fallen he was also limited to the knowledge available to fallen man. As the fallen poet with the omniscient voice he had recourse to the Homeric tradition of divine inspiration by the muse, but in dramatizing his own plight as poet and man he projected a personality far richer and more complex into the poem than did any of his predecessors. Dante, no doubt, was a vital example of the poet as epic voyager in his own poem, but the *Odyssey* provided a more influential model for the role of limited or delegated narrator. As the first epic beginning in medias res and employing extensively the mode of delegated narrative, the *Odyssey* was an even more crucial influence on *Paradise Lost* than it was on the *Aeneid*. With its thematic concentration on the experiences of *Man* it provided an equally important model for the reconciliation of the humanly individual with the representative. For our purposes, however, the most important aspect of the *Odyssey* is the use of the device of delegated narrative to permit the hero to tell his own story. In striking contrast to the *Iliad*, in which the hero's adventures are related by the omniscient voice, the psychological complexity of Odysseus requires that he tell us a great deal of his own story. Poised between the losses of the past and the hope of redemption in the future, Milton assumed the role of Odysseus on a cosmic scale:

> Of Man's First Disobedience, and the Fruit
> Of that Forbidden Tree, whose mortal taste
> Brought Death into the World, and all our woe,
> With loss of *Eden,* till one greater Man
> Restore us, and regain the blissful Seat,
> Sing Heav'nly Muse. . . .
>
> [1.1–6]

Virgil, of course, also imitated the in medias res structure of the *Odyssey* and began his epic with the hero poised between the disasters and trials of the past and the hope of the future—between ruined Troy and the voyage to Latium where Troy would be restored—but he did not implicate himself in the action in the way that Milton does. For Milton made the unusual claim that the ultimate heroic act was to create his epic of the fall and the promised redemption,

> Sad task, yet argument
> Not less but more Heroic than the wrath
> Of stern *Achilles* on his Foe pursu'd

Thrice Fugitive about *Troy* Wall; or rage
Of *Turnus* for *Lavinia* disespous'd,
Or *Neptune's* ire or *Juno's,* that so long
Perplex'd the *Greek* and *Cytherea's* Son.
[9.13–19]

Not only is Milton's *argument* more heroic than those of Homer and
Virgil, but his *telling* is a task more heroic than any imposed on Achilles, Turnus, Odysseus, or Aeneas.

   The prominence Milton gives to his role as heroic creator tends to
dissolve conventional distinctions of subjective and objective. It allows his epic to assume the form of an extended meditation in which
the divine story and his own experiences interact, a form, in fact, where
his own feelings and experiences are mingled with, illustrate, and become a vital part of the story he is telling.[4] Something like this occurs in
the *Odyssey* when the hero, in a pause between years of war and
shipwreck and marvelous adventures and his imminent return home,
recounts his experiences. While Homer's language is not nearly as
reflective as Milton's, it is clear that Odysseus has somehow been prepared for his triumphant return to Ithaca by assimilating and relating
his trials and adventures. In fact the good king Alcinous ventures to
remark that the purpose of wars and other such tedious havoc is to
provide material for good tales, a rather academic view which might
irritate some veterans:

But come, now, put it for me clearly, tell me
the sea ways that you wandered, and the shores
you touched; the cities, and the men therein,
uncivilized, if such there were, and hostile,
and those godfearing who had kindly manners.
Tell me why you should grieve so terribly
over the Argives and the fall of Troy.
That was all gods' work, weaving ruin there
so it should make a song for men to come!
[8.574–82][5]

As he starts to tell his story, Odysseus begins with the epic singer's
question about the disposition of his material: "What shall I / say first?
What shall I keep until the end?" (9.14–15) Next comes the pious
acknowlegment of suffering and mortality and *xenia*:

The gods have tried me in a thousand ways.
But first my name: let that be known to you,

and if I pull away from pitiless death,
friendship will bind us, though my land lies far.

[9.16–19]

Suffering, mortality, and love are the authenticating tokens of this
heroic teller, as they are of Milton. They also share the excruciating
torment of isolation, "from the cheerful ways of men / Cut off"
(3.46–47), and of alienation, "In darkness, and with dangers compast
round, / And solitude" (7.27–28). Both win deliverance through the
tales they tell.

While the emphasis of the Miltonic narrator on his Odyssean suffering and endurance is obvious, his Odyssean adventurousness and
lust for knowledge may be less apparent. Nonetheless, when we reach
the opening of book 3 our first reaction to the invocation, "Hail, holy
light," is to impute the words to Satan whom we have just seen at the
end of book 2 "by dubious light" beholding "Far off th' empyreal
Heav'n." So powerful is Milton's kinaesthetic evocation of Satan's
prodigious flight from hell through Chaos to the Empyrean that his
identity is temporarily merged with Satan's, and so is the reader's. This
sympathetic identification is intensified by a key allusion to the
Odyssey a few lines earlier:

He ceas'd; and *Satan* stay'd not to reply,
But glad that now his Sea should find a shore,
With fresh alacrity and force renew'd
Springs upward like a pyramid of fire
Into the wild expanse, and through the shock
Of fighting elements, on all sides round
Environ'd wins his way; harder beset
And more endanger'd, than when *Argo* pass'd
Through *Bosporus* betwixt the justling Rocks:
Or when *Uysses* on the Larboard shunn'd
Charybdis and by th' other whirlpool steer'd.

[2.010–20]

The latent association of the heroic voyages of Satan and Milton from
darkness and confinement ("on all sides round / Environ'd" anticipating "In darkness and with dangers compast round / In solitude") to
deliverance and light is reinforced by the allusion to Jason and the Ar-
gonauts but even more by the allusion to Odysseus threading Scylla
and Charybdis on his homeward journey. The association is inten-

sified in the following lines from the invocation to book 3 addressed to "holy Light":

> Thee I revisit now with bolder wing,
> Escap'd the *Stygian* Pool, though long detain'd
> In that obscure sojourn, while in my flight
> Through outer and through middle darkness borne
> With other notes than to th' *Orphean* Lyre
> I sung of *Chaos* and *Eternal Night*. . . .
>
> [3.13–18]

The complexity of Odysseus—rash and hubristic adventurer, insatiable seeker after knowledge, unprovoked slayer, on the one hand, and wise, pious, much-enduring home-seeker, on the other—could embrace the ruthless ambition of Satan and the consecrated ambition of Milton. As a recent critic puts it,

> The explicit comparisons of poet and devil in *Paradise Lost* are intended by Milton to demonstrate an undeluded recognition of the satanic potential of his poetic act. Within the epic, ambition and presumption dog the poet in the form of satanic resemblances to his attempt to understand and give poetic shape to the pattern of God's ways with men.[6]

Milton, building on the model of the *Odyssey* with its alternations of omniscient and delegated narrative, exploited and dramatized the dilemma of fallen and fallible man writing omnisciently about the Fall of Man.

A further aggravation of "the satanic potential of his poetic act" lies in Milton's peculiarly independent religious beliefs. While he took care in *Paradise Lost* to minimize disputed points of doctrine, a cursory knowledge of his life shows him frequently at odds with fellow Protestants on many issues of belief and fashioning his own special faith. His aversion to institutional authority made him an arch example of the dilemmas which the schismatic tendencies of liberal Protestantism could create. The idea which Milton shared widely with his fellow Protestants was that divine guidance was to be sought within the individual soul by prayer and meditation on the Bible. The opportunities for mistakenly erecting one's own inclinations into manifestations of God's will are obvious and became a source of such polemical satire as *Hudibras*. For Milton, as for many of his contemporaries, the dangers of falling into such heretical individualism in pursuit of the inner light were compounded by his championing of radical political freedom against duly constituted authority. Having narrowly escaped proscription at the Restoration for supporting the execution of Charles I, his voice in public affairs silenced, the blind poet was more isolated than ever, in double darkness bound. Whatever else it is, *Paradise Lost* is the instrument of Milton's deliverance, but unlike other great records of spiritual deliverance, it records the reassertion and consecration of the ego rather than its submission to external authority.

Of all Milton's biographers Hanford has traced most clearly and convincingly his development from a somewhat self-gratulatory champion of virtue who could resort to vituperation and innuendo (as in his reply to Salmasius) into a more serene and magnanimous servant and mouthpiece of God. Speaking of the autobiographical passages in *Paradise Lost* Hanford observes:

> The lineaments of this portrait are essentially the same, but there is a new depth in interpretation, a more complete confidence in execution. It is as if Milton, hitherto troubled by a weak desire for approbation from without, needed now no witness but all-judging Jove.[7]

Milton's most creative period seems to have been inaugurated with the writing of the *Second Defense of the English People,* published in 1654, a passionate oration defending and celebrating the cause of liberty and affirming himself as its spokesman and champion. The pamphlet represents "the beginning of a new cycle of self-exaltation, which has followed as natural reaction from the depression of the preceding years."[8] There Milton, according to Hanford, "rouses himself, throws off the intimations of despair, and turns the great affliction which has come upon him into a final seal of consecration."[9] The mark of Milton's transition from the defensive self-exaltation of the earlier pamphlets with their touches of narcissism to a serener conviction of his destiny as poet and prophet is the transformation of his blindness from an affliction to a token of divine favor:

> There is, as the apostle has remarked, a way to strength through weakness. Let me then be the most feeble creature alive, as long as that feebleness serves to invigorate the energies of my rational and immortal spirit; as long as in that obscurity, in which I am enveloped, the light of the divine presence more clearly shines, then, in proportion as I am weak, I shall be

invincibly strong; and in proportion as I am blind, I shall more clearly see. O! that I may thus be perfected by feebleness and irradiated by obscurity! And, indeed, in my blindness, I enjoy in no inconsiderable degree the favor of the Deity, who regards me with more tenderness and compassion in proportion as I am able to behold nothing but himself.[10]

As Hanford says, "the importance of the *Second Defense* is that it exhibits the actual struggle which led Milton to his final victory."[11] In his two sonnets on his blindness and in *Paradise Lost* he now proceeded to give the world a poetic interpretation of that "deeper vision of spiritual truth which had begun to come upon him in his solitary communion with the Most High."[12]

At the heart of *Paradise Lost* is the familiar Christian formula that *humilitas* equals *sublimitas*. Milton differs from his predecessors, however, in the energy with which he explores and displays his humbled and exalted self. More than that, he outdistances all his poetic models in the subtlety and fidelity with which he explores his own devilish inclinations. The result is a drama of the mind in which the self is chastened and disciplined by affliction and is then exalted in the knowledge and love and service of God. Milton's lifelong fascination with temptations and trials, which lies at the heart of *Comus, Lycidas, Paradise Regained, Areopagitica,* and *Samson Agonistes,* as well as *Paradise Lost,* is always focused on the attractions and dangers of unbridled egotism. The young Milton treated the temptations of sensual self-indulgence in *Comus* and the lust for poetic fame in *Lycidas.* The mature Milton dealt with uxoriousness in Adam. But the great temptation which obsessed him in his later years was the lust for power, and it is this drive which provides the dangerous energy we find in "On his Blindness," in Eve and the Satan of *Paradise Lost,* and at the center of *Paradise Regained* and *Samson Agonistes.* Again and again Milton reverts to the Promethean motif of the hero in chains, of the heroic activist immobilized, transfixed, incarcerated—the Lady frozen in her chair by Comus's spell and unable to utter a sound, Satan on the burning lake, immured in darkness visible, the blind Samson, a prisoner "in double darkness bound," the Son of God balanced on a spire of the Temple. But these physical afflictions of immobilization and blindness are metaphors for even more painful and dangerous ones. Once Satan has 'scap'd the dark Abyss, he discovers that wherever he goes he is his own prison:

> myself am Hell;
> And in the lowest deep a lower deep
> Still threat'ning to devour me opens wide,
> To which the Hell I suffer seems a Heav'n.
> [4.75–78]

As Abdiel sternly reminds Satan:

> This is servitude,
> To serve th' unwise, or him who hath rebell'd
> Against his worthier, as thine now serve thee,
> Thyself not free, but to thyself enthrall'd.
> [6.178–81]

After the Fall Adam's paroxysm of guilt and self-reproach sounds like Satan's: "O Conscience, into what Abyss of fears / And horrors hast thou driv'n me; out of which / I find no way, from deep to deeper plung'd!" (10.842–44). The state of sinful self-imprisonment is often expressed in *Paradise Lost* as frenetic, restless, and futile movement. Milton employs the Virgilian implications of the maze of Daedalus and loads the key word *error* with the associations it has in the *Aeneid* as *inextricabilis error* or *irremediabilis error*. A little earlier in Adam's speech from which I have just quoted he says: "all my evasions vain / And reasonings, though through Mazes, lead me still / But to my own conviction. . . ." (10.829–31). While Adam's reason at least leads him to his own conviction, the first step toward his regeneration, the more philosophical devils get nowhere:

> [They] apart sat on a Hill retir'd,
> In thoughts more elevate, and reason'd high
> Of Providence, Foreknowledge, Will, and Fate,
> Fixt Fate, Free will, Foreknowledge absolute,
> And found no end, in wand'ring mazes lost.
> [2.557–61]

At the heart of Milton's conception of deliverance from such bondage is obedience to the will of God. Adam and Eve can perform this act of atonement, but the devils cannot. Adam and Eve

> forthwith to the place
> Repairing where he judg'd them prostrate fell
> Before him reverent, and both confess'd

Humbly thir faults, and pardon begg'd, with tears
Watering the ground, and with thir sighs the Air
Frequenting, sent from hearts contrite, in sign
Of sorrow unfeign'd and humiliation meek.

[10.1098–104]

In the psychodynamics of damnation, egotism prevents Satan from making this essential act of submission and he continues to be a prisoner of the self:

Hadst thou the same free Will and Power to stand?
Thou hadst: whom hast thou then or what to accuse,
But Heav'n's free Love dealt equally to all?
Be then his Love accurst, since love or hate,
To me alike, it deals eternal woe.
Nay curs'd be thou; since against his thy will
Chose freely what it now so justly rues.
Me miserable! which way shall I fly
Infinite wrath, and infinite despair?
Which way I fly is Hell. . . .

[4.66–76]

It seems likely that Milton's disappointing political experiences as an unappreciated deliverer of the English people contributed profoundly to his preoccupation with the theme of the liberator in chains, while the schismatic tendencies of the Protestant sects taught him to scrutinize the motives of political and religious leaders and to project the destructive ones in the character of Satan. The projection could never have attained the imaginative power and the psychological subtlety it displays in *Paradise Lost* if Milton had not put a lot of his own feelings into Satan or recognized vital aspects of Satan as at least potentially present in himself. It is this self-knowledge that permits Milton to become the spokesman of things invisible to mortal sight in *Paradise Lost* without a trace of the self-sufficiency or smugness or priggishness to be found in some of his early accounts of himself and in the character of the Lady in *Comus*. It is his extraordinary combination of humility and soaring aspiration, in this poem tuned by an inner ear to the divine voice, that saves the poet from the ruinous pride of Satan and at the same time inspires him to sublimities that satanic pride could never reach. The collapse of Milton's hopes as spokesman for England's apocalyptic role can be seen as leading to a submission to *kairos,* to the working out of divine providence:

> Magnanimous Despair alone
> Could show me so divine a thing,
> Where feeble Hope could ne'er have flown
> But vainly flapt its Tinsel Wing.

Milton's most confident and challenging assumption of the role of omniscient poet and prophet is found in the opening invocation to the poem. Here he not only glances ironically at Ariosto's proud declaration as he "pursues / Things unattempted yet in Prose or Rhyme," but outdoes all epic predecessors in the boldness with which he associates himself explicitly with Moses (supposed author of Genesis) and implicitly with the author of the fourth Gospel. In weaving elements from the poems of Homeric and Virgilian epic into his own, Milton is also claiming for himself not only a greater subject than theirs but a much more active part in the creation of the poem. The anonymity of Homer is blended with the comparative self-assertiveness of Virgil in such a way that the divine sources of inspiration and the poet's creative role are both raised to a higher power. The invocation for the muse's aid is in no way incompatible with the sturdy self-assertiveness in "my advent'rous song" and the breathtakingly confident clause that amplifies the phrase: "That with no middle flight intends to soar / Above th' Aonian Mount." Milton's allusion to his own limitations is acknowledged, but not in a humble petition for assistance. Although he refers in a later invocation to the spirit who "nightly dictates to him / Slumb'ring," here it almost seems as if Milton were himself the dictator:

> What in me is dark
> Illumine, what is low raise and support;
> That to the highth of this great Argument
> I may assert Eternal Providence,
> And justify the ways of God to men.
>   [1.22–26]

Milton here calls spirits from the vasty deep and knows that they will come. There is no split or separation between the omniscient voice and the voice of mortal limitation here. Although Milton acknowledges his mortal limitations it may be said that he views them from the lofty perspective of the inspired Knower.

It is right that *Paradise Lost* should begin by displaying the poet in serene possession of his divine role. Milton's subsequent appearances in the poem are, as it were, autobiographical flashbacks in which we can trace his painful evolution toward this fully achieved and integrated persona. Since the perspective of this invocation is the most comprehensive of all—indeed it includes *everything,* from the creation of the world to the Second Coming—it is appropriate that the poet should manifest a personality to correspond. To the extent that *Paradise Lost* is concerned with Milton's own struggles and vicissitudes in writing it, his first appearance in the poem expresses the perfect fulfillment of his role as Christian epic poet.

The beginning in medias res does not conflict with this conception of the poet's dynamic evolution in the poem but rather enhances it. With a perspective that includes everything, Milton can express a serene confidence based on a total view of the workings of providence. The promise of redemption is, of course, at the heart of this confidence. The poet's subsequent appearances in the poem, being really earlier in time, are not nearly so untroubled. It is there that we can pursue the dramatic conflict between his doubts as a fallible and limited person and his intimations of immortality. Thus *Paradise Lost,* like the *Odyssey,* begins with an omniscient survey of the story, which reassures us that everything will turn out all right in the end, and then, through a succession of dissolves, focuses on the plights of various actors, who are, of course, unaware, or only partly aware, of divine providence. Taking the example of Odysseus, as narrator of his own experiences, Milton assumes for himself, in these subsequent appearances in *Paradise Lost,* the role of an Odyssean adventurer on a mission of the Spirit. In his new persona at the beginning of book 1 he thus combines the omniscience of Zeus with both the limited knowledge and the experiential wisdom Odysseus has acquired through his sufferings. Divine and mortal vision are there fused.

While the invocation of book 1 conveys a total vision of divine providence and introduces the entire poem, subsequent invocations show the more limited perspective characteristic of delegated narrative. They are also more narrowly focused on the specific difficulties of the narrator's situation. They thus dramatize the tension between the aspiration to divine knowledge and the fear of presumption in thus aspiring or the fear of failure. The proem of book 3 is not written from the serene and lofty perspective of the opening invocation, but after the arduous terrors of an ascent from hell. Its interrogatory mode suggests

the extent to which Milton's visionary confidence has been shaken by
his imaginative participation in Satan's heroic voyage:

> Hail holy Light, offspring of Heav'n first-born,
> Or of th'Eternal Coeternal beam
> May I express thee unblam'd? since God is Light,
> And never but in unapproached Light
> Dwelt from Eternity, dwelt then in thee,
> Bright effluence of bright essence increate.
> Or hear'st thou rather pure Ethereal stream,
> Whose Fountain who shall tell?
>
> [3.1–8]

The tentative, faltering movement of this passage reflects the uneasiness of a poet who, like Odysseus, Aeneas, Dante, or Guyon, has un-
dergone the ordeal of a descent to the underworld and a return to light.
The uneasiness stems as well from the uncertain quality of the light
Milton is hailing: it may be the ordinary light of day; or the "offspring
of Heav'n first-born" on the first day of the Hexaemeron; or it may be
a "Coeternal Beam" of the Eternal; or, since God is light, it may even
be God. In any case Milton approaches it with none of the assurance
with which he first hailed the muse, but with diffidence and awe. It is as
if he had only light enough to speculate cautiously about the light he is
addressing. He thus puts himself implicitly in the company of a succession of fallen witnesses to the various lights which glimmer in a series
of similes in the first two books:

> the Moon, whose Orb
> Through Optic Glass the *Tusca* Artist views
> At Ev'ning from the top of *Fesole,*
> Or in *Valdarno,* to descry new Lands,
> Rivers, or Mountains in her spotty Globe.
>
> [1.287–91]

> As when the Sun new ris'n
> Looks through the Horizontal misty Air
> Shorn of his Beams, or from behind the Moon
> In dim eclipse disastrous twilight sheds
> On half the Nations, and with fear of change
> Perplexes Monarchs.
>
> [1.594–99]

> As when from mountain tops the dusky clouds
> Ascending, while the North wind sleeps, o'erspread
> Heav'n's cheerful face, the low'ring Element
> Scowls o'er the dark'n'd lantskip Snow, or Show'r;
> If chance the Radiant Sun with farewell sweet
> Extend his ev'ning beam, the fields revive,
> The birds thir notes renew, and bleating herds
> Attest thir joy, that hill and valley rings.
>
> [2.488–95]

But the initial relief with which Milton (like the birds and cattle of the last simile) hails the returning light is overshadowed not only by the pervasive doubt we have noticed in the opening of the invocation to book 3 but also by the belated realization of his own blindness:

> Thus with the Year
> Seasons return, but not to me returns
> Day, or the sweet approach of Ev'n or Morn,
> Or sight of vernal bloom, or Summer's Rose,
> Or flocks, or herds, or human face divine. . . .
>
> [3.40–44]

Blindness is a symbol for Milton's limitations as a visionary narrator, but it is also the affliction that spurs him to seek a truer source of enlightenment than the visiting sun. The invocation to book 3, after its tentative opening, proceeds by a series of alternations between fears of presumption and dismay at his blindness to an increasingly resolute pursuit of the "Celestial Light." Although the movement may be uncertain, it is persistent:

> Yet not the more
> Cease I to wander where the Muses haunt
> Clear Spring, or shady Grove, or sunny Hill,
> Smit with the love of sacred Song. . . .
>
> [3.26–29]

While, as a recent critic has suggested, *wander* here carries ominous overtones,[13] its main force is to convey the blind poet's erratic but dogged pursuit of the true source of inspiration, a pursuit which is rewarded by the renewed serenity of the concluding injunction,

> So much the rather, thou Celestial Light
> Shine inward, and the mind through all her powers
> Irradiate, there plant eyes, all mist from thence

Purge and disperse, that I may see and tell
Of things invisible to mortal sight.

[3.51–55]

The "advent'rous Song" Milton confidently proclaims in book 1
gives place to the much more precarious feeling expressed in these lines
from book 3:

Thee I revisit now with bolder wing,
Escap't the *Stygian* Pool, though long detain'd
In that obscure sojourn, while in my flight
Through utter and through middle darkness borne
With other notes than to th' *Orphean* Lyre
I sung of *Chaos* and *Eternal Night,*
Taught by the heav'nly Muse to venture down
The dark descent, and up to reascend,
Though hard and rare. . . .

[3.13–21]

The "venture" of the first two books has been a hazardous and terrifying ordeal, and this passage clearly alludes to Aeneas's ascent from the
underworld which the Sybil tells him is arduous and difficult. Thus
Milton's Virgilian allusion implies that his own descent into and return
from the underworld is ultimately much more than a "venture" with
its associations of casual and perhaps foolhardy heroism. To the extent
that he is imitating Aeneas (who was imitating Odysseus) Milton's
hellish venture is a rite of passage, an initiation into the darker regions
of the spirit. It is a temptation which goes beyond that of Guyon in the
Cave of Mammon in that Milton's imagination actually responds to
the enticing manifestations of demonic power. In this regard Milton's
concept of temptation has become infinitely more complex than it was
in his earlier work, because of an imaginative and, up to a certain point,
sympathetic involvement in satanic heroism. The worst part of Milton's ordeal has been encountering the satanic part of himself, which
is, nevertheless, a precondition to his emancipation from it.

In turning to the proem of book 7 we find Milton even more intensely aware of the hazards of his epic enterprise. Where in 3 he lays
emphasis on the perils of the flight upward from the dark abyss, in 7 he
is deeply troubled by the dangers of a descent to earth. Whether climbing or gliding Milton displays none of the soaring confidence of the

opening invocation in these later ones. His address to Urania is filled
with a deep sense of his own fallibility and vulnerability:

> Up led by thee
> Into the Heav'n of Heav'ns I have presum'd,
> An Earthly Guest, and drawn Empyreal Air,
> Thy temp'ring; with like safety guided down
> Return me to my Native Element:
> Lest from this flying Steed unrein'd, (as once
> Bellerophon, though from a lower Clime)
> Dismounted, on th' *Aleian* Field I fall
> Erroneous there to wander and forlorn.
>
> [7.12–20]

This is very close to the Keatsian despair of the "Ode to a Nightingale," with its echoing *forlorn*, but it has a more than Keatsian sense of
peril in the intricately interwoven expressions of fear and pleas for
help. Thus the feeling is fearful, humble, and prayerful, and flying here
inspires Milton with dread. Although Antaeus-like he regains some
strength by his renewed contact with the earth ("Standing on Earth,
not rapt above the Pole") and by renewed confidence in the muse
who visits his slumbers nightly, Milton ends this invocation with an
agonized plea:

> But drive far off the barbarous dissonance
> Of *Bacchus* and his Revellers, the Race
> Of that wild Rout that tore the *Thracian* Bard
> In *Rhodope,* where Woods and Rocks had Ears
> To rapture, till the savage clamor drown'd
> Both Harp and Voice; nor could the Muse defend
> Her Son. So fail not thou, who thee implores:
> For thou art Heav'nly, shee an empty dream.
>
> [7.32–39]

Not only does this despairing allusion to Bacchus anticipate Keats's
"Away! Away! For I will fly to thee / Not charioted by Bacchus and his
pards," but, more significantly, it is the closest thing we find in Milton
to the Keatsian terror of abandonment and isolation.

The whole proem to book 7 should be seen as an imploring meditation on true guides and false ones, with the passage on Orpheus and
Bacchus serving as an extraordinarily vivid composition of place. The
tentative note on which it ends perfectly realizes the precariousness of

Milton's heroic venture, while the vitality and beauty of Raphael's subsequent account of the creation is a confirmation of the poet's prayer for guidance.

As Milton turns his notes to tragic in the last of his invocations, the voice of the bard becomes more authoritative and less personal, as if he shared the "distance and distaste / On the part of Heav'n / Now alienated." *Tragic* implies not only the catastrophe which Eve and Adam are to enact and suffer in books 9 and 10, but the essentially dramatic mode in which this portion of the story is presented. Now that the human protagonists are fully prepared for the encounter with temptation, the poet withdraws from the action and allows them to play out the tragedy. His introductory remarks have something of the detachment many readers have found in God's anticipatory comments on the fall in book 3. Like him Milton is forthright, precise, and succinct:

> I now must change
> Those notes to Tragic; foul distrust, and breach
> Disloyal on the part of Man, revolt,
> And disobedience: On the part of Heav'n
> Now alienated, distance and distaste,
> Anger and just rebuke, and judgment giv'n,
> That brought into this World a world of woe,
> Sin and her shadow Death and Misery
> Death's Harbinger.
>   [9.5–13]

While Milton's presence is still felt in these books in occasional Virgilian expressions of disapproval or dismay, his resumption of the role of omniscient narrator after the delegated narrative of Raphael in the preceding four books brings the poem back to the predominantly objective and dramatic mode of the opening books. The terse assurance of this proem, however, is quite different from the anguish and anxiety we noticed in the two preceding ones. Milton's role as epic creator is no longer threatened by the inner strife of fallibility and omniscience, although it is still contingent on his celestial patroness, "who deigns / Her nightly visitation unimplor'd, / And dictates to me slumb'ring, or inspires / Easy my unpremeditated Verse. . . . (9.21–24).

Milton's passive stance as the muse's instrument is not only compatible with a new assurance in the supreme value of his "argument," but marks his own deliverance from the heroic ordeals of Odysseus

and Aeneas as he takes leave of the themes of classical epic in "*Neptune's*
ire or *Juno's,* that so long / Perplex'd the *Greek* and *Cytherea's* Son." In
dismissing the strenuous exploits of Odysseus Milton implicitly
leaves behind the heroic phase of his role as creator. He now looks on
the risks of his venture with philosophical detachment:

> Mee of these
> Nor skill'd nor studious, higher Argument
> Remains, sufficient of itself to raise
> That name, unless an age too late, or cold
> Climate, or Years damp my intended wing
> Deprest; and much they may, if all be mine,
> Not hers, who brings it nightly to my Ear.
>   [9.41–47]

NOTES

1. Throughout this essay I am indebted to Anne Davidson Ferry, *Milton's Epic Voice* (Cambridge, Mass., 1963); Joseph H. Summers, *The Muse's Method* (Cambridge, Mass., 1962); Louis L. Martz, *The Paradise Within* (New Haven, 1964); Rodney Delasanta, *The Epic Voice* (The Hague, 1967), and William G. Riggs, *The Christian Poet in Paradise Lost* (Berkeley, 1972).

2. Homer, *Iliad,* trans. A.T. Murray (Cambridge, Mass., and London, 1924).

3. This and all subsequent quotations are from the edition of *Paradise Lost* by Merritt Y. Hughes (New York, 1962).

4. This point is developed by Martz in "The Voice of the Bard," *The Paradise Within* (New Haven, 1964), pp. 105–10.

5. *The Odyssey of Homer,* trans. Robert Fitzgerald (New York, 1963).

6. Riggs, *The Christian Poet,* p. 45.

7. James Holly Hanford, *John Milton, Englishman* (New York, 1949), p. 179.

8. Ibid., p. 146.

9. Ibid., p. 9.

10. Quoted in ibid., p. 147.

11. Ibid., p. 147.

12. Ibid., p. 149.

13. Leslie Brisman, "Serpent Error: *Paradise Lost* X, 216–18," *Milton Studies* 2 (1970): 27–35.

JANET ADELMAN

Creation and the Place of the Poet in *Paradise Lost*

Commentators have frequently noticed the degree to which Milton is implicated in the action of *Paradise Lost:* not only do the invocations make his presence virtually inescapable, but the moral dilemmas facing the characters within the poem are frequently reflections of those facing Milton himself.[1] But the degree to which the process of writing poetry implicates Milton in the subject of his poem has not always been recognized. For *Paradise Lost* is deeply concerned with varieties of creation and attitudes toward creation, with the kinds of imitation and image making that are the special province of the poet, and the kinds of dreams and inspirations that are his source. This essay attempts to deal with some of these concerns insofar as they reflect Milton's anxieties about his own creative process and about the special status of his poem.

Paradise Lost is a poem of reflections and imitations. The structure of imitation is everywhere apparent: in Satan's "God-like imitated State" (2.511),[2] his empire founded "In emulation opposite to Hev'an" (2.298), his heroism in volunteering to destroy man as Christ will volunteer to save him, his Trinity with Sin and Death, and his Incarnation (9.166); in the satanic versions of the fortunate fall (2.14–17) and the paradise within (1.254–55) that we meet eleven books before we meet their grand originals (12.469–78; 12.587); in Mammon, the type of the mimetic artist as literalist, imitating God's light in Pandemonium; in Eve's unwitting imitation of Satan's aspirations and Adam's unwitting imitation of Satan's mode of rationalizing argumentation as they fall;[3] in Enoch's and Noah's and Abdiel's imitation of Christ by their participation in the pattern of the "one just man" (11.818), an imitation to which Milton himself aspires, as he suggests in his self-portrait in the invocation to book 7.[4] The pattern of imitation throughout is partly dictated by—and partly creates—the sense that all events are shadowy types of one truly real event, as history before the Incarnation is filled with shadowy types of truth, and pagan myths are shadowy versions of the one true story. We are all, then, imitators. The structure of imitation implicates us in the moral dimension of the poem: it becomes our responsibility to recognize the ways in which acts and attitudes reflect and distort one another, to distinguish between the imitation and the prototype, and hence to discover the originals of our own actions, to learn who and how to imitate.[5] And our model in this learning is the figure of the poet himself, as he explores the status of his own poetic creation as imitative act.

God is, of course, the great creator in the poem; and the imitative structure of the poem itself reflects the universe he creates. For God's creation in *Paradise Lost* is, in a sense, creation by analogy or shadow: a movement from the invisible to the visible similitude. God, the unimaged maker of images,[6] creates in his own image through the agency of his son, the "Divine Similitude" (3.384) in whom "all his Father shone / Substantially express'd" (3.139–40).[7] Adam and Eve are created in God's image, although Eve is a less perfect similitude than Adam. The earth and all its creatures may be created in the image of God, or at least they may be his visible signs: Adam believes that "In contemplation of created things / By steps we may ascend to God" (5.511–12), a God who is, according to his morning prayer, "To us invisible or dimly seen / In these thy lowest works" (5.157–58). Raphael hints that earth may be "the shadow of Heav'n" (5.575); and even Satan sees the resemblance (9.99). The created world is "Earth conspicuous" (6.299; 7.63), the visible reflection of God's invisibility. And we later find out that, before the literal making of Godhead visible in the incarnation of Christ, history itself is a sequence of visible types of the truth to come: in the shadowy reality of the types, the truth is dimly seen (12.232–35, 303). God, then, creates in visible images that are in some sense the shadows of his light; he sends his "overshadowing Spirit" (7.165) with Christ as he goes to create the world.

This overshadowing spirit is the same one that Milton implores to guide his own creation; at the beginning of *Paradise Lost* he invokes his heavenly muse as the spirit who "from the first / Wast present, and with mighty wings outspread / Dove-like satst brooding on the vast Abyss / And mad'st it pregnant" (1.19–22). His creation, the new

world of his poem, is associated from the beginning with God's creation of the universe. And the analogy between God's creation and Milton's own depends not only on the identity of the spirit presiding over
both, but also on Milton's imitation of the means by which God creates
the world, his creation by analogy. The process of God's creation is a
descent down a scale of increasing incarnation, moving from God,
through Christ who expresses God substantially, into the substance of
the created world, the shadow of God; and this creation is the model for
the process that the poet must follow as he attempts to make God's
ways intelligible to fallen man, to speak of "things invisible to mortal
sight" (3.55). Milton's task—to convey spiritual truths through the
shadowy form of narrative—is a more general version of the task that
his angelic narrator Raphael faces in attempting to relate to Adam's
"human sense th'invisible exploits / Of warring Spirits" (5.565–66);
Raphael's solution, like the solutions of the poet writing the narrative
and the God dimly seen in his works, is to relate the invisible by the
visible: "and what surmounts the reach / Of human sense, I shall delineate so, / By lik'ning spiritual to corporal forms, / As may express
them best" (5.571–74). Creation, then, for God, for the angelic historian, and for the poet, is an incarnating descent into analogy, with the
recognition that the analogous forms are only shadows, that they cannot fully express the light, but that only they can serve to make it
visible.[8]

But the analogy of the poet's creation to God's is only one of the
possibilities that the poem presents; and God's overshadowing spirit is
not the only muse in the poem. When Milton tells us that his muse
visits him nightly and dictates to him slumbering, the resemblance to
the night spirit who dictates Eve's dream is uncomfortably close; and
our discomfort is increased by the realization that both night visitants
inspire dreams of flying, of attaining more than mortal power. Our
first view of Satan suggests that he may be an alternative muse, inspiring the poem: only two hundred lines after we have met the spirit of
God, who "with mighty wings outspread / Dove-like satst brooding
on the vast Abyss" (1.20–21), we meet Satan, with head uplifted, talking as usual, but with "his other Parts besides / Prone on the Flood,
extended long and large" (1.194–95), brooding his own hell. When we
see his "expanded wings" (1.225) as he rises from the flood, the resemblance to the spirit "with mighty wings outspread" is complete.
This resemblance forces us to ask from the first: which of the brooding

figures that we meet at the beginning of the poem is its inspiration?[9] And once we have posed the question, we become aware of the ways in which the inspiring spirit of Milton's creation seems satanic. Immediately before we meet Satan, who aspired "to set himself in Glory above his Peers" and "trusted to have equall'd the most High" (1.39, 40), we hear that Milton's adventurous song "with no middle flight intends to soar / Above th'*Aonian* Mount, while it pursues / Things unattempted yet in Prose or Rhyme" (1.14–16). The note of pride apparent in "things unattempted yet" is an echo of Satan's pride in his grand and original exploits; as Milton makes claims for the unique status of his poem, he sounds dangerously close to the Satan who cannot bear to have a competitor. If Milton's attempt to "see and tell / Of things invisible to mortal sight" (3.54–55) may be a commendable imitation of the creation of the God who makes himself visible for man, it may also be a fatal imitation of the curiosity to "see / What life the Gods live" (5.80–81) that Satan inspires in Eve, the curiosity to know "things not reveal'd" (7.122) that Raphael warns Adam against.

Milton's creation, then, may be divine or demonic: if his word may be analogous to God's, creating a new universe which shadows truth, it may also be analogous to Satan's, creating a hell for everyone who believes in its persuasive power, finally entrapping even himself in his own rhetoric. Indeed, the very attempt to imitate God's creation, unless it is divinely inspired, may be demonic: for Satan is not only the alternative muse of the poem; he also provides Milton with the model of a creative act imitative of God's creation and hence frighteningly like Milton's own. If God creates in his own image, so does Satan, whose creation of Sin from his own head and in his own image is not only a parody of the relationship between God and Christ but also of the whole process of divine creation, "Answering his great Idea" (7.557). And as God loves his begotten image, so Satan loves his: Sin tells him, "Thyself in me thy perfect image viewing / Becam'st enamor'd" (2.764–65). The model of Satan suggests that the creature as creator will attempt to imitate God by creating in his own image; and at the same time it suggests the terrible danger of such creation, the danger that one will substitute one's own created world, one's own image, for God's, and so embrace death. For this substitution is itself a kind of death, since it cuts one off from the generative possibilities of the "real" world outside oneself, the world of God's making, at the same time as it cuts one off from God's promise of everlasting life.

Satan's narcissistic love of his own created image in Sin necessarily implies death within it; the birth of Death from this union is merely the unfolding, the making literal, of this implication. As such, the relationship of Satan to Sin is the model for every creature who falls in love with his own created image; and it is a powerful reflection of Milton's fears about his own role as creator. Is the true analogy for his own work the creation of God or of Satan? Does his creation answer to God's Idea, or is it merely a sinful and self-deluding universe sprung from his own head, born from his self-love?[9]

Milton's awareness of the satanic possibilities inherent in his creation is reflected in the peculiar intensity and uncertainty of his invocations of the muse. Milton's need for his muse is implicit in Raphael's warning to Adam: "nor let thine own inventions hope / Things not reveal'd, which th'invisible King, / Only Omniscient, hath supprest in Night, / To none communicable in Earth or Heaven" (7.121–24). If the poem is Milton's own invention, his own attempt to communicate things not revealed, then it is deeply implicated in the thirst for wrong knowledge that is associated with the fall; and given his position as fallen and mortal, Milton's very claim to see and tell of things invisible to mortal sight becomes satanic in its aspiring egoism unless his poem is in fact inspired by a heavenly muse. The presence of the muse, then, is Milton's guarantee against the satanic model precisely because it ensures that the poem is not his own invention: in order to deny the possibility of satanic inspiration, Milton must deny his own authorship. Milton claims that he is the mediator of the poem but not in the fullest sense its agent; he dissociates himself from his work by stressing the ease with which it comes to him, unpremeditated, of its own accord (9.21–24). These denials of his authorship are ultimately attempts to dissociate himself from the satanic belief that oneself and one's powers are "self-begot, self-rais'd" (5.860), the satanic assertion that "Our puissance is our own" (5.864) which receives its answer in Gabriel's "Neither our own but giv'n" (4.1007). To claim the poem as his own, to deny the muse, would be an imitation of Satan that ensured his place as one of the artists condemned by Michael, the "Inventors rare, / Unmindful of thir Maker, though his Spirit / Taught them, but they his gifts acknowledg'd none" (11.610–12).

But precisely because acknowledgement of the gifts of the muse is Milton's guarantee against his participation in the satanic model, this

acknowledgement itself is deeply problematic: for Milton cannot ultimately be certain that the muse is in fact dictating his poem; and his
most confident assertions of divine inspiration are accompanied by his
fear of the consequences if he, not she, is the only author of his poem.
The invocation to book 7 is concerned with the kinds of fall to which
the poet will be subject if the muse withdraws her support; and in the
last lines of the invocation to book 9, the final invocation of the poem,
Milton quietly raises the possibility of his failure "if all be mine, / Not
Hers who brings it nightly to my Ear" (9.46–47). The final words of
the final invocation are characteristic in their incorporation of both
doubt and certainty: the assertion that the muse brings the poem to him
comes out of his fear that the work may be his alone, as though in
answer to it, so that the phrase that begins in "if" can end in firm assurance, but in an assurance that cannot quite undo the "if". Milton no
sooner questions the agency of his muse than he defines her in a way
that asserts her agency absolutely; and the movement here is echoed
elsewhere in the invocations to 7 and 9: "If rightly thou art call'd,
whose Voice divine / Following, above th'*Olympian* Hill I soar"
(7.2–3); "If answerable style I can obtain / Of my Celestial Patroness,
who deigns / Her nightly visitation unimplor'd, / And dictates to me
slumb'ring" (9.20–23). This oscillation from "if" to confident assertion is everywhere characteristic of the poem; for certainty and doubt
go together throughout. "Descend from Heav'n *Urania*," the invocation to book 7 begins boldly, as though the descents of the muse were
within the poet's power to command, as though her descents were not
analogous to God's "prevenient Grace descending" (11.3) and far outside his will. But this certainty dissolves immediately in the "if" cited
above, an "if" which questions the poet's power to call the muse at the
same time as it questions that right naming which is essential to his
attempt to communicate with us.[10] The "if" leads back to the certainty
of divine aid, which in turn leads to the poet's fear of falling if the aid
is withdrawn. Later in the invocation, Milton's contemplation of his
own dangerous solitude calls forth his comfort in the muse's visits; this
comfort in turn calls forth his fears of sharing the fate of Orpheus; and
the fear again calls forth the certainty that his muse will not allow such
things to happen to him. But even the final certainty of this invocation
is expressed in lines which insist on the possibility that his muse may be
similar to Orpheus's, that she might fail, even as they assert her absolute superiority to the pagan muse: "nor could the Muse defend / Her

Son. So fail not thou, who thee implores: / For thou art Heavn'ly, shee an empty dream" (7.37–39).

If the invocation to book 7 is striking partly because of the oscillation of doubt and certainty inherent in its imploring, the invocation to book 9 is striking partly because here Milton no longer implores. In place of the imploring commands of the earlier invocations—"Sing," "Shine inward," "Descend"—Milton now speaks in the language of statement, no longer praying for the muse's aid, but simply asserting that she aids him "unimplor'd" (9.22). This invocation contains the strongest statement of the muse's aid, and the one that most denies Milton's share in writing his own poem: he suggests not only that the muse comes unimplored, without the active participation of his will, but that he is scarcely present as she "dictates to me slumb'ring, or inspires / Easy my unpremeditated Verse" (9.23–24). But this confident invocation ends with the strongest statement of Milton's doubt of the muse's aid, his fear that he may be writing the poem by himself: "if all be mine". And it has begun with an extraordinary and peculiar assertion of Milton's agency, very different in tone from the fear expressed in the end. After describing the harmonious discourse of angel or God with man, Milton adds, "I now must change / Those Notes to Tragic" (9.5–6), as though he himself were dictating not only the style of his poem, but also the course of divine history.

The radical combination of self-assertion and self-denial in the invocation to book 9 is in fact characteristic of Milton's stance throughout the poem. At the same time that he insists that the poem is written through but not by him, he insists that we notice his presence everywhere, that we share in his sense of his own poetic task and his unique fitness for it, in his blindness and his solitude beset with enemies, even in his fears that the muse may not be dictating his poem after all. This double insistence, particularly intense in the first two invocations, suggests the extent to which Milton is both proud of and fearful of his own reflection in the poem; it bears witness to his struggle to allow his pride in his own creation to emerge in a non-satanic form. In the early invocations, the oscillation between language suggesting Milton's sense of his own agency and that suggesting his instrumentality reveals the interdependence of self-assertion and self-denial: so that Milton's pride in his own agency becomes pride in his special fitness to give up agency and become the muse's instrument; and this sense of his own instrumentality in turn allows him to make extraordinary claims for his agency.[11] The invocation to book 1, for example, is immediately striking in its suppression of the "I": the poet initially appears only modestly as one of "us," sharing "our" woe; he is indistinguishable, part of the fallen mass of mankind. In place of the characteristic epic "I sing" of Virgil, Ariosto, Tasso, and Spenser, we get "Sing Heav'nly Muse". Only after eleven lines do we meet the poet who has invoked the muse; and as soon as we have met him, his song replaces hers: "I thence / Invoke thy aid to my advent'rous Song, / That with no middle flight intends to soar / Above th'*Aonian* Mount, while it pursues / Things unattempted yet in Prose or Rhyme."[12] The sense of agency, here attributed to "my song" rather than directly to an "I," becomes overwhelming; and as though in response to it, the "I" immediately shrinks back and becomes mere instrument: "And chiefly Thou O Spirit . . . Instruct me." The emphasis is firmly on "thou" as agent, "me" as instrument, in the following lines (19–23); and as though protected by this emphasis, the "I" of agency can finally return without threat: "What in me is dark / Illumine, what is low raise and support; / That to the highth of this great Argument / I may assert Eternal Providence / And justify the ways of God to men."

The same alternation of "I" as agent with "thou" as agent shapes the invocation to book 3, although here the "thou" is not the heavenly muse but the functionally similar celestial light.[13] This invocation begins with the self-doubts of the "I": "May I express thee unblam'd?" But as it continues, the "I" of agency grows more confident. The movement of the pronouns even seems to suggest the failure of the "thou" to do its part and the constancy of the "I" in the face of this defect: "Thee I revisit . . . : thee I revisit . . . ; but thou / Revisit'st not these eyes. . . . Yet not the more / Cease I to wander."[14] At this point the object of Milton's address changes from the heavenly light, a "thou" whom he must implore, to an instrumental "thee" apparently wholly within his control: "but chief / Thee *Sion* . . . Nightly I visit." As the poet asserts his control, as he visits the haunt of his muse instead of imploring her visits, he seems to move into a sense of full agency. For the only moment in the poem, he allows himself to think openly of the earthly renown that might be the reward of his labors (34). And in an extraordinary gesture he invokes not the muse or the light but his own mind; the "thou" to whom he speaks becomes purely internal in a description of his creative process that totally omits outside agency: "Then feed on thoughts, that voluntary move / Harmonious numbers." Then, abruptly, this very confidence becomes its opposite; it is replaced by the sense of himself as acted upon rather than as actor. He becomes the object, not the subject, of the invocation; "me" replaces "I" (41, 46, 49). But this loss of agency produces as compensation the "thou" for whom Milton was seeking at the beginning of the invocation; as object, he can implore the light to revisit him, to make him its instrument: "So much the rather thou Celestial Light / Shine inward." And finally, as in the invocation to book I, the sense of himself as instrument rather than as agent allows the return of the "I," now claiming extraordinary powers for itself: "all mist from thence / Purge and disperse, that I may see and tell / Of things invisible to mortal sight." The "I" can emerge triumphant only when it is protected by a firm sense of its own instrumentality, as Abdiel can assert his power safely only with the simultaneous assertion that his power comes from God (6.119–20). Only thus can the "I" escape the egoism of Satan's "I therefore, I alone" (4.935); only thus can the poet be sure that his creation is not in imitation of Satan.

The poem itself provides Milton with a model of divine creation, only partly imitable by any creature, and satanic creation, fully imitated by virtually every fallen creature as he falls in love with himself, with his own image, and creates a universe of death in place of God's universe. But the poem also provides Milton with the model of a human creation of the kind to which he himself aspires in his reliance on his heavenly muse. For Eve is in some measure Adam's creation, answering his great idea as the universe answers God's and Sin answers Satan's. Part of the effect of the long debate between God and Adam on the subject of Adam's need for Eve is to make her creation contingent on Adam's desire, to give him a hand in the creation of Eve as Genesis does not, so that it is no longer wholly something that God does to him in a dream. Eve has in fact a double status as creature in the poem: she is the creature of God, but also of Adam, and in the image of them both. When we first see the human pair, there is no distinction made in the degree to which they both reflect the image of God (4.292). But it is clear that Eve is created less fully in the image of God than Adam is. Adam reassures Raphael that he knows his own superiority to Eve by pointing out her greater distance from the divine archetype: "In outward also her resembling less / His Image who made both" (8.543–44). For Eve is created in the image of God only insofar as that image is mediated through Adam. God tells Adam that he will bring him "Thy likeness, thy fit help, thy other self, / Thy wish, exactly to thy heart's desire" (8.450–51): and insofar as Eve is made exactly to Adam's wish and in his image, Adam stands as her human creator.

The creation of Eve, by God but through Adam, created from Adam's material nature and in his image, but while his conscious will is absent, in a dream, is analogous to Milton's vision of the creation of his poem, created through but not by him. If the creation of Sin provides Milton with a nightmare image of his own agency—"I alone"—then the creation of Eve provides him with a powerful image of his own instrumentality. But at the same time, the relationship between Adam and Eve suggests the danger to which the human creator is subject should he forget his own instrumentality. Eve unwittingly suggests the source of the danger in her first speeches to Adam. When we first hear her speak, she addresses Adam in terms which tacitly acknowledge that God has created her through Adam: he is "thou for whom / And from whom I was form'd flesh of thy flesh" (4.440–41). But two hundred lines later, God's authorship of her is acknowledged only very indirectly, insofar as he has ordained that Adam be her law as he is Adam's (4.636–37); Adam has become "My Author and Disposer" (4.635). Eve's address to Adam as her "Author" here may be no more than a reflection of the unfallen hierarchical relationship between man and woman, but it is slightly ominous in its suggestion that Eve may forget who her true Author is—and ominous also in its echo of Sin's characteristic mode of address to Satan as Author (2.864; 10.236).[15] Adam knows that God is "Author of this Universe" (8.360); the danger is that Eve's forgetfulness will become his own, that he too will begin to forget God's part in Eve's creation and will begin to regard her only as an extension of himself. When Adam addresses Eve as "Best Image of myself" (5.95), the phrase suggests not only the extent to which he conceives of Eve as formed in his image, but also the potential for self-love present in his love for Eve even before the fall. God has promised Adam an Eve who shall be his "other self" (8.450): and Adam greets her innocently as "my Self / Before me" (8.495–96). But the sense of Eve as part of himself, as inseparable from him, later becomes central to his fall: "I feel / The Bond of Nature draw me to my own, / My own in thee, for what thou art is mine; / . . . to lose thee were to lose myself" (9.955–59). For the moment, Adam acts as though Eve were wholly his. And when he substitutes himself in Eve for God, the consequence is death, as it is when Satan embraces his own image in Sin.

Insofar as Eve is at least partly Adam's creation and in his image, she poses the same temptation for him that Sin poses for Satan and the poem itself for Milton as author: the temptation to substitute his own created image for the universe created by God, the temptation of a self-love that is ultimately a form of idolatry. And in fact the temptress Eve herself is subject to a type of this temptation at the moment of her creation. When Adam is created, he immediately turns his eyes upward toward "the ample sky" (8.258); when Eve is created, she immediately looks downward, not toward the sky but toward its reflection in "the clear / Smooth Lake, that to me seem'd another Sky" (4.458–59).[16] Adam looks upward toward his source in heaven and springs to his feet "As thitherward endeavoring" (8.260); Eve remains prone, looking downward toward her own reflection, until the Voice raises her and joins her to Adam:[17]

> . . . there I had fixt
> Mine eyes till now, and pin'd with vain desire,
> Had not a voice thus warn'd me, What thou seest,
> What there thou seest fair Creature is thyself,
> With thee it came and goes; but follow me,
> And I will bring thee where no shadow stays
> Thy coming, and thy soft imbraces, hee
> Whose image thou art. . . .
>
>   [4.465–72]

When Eve is created, she is immediately drawn to the reflection rather than the real thing because her very nature allies her with reflections. The Voice tells Eve that what she sees is herself, not an image of herself: for Eve is the reflected image as she is the reflecting pool.[18] She is one degree further removed from the reality of God than Adam is: created in God's image, but only as that image is reflected through Adam; capable of serving God, but only by serving him in Adam ("God is thy Law, thou mine" 4.637). Her experience of God characteristically is mediated: she withdraws from Raphael's angelic discourse not because she can't understand it, but because she would rather hear the heavenly message indirectly from Adam than directly from the angel (8.48–57); while Adam is given the direct vision of the future by Michael, she receives her comfort, as she had received her first temptation, in a dream. She can know God only as his light shines through Adam: "Hee for God only, shee for God in him" (4.299). The physical analogy for the relationship between Adam and Eve is the relationship between sun and moon, "Communicating Male and Female Light, / Which two great Sexes animate the World" (8.150–51). Eve is the reflector, the moon who gives off light only insofar as she receives and reflects it from the sun of Adam, as the moon is the sun's "mirror, with full face borrowing her Light / From him, for other light she needed none" (7.377–78).

Eve's very nature as a reflected image seems to subject her to the temptation of loving her own image as though it were an act natural to her. Satan brilliantly exploits her affinity with the moon and the realm of shadows, as well as her love of her own image, in his initial temptation of her; he is shrewd enough to have learned of her pull toward the unreal from overhearing her account of her creation. He lures Eve into the night, the reign of fancy, by language particularly calculated to appeal to her:

> . . . now reigns
> Full Orb'd the Moon, and with more pleasing light
> Shadowy sets off the face of things; in vain,
> If none regard; Heav'n wakes with all his eyes,
> Whom but to behold but thee, Nature's desire,
> In whose sight all things joy, with ravishment
> Attracted by thy beauty still to gaze.
>   [5.41–47]

Satan's appeal here moves cunningly from an invitation to see the shadowy world under the aegis of the female light of the moon, to an invitation to be seen by heaven and all nature, a movement which demonstrates how closely he has listened to Eve's story. For the simultaneous impulse toward seeing and being seen[19] is inherent in Eve's fixt gaze on her own reflected image:

> As I bent down to look, just opposite,
> A Shape within the wat'ry gleam appear'd
> Bending to look on me, I started back,
> It started back, but pleas'd I soon return'd,
> Pleas'd it return'd as soon with answering looks
> Of sympathy and love; there I had fixt
> Mine eyes till now. . . .
>   [4.460–66]

The impulse here is innocent enough; but it suggests the beginnings of a kind of idolatrous self-love, and as such, it becomes the basis for Satan's major temptations of Eve. He appeals to her not only to see properly—to see how the gods live and behold the world with eyes undimmed (5.80, 87; 9.706–08)—but also to be properly seen. Adam will later attribute her fall to her "longing to be seen" (10.877); and however vicious his words, he is at least partly right. For Satan succeeds in teaching Eve to experience herself as an image, that is, in encouraging her to make herself into an idol to be seen and worshipped.

> Fairest resemblance of thy Maker fair,
> Thee all things living gaze on, all things thine
> By gift, and thy Celestial Beauty adore
> With ravishment beheld, there best beheld
> Where universally admir'd: but here
> In this enclosure wild, these Beasts among,
> Beholders rude, and shallow to discern
> Half what in thee is fair, one man except,
> Who sees thee? (and what is one?) who shouldst be seen
> A Goddess among Gods.[20]
>
> [9.538–47]

It is admiration for her "Divine Semblance" (9.606–07) that has caused him to "come / And gaze, and worship" her (9.610–11). After this introduction, it is no wonder that the fallen Eve immediately wonders how she should appear to Adam (9.816–17), what image of herself she should make.

Eve is justly taught to make herself into an idol by Satan, who has made himself an "Idol of Majesty Divine" (6.101) and whose followers will lead fallen men astray partly by persuading them to become idolaters. For idol worship is the epitome of the temptation to which all the creatures of the poem are subject: it is precisely a substituting of one's own self-made image for God. Michael tells Adam of the stupidity of men who "forsake the living God, and fall / To worship thir own work in Wood and Stone / For Gods" (12.118–20). "To worship thir own work": as Satan worships the image of himself as "majesty divine," self-begotten; as Adam substitutes his creation Eve for God and momentarily worships her ("Was shee thy God" 10.145). This is the temptation to which the creature as creator of images is prone: a temptation for us and for Milton no less that for the characters in the poem. It is the temptation explicated for us when Eve is first created: for Eve's reflection in the water is itself a kind of idol, both in the sense that it is an insubstantial imitation, a false appearance,[21] and in the sense that it is, although Eve cannot know it, self-generated. The education that leads Eve away from this idol can therefore stand as the educative model of the poem, for its creator and its readers as well as for its characters:

> . . . follow me,
> And I will bring thee where no shadow stays
> Thy coming, and thy soft imbraces, hee
> Whose image thou art, him thou shalt enjoy
> Inseparably thine, to him shalt bear
> Multitudes like thyself, and thence be call'd
> Mother of human Race.
> [4.469–74]

If Eve remains looking downward in self-love toward her own shadowy image, she embraces the death implicit in the analogy with Narcissus and fulfilled in the poem by Satan and Adam as they embrace death in their own images. But instead she is led back toward her source in Adam—he whose image she is—toward a reality where no shadow stays her coming, and away from the shadowy realm that promises death. And by moving back toward her source, she can take her place as part of God's generative universe and become truly creative. In place of the sterile contemplation of her own image, she is given the promise of a boundless pouring forth of multitudes like herself, her own images, sanctioned, like Adam's creation of Eve herself and Milton's creation of his poem, because made through but not by her.

Eve's education away from her own image stands as an answer to the dangers posed by creaturely creation throughout the poem; it is in this sense at the imaginative center of the whole. And it is fitting that Eve should provide the occasion for this education: throughout the poem the female has been associated with the realm of shadow and reflection and the dangers it poses. For the female creature is throughout projected from the male creator, and in his image: as the universe from God, Sin from Satan, and Eve from Adam.[22] And insofar as all three of these female creations serve as potential models for Milton's creation of his poem, his descent into shadows, they reflect his concern with the source and end of his own creativity, a creativity apparently felt as an expression of the female in his own nature and presided over by a female muse.[23] For the nature of creativity in the poem is allied to the double nature of woman herself: the female realm of reflections is beneficent or destructive, depending on how it is used, as the woman Eve is the agent both of destruction and redemption (12.621–23). The celestial muse who comes to Milton at night, who associates herself with fancy's realm of moon, shadow, and dream, is the expression of Milton's belief that this female realm can be beneficent, that it can lead toward God as well as away from him, provided only that we acknowledge it as his gift. And as his gift, the poem itself can become a kind of shadowy type, designed ultimately to lead us away from itself and toward truth, where no shadow stays our coming.

Notes

1. Many critics, for example, find in the poet's illumination through blindness the pattern of the fortunate fall; among the multitudes, see Jackson I. Cope, *The Metaphoric Structure of Paradise Lost* (Baltimore, 1962), p. 164, and Anne Davidson Ferry, *Milton's Epic Voice* (Cambridge, 1963), p. 38. I have not attempted to acknowledge all the critics who have anticipated elements in my argument because they are legion. But the work of William G. Riggs on the resemblances between the narrator and Satan is so close to my own that it deserves special mention (*The Christian Poet in Paradise Lost* [Berkeley, 1972], pp. 15–45).

2. *Paradise Lost,* ed. Merritt Y. Hughes (New York, 1962). All citations of the text are to this edition.

3. After he falls, Adam imitates another satanic mode of argumentation: the soliloquy. Soliloquy is the badge of the fallen in *Paradise Lost*: only after the fall is the creature sufficiently self-divided and sufficiently divided from his surroundings to engage in dialogue with himself.

4. I use the term "Milton" loosely, to cover both the entity sometimes known as "the narrator" and the historical figure John Milton, because these entities seem to me impossible to disentangle. It is clear that the narrator is a consciously controlled character in the poem; but it is equally clear that Milton is anxious to ensure that we recognize him in the narrator.

5. Our education is given particular force by the fact that we are introduced to the imitation before we see what it imitates: hell before heaven, Satan's heroism before Christ's. The placing of the books in hell before those in heaven tempts us to accept the imitation on its own terms: only when we get to book 3 are we forced to realize that we have mistaken the mirror image for the real thing. We can in fact learn to recognize the structure of imitation only insofar as we are able to imitate the vision of God, to see all narrative time at once.

6. When Milton tells us of the angels' song, "Loud as from numbers without number, sweet / As from blest voices" (3.346–47), he creates an image of that which cannot be imaged, that which is comparable only to itself, by leading us to expect similitude and giving us identity: his use of the form of the simile emphasizes the degree to which heavenly things are like themselves alone.

7. The pun on *shone* / *shown* suggests the mystery of the light made visible in the Son.

8. The ambiguity inherent in the idea of shadows is closely related to the complexity of Milton's attitude toward the visible world and hence toward his own blindness. God may be dimly seen in his shadowy lowest works; and Milton laments that his blindness cuts him off from this source of knowledge (3.47–50). But blindness itself may be a source of knowledge: the angels hymn God in a song which becomes Milton's own (3.413) partly because it shows so clearly the virtue of blindness; they tell us that God's light is visible only when shaded, only through a veiling of the senses, in a paradox impossible to mortal sight. For the fountain of light is invisible except when he shades his beams and appears "dark with excessive bright" (3.380); even "brightest Seraphim / Approach not, but with both wings veil thir eyes" (3.381–82). The poem teaches us to see God in darkness, even in the shadow of death (2.669–70): and as Adam receives true vision from Michael only after his mortal sight has failed (12.9), so Milton hopes that his blindness, the "dim suffusion" that has "veil'd" his eyes (3.26), will make him the appropriate vehicle for divine illumination.

9. The model of true inspiration is of course God breathing his Spirit into Adam (7.525–26). Images of false inspiration abound in the poem. They are implicit in the winds, whirlwinds, volcanos, and earthquakes associated with the fallen angels (see, for example, 1.230; 2.286 and 541). Mere wind, especially wind self-generated by the passions and delusions of fallen creatures, stands as a kind of literalistic parody of God's spirit, and hence as an emblem of false inspiration: those who have attempted to win heaven by purely physical means fly up to the Limbo of Vanity like "Aereal vapors" (3.445); instead of receiving the spirit, they receive a fittingly literal punishment in becoming "the sport of Winds" (3.493). Raphael's digestive analogy for right and wrong uses of knowledge depends, somewhat comically, on the same cluster of concepts. If food is properly used, corporal is turned to incorporal (5.413); the process is a transubstantiation (5.438) which is the inversion of incarnation and provides a model for the way in which man's "bodies may at last turn all to spirit" (5.497). But when man is gluttonous in the use of knowledge or food, the surfeit "turns / Wisdom to Folly, as Nourishment to Wind" (7.129–30). The fullest model of an inspiration false because mechanical and proceeding entirely from the self is the machine which creates Pandemonium in the way that "an Organ from one blast of wind / To many a row of Pipes the sound-board breathes" (1.708–09). The joke here is that Pandemonium is "like an Exhalation" (1.711) rather

than an inspiration: mere wind breathed out of the self rather than spirit breathed into it.

10. In an invocation largely concerned with right and wrong uses of the voice, fittingly a prelude to Christ's creation of the world by his voice, the initial source of anxiety is about right naming. When Milton says "The meaning, not the Name I call" (7.5), he raises doubts about the efficacy of his own poetic process, since the reader is, after all, dependent on his words. Right naming should be the province of the poet, as it is the province of Adam in paradise; but neither unfallen man nor fallen poet can name what is above him on the scale of being. Confronted by God, Adam does not know what to call him (8.357–59), any more than Milton knows how to express the light unblamed (3.3) or by what name to call his muse.

11. The dilemma that Milton faces here is a specialized form of the dilemma faced by the human creature, who must somehow reconcile his sense of his own agency with his sense that he is a dependent being, not self-created but made by others. Hugh M. Richmond, in *The Christian Revolutionary: John Milton* (Berkeley, 1974) sees the tensions between self-assertion (associated with Platonism and the belief in the sufficiency of reason) and humility (associated with Christianity and the recognition of the insufficiency of the individual and the need for God's grace) as the central issue in Milton's career; according to his argument, Milton's success in *Paradise Lost* depends on his failure of self-confidence and his consequent rejection of "any aspiration to conscious achievement" (p. 137), a rejection embodied in the stress laid on the role of the muse. Although I do not find the rejection as unequivocal in *Paradise Lost* as Richmond does, our arguments are obviously parallel; his is useful in that it sets the issue in a larger context (see pp. 44–47 and 122–54).

12. The word *advent'rous* links the poet's song to another adventurous and dangerous act of agency: "advent'rous" Eve's eating of the apple (9.921). I am indebted to Joseph H. Summers, in *The Muse's Method* (Cambridge, Mass., 1962), for pointing out the use that Milton makes of the word, although he does not refer to Milton's own adventure in his discussion (p. 64).

13. In fact, Milton can assert without fanfare that he has been taught by the muse (ll. 19–20), that she has performed the function for which she was invoked in book 1, partly because his anxieties about agency here have been displaced from her to the figure of the Celestial Light.

14. The echo of *I / eyes* emphasizes the shift of the "I" from agent to instrument.

15. This echo asks us to notice the parallels in the modes of creation of the two women, both in the image of their men. Indeed, Milton ensures that the birth of Sin will look forward to the birth of Eve even at the risk of making the anatomy of the event somewhat confusing: Satan's left side opens wide (2.755) and Sin springs out of his head (2.758), an image which seems designed to suggest both the likeness to and the difference from Eve's birth

from Adam's left side (8.465). After her fall, Eve again echoes Sin: Sin has boasted to Satan, "Out of thy head I sprung" (2.758); Eve welcomes Adam's decision to share her fall by addressing him as "Adam, from whose dear side I boast me sprung" (9.965). In both cases the word *sprung* suggests a self-willed act, as though the two creatures willed themselves into existence without any outside help. Eve's association here with Satan's claim that he is "self-begot" is an index of her new kinship with him and his daughter.

16. Milton emphasizes that the lake's appeal to Eve lies in its status as analogue to heaven by anticipating this image a few lines earlier: the lake "stood unmov'd / Pure as th'expanse of Heav'n" (4.455–56).

17. The newly created Eve finds herself lying down and presumably must stand up to get to the pool, but Milton suppresses this movement: we see her lying down, then lying down again, in dramatic contrast to the male assertiveness implicit in Adam's springing to his feet.

18. The scene of Eve's creation reflects Eve's female nature in all its details: the shade of flowers, the waters rushing from the cave, and the pool.

19. So exhibitionism and scopophilia or voyeurism are two forms of the same impulse and often occur together, according to Freud.

20. Satan's address to Eve as "Fairest resemblance of thy Maker fair" works beautifully on Eve's latent capacity to resent her inferiority by suggesting, first, that Eve may be a better image of God's fairness than Adam is (she is the fairest resemblance of his fairness), and secondly, contrary to all logic, that she may be even fairer than God (he is fair, while she is fairest.)

21. John M. Steadman, in *Milton's Epic Characters: Image and Idol* (Chapel Hill, 1959), identifies idol with *eidolon,* false appearance (pp. 236–40), and cites Eve's reflection as an instance of an *eidolon* (p. 239.) In this sense, Eve herself is an idol; she is twice identified with the lure of the false show as opposed to reality (8.575; 10.883).

22. Although the creation must logically include male and female, the stress throughout on the female nature of the created light (7.245, 360) and on Earth as the great mother (7.281), as well as the density of occurrences of the word *her* in the passage from lines 311 to 331, create the sense that the universe itself is female. The sun is the first created thing that is conspicuously male (7.370), possibly because of his status as analogous to God. Northrop Frye says, "The relation of man to woman symbolizes, or dramatizes, the relation of creator to creature. . . . We think of God as male primarily because he is the Creator; we think of Nature as female, not merely as the mother from whose body we are born, but as a creature of God" ("The Revelation to Eve," in *Paradise Lost, A Tercentenary Tribute,* ed. B. Rajan [Toronto, 1969], p. 20).

23. That Milton may have thought of his own creativity as female is suggested by an odd phrase used by an anonymous contemporary biographer: if his amanuensis came to him later than usual, Milton "would complain, saying *he wanted to be milked."* (Cited in *English Masterpieces: Milton,* ed. Maynard Mack, [Englewood Cliffs, N.J., 1961], p. 3.) The biographer's

obvious surprise at the oddness of the phrase suggests that he may not have made it up, although of course it is impossible to conclude that he heard it from a reliable source. Maud Bodkin comments on Milton's tendency to experience his own poetic creativity in feminine terms, and associates this tendency with his representation of the feminine element in divine creativity (*Archetypal Patterns in Poetry* [Oxford, 1934], p. 155).

LOUIS L. MARTZ

Paradise Lost: The Solitary Way

"In my end is my beginning," T. S. Eliot wrote in *East Coker,* "In my beginning is my end"—adapting an ancient motto said to belong to Mary, Queen of Scots. I should like to think of *Paradise Lost* from this standpoint, as a poem approachable either from its end or its beginning—after a first reading, of course. Consider the closing lines of the poem, which tell of Adam and Eve's departure from Eden to begin life in the world we all know. I would rather use the word *departure* instead of the more traditional term *expulsion*—that is to say, the driving out—for it is essential to notice how different Milton's ending is from the stark and simple words of Genesis: "so he drove out the man; and he placed at the east of the garden of Eden cherubims, and a flaming sword which turned every way, to keep the way of the tree of life."

How different, too, Milton's presentation is from the usual pictorial representations of the Expulsion in Renaissance or Baroque art, as in the earliest English illustration of that scene, which appeared in 1688.[1] Here the stern-faced angel with his left hand grasps Adam firmly by the shoulder, as though partly pushing and partly steadying an Adam whose hands cover his face and whose body seems about to drop to the ground with anguish. Meanwhile, in his right hand the angel holds a sword toward Adam's leg, threatening any effort at return. Or consider Michelangelo's Expulsion, on the Sistine Chapel ceiling, where the angel seems to hold the point of his sword against the back of Adam's neck, while Adam strikes a gesture of fear and pleading, with an expression of poignant regret and remorse, and Eve cowers at his side. Or, farthest of all from Milton's conception, recall Masaccio's fresco in the church of the Carmine at Florence, where Eve expresses by her ragged, open mouth a cry of grief almost beyond bearing.

But Milton, as always, does things in his own way. He has shown the horror of the Fall throughout the length of his last two books, with their oppressive tale of human wickedness, which evokes Adam's cry when in his vision he sees the murder of Abel:

Alas, both for the deed and for the cause!
But have I now seen Death? Is this the way
I must return to native dust? O sight
Of terror, foul and ugly to behold,
Horrid to think, how horrible to feel!
[11.461–65]

Milton will not end his poem in such a mood. The angel does not drive the human pair, but rather saves them from a burning residence, as the angels in the book of Genesis (chapter 19) escort Lot and his family from the doomed city of Sodom, taking them by the hand; or as Aeneas in a different fashion escorts his son and his father from burning Troy. Here are Milton's words, beginning with the ominous scene in which a group of cherubim are seen afar off:

High in Front advanc't,
The brandisht Sword of God before them blaz'd
Fierce as a Comet; which with torrid heat,
And vapor as the *Libyan* Air adust,
Began to parch that temperate Clime.

Notice that the sword is not held in this archangel's hand; the sword is a manifestation seen at a considerable distance from Adam and Eve. But the archangel is near; he grasps Adam by one hand and Eve by the other, and he leads them to safety through the east gate of Paradise and down to the "subjected plain," that is, to the plain of Eden that lies below the mount of Paradise:

In either hand the hast'ning Angel caught
Our ling'ring Parents, and to th' Eastern Gate
Led them direct, and down the Cliff as fast
To the subjected Plain; then disappear'd.

This is an act of rescue, a sign of mercy, and it does not evoke horror or terror in our first parents:

They looking back, all th' Eastern side beheld
Of Paradise, so late thir happy seat,

Wav'd over by that flaming Brand, the Gate
With dreadful Faces throng'd and fiery Arms:
Some natural tears they dropp'd, but wip'd them soon;
The World was all before them, where to choose
Thir place of rest, and Providence thir guide:
They hand in hand with wand'ring steps and slow,
Through *Eden* took thir solitary way.

And they will find a place of rest, as Milton has implied by a complex simile that he has placed within this ending, the simile in which he compares the assembling cherubim to the evening mist that a field-laborer sees as he returns home from work in the English countryside:

So spake our Mother *Eve,* and *Adam* heard
Well pleas'd, but answer'd not; for now too nigh
Th' Arch-Angel stood, and from the other Hill
To thir fixt Station, all in bright array
The Cherubim descended; on the ground
Gliding meteorous, as Ev'ning Mist
Ris'n from a River o'er the marish glides,
And gathers ground fast at the Laborer's heel
Homeward returning.

One may feel something ominous in this glowing mist, for meteors were traditionally regarded as ominous; but there is much more in the simile than dread. There is here the sense of a fertile river valley in which the mist counteracts the effects of threatening fire and parching heat. And there is the promise of a peaceful homecoming after a hard day of labor. All this provides an implicit answer to the question: what lies ahead for Adam and Eve? We notice how the emphasis has fallen on that word *choose,* in the lines "The World was all before them, where to *choose* / Thir place of rest, and Providence thir guide." The word *choose* not only receives a special stress here by coming at the end of the line; at the same time, as critics have noted,[2] it also seems to govern the word *Providence.* That is to say, Providence will be their guide if they choose to accept the guidance. One notices too a paradox in the word *solitary:* they are a solitary *pair,* hand in hand, and they may if they choose also have the presence of Providence to be their guide. Furthermore, those final two words in the poem, *solitary way,* and the word *wand'ring,* despite their apparent gloom and bleakness, are lighted with some hope in their full context of allusion, for these words echo Psalm 107, speaking of the Hebrew people:

> They *wandered* in the wilderness in a *solitary way;*
> They found no city to dwell in.
> Hungry and thirsty,
> Their soul fainted in them.
> Then they cried unto the Lord in their trouble,
> And he delivered them out of their distresses.
> And he led them forth by the right way,
> That they might go to a city of habitation.
> Oh that men would praise the Lord for his goodness,
> And for his wonderful works to the children of men!

The total context of that phrase *solitary way* is thus one of hope and faith. And that sentence of the psalm, "Oh that men would praise the Lord for his goodness, and for his wonderful works to the children of men," is repeated three more times in this psalm, so that one cannot miss the feeling of hope. It is, then, in this setting of hope and faith and love that Adam and Eve begin what we might call the pilgrimage that is their life, while those closing words, *wand'ring* and *solitary way,* seem to take us back to the beginning of the poem. For those words may remind us that the poem contains two other figures that move in a "solitary way."

The first of these is Satan, who, after his expulsion from the Heavenly Paradise, makes what one might call a pseudo-pilgrimage from hell to earth—and certainly in his case the word *expulsion* is appropriate, for we recall the words near the beginning of Milton's poem:

> Him the Almighty Power
> Hurl'd headlong flaming from th' Ethereal Sky
> With hideous ruin and combustion down
> To bottomless perdition, there to dwell
> In Adamantine Chains and penal Fire,
> Who durst defy th' Omnipotent to Arms.
>
> [1.44–49]

The contrast between the treatment of fallen angel and fallen man could hardly be more pointed. Yet Satan undertakes what we may well call a pilgrimage of sorts, for Satan offers the pretense that he is making his journey from hell to earth in order that he may rejoice in the wonderful works of the Lord—and this is the true meaning of the word *pilgrimage:* "a journey (usually of considerable duration) made to some sacred place, as an act of religious devotion." Such is the motivation that Satan in book 3 offers to Uriel, the angel of the sun, after Satan has adopted his disguise of a traveling cherub, looking like an angel in a Renaissance painting:

> Under a Coronet his flowing hair
> In curls on either cheek play'd, wings he wore
> Of many a color'd plume sprinkl'd with Gold,
> His habit fit for speed succinct, and held
> Before his decent steps a Silver wand.
>   [3.640–44]

It is a ludicrous and ironical scene, if we remember the enormous size and baleful, blazing eyes of Satan in hell. But here he has "His habit fit for speed succinct"—his clothing is tied up or close-fitting so that he can make all speed in his pilgrimage. And in this neat and humble garb he addresses Uriel, in the very attitude of Psalm 107:

> Unspeakable desire to see, and know
> All these his wondrous works, but chiefly Man,
> His chief delight and favor, him for whom
> All these his works so wondrous he ordain'd,
> Hath brought me from the Choirs of Cherubim
> Alone thus wand'ring.

It is the very language found in Psalm 107 and in a score of other places in the psalms or other books of the Bible where we find that phrase "wonderful works" or "wondrous works." Uriel is taken in (and how, we may ask in passing, can we blame Eve very severely for falling for Satan's line later on in book 9, when here the very archangel of the sun is thus deceived: "The sharpest-sighted Spirit of all in Heav'n"?). So Uriel replies, happily, also using the language and the lesson of Psalm 107:

> Fair Angel, thy desire which tends to know
> The works of God, thereby to glorify
> The great Work-Master, leads to no excess
> That reaches blame, but rather merits praise
> The more it seems excess, that led thee hither
> From thy Empyreal Mansion thus alone,
> To witness with thine eyes what some perhaps

Contented with report hear only in Heav'n:
For wonderful indeed are all his works,
Pleasant to know, and worthiest to be all
Had in remembrance always with delight.

[3.694–704]

Here we seem to find an exact echo of Psalm 111, verse 4: "He hath made his wonderful works to be remembered." All this is the true end of any pilgrimage—to grasp and to appreciate the wonder of the works of God. But of course Satan's pilgrimage is hardly one of love and delight, for, as we come to see, he hates the beauty of the earth and he sees "undelighted all delight" (4.286), as in his address to the sun, at the beginning of book 4.

There is, however, another pilgrim in this poem, who also walks a solitary way; he is introduced to us very plainly at the opening of book 3, although in fact he has been with us from the very first line of the poem and he will remain until the last. He is the singer in darkness who tells this tale, and who, though blind, sees things invisible to mortal sight, as he tells us in his hymn to light:

Thee I revisit now with bolder wing,
Escap't the *Stygian* Pool, though long detain'd
In that obscure sojourn, while in my flight
Through utter and through middle darkness borne
With other notes than to th' *Orphean* Lyre
I sung of *Chaos* and *Eternal Night*,
Taught by the heav'nly Muse to venture down
The dark descent, and up to reascend,
Though hard and rare: thee I revisit safe,
And feel thy sovran vital Lamp; but thou
Revisit'st not these eyes, that roll in vain
To find thy piercing ray, and find no dawn.

[3.13–24]

Through his blindness, he says, he is now cut off from seeing the wondrous works of God, and yet with the eyes of the mind he makes his pilgrimage to paradise—revealing in his own response the delight in God's works that Satan cannot feel. It is a journey of remembrance, using all the aids that divine grace and human knowledge can provide. Thus he is no distant teller of the tale, no detached observer.[3] This singer is an active participant in the poem, so much so that at the begin-

ning of book 4 he is overwhelmed with pity at the success of Satan's
hypocrisy, and he wishes that someone, somehow, could help:

> O for that warning voice, which he who saw
> Th' *Apocalypse,* heard cry in Heav'n aloud,
> Then when the Dragon, put to second rout,
> Came furious down to be reveng'd on men,
> "Woe to the inhabitants on Earth!" that now,
> While time was, our first Parents had been warn'd
> The coming of thir secret foe, and scap'd
> Haply so scap'd his mortal snare; for now
> *Satan,* now first inflam'd with rage, came down,
> The Tempter ere th' Accuser of man-kind,
> To wreck on innocent frail man his loss
> Of that first Battle, and his flight to Hell.
>   [4.1–12]

The poet, as it seems, has become so deeply immersed in the present
action of his story that he does not seem to know that of course Adam
will be warned by Raphael later on in the poem. Perhaps, though, this
only shows the error of calling the speaker "the poet," or "John Milton," or even "the bard," or the "singer," as some of us like to call him.
Perhaps it is better to speak only of a human voice who does not quite
know what lies ahead and who waits for the muse to prompt his "unpremeditated Verse," as Milton calls his writing later on in the poem
(9.24). And yet even a disembodied human voice ought, it seems,
somehow to remember what he has just said through the voice of God
in the third book, where Milton has God say, "I made him just and
right, / Sufficient to have stood, though free to fall" (3.98–99). But
notice that the voice of the singer in book 4 has called man *frail.* And the
voice of pity here seems to draw out all the implications of the word,
not just simply the basic meaning, "liable to break or to be broken"
("free to fall"), but all the weight of all the other meanings of that word:
"easily crushed or destroyed," "weak, subject to infirmities: wanting
in power, easily overcome," or worse yet, "morally weak; unable to
resist temptation; habitually falling into transgressions." We may well
ask: how can a man be made sufficient to have stood, though frail? But
the impact here is not theological. And the contradiction may well pass
unnoticed, for the main point of the speaker's cry seems to be to call our
attention to the singer's presence, to tell us of his love and pity, so

different from Satan's hate and envy. So now this singer guides his readers toward a true response, as he presents the true pilgrim's vision of a paradise of perfect beauty regained in memory.

Here in book 4 is perhaps the greatest challenge of the entire poem, for in this vision Milton must transcend the fallen, but heroic, grandeur of Satan, as we have seen him defying God in books 1 and 2. Would not a scholar and a writer, struck blind as Milton was in the prime of life, be tempted to curse God as Satan does, and turn to despair? Milton has given us a glimpse of that possibility in his sonnet "When I consider how my light is spent." Now he shows that frailty overcome as he draws upon his memories of books and paintings and his own earlier visual experience of the book of nature to show how the wondrous works of God may be had in remembrance always with delight. These paradisal scenes of perfect beauty in books 4 and 5, along with the story of creation in books 7 and 8, constitute a long psalm in praise of the wondrous works of God; they constitute the goal of this singer's pilgrimage, a goal in which the redeemed man may sing the praises of his creator and his recreator, before the shrine of the great created universe. The redeemed man, as represented in this blind singer, reaches his goal, we must note, sings his hymn of praise, *before* he relates the story of man's fall. The evidence of man's redemption precedes the evidence of man's condemnation.

We must note also that this is a song of praise which persists throughout a series of violent interruptions, as Satan in his soliloquies reveals his torment, his hell on earth, and his ruthless determination to destroy mankind. The hymn of praise is also interrupted, at much greater length, by the angel Raphael's account of the war in heaven. Nevertheless, a rising tide of irresistible creative power runs from Satan's account (in book 3) of his false pilgrimage, through Uriel's true account of the aims of pilgrimage, to the realization of that true pilgrimage in the singer's account of paradise. Indeed, considering the alternations between the poet's praise and Satan's hatred, we might say that a battle between light and dark is framed between two angelic psalms in praise of creation—psalms that foreshadow and complete the imperfect human apprehension of paradise that lies between these two angelic poems. The first of these angelic hymns is that spoken by Uriel at the very close of book 3:

I saw when at his Word the formless Mass,
This world's material mould, came to a heap:

Confusion heard his voice, and wild uproar
Stood rul'd, stood vast infinitude confin'd;
Till at his second bidding darkness fled,
Light shone, and order from disorder sprung:
Swift to thir several Quarters hasted then
The cumbrous Elements, Earth, Flood, Air, Fire,
And this Ethereal quintessence of Heav'n
Flew upward, spirited with various forms,
That roll'd orbicular, and turn'd to Stars
Numberless, as thou seest, and how they move;
Each had his place appointed, each his course,
The rest in circuit walls this Universe.
                    [3.708–21]

Notice that the angel places the stress on order, rule, form, design, purpose, and thus on the wondrous power of God to control such plenitude, such rich fertility of being. Perfect beauty exists within a powerful design; the bounty of the material universe is beautiful only within an orderly and appointed plan.

Book 7 of *Paradise Lost* represents the detailed fulfillment of that vision, told by another angel, Raphael, who reveals all the richness of the six days of creation, and then concludes his account of creation near the close of the book with these words:

So Ev'n and Morn accomplish'd the Sixt day:
Yet not till the Creator from his work,
Desisting, though unwearied, up return'd
Up to the Heav'n of Heav'ns his high abode,
Thence to behold this new created World
Th' addition of his Empire, how it show'd
In prospect from his Throne, how good, how fair,
Answering his great Idea.
                    [7.550–57]

What Milton is celebrating here is basically the pure idea of beauty—the Platonic idea of creation that existed in the mind of God and is now recreated here within the poet's mind and in our own minds, as we read. But this idea, in its full grandeur and power, Milton allows the two angels to tell; it is beyond human vision, except, of course, for a divinely inspired poet and prophet.

By contrast, in books 4 and 5, we watch the human singer attempting to grasp and to convey a glimpse of that divine idea of perfect beauty; we watch Adam's descendant, in his own imperfect way, at-

tempting to fulfill the original impulse of joy and gratitude which
Adam himself remembers as his earliest emotion. Thus Adam recounts his first sensations of life to the angel Raphael in book 8:

> Thou Sun, said I, fair Light,
> And thou enlight'n'd Earth, so fresh and gay,
> Ye Hills and Dales, ye Rivers, Woods, and Plains
> And ye that live and move, fair Creatures, tell,
> Tell, if ye saw, how came I thus, how here?
> Not of myself; by some great Maker then,
> In goodness and in power preëminent;
> Tell me, how may I know him, how adore,
> From whom I have that thus I move and live,
> And feel that I am happier than I know.
>
> [8.273–82]

So every part in this portion of the poem, extending from the hymn
to light at the outset of book 3 to this address to light by Adam in book
8, is held together by the voice of praise, which rises above the satanic
voice of hate. This contrast is especially evident in book 4, as Adam's
descendant, the modern singer, struggles to express his love and wonder at this answer to his pilgrimage of remembrance:

> And of pure now purer air
> Meets his approach, and to the heart inspires
> Vernal delight and joy, able to drive
> All sadness but despair.
>
> [4.153–56]

The word *his* refers literally to Satan, as the poet follows his approach
to paradise, but the word *heart* (that is, the response to the vision of
beauty) does not apply to Satan. Satan is only a foil to the redeemed
vision of the bard, who now, overcome with delight and joy, is able to
create a vision of the earthly paradise out of his knowledge of the Bible
and of human history and mythology. Here again we have the distinction between Satan's point of view and that of the *human* viewer:

> Beneath him with new wonder now he views
> To all delight of human sense expos'd
> In narrow room Nature's whole wealth, yea more,
> A Heaven on Earth. . . .
>
> [4.205–08]

The wonder that Satan feels here is not the wonder of the psalms; Satan
feels amazement, astonishment, but not delight. Such delight is re-

served for the vision of the redeemed man who now goes on to tell us in his human voice what we may already know from our readings in the Bible and in human history:

> for blissful Paradise
> Of God the Garden was, by him in the East
> Of *Eden* planted; *Eden* stretch'd her Line
> From *Auran* Eastward to the Royal Tow'rs
> Of Great *Seleucia,* built by *Grecian* Kings,
> Or where the Sons of *Eden* long before
> Dwelt in *Telassar.* . . .
>
> [4.208–14]

But now the poet goes on to tell us something that we do not necessarily know and therefore he imagines it for us; he now shows us how paradise was irrigated:

> Southward through *Eden* went a River large,
> Nor chang'd his course, but through the shaggy hill
> Pass'd underneath ingulft, for God had thrown
> That Mountain as his Garden mould high rais'd
> Upon the rapid current, which through veins
> Of porous Earth with kindly thirst up-drawn,
> Rose a fresh Fountain, and with many a rill
> Water'd the Garden; thence united fell
> Down the steep glade, and met the nether Flood,
> Which from his darksome passage now appears,
> And now divided into four main Streams,
> Runs diverse, wand'ring many a famous Realm
> And Country whereof here needs no account. . . .
>
> [4.223–35]

The poet's familiar manner indicates that we may well know all about these famous realms and countries from our studies in history and geography. But here the problem is, he goes on to say, how to deal with something that lies beyond the limits of art:

> But rather to tell how, if Art could tell,
> How from that Sapphire Fount the crisped Brooks,
> Rolling on Orient Pearl and sands of Gold,
> With mazy error under pendant shades
> Ran Nectar, visiting each plant, and fed
> Flow'rs. . . .
>
> [4.236–41]

What kind of flowers? Well, simply, "Flow'rs worthy of Paradise."
The poet cannot imagine any further detail than this, and he ends his
scene with a summary: "Thus was this place, / A happy rural seat of
various view." Notice all those humanizing touches: the embedding
of this account in a specific geographical place amidst the events of
human history; the imaging of the mount of paradise as a sort of
human organism with thirst and veins; and then, after admitting the
limitations of art, the poet comes to rest in the image of a happy English
country estate—not, of course, an adequate image (nothing is), but at
least it is a vestige of paradise. It is something man has made by art out
of nature—though here in paradise is a scene that surpasses all the efforts of human imagination in gardening or architecture. The main
effect is simply this: here is one of us trying to tell the story—impossible to tell.[4] "Not that fair field / Of *Enna*" nor "that sweet Grove / Of
Daphne by *Orontes*," "nor that *Nyseian* Isle," "Nor where *Abassin*
Kings thir issue Guard," none of these, says the singer, "might with
this Paradise / Of *Eden* strive." The description does not matter. The
very admission of the speaker's inadequacy indicates his appreciation
and his gratitude for the gift. What matters is his love for the creator as
conveyed by his love for all created things. The expression of this love
is the goal of the speaker's pilgrimage, and he conveys it all to us as he
joins with Adam and Eve in their morning hymn in praise of the wondrous works of God, which appears in book 5:

> These are thy glorious works, Parent of good,
> Almighty, thine this universal Frame,
> Thus wondrous fair; thyself how wondrous then!
> . . . .
> Join voices all ye living Souls; ye Birds,
> That singing up to Heaven Gate ascend,
> Bear on your wings and in your notes his praise;
> Yee that in Waters glide, and yee that walk
> The Earth, and stately tread, or lowly creep;
> Witness if I be silent, Morn or Even,
> To Hill, or Valley, Fountain, or fresh shade
> Made vocal by my Song, and taught his praise.
> Hail universal Lord, be bounteous still
> To give us only good; and if the night
> Have gather'd aught of evil or conceal'd,
> Disperse it, as now light dispels the dark.
> [5.153–55, 197–208]

As long as a living poet can sing that song, the continuity between human beings, nature, and God will persist, and each human being may reach the proper goal of his solitary way—which is of course solitary only in the sense that it must be followed in accordance with each individual's deepest inner being. But Satan is truly solitary, cut off by his pride even from his followers: "this enterprise," he says as he departs from hell upon his pilgrimage of hate, "this enterprise / None shall partake with me" (2.465–66). Milton's hell is populated by individuals isolated by their crimes against creation.

For humankind, in Milton's view, the way need not be solitary in this literal, single sense. The rich paradox and ambiguity of Milton's ending has nowhere been captured better than in William Blake's two great drawings of Adam and Eve leaving Paradise.[5] In both drawings a sorrowing angel leads Adam and Eve forth gently by the hand. In both drawings Blake presents a sheet of flame behind the human pair, with terrifying effect. Hand in hand with the angel, Adam and Eve step forward toward us, their descendants. In one of Blake's drawings they look upward, not without hope, but with considerable apprehension and uncertainty. In the other version they look downward at the serpent writhing between them on the ground, and their look is one of horror, fear, and repugnance. Will they go the way of Satan, they seem to be asking. Behind them, in both drawings, the four staring figures on horseback that guard the wall present no answer to that question. Their eyes are full of enigma and mystery. They look into a future that Adam and Eve must choose to make.

NOTES

1. The illustration is derived from Raphael: see Marcia R. Pointon, *Milton and English Art* (Manchester, 1970), p. 15; and Helen Gardner, "Milton's First Illustrator," *Essays and Studies* (1956), pp. 34–35. See also Merritt Y. Hughes, "Some Illustrators of Milton: The Expulsion from Paradise," *Journal of English and Germanic Philology* 60(1961): 670–79; and Kester Svendsen, *Milton and Science* (Cambridge, Mass., 1956), pp. 107–13.

2. See the note on book 12, line 647, in *The Poems of John Milton,* ed. John Carey and Alastair Fowler (London, 1968).

3. For previous studies of the role of the narrator in *Paradise Lost* see the works listed in the first note to the preceding essay by George Lord; in particular, some of the points mentioned in my discussion are treated, in a different context, by Anne Ferry.

4. See C. S. Lewis, *A Preface to Paradise Lost* (London, 1942), pp. 47–50.

5. See Pointon, *Milton and English Art,* p. 159. Quotations from *Paradise Lost* throughout this essay are taken from the edition by Merritt Y. Hughes (New York, Odyssey Press, 1962).

KENT T. VAN DEN BERG

"The Counterfeit in Personation": Spenser's *Prosopopoia, or Mother Hubberds Tale*

In *The Arte of English Poesie* (1589), George Puttenham translates *prosopopoeia* as "the counterfeit in personation," distinguishing it from *prosopographia,* which is the description of historical persons "according to the truth and not by fiction":

> But if ye wil faine any person with such features, qualities and conditions, or if ye wil attribute any humane quality, as reason or speech to dombe creatures or other insensible things, and do study (as one may say) to giue them a humane person, it is not *Prosopographia,* but *Prosopopeia,* because it is by way of fiction, and no prettier examples can be giuen to you thereof, than in the Romant of the rose translated out of French by *Chaucer,* describing the persons of auarice, enuie, old age, and many others, whereby much moralitie is taught.[1]

This definition conflates imaginative operations that are logically distinct and can occur independently: (1) the characterization of any fictive, as opposed to historical, person; (2) personfication in the sense of treating animals or things as human by making them think and speak, like the beasts in Aesop's *Fables;* (3) personification in the different sense of using animals, things, or humans as allegorical embodiments of universals, like Avarice and Old Age in Chaucer's *Romant.* Puttenham's rubric, "the counterfeit in personation," also suggests: (4) impersonation in the sense applied to an author when he adopts a persona, like Chaucer's pilgrim story tellers; (5) impersonation in the sense applied to a character who assumes a disguise. Spenser's *Prosopopoia, or Mother Hubberds Tale* employs Puttenham's figure in all of these ways: the descriptions of the farmer, priest, courtier, and Mercury provide a range of fictive characterizations; the narrator impersonates Mother Hubberd's distinctive style; the Fox and Ape in her beast

fable are given the human qualities of reason and speech, they imper-
sonate men by assuming disguises, and they personify cunning and
greed. Spenser makes these different uses of *prosopopoeia* aspects of a
single act of mind by which the world's vanity is comprehended in the
fictive image of a beast fable. He does so by treating Puttenham's figure
of speech as a metaphor: the "counterfeit in personation" is not only a
rhetorical resource for the poet but also the modus operandi of Fox and
Ape, who assume "False personages fit for euerie sted" (line 861),[2] as
they rise by dexterous fraud through the four estates of Elizabethan
society, from the peasantry to the clergy to the court to the throne. If
Mother Hubberds Tale is Spenser's most extensive satire, exposing
abuses in Elizabethan social life, it is also what Louis Martz calls
"poetry of the interior life, where the mind, acutely aware of an outer
world of drifting, unstable forms, finds within itself the power to
create coherence and significance."[3] As a comprehensive persona
making, *Mother Hubberds Tale* sets the poet's power to personify
against his disdain for the counterfeit self, and thereby exemplifies his
struggle to maintain moral and aesthetic integrity in the face of a fragmented and deceptive world, "Continuallie subiect vnto chaunge"
(92).[4]

The prologue places Mother Hubberd's original recital far in the
past and presents the poem as Spenser's effort at a later time to reconstruct the story:

Ile write in termes, as she the same did say,
So well as I her words remember may.
No Muses aide me needes heretoo to call;
Base is the style, and matter meane withall.

[41–44]

He distinguishes himself as narrator of the poem from Mother Hubberd as teller of the story, and thereby gives the narration a richly subjective resonance: the narrative is both Mother Hubberd's story as it
echoes in his memory and his own attempt to write in her style. He
does not consistently "remember" her words; the distinction of story
teller and narrator is emphasized by several passages—the humanist
description of an ideal courtier (711–93), the overtly personal suitor's
complaint (891–918), and the epic descent of Mercury (1225–
1332)—which are so out of keeping with the low style of the beast fable
and the homely character of Mother Hubberd that we must read them

as the narrator's additions to her story. Critics have assumed that these passages were hastily added in 1590 to a poem Spenser said he wrote long before "in the raw conceipt of . . . youth."[5] Whatever the truth about the poem's composition, Spenser makes a process of revision—the narrator's revision of Mother Hubberd's story—a part of the fiction. He presents the poem as his transformation of an oral performance into a more thoroughly literary mode: "Ile *write* in termes, as she the same did *say*." The management of the narrative and modulations of its tone characterize not the fictive personality of Mother Hubberd as a speaker but the changing responses of the narrator as a writer recollecting her tale and setting it down in verse.

The narrator's interpretative response to the beast fable as an image of life is evident in the systematic progression of its episodes through the four estates. This progression does not result from any coherent plan of action put in effect by the characters. They do not approach the farmer as a means of advancing to the clergy, or enter the clergy as a way of getting to court, or use the court as a stepping stone to the throne. This sequence is, from their point of view, quite haphazard:

> At last they chaunst to meete vpon the way
> A simple husbandman
> . . . .
> At length [they] chaunst with a formall Priest to meete
> . . . .
> At last they chaunst to meete vpon the way
> The Mule
> . . . .
> Whilst through the forest rechlesse they did goe,
> Lo where they spide, how in a gloomy glade,
> The Lyon sleeping lay.
>   [227–28, 361, 581–82, 950–52]

This iteration of *chaunst* emphasizes their abject surrender to the world of change. It is only from the detached and contemplative viewpoint shared by narrator and reader that their random adventures reveal a comprehensive survey of Elizabethan society.

The episodes are not run together in a single action but are held apart by long periods of aimless wandering and "manie haps, which needs not here to tell" (360). Each episode is a self-contained unit that repeats the same pattern of action: Fox and Ape present themselves in disguise, their false appearances are accepted for true, and they thereby gain undeserved benefits at others' expense. In every instance, they exceed themselves and are, at last, "descryed" (see 345–48, 559–74, 919–37, 1225–384), so that they must steal away by night (see 339–40, 574, 937). Other repeated words and themes impede the forward movement of the action by making the latter episodes seem reflections of the earlier ones. There are three elaborate descriptions of the Ape's costumes (as soldier, courtier, and king), and three times we watch him step deftly into a new adventure:

> Eftsoones the Ape himselfe gan vp to reare,
> . . . .
> And stoutly forward he his steps did straine,
> That like a handsome swaine it him became.
>   [237, 241–42]

> the fond Ape himselfe vprearing hy
> Vpon his tiptoes, stalketh stately by,
> As if he were some great *Magnifico*.
>   [663–65]

> Vpon his tiptoes nicely he vp went.
>   [1009]

Conspicuous figures of speech recur, especially the figures of repetition; the rhetorical high point of each episode is punctuated by a figure that packs a verb into every foot: "To plough, to plant, to reap, to rake, to sowe, / To hedge, to ditch, to thrash, to thetch, to mowe" (263–64; see also 505–08, 905–06, 1012, 1340). The repetition of these elements makes the episodes look like successive reconsiderations and revisions, even though the contrary impression of forward movement is never entirely lost. The two impressions combine to produce a more complex sense of incremental repetition, as the basic action is repeated at higher levels of society and deeper levels of understanding.

The second episode, in relation to the first, illustrates the process by which the fiction is simultaneously brought closer to its referents in the actual world and more thoroughly immersed in the subjective responses of writer and reader. This episode subsumes and revises the first at a metaphoric level by moving from false shepherds to false pastors and from the slaughter of a flock to the exploitation of a congregation. This metaphoric revision enriches characterization. In the priest the virtues and vices represented earlier by exemplary and allegorical figures meet and interact. He combines the Fox's cunning and the Ape's greed with something like the plain and simple honesty exemplified by the farmer in the first episode. In the following lines, the narrator pretends to praise such a virtue in the priest:

> Of such deep learning little had he neede,
> Ne yet of Latine, ne of Greeke, that breede
> Doubts mongst Diuines, and difference of texts,
> From whence arise diuersitie of sects,
> And hatefull heresies, of God abhor'd:
> But this good Sir did follow the plaine word,
> Ne medled with their controuersies vaine;
> All his care was, his seruice well to saine,
> And to read Homelies vpon holidayes:
> When that was done, he might attend his playes;
> An easie life, and fit high God to please.
>
> [385–95]

This mock praise, occasioned by the priest's inability to read the Ape's forged *bona fides,* is an impressive display of double irony. At one level, it exposes the hypocrisy of the priest, who is pretending to scrutinize the Ape's credentials while the narrator praises his illiteracy. At another level, the passage questions the adequacy of plain honesty itself as a moral norm. The insidiously smooth transition from following the plain word to enjoying the easy life suggests how susceptible a genuinely simple soul is to corruption by the Fox and Ape within. The irony intensifies when the priest assures the Ape that the Reformation's zealous purification of the liturgy has greatly improved the religious life:

> They whilome vsed duly euerie day
> Their seruice and their holie things to say,
> At morne and euen, besides their Anthemes sweete,
> Their penie Masses, and their Complynes meete,
> Their Dirges, their Trentals, and their shrifts,
> Their memories, their singings, and their gifts.
> Now all those needlesse works are laid away;
> Now once a weeke vpon the Sabbath day,
> It is enough to doo our small deuotion,
> And then to follow any merrie motion.
>
> [449–58]

These lines expose the moral complacency of both the old and the new order. The catalogue of "all those needlesse works" expresses the reformer's scorn for the claptrap of medieval Catholicism; yet the Protestant dispensation has left this simple priest helpless to resist his penchant for laziness and self-deception by granting him more "libertie" than his weak soul can handle.

The reader is directly implicated in the complex moral vision of this episode by its sophisticated mode of narration. The first episode, by contrast, was related in a simpler mode, more closely confined to the objective norms of oral presentation. A speaker's physical presence to his audience tends to keep his attitudes toward and presentation of the story distinct from the events themselves, which are not present but have to be imagined. In the first episode, the speaker's commentary is clearly stated to us in direct address, and is held apart from the fictive substance of the story, as when an indulgently detailed description of the Ape's soldier costume is followed by a brief editorial condemnation:

> Shame light on him, that through so false illusion,
> Doth turne the name of Souldiers to abusion,
> And that, which is the noblest mysterie,
> Brings to reproach and common infamie.
>
> [219–22]

In the second episode, judgments of this sort are implicit in the dialogue or in passages of descriptive narration that are closely keyed to the characters' point of view, as when the narrator ironically justifies the priest's inability to read. Spenser adopts a Chaucerian narrative mode that subsumes oral presentation by making it part of the fiction, so that a single utterance expresses both the character's speech to the fictive audience and the narrator's implicit judgment for the reader. Thus the very words the priest speaks to Fox and Ape in praise of his vocation elicit the reader's condemnation. The indirection of Chaucerian irony grants the reader liberty of interpretation and invites his active response, through which the moral significance of the events must be established. The reader is challenged to accept responsibilities not required of him in the first episode and to shun the weakness of spirit that allows the priest to abuse, by willfully misinterpreting, "the Gospell of free libertie" (478).

Each of the four episodes is longer and more elaborate than the last and burdens the fable with a more comprehensive metaphoric reference to Elizabethan society. In the first, Fox and Ape are the sole perpetrators of evil, and their crime, devouring the farmer's sheep, is merely the instinctive reflex of the animal predator: "For that disguised Dog lou'd blood to spill" (319). But in the second episode, they need to be instructed at length by the priest, because animal greed and guile are not sufficient guides to action in the more complex world of the clergy, where corrupt practices are widespread and well established. Court society in the third episode is so intricate in its modes of exchange that Fox and Ape must diversify their functions to exploit it: the Ape plays the great and influential courtier, while the Fox, as his groom, entraps those who seek the Ape's favor. The same division of labor is more widely effective in the final episode, where the Ape as king and the Fox as first minister tyrannize an entire kingdom.

The changing relationship of fiction and reality is made conspicuous, especially in the third and fourth episodes, by an inconsistency in the presentation of Fox and Ape. In the first episode, the Ape presents himself as a soldier because his "manly semblance" (200) makes him fit for the part, while the Fox must disguise as his "Curdog" (294); but in the second episode both animals can pass themselves off as clerks and converse at length with the priest. As the third episode begins, they meet the Mule who tells them which beasts are most in favor at the Lion's court; but the court, when they reach it, turns out to be an all too human society realistically presented. The final episode brings Fox and Ape to the animal kingdom, where they steal the sleeping Lion's royal insignia; yet, even here, they base their claims to the Lion's throne on their resemblance to man, "the Lord of euerie creature" (1030). One scholar finds this shifting between human and animal worlds "a defect so obvious that it is hard to understand how a skilled writer could have overlooked it"; others attribute the defect to "hasty and radical revision."[6] But could Spenser have been so careless?

The inconsistency was probably deliberate and need not be regarded as a defect. It displays the different ways that a beast fable can be related to actual life and makes the process of representation, the *prosopopoeia,* part of the fiction. The animals represent humans by convention, but they enter the human world itself through disguise; the credibility of their impersonations results in part from their own cleverness, but in part also from the narrator's satiric perspective: the Fox can easily become a priest in a world where priests are foxes, and the Ape will be readily accepted by courtiers who are themselves an "Apish crue" (731). The changes in the relation of fiction to reality

conform to a significant pattern by moving from the recreative fiction
that animals are like men to the satiric complaint (most prominent in
the court episode) that men are like animals. The final episode combines these alternatives: on the one hand, it retreats from the human
world to the animal kingdom; on the other, it engages the human
world more directly through sustained topical allusions to actual persons and specific abuses.

The prologue to *Mother Hubberds Tale* invites us to attribute the
recreative fiction of animals as men to Mother Hubberd's "honest
mirth" (35) and the satiric perception of men as animals to the narrator's melancholy. His sickness suggests the "inward sorrow" and
"deep dismay" that Spenser elsewhere attributes to an awareness of
mortal decay (see *The Ruines of Time*, lines 470–90): his body is "set on
fire with griefe" (15), his senses troubled with "vnquiet fancies" (24),
and his spirit "heauie and diseased" (40). "Gladsome solace" (20) is
provided for the narrator by some friends who gather around the sickbed and distract him from his solitary and obsessive brooding with
"talke" (24) and "pleasant tales . . . to waste the wearie howres" (26,
27). The surpassing mirth of Mother Hubberd comes mostly from her
ability to project the actual situation of oral communication into her
tale; she indulges at length the pleasure of making her characters talk
and shows them relishing their own rhetorical skill. The priest, for
example, ends his lengthy monologue by addressing a wonderfully
smug *plaudite* to the Fox:

> How saist thou (friend) haue I not well discourst
> Vpon this Common place (though plaine, not wourst)?
> Better a short tale, than a bad long shriuing.
> Needes anie more to learne to get a liuing?
>
> [541–44]

By making them talk, Mother Hubberd asserts their presence as fictive
characters and thereby affirms the imagination's recreative power.
This affirmation acts as a counterweight to the satiric recognition
that what her characters are saying typifies the hypocrisy and self-
deception that contaminate the actual world.

This equipoise of fictive presence and satiric representation is not
maintained in the third episode, where (after the initial conversation
with the Mule) no fictive speech is actually rendered, while the Ape's
abuse of speech is described at length and vigorously condemned (see

698–99, 703–10, 809–43). As a result, the fiction nearly collapses under its growing burden of actuality, and Mother Hubberd's "honest mirth" is obscured by the narrator's plaintive description of court life. Fox and Ape lose their substance and become nearly transparent symbols of corruption diffused throughout the court. Descriptions of the Ape break down into lists of degenerate pastimes:

> For he could play, and daunce, and vaute, and spring,
> And all that els pertaines to reueling,
>
> . . . .
>
> A thousand wayes he them could entertaine,
> With all the thriftles games, that may be found,
> With mumming and with masking all around,
> With dice, with cards, with balliards farre vnfit,
> With shuttelcocks, misseeming manlie wit,
> With courtizans, and costly riotize.
>
> [693–94, 800–05]

The Fox becomes so "slipprie" in taking on the "False personages" of a merchant, lawyer, broker, farmer (see 859–76) that his identity disappears into a pervasive force of negation that exploits and undermines the social forms assumed in good faith by others.[7] His counterfeit reality spreads like an infection through the court.

The story of Fox and Ape is abandoned altogether in two long passages: the portrait of the ideal courtier (711–93), and the suitor's complaint (891–918). Spenser deliberately makes both passages look like digressions, so that we will take them not as part of the story but as the narrator's subjective responses to the reality that the story has called too powerfully to mind. He could have brought the courtier into the action by making him the one to expose and banish Fox and Ape, but he does not. The portrait is included not for the story's sake but for the narrator's; the courtier is an ideal countertype to the prevailing corruption. If the description of the courtier shows the narrator swerving away from his story, the suitor's complaint moves in the other direction, from avoidance to obsession. In this remarkable passage, Spenser dramatizes the narrator in the act of losing self-control. The complaint is preceded by a straightforward account telling how the Fox cheated suitors by encouraging them to buy useless favors from the Ape. The whole subject seems to come to a decisive end in the following lines:

So would he worke the silly man by treason
To buy his Masters friuolous good will,
That had not power to doo him good or ill.

[888–90]

The couplet is so emphatically closed ("good will . . . good or ill")
that we expect the narrator to move on to a different topic. But he
bestows another line on the suitor, as if reacting to his own description:
"So pitifull a thing is Suters state" (891). He then develops the theme in
a tirade overtly based on personal experience; the narrator was himself
a suitor:

Full little knowest thou that hast not tride,
What hell it is, in suing long to bide:
To loose good dayes, that might be better spent;
To wast long nights in pensiue discontent;
To speed to day, to be put back to morrow;
To feed on hope, to pine with feare and sorrow;
. . . .
To fawne, to crowche, to waite, to ride, to ronne,
To spend, to giue, to want, to be vndonne.

[895–900, 905–06]

Spenser's ideal courtier offers a significant contrast not only to the
"Apish crue" but also to the narrator himself. The courtier, unlike the
narrator, maintains a stable, deftly poised relation to the treacherous
society of the court. His integrity depends in large measure on his
ability to disengage himself from that world:

He stands on tearmes of honourable minde,
Ne will be carried with the common winde
Of Courts inconstant mutabilitie.

[721–23]

As the description unfolds, Spenser presents a series of progressively
more thorough modes of withdrawal. The first is a prudent aloofness
that allows a considered view of a complex social scene and makes
room for second thoughts: the courtier does not credit "euerie tattling
fable," "But heares, and sees the follies of the rest, / And thereof
gathers for himselfe the best" (725–26). He turns from court society to
a variety of physical exercises that are partly basic training for combat
but mostly means of avoiding idleness and dissipation. After his exercise, he "doth recoyle / Vnto his rest" (754–55) and "reuiues his toyled

spright" (756) with music and "Ladies gentle sports" (757). Finally, "His minde vnto the Muses he withdrawes" (760). He retires to the solitude of reading and learns

> Of Natures workes, of heauens continuall course,
> Of forreine lands, of people different,
> Of kingdomes change, of diuers gouernment,
> Of dreadfull battailes of renowmed Knights.
>
> [764–67]

This "Heroicall" poem (is it *The Faerie Queene?*) has the effect prescribed by Sidney:

> For indeede Poetrie euer setteth vertue so out in her best cullours, making Fortune her wel-wayting hand-mayd, that one must needs be enamored of her. . . . The Heroicall . . . [is] the best and most accomplished kinde of Poetry. For as the image of each action styrreth and instructeth the mind, so the loftie image of such Worthies [as Cyrus, Aeneas, and others] most inflameth the mind with desire to be worthy, and informes with counsel how to be worthy;[8]

it

> kindleth his ambitious sprights
> To like desire and praise of noble fame,
> The onely vpshot whereto he doth ayme:
> For all his minde on honour fixed is,
> To which he leuels all his purposie.
>
> [768–72]

Poetry allows the courtier to shape himself from within according to an ideal pattern and thereby avoid the fate of Fox and Ape, who, by surrendering to the changeful world, make its deceptive and mutable character their own. By withdrawing from the world, the courtier can return to it on his own terms, "of honourable minde," prepared not only for warfare but also for more difficult diplomatic struggles in the world governed by Fox and Ape, the world of "policie . . . and the change / Of states . . . Supplanted by fine falshood and faire guile" (783, 786–87, 788).

In the final episode, the poem achieves a literary equivalent of the courtier's poise by combining imaginative detachment with effective satiric engagement. This episode turns from the court where the poet himself had been a frustrated suitor to the animal kingdom where the worst that Fox and Ape might do can be displayed in a world he creates

and controls. The overtly fictive quality of this world emphasizes the
narrator's control, as does the leisurely pace of the narration. Each step
in the rise and fall of Fox and Ape is elaborately described. They encounter the sleeping Lion; the Fox persuades the Ape to steal the royal
insignia; the Ape, very gingerly, does so; they argue about which of
them should be king; they make a royal progress to test the effectiveness of the disguise; they secure their power and tyrannize the kingdom; Mercury awakens the Lion who expels the usurpers. All of this is
quite unhurried, and we are invited to regard the action with amused
detachment:

> Loath was the Ape, though praised, to aduenter,
> Yet faintly gan into his worke to enter,
> Afraid of euerie leafe, that stir'd him by,
> And euerie stick, that vnderneath did ly;
> Vpon his tiptoes nicely he vp went,
> For making noyse, and still his eare he lent
> To euerie sound, that vnder heauen blew;
> Now went, now stept, now crept, now backward drew,
> That it good sport had been him to haue eyde:
> Yet at the last (so well he him applyde,)
> Through his fine handling, and cleanly play,
> He all those royall signes had stolne away.
>
> [1005–16]

Even the topical references to Lord Burghley in the account of the
Fox's ministry (1137–224) emphasize narrative control. They differ in
effect from the topical allusions in the third episode. The Mule's remarks about the gold chains (623–630) and the reference to Burghley's
interference in the suitor's complaint ("To haue thy Princes grace, yet
want her Peeres; / To haue thy asking, yet waite manie yeeres," 901–
02) are brief and cryptic allusions to specific and isolated circumstances
in real life that are not fully accounted for within the fictive world.[9] By
contrast, the final episode organizes a series of allusions into a unified
exemplum of abuse that is consistent with the fiction as a whole.[10] The
Fox's ministry is of a piece with his earlier conduct at court; it is a logical
counterpart of the Ape's rule, and is a further development of his relation to the Ape in the previous episodes. In the final episode, the fiction
has sufficient substance and internal coherence to stand by itself.
Spenser uses Burghley's ministry as raw material from which to construct an emblem of bad faith in government and increases the poem's
power as satiric exposure by making it appear that life, in this instance,

imitates art. If the Fox resembles Burghley, Burghley also resembles the Fox. Here, more than anywhere else, Spenser has it both ways at once. The topical references in this episode are an indication that the narrator has finally stabilized the previously shifting relationship between the recreative fiction of animals as men and the satiric perception of men as animals.

The boldest display of the narrator's control is, of course, the *deus ex machina* by which the Lion is awakened and the Fox and Ape expelled. The descent of Mercury is an important convention in epic poetry, and Spenser's version of it here is as elaborate as Homer's and Virgil's. Mercury's appearance in a beast fable is, as Thomas Greene remarks, "an extraordinary breach of decorum."[11] It cannot be entirely accounted for as an instance of Spenser's habitual syncretism that prompted him to mingle genres. Spenser wants the descent of Mercury to appear imposed on the story as an artificial means of securing a final victory over Fox and Ape that he knows is impossible in real life. The episode is so obviously an indulgence of wishful thinking on the narrator's part that it clearly distinguishes the fiction from the actual world in which social evils cannot be so decisively encountered.

The conclusion, immediately following the descent of Mercury, displays both the value and the limits of the poem as a fiction. The poem's value inheres less in the satiric warning Spenser may have wished to convey to his sovereign about abuses in her kingdom than in the exercise of imaginative power that recreates those abuses in the fictive form of Fox and Ape; as Yeats would say, "Only when we are gay over a thing, and can play with it, do we show ourselves its master, and have minds clear enough for strength."[12] After a comic chase worthy of an animated cartoon, Fox and Ape are captured and brought to justice. They are punished by being exposed and shamed—but then they are set free:

> The Foxe, first Author of that treacherie,
> He [the Lion] did vncase, and then away let flie.
> But th'Apes long taile (which then he had) he quight
> Cut off, and both eares pared of their hight;
> Since which, all Apes but halfe their eares haue left,
> And of their tailes are vtterlie bereft.
>
> [1379–84]

This is honest mirth indeed; the poem assumes a playful Ovidian tone in turning the Ape's punishment into a fictive explanation of his appearance. But without his tail and long ears the Ape will have even greater "manly semblance" (200) than before, and the Fox uncased will scarcely be recognized for what he is, except by his "slie wyles and subtill craftinesse" (1045). As the poem concludes, the human guile and greed that had been concentrated in the emblematic forms of Fox and Ape are released into the diffuse and multifarious forms they assume in real life.

Spenser symbolizes in Mercury an ambivalent attitude toward the nature of the poet's power. He could not altogether abandon an archaic confidence in poetry as direct and effectual utterance or the attendant belief in the poet's "celestiall inspiration."[13] Mercury, as a superpoet, is an omnipotent admonitory force sent by Jove; he shouts the scandal of disorder and corruption into the ear of a sleeping monarch who is promptly roused to action:

> Arise (said *Mercurie*) thou sluggish beast,
> That here liest senseles, like the corpse deceast,
> The whilste thy kingdome from thy head is rent,
> And thy throne royall with dishonour blent:
> Arise, and doo thy selfe redeeme from shame,
> And be aueng'd on those that breed thy blame.
> Thereat enraged, soone he gan vpstart,
> Grinding his teeth
> . . . .
> Therewith he gan fully terribly to rore
>
> [1327–34, 1337]

The Lion's roaring is an exuberant dramatization of oral power.

Mercury is also devious, disguised, or invisible. As such, he is an emblem of the poet committed to the written medium whose relation to society is therefore oblique and problematic. In the Euhemeristic tradition, Mercury is credited with the invention of the alphabet. This tradition is given striking emphasis in Thomas Nashe's *Summers Last Will and Testament,* where Winter, an enemy of learning and poetry, sardonically states that Mercury "Invented letters to write lies withall."[14] Winter implies a relationship between Mercury as founder of literacy and as master of disguise. Writing entails indirection, even if not lying; as Walter Ong has shown, it is necessarily a kind of *prosopopoeia:*

> Masks are inevitable in all human communication, even oral. Role playing is both different from actuality and an entry into actuality. . . . No matter

what pitch of frankness, directness, or authenticity he may strive for, the writer's mask and the reader's are less removable than those of the oral communicator and his hearer. For writing is itself an indirection. Direct communication by script is impossible. This makes writing not less but more interesting, although perhaps less noble than speech. For man lives largely by indirection, and only beneath the indirections that sustain him is his true nature to be found.[15]

Mercury embodies "the counterfeit in personation" in all its ambivalence by uniting the poet's power and the Fox's. His magic hat gives him a divine equivalent of the Fox's craft:

Through power of that, his cunning theeueries
He wonts to worke, that none the same espies;
And through the power of that, he putteth on
What shape he list in apparition.
[1286–90]

His magic wand, the Caduceus, may be for Spenser, as it was for Comes, a symbol of concord achieved through government of self and society,[16] but its force is potentially as harsh as the tyranny of Fox and Ape. With his wand, he

causeth sleep to seize the eyes,
And feare the harts of all his enemyes;
And when him list, an vniuersall night
Throughout the world he makes on euerie wight.
[1295–98]

This wand has its counterpart in the "wicked weed" (1321) the Fox used to prolong the Lion's slumber, so that he and the Ape could bring darkness and confusion to every wight in the animal kingdom. When he arrived in that kingdom, Mercury "gan . . . to himselfe new shape to frame" (1266), doffing his godlike appearance as "vnfit for that rude rabblement" (1270) and assuming a "strange disguize" (1271). The poet likewise has assumed the guise of Mother Hubberd, adopting her base style as a way of entering the world corrupted by Fox and Ape. Through its multiple uses of "the counterfeit in personation," *Mother Hubberds Tale* has explored without evasion the affinity of the poet's highest aspirations to creative power with the lowest forms of greed and guile. It is Spenser's most tough-minded poem.

Both the exploration and the tough-mindedness required Spenser to respond to his poem more as a subjective experience unfolding deep within the mind than as a rhetorical communication of speaker and audience. This response is authenticated by his actual isolation as a writer. The writer has no audience; he is alone, and his reader is also alone. The medium of writing internalizes the social relationship of the speaker and his audience, making it a "dialogue of one" in the privacy of consciousness. It is natural to mitigate the solitude of literature by pretending that the written narrative is spoken. The fictions, in literature and in critical theory, of the writer as speaker and the reader as listener manifest what Walter Ong calls "habits of thought and expression tracing back to preliterate situations or practice, or deriving from the dominance of the oral as a medium in a given culture, or indicating a reluctance or inability to dissociate the written medium from the spoken."[17] One might even speculate that literary fiction itself is a response to the isolation of consciousness that is intensified by literacy, a response that begins by filling the void with the presence of a fictive speaker to a fictive audience, and proceeds to the presentation of characters, who (in impersonal narration) finally displace the speaker and audience. In this view, the writer's persona, his characters, and all his resources of representation are not only means of communication but also means of establishing an imagined relation to the world from which through literature he and the reader withdraw.[18] Spenser's multiple uses of *prosopopoeia* in *Mother Hubberds Tale* offer an unusually explicit instance of this subjective dimension of fiction.

NOTES

1. *The Arte of English Poesie,* ed. Gladys Doidge Willcock and Alice Walker (Cambridge, 1936), pp. 238–39. In quoting from this edition, I have expanded printer's contractions.

2. I quote Spenser throughout from *The Works of Edmund Spenser: A Variorum Edition,* ed. Edwin Greenlaw, et al., 10 vols. in 11 (Baltimore, 1932–57). *Mother Hubberds Tale* is in *The Minor Poems, Volume 2,* ed. Charles G. Osgood, Henry G. Lotspeich, and Dorothy E. Mason (1947), which is the eighth volume of the *Works.*

3. *The Poem of the Mind* (New York, 1966), p. ix.

4. See Harry Berger, Jr., "The Prospect of Imagination: Spenser and the Limits of Poetry," *Studies in English Literature* 1 (1961): 93–120, especially pp. 109–10: "The great minor poems present Spenser as both poet and man, faced with the problem of establishing the correct decorum . . . between the brazen world and the golden. They deal with the difficulties imposed by life on a mortal who wants completely to transform the one world into the other." I am indebted to Berger throughout this essay.

5. See the dedicatory epistle to Lady Compton and Mountegle. The most important studies that concern the poem's composition are: Edwin Greenlaw, "Spenser and the Earl of Leicester," *PMLA* 25 (1910): 535–61, and *"The Shepheardes Calender, 11,"* *Studies in Philology* 11 (1913): 14–22; Edmund Spenser, *Complaints,* ed. W. L. Renwick (London, 1928), pp. 227, 229–30, 239, 243; Harold Stein, *Studies in Spenser's Complaints* (New York, 1934), pp. 55–62, 78–100; A. C. Judson, "Mother Hubberd's Ape," *Modern Language Notes* 63 (1948): 145–49; William Nelson, *The Poetry of Edmund Spenser* (New York and London, 1963), pp. 12–16, 81–83.

6. Nelson, *The Poetry of Edmund Spenser,* p. 83; see also *Complaints,* ed. Renwick, p. 227. Kenneth John Atchity, in "Spenser's *Mother Hubberds Tale:* Three Themes of Order," *Philological Quarterly* 52 (1973): 161–72, anticipates my suggestion that the inconsistency Nelson complains of is deliberate. Atchity accounts for it by positing a threefold distinction between Mother Hubberd's story about the animals, the narrator's story about Mother Hubberd, and Spenser's story about the narrator. My own interpretation is necessarily more complicated, because I find that the narrator, in retelling Mother Hubberd's story, imposes his own responses on it.

7. See Berger, "The Prospect of Imagination," p. 105: "fox and ape have no reality, no interior form at all. The deliberately inconsistent portrayal, oscillating rapidly between literal and symbolic narrative, reveals them as protean figures whose reality consists in their manifold appearances. They are impelled to knavery by their privation. . . . Their emptiness . . . makes them parasites on the reality of others."

8. *Elizabethan Critical Essays,* ed. G. Gregory Smith (London, 1904), 1:170, 179.

9. Possible explanations of the Mule's references to the gold chains are surveyed by Charles E. Mounts, "The Ralegh-Essex Rivalry and *Mother Hubberds Tale,"* *Modern Language Notes* 65 (1950): 509–13. For Spenser's references to Burghley, see the studies cited above in note 5 and Frederick Hard, "Spenser and Burghley," *Studies in Philology* 28 (1931): 219–34.

10. The Fox's ministry alludes to Burghley's pride in his "long experience" (1168), his disregard for the nobility and their ancestral houses, his disrespect for soldiers and scholars, and his efforts to secure high office for his son, Robert.

11. *The Descent from Heaven* (New Haven and London, 1963), p. 303. Greene provides a detailed account of Spenser's Mercury in relation to the epic tradition, pp. 301–11. I am also indebted to Robert A. Bryan, "Poets, Poetry, and Mercury in Spenser's *Prosopopoia: Mother Hubberd's Tale,"* *Costerus* 5 (1972): 27–33, especially p. 31: "Mercury fulfills the role of the poet, the shepherd-priest, the cleanser of society. . . . Mercury does, in effect, what the satiric poet must do; he prescribes a course of action that will cleanse and scourge the kingdom."

12. *Essays and Introductions* (New York, 1961), p. 252, quoted by John Creaser in "Volpone: The Mortifying of The Fox," *Essays in Criticism* 25 (1975): 350.

13. See the Argument to the October eclogue in *The Shepheardes Calender*.

14. *The Works of Thomas Nashe,* ed. Ronald B. McKerrow, corrected edition, ed. F. P. Wilson, 5 vols. (Oxford, 1958), 3:273. Other Renaissance allusions to Mercury as patron of literacy are cited by Bryan, "Poets, Poetry," p. 32, and by Malcolm Evans, "Mercury Versus Apollo: A Reading of *Love's Labor's Lost,*" *Shakespeare Quarterly* 26 (1975): 113–27.

15. "The Writer's Audience Is Always a Fiction," *PMLA* 90 (1975): 20.

16. See Greene, *The Descent from Heaven,* p. 310.

17. *Rhetoric, Romance, and Technology* (Ithaca and London, 1971), pp. 25–26. William Nelson argues that Father Ong's distinction between oral and written modes is blurred in Renaissance literature by the practice, common throughout the period, of reading aloud to groups of listeners, and that most Renaissance poems, including Spenser's, were written with the requirements of oral presentation in mind; see "From 'Listen, Lordings' to 'Dear Reader'," *University of Toronto Quarterly* 46 (1976-77): 110–24. Even so, Spenser states his awareness of the differences between the two modes, not only in the prologue to *Mother Hubberds Tale* but also at the conclusion: "So Mother *Hubberd* her discourse did end: / Which pardon me, if I amisse haue pend, / For weake was my remembrance it to hold, / And bad her tongue that it so bluntly tolde" (1385–88). Spenser's residence in Ireland isolated him from his courtly audience and may have encouraged his penchant, already evident in *The Shepheardes Calender,* for the writer's indirect mode of communication. He emphasizes this indirectness not only through pseudonyms and personae ("Immerito," "Colin Clout"), but also through elaborately printed publications presented "to the gentle reader" by intermediaries like "E.K." or the printer. At the same time, Spenser's minor poems contain several idealized and nostalgic images of the more direct communion between an oral presenter and his listeners (the prologue to *Mother Hubberds Tale* is a notable instance); he recreates the oral within the written mode.

18. See Geoffrey H. Hartman on literary representation and the idea of presence in *The Fate of Reading* (Chicago, 1975), pp. 35–40, 74–78, 96–98.

RONALD PAULSON

Rochester: The Body Politic and the Body Private

A man could not write with life, unless he were heated by Revenge; for to make a Satyre *without Resentments, upon the cold Notions of* Phylosophy, *was as if a man would in cold blood, cut men's throats who had never offended him.*[1]

In these words spoken by the Earl of Rochester to Gilbert Burnet during their conversion dialogues it is not difficult to detect the stereotype that underlies the satirist's apologia: it may take an evil man to detect evil in others, though only out of a desire to revenge himself for their greater success. "*Heated by* Revenge," however, seem to be Rochester's operative words. There is another interesting remark he dropped to Mr. Giffard, his tutor:

> My Ld. had a natural Distemper upon him which was extraordinary, . . . which was that sometimes he could not have a stool for 3 Weeks or a Month together. Which Distemper his Lordship told him [Giffard] was a very great occasion of that warmth and heat he always expressed, his Brain being heated by the Fumes and Humours that ascended and evacuated themselves that way.[2]

The problem of evacuation carries over into Rochester's poems. In the persona of M.G. (Mulgrave) he writes to O.B. ("Old Bays" or Dryden) that "Perhaps ill verses ought to be confined / In mere good breeding, like unsavory wind," and concludes:

> What though the excrement of my dull brain
> Runs in a costive and insipid strain,
> Whilst your rich head eases itself of wit:
> Must none but civit cats have leave to shit?

And this is very close to the sense of his own argument (in the persona of Horace) with Dryden in "An Allusion to Horace," where, for example: "Yet having this allowed, the heavy mass / That stuffs up his loose volumes must not pass. . . ." He is criticizing Dryden's "looseness" against the norm of his own costiveness, as Horace did with Lucilius. The "warmth and heat he always expressed," however, refer to both sexual and literary activity, emphasizing the naturalness of both but also the particular situation of a body for whom catharsis has a special meaning.

Horace writes satiric verses to ward off insomnia ("verum nequeo dormire") and Pope responds to a fool or a knave as "Bulls aim their horns, and Asses lift their heels." Rochester tells us he "never rhymed but for [his] pintle's sake." Unlike Pope, who was "dipp'd in ink" as his baptism into literature, Rochester says he "dip[s his] pen in flowers" (semen or menstrual discharge). The symptoms he describes are, needless to say, those of melancholy, for which the natural outlet is ordinarily sexual fulfilment. He might have served as a case history for Robert Burton.

Rochester is the difficult transitional figure, in some ways the father of the Augustan mode of satire, in others still an Elizabethan in the tradition of the melancholy satyr-satirist of Jonson and Marston. Some poems—the satires on Sir Carr Scroope come to mind—exist simply as the vivid expression of an individual's disgust, in the ancient tradition of Archilochus's iambics, rather than as the exposure of some general truth about man. It may, of course, take an excitation of the subject to elicit a truth otherwise not noticed in the object—something like the heightened awareness arrived at by a conscious disarranging of the senses. And we have here the alternative possibilities that he associates himself so thoroughly with a particular type, a melancholiac or a Mulgrave or a "hater of Scroope," that via impersonation a transference takes place; or that Rochester's hatred is a kind of attraction leading into the projection of an aspect of himself that he must exorcise or explore. Indeed, the relationship between his poems and his own actions (as distinct from the experience from which they may have emerged) involves the question: do the poems act as a self-criticism, a confession, and a penance for the actions; or are the actions meant to extend the disruptive effect of the satires? Rochester's involvement in the murder of Captain Downs argues for the former; his confrontation with the glass chronometers in the garden of Whitehall Palace, with his obscene but pertinent question followed by his shattering of the mechanism, argues for the latter.

Acknowledging that in his case there often seems to be a physical action in his life that corresponds in some way to a literary expression, we may start by enumerating the conventional aspects of his satires to see if anything remains that is not convention. The obscenity, for a start, was a facet of the low burlesque or travesty mode; the shock has the satiric function of awakening the reader and, by laying bare in the most vivid way his animal origins, making him reassess customary humanist values. Reacting politically and emotionally against the repressive years of the Commonwealth, many Englishmen—but most of all the Cavaliers—encouraged an attitude that was bent on exposing old pious frauds and treating grave subjects like love or life with disrespect. Long before Charles II's return from his travels, the discrediting of something so ostensibly upright as the Puritan led naturally to travesty as a satiric form. The Puritans presented and regarded themselves as paragons, and so allying them with greed for money or power and secret sexual proclivities was intended to expose the real man under the false appearance of saintliness. Begun by *Rump Songs,* the tradition was carried on by Samuel Butler's attacks on the Puritans in *Hudibras,* Cotton's irreverence for heroic attitudes in his *Scarronides,* and Rochester's attacks on the court and the morals of his age in both word and deed.

Elsewhere I have argued that travesty as a satiric device was as necessary for the anti-court forces as the mock-heroic was for the pro-court forces.[3] The latter began with an assumption of the high position of king and court and showed the upstart's presumption in aspiring toward that unassailable position. The aim of the anti-court satire was to show the real hollowness, human weakness, and corruption beneath the rich and respectable, supposedly divine, facade of the court. The obvious corruption of Charles II's court and his personal predilections, like the worldliness of many of the most pious Puritans, made such an approach almost irresistible.

It is a revealing fact that the best of the anti-court satirists were also "court wits" who, though having gone over to the Opposition, shared Charles's libertine skepticism and had helped to give his court the bad name at which they leveled their diatribes. The belief in the efficacy of release and reliance on instinct that contributes to the libertine complex led to the cynical dictum that reality can be found only in the crudest sensuality; the close scrutiny of kings and their mistresses offered another way to this insight. Travesty then ends as a double revelation, of a gross reality masquerading under a glittering appearance, and of the only true reality. Love becomes obscene and life scatological in order to expose certain simpleminded illusions (or hypocrisies), but also because experience proves that love and life are no more than obscene and scatological, that perhaps this is all there is.

Obscenity, though at the center of Rochester's best poems, almost never appears alone; it is the private half of a basic analogy between public and private life.[4] Sexuality offered the most impressive symbol available for the private world, drawing upon an impressive tradition of satirists who wished to remind man of his unheroic, animal self. Even the "gentle" Horace had used sexual lust as a metaphor for a general lack of control in man (satire 1.2). The Puritan emphasis on sexual violation as the darkest of sins, and the court's opposite view, served as further authorities for the intensity of the symbol at this moment of history. There have been few occasions when sex as a vehicle has been closer to the tenor of the satire.

"The Scepter Lampoon" begins with a negative simile relating two kings—Charles II of England is *not* like the foolish Louis XIV of France—and then proceeds to prove that they are precisely alike. The first couplet gives us the generalization that England is famous "For breeding the best cunts in Christendom," as the second couplet parallels this fact about England with the wonderful appropriateness of its king, Charles, the "easiest King and best-bred man alive." The third couplet then contrasts the peaceful Charles with the war-loving Louis, who is characterized by his frantic, meaningless soldiering: he "wanders up and down / Starving his souldiers hazarding his Crown." Opposed to him is Charles: "Peace is his aim, his gentleness is such, / And love he loves, for he loves fucking much." The equation becomes explicit when we are told of Charles that (like Louis who "wanders up and down" fighting wars) "Restless he rolls about from whore to whore, / A merry monarch, scandalous and poor."[5] Kingship is the subject of the poem: Louis's kind of kingship is compared with Charles's, the one a game of war, the other a game of love, and the conclusion is, "All monarchs I hate, and the thrones they sit on, / From the hector of France to the cully of Britain." They share a common lack of serious purpose, abdication of the duties of kingship, and a frenzied, compulsive, and altogether pointless activity.

The initial analogy between war and lust remains implicit, but our attention is focused in the larger part of the poem on Charles and the second half of the comparison, which becomes an equation of Charles's scepter with his sexual organ (and, by implication, Louis's scepter with his sword). Since the king *is* in an important sense the state, public and private life are one, and the king's body is the body politic; and so quite appropriately for Charles, "His scepter and his prick are of a length." The vehicle of the metaphor—as befits an effective lampoon—is taken from the material of the tenor or subject: Louis did wage wars and Charles did have numerous whores. The metaphor is based on a physical resemblance and on a causality between private and public actions. The whore "may sway the one who plays with th' other," and, in effect, Charles's lust determines policy; conversely, his policy is characterized by the changeableness of his passion. And so when Rochester says that Charles's lust is now so jaded that Nell Gwynn can barely arouse it to action, he is saying the same for Charles's rule of the country.

Rochester begins the "Scepter Lampoon" with a contrast of war and lust, which could appear to be public as opposed to private activities (war is traditionally a public duty of kings). By equating them he not only exposes the frantic meaninglessness of Charles's lust (this is the part that adheres to Charles from the "war" half of the equation), but also reduces the idea of war to a level with whoring. The official view was that war was public and whoring private, that a king's public acts were separate from his private. Charles replied to Rochester's lines "He never said a foolish thing, / Nor ever did a wise one" that *he* was responsible for his words, his ministers for his actions. Rochester demonstrates that they are a unity.[6]

Rochester follows the same procedure in a nonpolitical poem, one of those that used to be taken as autobiographical, "The Disabled [or Maimed] Debauchee." Again he begins with the false praise of his subject, in this case debauchery:

> As some brave admiral, in former war
>   Deprived of force, but pressed with courage still,
> . . . .
> So, when my days of impotence approach,
>   And I'm by pox and wine's unlucky chance. . . .

It takes six stanzas, however, to connect the retired admiral and the old poxed rake—six stanzas which elevate debauchery to the level of a heroic duty, war. The continuum is somewhat ambiguous to be sure: debauchery and war share such noble attributes as "courage," "daring," "boldness," "glory," and ideas of excitement and vigor, as opposed to "the dull shore of lazy temperance." And yet both are clearly dangerous, causing disabling wounds, and with the "honorable" scars of the syphilitic that are paid for by "past joys" a mock-heroic effect emerges.

Then in stanzas 9 to 11 the speaker presents a close-up of love-war, only indicated before through the admiral's rose-tinted telescope, and a different kind of soldiering emerges. It is no longer the beautiful abstraction of war but the physical reality of pillaging, reminiscent of Callot's *Misères de la guerre:* "whores attacked, . . . Bawds' quarters beaten up, and fortress won; / Windows demolished, watches overcome; . . . some ancient church [put] to fire. . . ." As these images suggest, the references are to lovemaking as a frenzied, destructive, pointless activity, which reaches its nadir in the link-boy episode, with the matter of whether the rake or his mistress will enjoy the link-boy's favors, a matter to be decided by whose kiss is the better (37–40).[7]

The debauchery and the love-war parallel are the same as Charles's rolling about "from whore to whore" and Louis's warring. The metaphor begins again with a clearly separated tenor and vehicle, but the two parts merge into a single image of debauching soldiers; what starts as a comparison or a contrast becomes a unity, or a mutual travesty. If the reality beneath the rake's glamor is squabbling with whores, it is much the same with the soldier. In both the public and the private parts of the comparison, a public aspect—a glamorous appearance—is reduced to a private, which is a squalid reality. The assumed but invisible term that joins the rake and the admiral is gallantry or some such attractive abstraction. The poem is composed in the stanzaic form of *Gondibert,* Davenant's heroic poem which contains all the "gallantry" of the sort Rochester is referring to, but treated grandiosely. Davenant portrays the kind of battle "Where even the vanquish'd so themselves behave, / The victors mourn for all they could not save."[8] Rochester begins by setting up a high ideal against which to measure debauchery; but very soon both soldiering and debauchery are exposed as the ugly reality underlying the gallant *Gondibert* stanzas and the heroic talk of old poxed rakes. The whoremonger talks like an admiral; but, as the mock-heroic effect changes to travesty, the admiral behaves like a whoremonger.[9]

The metaphor of love-war is, of course, an ancient Petrarchan cliché. Rochester's use of it is still close to conventional love parlance in "Second Prologue to the 'Empress of Morocco'": when he addresses the king with "your prosperous arms" he refers both to Charles's war with the Dutch and his amorous powers. The "Millions of cupids, hovering in the rear" are "like eagles following fatal troops," both awaiting "the slaughter" of the warriors in the play and the lovers of the outside world, including the audience in the theater and the king. Rochester's translation of Ovid's *Amores* 2.9 demonstrates his appropriation of the metaphor. Ovid's lines (in Humphries's translation),

> Old soldiers, their long term of service over,
> Retire to acres given by the state,
> And an old race horse kicks his heels in clover
> When he is done with breaking from the gate,

which refer to the peace an old lover desires, become in Rochester's translation:

> But the old soldier has his resting place,
> And the good battered horse is turned to grass.
> The harassed whore, who lived a wretch to please,
> Has leave to be a bawd and take her ease.
> For me, then, who have freely spent my blood,
> Love, in thy service, and so boldly stood. . . . [etc.]

The last four lines, Rochester's addition of his own metaphor, carry the matter into "Celia's trenches" and toward another "Disabled Debauchee." In his rendering of Ovid, the love-war relationship is causally linked: "With doubtful steps the god of war does move / By thy example led, ambiguous Love." Cupid is directing Mars as Charles's sexual organ does him.

Rochester's poetry projects a situation in which the two areas of experience, public and (illustrated by sexuality) private, are for all practical purposes one. In "Timon" a bore's attempt to lure a gentleman to his dinner party is compared to a whore's soliciting; the meat and carrots served are arses and dildoes; the lady's question to Huff ("if love's flame he never felt") is answered, "Do you think I'm gelt"; the diners go into heroic verses about war from plays, which lead into talk about actual war (Huff and Dingboy at dinner are the equivalent of kings and generals and admirals running the war), and a squabble among the diners ends with a "peace" treaty. The correspondence appears in the most incidental imagery. In "The Imperfect Enjoyment" the speaker's organ would "invade, / Woman or Boy";[10] it "Breaks ev'ry stew, does each small whore invade." In "Satyr against Reason and Man-kind" the distrust accorded wits is like that accorded whores by the clients who fear the consequences of their pleasure;[11] and in "Ar-temisia to Chloe" "whore is scarce a more reproachful name / Than poetess." In all of these "whore" is connected with a perversion of natural feeling that reflects on a similar perversion in the tenor of the comparison. By inference, friendship and not social climbing should be the occasion for dinners, as true love and not prostitution should be for sexual satisfaction.

The distinction between nature and its perversion points to the meaning of Rochester's sexual metaphor. In the example of Charles and Louis the terms would be freedom (nature) and license (perver-sion). Charles's behavior is to the ideal (or in his terms, the romantic illusion) of kingship as uncontrolled lust is to love. The relationship between the terms becomes somewhat more complex in "The Dis-abled Debauchee." The squabbling, the destruction, and the treatment of the link-boy might easily have been presented as praiseworthy free-dom, opposed to the chains of custom; even the burning of "some Ancient Church" might have been shown to be a laudable gesture. But the poem presents such actions as mechanical parts of a rigid pattern of behavior passed down from debauched rakes (or retired admirals); their libertine function of freeing the human spirit is not operative.

Rochester makes his point by the comparison in the last stanza of the impotent debauchee to a statesman who sends out youths to battle. Both stand back and watch others killed for an abstraction that was once perhaps real to them: "And being good for nothing else, be wise." It is *wise* to stay out of these actions but wisdom is actually mere impo-tence, since as long as one is able he does the unwise thing. Implicit is a contrast between two kinds of wisdom, natural (the instinct that drove the old debauchee to "Love and Wine" in his youth); and the so-called wisdom of counsellors and statesmen who curb the instinctive actions of others.

However meaningless the rake's actions in the past, Rochester im-plies a moral distinction between them and his present generalizations. The fact that the admiral is so feeble that he "crawls" up the hill is contrasted with his eyes that cannonlike emit "flashes of rage"; and, to the accompaniment of the rhymes "courage still" and "adjacent hill," he shows his courage by climbing a safe hill and watching the combat through a telescope. There was something good in the vice at the time—it was at least a self-fulfillment of some kind—which has been completely expunged now in the old impotent rake's proselytizing. He has himself become a symbol of the custom he flouted. (Even the stanza form underlines the formalized quality of the vice now that it is promulgated as a doctrine by the impotent debauchee.) To generalize from one's own experience is probably the greatest sin represented in the poem, coming close to Rochester's definition of custom (and also underlying his lines on Charles II, who never *said* a foolish thing, nor ever *did* a wise one).[12]

If to generalize from one's own experience is the greatest sin, what then is the "Rochester" in his works? His own ambivalence about the difference between saying and doing, or between public and private parameters, is expressed in the following lines:

> Should hopeful youths[13] (worth being drunk) prove nice,
>   And from his fair inviter meanly shrink,
> 'Twill please the ghost of my departed vice
>   If, at my counsel, he repent and drink.

Here "hopeful," "worth," "fair," "meanly," and "repent" are so ambiguous as to be pivotal words between the two parts of the poem. In terms of Rochester's own experience there was the heroic sea battle in which he *had* fought bravely but also witnessed the bloody death of Montagu; there were the later shadowy acts which were called (at least by some) cowardice and the fact that he was ill and prematurely aged.[14]

In "The Imperfect Enjoyment" the "brave Youth" who may "meanly shrink" has become the speaker's own sexual organ which "shrinks, and hides his head." He addresses it to curse it:

> When vice, disease, and scandal lead the way,
> With what officious haste dost thou obey!
> Like a rude, roaring hector in the streets
> Who scuffles, cuffs, and justles all he meets,
> But if his King or country claim his aid,
> The rakehell villain shrinks and hides his head.

Here is the resumé of all we have seen associated with evil in Rochester's satires. The activity of the "roaring hector" is exactly that of the debauching soldiers in "The Disabled Debauchee"; and any old whore versus the woman he loves is the private part of a comparison with king or country, street fights, and civil chaos. But the poem is not about whores and street fights but the poet's unruly organ, which can succeed with whores but not with his true love (and, by the terms of the comparison, cannot serve his king and country as it ought). We might say that when he talks about a personal problem like his impotence he is really talking about a much larger issue, which he can feel so strongly because of the analogy to his own plight. The king's body (body politic) is also manifest in the microcosm of the body-Rochester.

In "The Imperfect Enjoyment" and "A Ramble in St. James's Park" the public half of the analogy can only be inferred; or, rather, the sexual experience has become a synecdoche for more general considerations of life. The "Ramble" begins with a short history of St. James's Park and a situation parallel to that of the speaker. The origin of the park, according to legend, was "an antient pict" lover who was jilted by his love. His natural object being thwarted, he resorted to masturbation, fertilizing the ground and giving birth to the sinister foliage which now conceals such lewd, unnatural behavior as the pict was forced into: "And nightly now beneath their shade / Are buggeries, rapes, and incests made." These—like the link-boy episode in "The Disabled Debauchee"—are the unnatural outlets for man's normal and natural passion for women. The speaker himself has been jilted by Corinna for a pair of fops, and while he admits "There's something generous in mere lust," he rails at this "abandoned jade" who mechanically copulates with any male who happens along, engaging in a meaningless activity divorced from affection or love, and his railing points ultimately toward the leather phallus of "Signior Dildo" which replaces the human agent entirely. The speaker's romantic love is an ideal behind the indictment of the restless woman, but his own reaction is as sterile and aimless as the ancient pict's: he merely loads curses on Corinna's head, and the outlet of outraged and pointless ejaculation is paralleled by this outpouring of invective.

Rochester's explanation for the perversion of love—and so of all other human relationships—develops in two divergent lines. One in purely satiric terms, as in the poems we have mentioned so far, places the blame on the opposite extremes of license and custom. The Restoration gentleman presumably follows the middle road of libertine love, hindered by neither marriage, indiscriminate lust, nor ideal love.

This is part of the pose that connects Rochester's satires with the great comedies being written by Etherege and Wycherley.

The other explanation is hinted at in the implication that the speaker of the "Ramble" could not get together with Corinna because of a similar but unfortunately definitive trouble between Adam and Eve. Rochester's fable, turning St. James's Park into a version of Eden, suggests a certain hopelessness in the situation of present-day man, a hopelessness which surfaces in his letters when he remarks that there is "soe great a disproportion 'twixt our desires and what is ordained to content them" that love is impossible.[15] The various unnatural channels chronicled are all that is left: masturbation, invective or satire, and whores.

"The Imperfect Enjoyment," a pessimistic resolution to the problem of the "Ramble," is an adaptation of Ovid's *Amores* 3.7. The latter celebrates the impossibility of controlling the flesh, but though it recalls the speaker's past successes with other women, it makes no distinction between them and the present one; this one is a whore, and so presumably were all the others. In Rochester's poem the whores are contrasted with the true love in whose arms he now lies, as lust with romantic love. In effect, Rochester says that even if the girl of the "Ramble" came to him he would be unable to achieve a consummation *because* he loves her, *because* he has an ideal image of her; not only do we have no control over our bodies, but they can satisfy only the pattern of lust, not the patternless complexity of love. This is an extreme statement, which even Swift does not approach, of a Strephon who doesn't need to get into Chloe's dressing room; under the most felicitous circumstances he simply could not bridge the gap between ideal and real.

Something is to be said about the relationship between the impotence in these poems (sexual, royal, moral) and the profligacy or license of the mistress who is merely a "passive pot to spend in" or "The joy at least of a whole Nation": "On her no Showers unwelcome fall, / Her willing womb retains 'em all." The receptivity of the woman is matched by the "looseness" of Rochester with any passing whore, of other "lovers" like Charles II, and, to extend the metaphor, of writers like Dryden (in the "Allusion to Horace"). For impotence / constipation is a general malady of Rochester / Charles, who say wisely but act foolishly, while the world around is full of mere "looseness." The custom of respect or "love" is the trap in which such as

Rochester and the king, and many of his subjects, find themselves when confronted by "king" or "loved one" or any hallowed ideal. The organ will not respond. The only alternative to the costive, in love or art or politics, is the loose.

"Kings and Princes," Rochester wrote to Henry Savile, "are only as Incomprehensible as what they *pretend* to represent; but apparently as Frail as Those they Govern."[16] It is certainly noticeable that Rochester attacks in others (like Charles) what he comes around to attacking in himself. Their mutual impotence and inability to relate public and private life become the insight that one must be satisfied with whores and link-boys; Rochester turns this knowledge into a private version of the body politic metaphor, an image of the whole world's decline that looks forward to Swift's use of his own body in his Irish poems. We might, in fact, say that Rochester projects his plight into poems about the monarchy in the same way that Swift projects his into poems extending from political lampoons to "A Beautiful Young Nymph going to Bed." Rochester must have seen himself as a representative man (certainly so by 1676, when Dorimant appeared), fully as representative as the king: and it is at this point that he begins to project his alternative selves—versions of damnation, pride, and conversion. When he enquires of the postboy the way to hell, he is told: "The readiest way, my Lord, 's by Rochester." That is, by way of the city of Rochester, toward the sea and France; but also by *playing* the Earl of Rochester, or by his example, or by being himself.

Rochester's career comes to a climax, or a watershed, in 1675–76: his greatest poems are written around this time and he begins seriously to extend his poetry into life in various forms, looking toward his conversion and death. It is also the time when the two great comedies of the Restoration, *The Country Wife* and *The Man of Mode,* are first performed, reflecting Rochester mimetically and metaphorically. We know from contemporary evidence that he was seen as the model for Dorimant,[17] but Horner is equally Rochester, because Wycherley makes him a symbol in precisely the way that Rochester was making himself one. The most immediate analogue (whether source or allusion is not certain) is Harcourt's remark that Horner, like "an old married general, when unfit for action, is fittest for counsel" (3.2). Horner is a symbol that combines the repletion or retention with the covert release by both sexual and satiric catharsis that we have seen in Rochester's satire. The pose of impotence is a device for exposing the lust of the hypocritical women and the complaisance of their husbands, an outlet equally for his sexual and for his satiric satisfaction. The satire depends on the private-public analogy of Horner and the world, as of sex and china, which is painted, decorated, and collected to conceal its earthy origins.

But this is a masquerade which also educes a reality, an otherwise invisible aspect of the man. Horner's pose of impotence is a symbol of his own real moral impotence, and with him the moral (and social and political) impotence of English society as a whole. The sense in which Horner is really impotent is like that in which Volpone is really sick. Moreover, Rochester's masquerade as Alexander Bendo is very reminiscent of Horner, who derives in more ways than one from Volpone, another actor whose repertory included the role of mountebank, a self-disguise to expose politicians and clergymen and other more respectable mountebanks. In Rochester's (Bendo's) words, "the Politician is, & must be a Mountebank in State Affairs, and the Mountebank no doubt . . . is an errant Politician in Physick."[18] Bendo begins by distinguishing true physician and quack but then blurs them into one, together with politicians and clergymen. Rochester's impersonations transform the private man momentarily into the public; they extend from mountebank and city merchant to naval hero, peer sitting in the House of Lords, rake "some years always drunk, and . . . ever doing some mischief,"[19] coward refusing to duel with Mulgrave, and atheist turned convert.[20] Etherege and Wycherley recorded some aspects of the impersonation, as later Gilbert Burnet and Robert Parsons recorded the drama of conversion and a "good death," mixing life and art in a way that is central to Rochester.

Parsons, Rochester's mother's chaplain, stresses Rochester's "commands to me, *to preach abroad, and to let all men know* (if they knew it not already,) *how severely God had disciplined him for his sins by his afflicting hand.*"[21] I have no doubt that Rochester's urge for publication was conscious: both Burnet and Parsons were his amanuenses, the first of the conversations leading up to conversion, the second of the funeral sermon describing the conversion, with the appropriate text from the parable of the prodigal son. The passage from Isaiah 53 which converted Rochester did so, I rather suspect, because of its transference of his own situation to the "Suffering Servant" of Jahveh who is a prophecy of the suffering Christ:

He is despised and rejected of men, a man of sorrows, and acquainted with grief . . . he was despised, and we esteemed him not. Surely he hath borne our griefs, and carried our sorrows; yet we did esteem him stricken, smitten of God, and afflicted. But he was wounded for our transgressions, he was bruised for our iniquities: the chastisement of our peace was upon him, and with his stripes we are healed.[22]

Rochester must, at some level of consciousness, have remembered Lady Fidget's words to Horner:

But, poor gentleman, could you be so generous, so truly a man of honour, as for the sakes of us women of honour, to cause yourself to be reported no man? No man! And to suffer yourself the greatest shame that could fall upon a man, that none might fall upon us women by your conversation? [2.1]

The portrait Rochester commissioned of Huysmann (c. 1675) shows the poet with an ape. In a reciprocal action he offers the ape his bays, and the ape (emblematic of imitation) offers the poet a page he has torn out of a book; he is aping the poet, sitting on a pile of books with another in his hand, a finger marking the place where he has stopped reading or has torn out pages. Rochester himself, however, is holding in his other hand a number of manuscript pages, aping the ape. Sir John Vanbrugh was later to put an ape holding a mirror atop his monument to Congreve at Stowe, but that ape could be Congreve's subject ("Vitae imitatio, / Consuetudinis Comoedia"). Rochester juxtaposes himself with the ape in a gesture of mutual give-and-take: the ape is his double.[23] Rochester has chosen not a satyr, in either of its aspects, but an emblem of the satirist's imitative faculty and his own apish aspect, which reaches into his poems ("like an ape's mock face, / By near resembling man do man disgrace") and into his life (he owned an ape and remarked to Savile that it is "a Fault to laugh at the Monkey we have here, when I compare his Condition with Mankind").[24]

Barely glimpsed in the upper right corner, beyond the pillar before which Rochester stands, are an arch and trees and sky—hints of another life. The reference is to Rochester in the country, his wife, and his recoveries from life in the court and city. The country, he writes to Savile, becomes the place "where, only, one can think; for, you at Court think not at all; or, at least, as if you were shut up in a drum; you can think of nothing, but the noise that is made about you."[25] Country seems to be almost outside the public-private division; or at least it serves Rochester, as it later did Pope, as a place to stand from which to look back at the riot of the city. He told Burnet that "when he was well furnished with materials [from the city], he used to retire into the country for a month or two to write libels."[26]

But *in* the country there was also the distinction between Adderbury, the retreat with his wife and children, and Woodstock, where with his wilder companions he revived the city in the country—or, perhaps, with friends like Buckingham plotted Country Party strategy against the court. Woodstock was near Ditchley, the house in which he spent his childhood and in which his mother lived, separated (as the name implies) from Woodstock by a ditch—with beyond the ditch the pious dowager Lady Rochester; and then at some distance further north, almost to Banbury, the wife and family waiting at Adderbury.[27]

We have strayed from the poetry into the conversations and letters and beyond. Since we will never know what Rochester really was, any more than what Charles II or the times were, we ought to prefer the fictions that derive from Rochester himself. His two earliest surviving poems, of 1660, associate him and Charles II as son and father. He was born into a relationship with the great world of the court, and specifically with Charles II: his father, Lord Wilmot, had saved Charles at Worcester. In that scene Wilmot was to Charles as father to son, and Rochester becomes, in his own terms at least, both son and brother (or alter ego) to Charles. Whether Rochester wrote these verses of 1660 (he would have been only thirteen), or whether they were revised or even dictated by his mentor Robert Whitehall, nonetheless the two poems express the essential relationship that emerged. The king took over the dead father's role, supervised Rochester's education at Oxford, his grand tour, his life at court thereafter (navy and pension), and chose a wife for him. But this father / brother was also a slave to his lusts, and his energies were scattered when they should have been focused on his duty / queen / kingdom / son / subjects—and so it is no surprise that Rochester wrote attacks on the king that could have been directed at himself and eventually, in his last year, went over to the Opposition—which was, of course, centered on the crisis of the Succession, the replacement of the brother York with the bastard son Monmouth.[28] The protagonist of "A Ramble through St. James's Park" and "The Imperfect Enjoyment" could have been either Rochester himself or Charles II: as the kind of projection of omnipotence in Bajazet could have been of the illusory power and real impotence of either.

The poems show Charles II, the father surrogate, transformed from a threatening figure to the other side of the poet, the harmless, impotent, castrated, uxorious man—the costive man of wise words and bungled deeds, safer in the country but always yearning for the city.[28] What we do know is that Rochester's mother's ancestral sympathies were Puritan, while his father (whom he can have met no more than once, when he was eight) was the staunchest of cavaliers, who saved and served Charles until his death, separated from his wife and son (when he returned that once he was travelling in disguise on a secret mission directing Royalist conspiracies to undermine the Puritan Commonwealth). Perhaps the father, in that one return, seemed a threat to the son's own monopoly of his mother, or a threat to his own identity. Presumably something of Rochester's association with his father and his glamor persisted in the life at court in London and at sea, but Rochester always followed it with a return to the country to be near his mother, to meditate and write (although keeping Woodstock at hand in which to live like a cavalier).

He disguised himself as the low to expose the low in everyone, even the highest; but also to destroy—or replace or atone for—his own identity as John Wilmot, Earl of Rochester, or as Dorimant or Bendo, moving toward what the Puritans would have considered a conversion and rebirth. But only the final conversion of many, if we look back at the poems and masquerades. The satirist perhaps requires (as Evelyn Waugh's diaries of the 1920s show) the pleasure of debauchery followed by deep Puritan hangovers. Certainly from his mother's letters we see that his "conversion" (which remains as ambiguous as Dorimant's retreat to the country with Harriet), the final immolation of the father, brought him home to her. There remained a ditch between Woodstock, where he died, and Ditchley and his pious childhood; but he broke, with his final gesture, the Puritan aim of private but exemplary salvation away from the cavalier's public duty to crown.

NOTES

1. Gilbert Burnet, *Some Passages of the Life and Death of Rochester* (1680), in *Rochester: The Critical Heritage,* ed. David Farley-Hills (London, 1972), p. 54.

2. *The Remains of Thomas Hearne,* ed. John Bliss, rev. John Buchanan-Brown (Carbondale, 1966), p. 122. One thinks at once of Swift's "Digression on Madness" but also of Freud's Wolf-Man. The latter suggests that, like the Wolf-Man, Rochester was unable to have a bowel movement for long periods without the assistance of an enema: " . . . spontaneous evacuations did not occur for months at a time," writes Freud, "unless a sudden excitement from some particular direction intervened, as a result of which normal activity of the bowels might set in for a few days. His principal subject of complaint was that for him the world was hidden in a veil, or that he was cut off from the world by a veil. This veil was torn only at one moment—when, after an enema, the contents of the bowel left the intestinal canal; and then he felt well and normal again" (Freud, Standard Edition, trans. James Strachey, vol. 17 [1955], pp. 74–75). In other details as well the two cases may be similar; but the conventionality of the metaphor, as it extends from medical treatises to Burton's *Anatomy of Melancholy* to Swift's *Tale of a Tub,* needs little documentation.

3. See my *Fictions of Satire* (Baltimore, 1967), pp. 106–07, from which the present essay takes off.

4. David Vieth has done more than anyone else to make Rochester available to us in his *Attribution in Restoration Poetry: A Study of Rochester's Poems of 1680* (New Haven, 1963) and his edition, *The Complete Poems of John Wilmot, Earl of Rochester* (New Haven, 1968). One full-length study, Dustin H. Griffin's *Satires against Man: The Poems of Rochester* (Berkeley, 1973), has appeared, as have a number of enlightening essays. Some of these will be mentioned in the notes that follow; here I shall mention only Vieth's "Toward an Anti-Aristotelian Poetic: Rochester's *Satyr against Mankind* and *Artemisia to Chloe,* with Notes on Swift's *Tale of a Tub* and *Gulliver's Travels,*" *Language and Style* 5 (1972): 123–45, because Vieth has gradually changed his view from that of Rochester as proto-Augustan to something much closer to the view expressed in this essay. For two essays that are close to my own view of Rochester, see Carole Fabricant, "Rochester's World of Imperfect Enjoyment," *Journal of English and Germanic Philology* 73 (1974): 338–50, and "Rochester's *Valentinian* and the Subversion of the Augustan Hierarchy," *MLR,* forthcoming, on the demythologizing mode in Rochester.

5. My text is Vieth's *Complete Poems,* where he calls the poem "A Satyr on Charles II." For the problem of the arrangement of the lines, see p. 193 and Vieth, "Rochester's 'Scepter' Lampoon on Charles II," *Philological Quarterly* 37 (1958): 424–32.

6. Swift may have had the "Scepter Lampoon" in mind when he wrote: "The very same Principle that influences a *Bully* to break the Windows of a Whore, who has jilted him, naturally stirs up a Great Prince to raise mighty Armies, and dream nothing but Sieges, Battles, and Victories" (*Tale of a Tub,* ed. A.C. Guthkelch and D. Nichol Smith [2d ed., 1958], p. 165).

7. The link-boy may be a Rochester confessional purging or merely another way to outrage. It was not part of the rake's image, except perhaps for some innuendos in *The Country Wife,* where Marjorie dresses as a boy and is attacked by Horner, and in the character of Fidelio in *The Plain Dealer.*

In general we must regard the link-boy in Rochester as we would in a satire of Juvenal, as a perversion of normal human activities.

8. Argument to Canto 5. The possibility must not be overlooked, however, that Dryden's *Annus Mirabilis,* with the same stanzaic form, intervened; and the reference could as well be to that glorification of specifically British arms. Rymer noticed the allusion to *Gondibert* in his preface to Rochester's *Poems on Several Occasions* (London, 1691), p. A4, as did Pope in his copy of Rochester's *Poems* (1696, p. 97); noted by Griffin, *Satires against Man,* p. 48.

9. This sort of metaphor may have been a reflection of the virtual consonance felt by Dryden and many of his contemporaries among the worlds of politics, religion, art, and literature. Rochester participates in this tradition but with a conclusion far less sanguine than Dryden's—perhaps because he chooses the two parts of a travesty contrast, public and private, whereas Dryden relates science/politics or literature/politics in a concordia discors, or a way of showing the unity within apparently disparate areas of experience.

10. I prefer the 1680 edition's "boy" to Vieth's "Man."

11. This, the most anthologized of Rochester's poems, first attacks man's feigned and boasted reason and then exposes the personal fear which is the reality under this pose (as under the masks of knavery and all others that separate man from the beasts), and then it extends this personal, private situation to the public one of the court, statesmen, and clergymen.

12. One other sense of "private/public" for the king should be mentioned. Christopher Goodman, the Puritan apologist, wrote long before the Civil War that if rulers failed in their duty they would "be accounted no more for kings or lawful magistrates, but as private men: and to be examined, accused, condemned and punished by the law of God" (*How Superior Powers Ought to be Obeyed* [1558, reproduced Facsimile Society, New York, 1931], p. 139). With the trial and condemnation of Charles I this doctrine became real: he was judged not by his own but by a different law; and for this to happen, he had to become a private citizen, just as the private men who judged him became public.

13. "Hopeful" is my emendation, from the 1680 edition, for Vieth's "any."

14. Of the naval heroics, he told Gilbert Burnet that "He thought it necessary to begin his life with those Demonstrations of his courage in an Element and way of fighting, which is acknowledged to be the greatest trial of clear and undoubted Valour" (*Some Passages,* in *Critical Heritage,* p. 50); of his health, he wrote to Savile: "I am *almost Blind, utterly Lame,* and scarce within the reasonable hopes of ever seeing *London again*" (Oct. 1677, in John Hayward, ed., *Collected Works of John Wilmot, Earl of Rochester* [London, 1926], p. 252).

15. To his wife, in Hayward, *Collected Works,* p. 288. Cf. Fredelle Bruser, "Disproportion: A Study in the Work of John Wilmot, Earl of Rochester," *University of Toronto Quarterly* 15 (1945–46): 384–96.

16. Hayward, *Collected Works*, p. 252.

17. John Dennis, "Defence of Sir Fopling Flutter" (1722), in *The Critical Works of John Dennis*, ed. E.N. Hooker (Baltimore, 1943), 2:248.

18. *The Famous Pathologist, or the Noble Mountebank*, ed. V. de Sola Pinto (*Nottingham University Miscellany*, no. 1 [Nottingham, 1961]), p. 34.

19. Burnet, *History of his own Time* (1753), 1: 370–72.

20. The subject of Rochester's masquerades and their meaning has been well treated by Anne Righter, "John Wilmot, Earl of Rochester," *Proceedings of the British Academy* 53 (1967): 47–69; Griffin, *Satires against Man;* and Carole Fabricant, "John Wilmot, Earl of Rochester: A Study of the Artist as Role-Player" (Ph.D. diss., Johns Hopkins University, 1972), especially chap. 3, pp. 153–225.

21. Robert Parsons, *A Sermon Preached at the Funeral of the Rt. Honorable John Earl of Rochester . . .* (1680), p. 30.

22. Parsons, *A Sermon*, p. 24. Rochester stressed the passage to Burnet, "He hath no form nor comeliness and when we see him there is no beauty that we should desire him," glossing it: "The meanness of his Appearance and Person has made vain and foolish people disparage him, because he came not in such a Fool's-Coat as they delight in" (*Some Passages*, in *Critical Heritage*, p. 142).

23. Sir Thomas Killigrew, the last royal jester, with whom Rochester once exchanged identities to deceive two maids of honor, appears in *his* engraved portrait with a monkey sitting on the table imitating his pose, both heads supported by hands in the iconography of melancholy. See *British Museum Catalogue of Satiric Prints*, no. 1681; reproduced, Graham Greene, *Lord Rochester's Monkey* (London, 1974), p. 68.

24. "Epilogue to 'Love in the Dark,' " Vieth, *Complete Poems*, p. 92; to Savile, June 1678, in Hayward, *Collected Works*, p. 256.

25. Hayward, *Collected Works*, pp. 252, 258.

26. *History of his own Time*, in *Critical Heritage*, p. 93; see also *Some Passages*, in *Critical Heritage*, p. 54.

27. An old ditch ran directly by the house, which so fascinated Thomas Hearne when he visited the house in 1718 that he looked into its history. Ditchley got its name, he learned, from this ancient boundary-line ditch or dike, and he examined one "great Ditch, or Trench, of a vast Extent," a mile from Ditchley House, which "parts the two Manors of Ditchley and Woodstock" (*The Remains of Thomas Hearne*, p. 206).

28. But in a letter to Savile he relates Oates's trial for buggery to his accusations at King's Bench two days later "for the Honour of the Protestant Cause." The "Lowsiness of Affairs," he tells Savile, is such as " 'tis not fit to entertain a *private* Gentleman, much less one of *a publick Character*, with the Retaile of them" (Hayward, *Collected Works*, p. 263).

29. For a much more elaborate attempt to place Rochester in a Freudian context, see Griffin, *Satires against Man*, pp. 120–29.

R. A. FOAKES

"The Power of Prospect":
Wordsworth's Visionary Poetry

In responding to Wordsworth's poetry it is not easy to resist the temptation to define and homogenize his ideas and the terms he uses to convey the significance of what the poems enact. Poems which contain many reflective and generalizing passages may seem to encourage the critic to generalize also. This essay is concerned with what was to Wordsworth a centrally important concept, that of "vision," and its related vocabulary concerned with images, what is seen and the act of seeing, and imagination. The experiences described in poems that bear on this concept are so various that they should make us suspicious of all generalizing about it. Wordsworth was more tentative, shifting, and exploratory in his use of terms like "vision" and "imagination" than is generally acknowledged, and some well-known comments relating to these should not be taken simply at face value. One of these is Geoffrey Hartman's definition of Wordsworth's idea of imagination, based on his reading of the 1850 version of a passage in *The Prelude*, book 6, as "consciousness of self raised to apocalyptic pitch"[1]; another is Colin Clarke's statement that it was "essential" to the poet "that images should be solid if they were to be effective vehicles of moral meaning. *Merely* tenuous and dream-like landscapes were of little interest to him."[2]

An examination of some versions of "seeing" or "vision" in Wordsworth's poetry will illustrate the critical problem in arriving at any generalization about these notions, and will serve as preface to a consideration of two sonnets that engage directly with the poet's own difficulties in this matter. It may be useful to begin by commenting on versions of "seeing" in relation to another generalization about Wordsworth that seems at first glance acceptable enough, namely that the poet's "imagination"—in the sense of inner vision or "inward eye"—seems to have been most active when the outward vision was also engaged[3]". One version of seeing begins from the object, impressing itself on the eye as a passive receiver of images: "The eye it cannot choose but see" ("Expostulation and Reply"). In this sense the eye transmits images to the mind, but *feeds* it in a "wise passiveness." A characteristic mode of experience recorded in Wordsworth's poetry relates to times when a particular scene, object, or person impressed itself on his view. A notable example, also from *Lyrical Ballads,* occurs in the lines beginning "There was a boy"; during the pauses in his noisy enjoyments and "jocund din," it sometimes happened that

> the visible scene
> Would enter unaware, into his mind.
> With all its solemn imagery, its rocks,
> Its woods, and that uncertain heav'n, receiv'd
> Into the bosom of the steady lake.

The boy is not conscious of seeing, yet the effect is "solemn," the transposed adjective recording the effect on the boy rather than the scene, just as the final image, of the sky as an "uncertain heav'n" (uncertain, as sky, in its rapid changes from storm to sunshine? or uncertain, as heaven, in its frowns or blessings?—the adjective again transposes readily to attach itself to the boy), enacts the idea of "wise passiveness," and the imagery is received not only by the lake, but finds its way into the boy's "bosom" or heart, and so feeds the mind by planting images there, as Wordsworth claimed in his comment on these lines in his preface to *Poems* (1815).[4]

There are several famous passages in the first books of *The Prelude,* like the boat-stealing episode in book 1, which describe experiences of a similar kind, when the "visible scene" impressed the boy in a "solemn" way with a sense of significances not then grasped, but also feeding the mind. Wordsworth seems to record faithfully and exactly what he felt as a boy, the sense of "huge and mighty forms" (1.425) invading his mind; the adult poet adds a commentary, translating the experience into moral or spiritual terms, as an effect of nature's "ministry" (1.494). Here already in the boy's impressions the beginnings of what is later called a "wise passiveness" are glimpsed:

> even then I felt
> Gleams like the flashing of a shield; the earth

And common face of Nature spake to me
Rememberable things.
          [*Prelude* 1.613–16]

The eye as intermediary has disappeared from this image, and the "Gleams" are immediately "felt" in the mind or heart. The telescoping of the image seems appropriate and natural, for the eye has no other function than to transmit sights that are turned in the mind into "Rememberable things." Such images occur again, as in Wordsworth's account of rowing out on Windermere during an evening when

          the sky
Never before so beautiful, sank down
Into my heart, and held me like a dream.
          [*Prelude* 2.178–80]

The visible scene affected him without any conscious activity of eye or will or thought on his part, and could "fill" his heart, as in book 4, line 341, "My heart was full."

At the same time, another mode of seeing is at least as important in Wordsworth's poetry, a mode requiring effort to search out or attend to objects worth seeing, like the small celandine, not easily noticed because it is so "humble," as contrasted with "Buttercups that will be seen / Whether we will see or no." So although some sights impress themselves involuntarily upon the poet as unique, having an effect unexpected or unforeseen, with the eye serving as transmitter, like the "memorable pomp" of the morning scene in *The Prelude,* 4.331; and some sights also may, though repeated, produce a similar effect ("My heart leaps up when I behold / A rainbow in the sky"), yet other sights become significant only as consciously noticed by the poet. So he often seems strenuously to make us see what we ordinarily would not observe. It was, of course, Wordsworth's object in *Lyrical Ballads,* as described by Coleridge, to awaken "the mind's attention from the lethargy of custom" by "directing it to the loveliness and the wonders of the world before us," breaking through the "film of familiarity" because of which we "have eyes, yet see not."[5]

Many of the poems in *Lyrical Ballads* do indeed draw attention to figures, incidents, or objects we might not ordinarily regard but which become vehicles of moral significance. The whole of *Michael,* for instance, turns on the image of the unfinished sheepfold the old shepherd hopes to complete with his son Luke; in an otherwise unremarkable and solitary valley, this object alone deserves attention, but does not volunteer itself; it is a valley not worth mentioning but for "one object which you might pass by, / Might see and notice not (l. 15). The appearance is itself important when what is observed comes to have for the poet a significance that emerges in the act of watching or "espying." This is exemplified in the poem beginning "A whirl-blast from behind the hill"; in this Wordsworth draws the reader with him into the bower in which he sits in winter, and invites him to join in the act of seeing the dead leaves come to life: "But see! where'er the hailstones drop / The wither'd leaves all skip and hop." The act of noticing the movement of the leaves becomes simultaneously an animation of them into life, so that they "jump and *spring*," as if containing the new life that will burst out in the next season. The poem ends with the hope that the poet

> may never cease to find,
> Even in appearances like these
> Enough to nourish and to stir my mind!

Again the eye metaphorically feeds the mind with what it sees.

These two modes of seeing, passive and active, both feed the mind or imagination, but in one mode things seen sink unconsciously into the poet's heart, while in the other mode we are invited to notice by conscious effort and interpret objects, people, and incidents the poet has chosen to observe and make us see, brushing aside the "veil of familiarity." Other variants of "seeing" are also prominent, notably the perception not of "appearances," of what is there, but of a fancied spectacle. A boyhood experience of this kind is recorded in *The Prelude*, book 8; again and again, "a hundred times," the boy gazed at a "sparkling patch of diamond light" that shone inexplicably from a dark wood on summer afternoons, and found meanings there:

> And now it was a burnished shield, I fancied,
> Suspended over a Knight's Tomb, who lay
> Inglorious, buried in the dusky wood;
> An entrance now into some magic cave
> Or Palace for a Fairy of the rock;
> Nor would I, though not certain whence the cause
> Of the effulgence, thither have repair'd
> Without a precious bribe, and day by day
> And month by month I saw the spectacle,
> Nor ever once have visited the spot

Unto this hour. Thus sometimes were the shapes
Of wilful fancy grafted upon feelings
Of the imagination, and they rose
In worth accordingly.

[572–86]

What Wordsworth saw was perhaps merely the sun reflected on a wet rock, but he never "visited the spot" to find out, preferring to enjoy the varying spectacle as shaped by fancy in magic and romantic visions, visions nevertheless also valuable, and enriching the imagination. Such visions might spring from fancy, or arise wholly in the "inner eye," and yet to feed the mind, as one, for instance, enabled the poet when a boy to encounter the terrible figure of a drowned man without "vulgar fear":

for my inner eye had seen
Such sights before, among the shining streams
Of Fairy Land, the Forests of Romance.

[5.475–77]

Alternatively, a preconceived vision of an actual object may be preferred to seeing it, as, in "Yarrow Unvisited," it is better that the river valley remain unseen: "We have a vision of our own; / Ah! Why should we undo it?" The idea of the unknown beauty of Yarrow remains as an image to soothe care and relieve melancholy. So again, in "To the Cuckoo," the bird remains invisible, a mystery, "never seen," and telling of "visionary hours," it makes the earth seem "An unsubstantial, faery place." Both Yarrow and the cuckoo were real, and could have been seen, but, as with the vision of the cottage, something would be lost if they were seen plain; yet in some sense these poems are about seeing them as images in the inner eye, and about them as feeding the mind.

The relation between what is *there,* the object, and what is seen, the vision, also varies. In a striking simile in *The Prelude,* Wordsworth compared his progress with that of someone looking down from a boat through calm water to take pleasure in "such discoveries as his eye can make" in the bottom of the "deeps," and who

Sees many beauteous sights, weeds, fishes, flowers,
Grots, pebbles, roots of trees, and fancies more;
Yet often is perplex'd, and cannot part
The shadow from the substance, rocks and sky,

Mountains and clouds, from that which is indeed
The region, and the things which there abide
In their true dwelling.

[4.252–58]

The eye "discovers" objects in the bottom, and "fancies" more, but cannot separate what is there from what is reflected or imagined. Here there is a fusion of actual objects with visionary sights, so that it becomes impossible to say what is *seen;* but the notation that one "cannot part / The shadow from the substance" points to an effort to do just that, to make discriminations. This may be set against the lines in "The Brothers" which describe how Leonard, the shepherd turned sailor, filled with longing for his home, would hang over the vessel's side and stare into the sea in the far tropics:

And, while the broad green wave and sparkling foam
Flash'd round him images and hues, that wrought
In union with the employment of his heart,
He, thus by feverish passion overcome,
Even with the organ of his bodily eye,
Below him, in the bosom of the deep
Saw mountains, saw the forms of sheep that graz'd
On verdant hills, with dwellings among trees,
And Shepherds clad in the same country grey
Which he himself had worn.

[53–62]

Here the vision obliterates the actual scene, and Leonard sees simply what is imagined, the "forms" of his homeland. In the passage from *The Prelude,* a conscious play of fancy is involved, and though the distinction between reflections and fancies and "the things which there abide / In their true dwelling" is virtually lost, the very consciousness of the difference between them marks this off from Leonard's vision in the deeps. In the first passage the poet is conscious of two modes of seeing at work simultaneously, and this consciousness seems to produce a kind of anxiety about the visionary mode, a sense of "wilful fancy." In the second passage, Leonard sees only one sight, not what is actually there in the sea, but a vision of home. Only the word *feverish* sets up any critical challenge to an experience which seems to belong with what is associated in *The Prelude* with imagination rather than fancy.

A vision in this sense need neither be seen, as it were, through the actual objects presented to the eye, as Leonard looks at the sea and sees his homeland, nor be something distinct from the actual object, like a patch of sunlit rock observed simultaneously with what is "fancied"; the actual scene itself could become a vision. So, for instance, in *Lines written near Richmond,* the "lovely visions" seen by the bard apparently coincide with the spectacle before him of the Thames (or Cam, which is where it really happened, according to Wordsworth), at sunset. The image of the boat heading westward and leaving darkness behind suggests the passage of time and life, but the "visions" are of colors that endure, or time stayed: "Oh glide, fair stream! for ever so." The recognition in the poem of this as "fond deceit" and "vain thought" hardly disturbs the evident delight in the "visions" which "course" like a benediction, unsought, and are not distinguished here from the *actual prospect.* There are several notable examples in *The Prelude* of a natural scene experienced as visionary, like the famous description of descending the Alps into Italy in book 6, 549–72, where the "giddy prospect" is rendered as apocalyptic. Such experiences stored in the memory could become what Dorothy Wordsworth called "inner visions" in a passage written in 1802:[6]

When we passed through the village of Wensley my heart was melted away with dear recollections—the Bridge, the little waterspout, the steep hill, the Church. They are among the most vivid of my own inner visions, for they were the first objects that I saw after we were left to ourselves [Dorothy and William in 1799] and had turned our whole hearts to Grasmere as a home.

The very objects seen become *inner* visions in the mind.

In these examples (and more might be cited from the familiar poems of Wordsworth's central creative years) there can be found a variety of different versions of "seeing." Some scenes impinge like visitations, and sink of their own accord through the eye to affect the heart; some sights are looked for, searched out, and consciously noticed. Alternatively, what is seen shifts into things fancied or imagined, either as seen at the same time as the actual object, or as cutting out and replacing what is actually being looked at. Such visions can also be coincident with and seemingly undifferentiated from the object or person actually seen. In addition, there are visions of things unseen, and preferred so, like Yarrow or the cuckoo, which can have nothing to do with the "eye" of memory, and reveries, dreams, or visions that arise from the recesses of the mind, and are unconnected with what the bodily eye sees at the time, or effectually replace the sight of the closed or sleeping eyes with that of the "inner" or "inward" eye.

In his reflective and quasi-philosophical writing, in, for example, many passages in *The Prelude,* or in the *Ode on Intimations of Immortality,* Wordsworth tended to simplify and make too consistent and neat his accounts of "seeing." The emphasis in the *Ode* on the fading of the boyhood vision into the light of common day is not supported by the poems cited above; so, too, in *The Prelude,* the sharp distinction drawn between the child as having "unconscious intercourse" with beauty, and the adult as conscious, is not borne out by his other poems and seems to be rather a rationalization of his own development into a recognizable growth by stages. The passages commenting on the poet's growth emphasize the notion of the mind's supremacy over the senses and the natural world, which, however "active" the world around may be,

> Even as an agent of the one great mind
> Creates, creator and receiver both,
> Working but in alliance with the works
> Which it beholds.
>
> [2.272–75]

The creative mind works "in alliance" with what is seen, but the very terms "creator" and "receiver" register the dominance of the active mind. So although in a fine passage at the end of book 12 Wordsworth speaks of "an ennobling interchange / Of action from within and from without," (376–77) relating the "object seen" and "eye that sees," the movement of the poem is to reinforce the passage quoted from book 2, in the sense that "thou must give, Else never canst receive" (11.333). Those spots of time in which

> We have had deepest feeling that the mind
> Is lord and master, and that outward sense
> Is but the obedient servant of her will,
>
> [11.271–73]

are to be treasured with "gratitude," while periods in which "the eye was master of the heart," and that "most despotic" of the senses held sway (11.172) are regretted as times of weakness. To this extent the poem progresses from the boy's unconscious receptivity of seeing, "drinking in" a pure pleasure from the natural scene (1.591), and "drinking" also a "visionary power," an "obscure sense of possible sublimity" (2.330, 336), as these images fed his mind, to the adult's creative vision, and it fittingly concludes with the fine celebration of the ascent of Snowdon in book 13. This becomes an image of "a mighty Mind" in the exercise of "Power," and the magnificent spectacle which nature thrust on the poet's senses symbolizes the working of the imaginative faculty, making it "visible" (13.88); but however it may be momentarily acclaimed as

> a genuine Counterpart
> And Brother of the glorious faculty
> Which higher minds bear with them as their own,
> $\qquad$ [13.88–90]

its office is to feed the mind, which in turn "feeds upon infinity" (13.71).[7]

In this way one appropriate overall shape is given to *The Prelude,* even if it is a rather too neat one in relation not only to the variety of versions of seeing noted earlier, but also to other potential shapings of the poem.[8] Such a scheme appears to be at odds with another powerful sense the poem conveys, partly in the diminishing vitality of much in the middle books, of a development from the "seeing" boy to the adult as one who sees "by glimpses now" (11.338). It is also clouded by the issue of the taught or untaught eye. Nature schooled the poet's "unpractis'd sight" (3.583) as a child, and thwarted the tyranny of the eye, though how this effect was wrought remains unclear, and is "matter for another Song" (11.185). At the same time, the poem moves in terms of another schooling of the eye and imagination in its account of the poet's growing up through the experiences of Cambridge, London, and the French Revolution, even as it claims to emerge "from the depth of untaught things" (12.310).

The idea of an "ennobling interchange" in book 12 refines upon the prose commentary Wordsworth wrote in 1815 on "There was a Boy"; there he remarked, "I have represented a commutation and transfer of internal feelings, co-operating with external accidents to plant, for immortality, images of sound and sight, in the celestial soil of the Imagination." In the poem the "visible scene" enters "unawares" into the

boy's mind, and there is little sense of a transfer of "internal feelings."
The passage in book 12, and these lines, included in *The Prelude*, book
5, lines 389–413, might seem to offer useful formulae for an understanding of the relation between what is created in the mind, the activity of the fancy or imagination, and what is perceived, but no formula
covers the variety of versions of vision as recorded in the poems, and
each definition or generalization seems too inflexible or reductive.

At the same time, such passages arise from Wordsworth's continuing struggle to identify a process by which the mind, often imaged as
being nourished or fed, as itself creative or seemingly identified with
the imagination, or alternatively imaged as the soil in which the imaginative power grows, can have visionary experiences which may stem
from a direct interchange with the natural scene, may sometimes appear to be an immediate "creation in the eye,"[9] and at other times seem
to bypass the eye altogether, and arise as a prospect in the mind, when
"bodily eyes" are forgotten (*Prelude* 2.369), or the body itself "laid
asleep." So the "Inscription for the House (an outhouse) on the Island
at Grasmere," published in *Lyrical Ballads,* depicts the poet as lying at
noon on a summer's day in a shepherd's hut there,

> nor, while from his bed
> He through that door-place looks toward the lake
> And to the stirring breezes, does he want
> Creations lovely as the work of sleep,
> Fair sights, and visions of romantic joy.

The breezes may stir his activity of mind, but the "sights" and "visions" seen appear to be unconnected with the solid images around
him, and are rather "creations" like dreams.[10] The association of visions with dreams, so common in Wordsworth's poetry, certainly
helps on occasion to fortify that blending of outer and inner worlds, of
substance and spirit, so well analyzed by Colin Clarke in *Romantic
Paradox*[11]; at the same time the inner vision as dream may, as in these
lines, be no more than triggered by the external scene. It may even be
better if the external scene is not witnessed at all, and Yarrow remains
unvisited, or Mont Blanc, to judge by the curious lines in *The Prelude*
about Wordsworth's first sight of the mountain:

> That day we first
> Beheld the summit of Mont Blanc, and griev'd
> To have a soulless image on the eye

Which had usurp'd upon a living thought
That never more could be.

[6.452–56]

The following day the "Vale of Chamouny" reconciled Wordsworth
"to realities" (461). Whether we take it as the "image" or the "eye"
that "usurp'd" on the idea of Mont Blanc, the general effect is not
altered, of the real, solid image of the mountain as "soulless," and dis-
placing a "living" idea or vision of it.

It can be argued then that neither the notion of the interchange of
natural scene with the mind or seeing eye nor the connection of visionary experience with solid images is central in Wordsworth's processes
of significant seeing; no more can the claim stand that the poet's imagination was most active when the outward vision was also engaged.

On at least one memorable occasion, the evening of the day he was
married, 4 October 1802, Wordsworth was so fascinated by a landscape that was in one sense tenuous and dreamlike that he wrote two
sonnets (published in 1807) about it, and revised the first of them a
number of times prior to the publication of his *Poetical Works* in 1836–
37. He was also troubled by the nature of this experience, and the sonnets seem to struggle with his reaction to what he saw, what sort of
a vision he had, and how it related, or rather failed to relate to, his imagination. These sonnets are not distinguished poems, but they are
peculiarly interesting because they show the poet reacting very uncomfortably to a particular visionary experience.

The first was printed in the *Poems* (1807) as follows:[12]

Composed
after a Journey across
THE HAMILTON HILLS
Yorkshire

Ere we had reach'd the wish'd-for place, night fell:
We were too late at least by one dark hour,
And nothing could we see of all that power
Of prospect, whereof many thousands tell.
The western sky did recompence us well
With Grecian Temple, Minaret, and Bower;
And, in one part, a Minster with its Tower
Substantially distinct, a place for Bell
Or Clock to toll from. Many a glorious pile
Did we behold, sights that might well repay

All disappointment! and, as such, the eye
Delighted in them; but we felt, the while,
We should forget them: they are of the sky,
And from our earthly memory fade away.

Crossing the Hambleton Hills at dusk, too late to see the famous view of the Vale of York to the west, and disappointed in an expected "power of prospect," Wordsworth was greeted with an extraordinary landscape in the sky, which he felt he would "forget," but went out of his way to commemorate, and render unforgettable, by describing it in this sonnet. In the various redraftings of the sonnet much was changed, and the final version includes an "Indian citadel," while the "glorious pile" becomes "a tempting isle / with groves that never were imagined." Only the final lines remained unchanged throughout the various versions, conveying a kind of rejection of the vision as having no deeper resonance or continuance beyond the immediate delight of the moment.

The western sky became a kind of eastern city, or composite rather of east and west, pagan and Christian, the overall effect perhaps including a hint of Xanadu (Dorothy noted that there was a "dome,"[13] and this appears also in the second sonnet Wordsworth wrote on this experience), and of a "Bower" of bliss, and this may go a little way to account for Wordsworth's strong reaction against the vision, even as he recorded it in a sonnet which guaranteed that it would not fade from "our earthly memory." The late alteration of "glorious pile" to "tempting isle" adds a further suggestion of indulgence, of the Sirens, or Phaedria's idle lake with its floating island in *The Faerie Queene,* and it recalls also passages in *The Prelude* which associate periods of "loose indifference" and self-reproach with an image of an "enticing Island" that proves to be rotten and unsound.[14] The "isle" in the sonnet is "tempting," presumably, in the sense that the "sights" Wordsworth witnessed, though "of the sky," and so heavenly or paradisal in one sense, in another sense seem to offer a self-indulgent and idle enjoyment. However, these possible connections, which lie, if they exert any pressure at all, below the surface of the poem, do not adequately account for Wordsworth's distrust and repudiation of the vision, and it may have been his uneasiness about larger issues hinted at but not fully realized in the poem that made him go on tinkering with it.

Here the "sights" seem held in the eye as if by a barrier not allowing access to heart or mind. At some later time Wordsworth wrote another sonnet that takes off from the closing lines of this one. It was published with the first sonnet in 1807:

> *. . . they are of the sky,*
> *And from our earthly memory fade away.*

These words were utter'd in a pensive mood,
Even while mine eyes were on that solemn sight:
A contrast and reproach to gross delight,
And life's unspiritual pleasures daily woo'd!
But now upon this thought I cannot brood:
It is unstable, and deserts me quite;
Nor will I praise a Cloud, however bright,
Disparaging Man's gifts, and proper food.
The Grove, the sky-built Temple, and the Dome,
Though clad in colours beautiful and pure,
Find in the heart of man no natural home:
The immortal Mind craves objects that endure:
These cleave to it; from these it cannot roam,
Nor they from it: their fellowship is secure.

The repudiation of the vision implicit in the first sonnet is made much more emphatic in the sequel. Again the sonnet struggles with the nature of Wordsworth's objection, without very successfully expressing it. He seems to try in both poems to allow the vision its full attractiveness and spiritual quality, as a spectacle of delight, heavenly, a "solemn sight," hinting at a religious or awesome aspect, and as opposed to "life's unspiritual pleasures." Yet he could not simply rest in delight, but tried to account for a troubled and ambivalent response. The syntax of the second sonnet is difficult, and it is not clear whether "this thought" in line 5 refers to the vision, the lines quoted from the previous sonnet, or the sense of the vision as a reproach to bodily pleasures. The vision did not desert him, since he was at such pains to record it, but equally at pains here to insist that it was a mere "Cloud," and thus evanescent; this conflicts with the solidity of the "Grove, the sky-built Temple, and the Dome," and it is not immediately clear why praise of the vision requires disparagement of "Man's gifts." Perhaps the key to Wordsworth's anxiety lies here, in this notion of disparagement, and also in the sonorous but not very lucid last lines.

These provide a rhetorical "lift" to the end of the sonnet, but remain rather ineffectual, since it is not clear what "objects" endure, or how they could "roam";[15] the lines seem rather clumsily reductive, for so often in his poems Wordsworth celebrates without any hint of disquiet visions that in their "passing forms" have nothing to do with "objects that endure," as for example in these lines:

> O happy state! what beauteous pictures now
> Rose in harmonious imagery—they rose
> As from some distant region of my soul
> And came along like dreams; yet such as left
> Obscurely mingled with their passing forms
> A consciousness of animal delight,
> A self-possession felt in every pause
> And every gentle movement of my frame.
>   [*Prelude* 4.392–99]

What the last lines of the sonnet seem to be crudely emphasizing is the craving of the mind for intuitions of transcendence, of something that endures, of immortality, which is registered in more subtle ways again and again in Wordsworth's poetry, as at the end of *The Prelude* where he describes the "higher mind" as one

> By sensible impressions not enthrall'd,
> But quicken'd, rouz'd, and made thereby more apt
> To hold communion with the invisible world.
>
>   [13.103–05]

The question remains why the vision in the sky did not quicken and arouse him.

The answer does not, I think, have to do with its lack of solidity, or its transience, for many of Wordsworth's most cherished visions, those that seemed to give him access to what he sometimes called the "invisible world" (*Prelude* 6.536), occur as reveries or dreams, when the light of the senses is extinguished, or arise in relation to transitory spectacles. It has to do rather with the idea of "disparaging man's gifts and proper food." The vision had no "natural home" in, or access to, his heart because it was simply given, and demanded no activity or participation on his part. What nearly all the various visions celebrated by Wordsworth in relation to external scenes have in common is that, passive or active, they feed or stir the mind, in some chemistry of interaction. This operates across a spectrum, and cannot always be described as "interchange," as if in some equal partnership; at one end of the spectrum the mind is relatively passive and receptive to impressions from the "active universe," and at the other end the eye or mind is actively creative, and the natural world passive. However, the mind is always engaged, whether quietly nourished, or itself busy, and increasingly Wordsworth insists on the importance of the mind's activity, in images of its working in "fellowship," by "ennobling interchange" with what is seen, or by "commutation and transfer of internal feelings," so creating the visionary experience. The cloudscape he saw over the Vale of York was already transfigured, as by some other agency, into a vision, and gave his mind no share in creating it; as a vision it was wholly external to him. So, although the spectacle was celestial, "of the sky," spiritual even, and delightful, Wordsworth could not rest in what might by another man have been greeted as a vision of the heavenly city, or regard it as properly feeding the mind. The sense of unity "In all which we behold, and feel, and are" (*Prelude* 13.255) towards which his poetry directs us had to arise from the creative energy and involvement of his own mind or imagination, not from outside, but from "man's gifts," from himself. Hence that sense of disparagement expressed in the second sonnet.

At the apocalyptic end of the spectrum, the visionary experience becomes an overwhelming usurpation over ordinary consciousness, in a sense of access momentarily to an "invisible world" (*Prelude* 6.536); at other points on the spectrum the vision may coincide with a consciousness of joy or "animal delight." What, again, the visions seem to share is some sense of the breakdown of the gap between man as subject and the world around him as object. This relates closely, as Colin Clarke points out, to Coleridge's attempts in *Biographia Literaria* to solve philosophically the problem of this dualism, arguing that the existence of things outside us is "one and the same thing with our own immediate self-consciousness."[16] This is not to support Geoffrey Hartmann's definition of Wordsworth's imaginative power in terms of "consciousness of self," for Wordsworth's grandest visions involve loss of that consciousness; nor is it to support Kenneth Johnston's idea of Wordsworth as standing as a link between heaven and earth: "The traveler does not simply apprehend or suffer this dualism, he *is* the dualism—without him it does not exist,"[17] for this in fact is to propose a triad, with man in the center. The sonnets emphasize, I believe, that for Wordsworth a sense of heaven, of infinity, had to come from the mind, as he rejects the heavenly vision presented to him without any participation on his own part, but already transfigured as by some external power. The idea of infinity, of heaven, proceeds from the mind, though fostered by and expressed in visionary experience ranging from dreams and inner visions to transfigurations of the natural scene. Consequently the mind is primary, not as a reflection of egotism, but simply as the source of all significant perception, and because, as Coleridge said, "the act of self-consciousness is for *us* the Source and principle of all *our* possible Knowledge."[18]

What Wordsworth's visionary poetry points towards is not what Kenneth Johnston finds there, when he claims it is "simultaneously disjunctive and conjunctive, the very type of a great consummation in which Mind and Nature are imagined as exquisitely fitted to each other, yet remain distinct,"[19] but rather more like what the poet wrote in drafts of about 1800 for a passage in *The Prelude,* book 2,[20] where he refers to

> The one interior life
> Which is in all things, from that unity
> In which all beings live with God, are lost
> In god and nature, in one mighty whole
> As undistinguishable as the cloudless east
> At noon is from the cloudless west when all
> The hemisphere is one cerulean blue.

In a manuscript revision, the third and fourth lines were changed to read: "In which all beings live with god, themselves / Are god, existing in one mighty whole. . . ." Although Wordsworth modified the idea expressed here that God and nature are one, undistinguishable, he continued to reject the idea of God as a separate being, and as maker of the universe, distressing Coleridge by so doing in a heated argument in October 1803.[21] While it is true in some sense that when Wordsworth "depicts an object he is also depicting himself,"[22] his imagination is not "consciousness of self," but seeks to lose that consciousness in a larger sense of unity with the universe, of "one mighty whole." In this he does not deny the existence of objective reality, the world around us, but emphasizes rather that the source of all ideas of unity, of all vision, of whatever sense we have of God and infinity, is the mind. He summed this up neatly himself in the "Answer to Mathetes" published early in 1810 in *The Friend,* where he commented on the education of a youth in terms recalling his own development as portrayed in *The Prelude;* the use in this passage of the images of "feeding" and "planting," and the emphasis on the mind as "infusing" life into objects, bring out its lively connection with that poem, and with the issues raised in this essay:[23]

> In such disposition of mind let the youth return to the visible universe . . . and let him feed upon that beauty which unfolds itself, *not* to his eye as it sees carelessly the things which cannot possibly go unseen, and are remembered or not as accident shall decide, but to the thinking mind; which searches, discovers, and treasures up,—infusing by meditation into the objects with which it converses an intellectual life; whereby they remain planted in the memory, now, and for ever.

NOTES

1. *Wordsworth's Poetry 1787–1814* (New Haven, 1964), p. 17. In *New Perspectives on Coleridge and Wordsworth,* ed. Geoffrey Hartman (New York, English Institute Essays, 1972), pp. 1–39, Kenneth Johnston's essay "The Idiom of Vision" takes off from this definition, which he calls "one of the most vexing phrases in recent Wordsworth criticism" (pp. 6–7, 31), and though he would qualify it in different terms from those I suggest, I am concerned with some questions raised by him, and by Colin Clarke in *Romantic Paradox* (London, 1962), a book Mr. Johnston does not seem to have encountered. In my essay all quotations from *The Prelude* refer to the 1805 version.

2. *Romantic Paradox,* p. 69.

3. Ibid., p. 15.

4. See *Lyrical Ballads,* ed. R.L. Brett and A.R. Jones (London, 1963), p. 293.

5. Coleridge, *Biographia Literaria,* chapter 14, ed. J. Shawcross (Oxford, 1907), 2:6.

6. *Journals,* ed. E. de Selincourt, 2 vols. (London, 1959), 1:180.

7. Geoffrey Hartman comments interestingly on this sequence, noting how Wordsworth displaces "first the locus and then the meaning of the poet's apocalyptic feelings," the latter when he says that "Nature" had lodged the "Imagination" of the whole vision in a "blue chasm" in the mist; see *Wordsworth's Poetry,* pp. 256–57.

8. Recently another shaping of *The Prelude* in relation to "The Tyrant Eye" has been proposed by F.D. McConnell in *The Confessional Imagination* (Baltimore, 1974), pp. 127–45; he sees the poem as describing a progressive enslavement of imagination to the eye, and release from that enslavement

into a "higher kind of vision" (p. 128), a reading which also seems too neat and schematic to me, for the same reasons.

9. This phrase comes from a verse fragment related to *The Prelude* which goes on to describe our "godlike faculties" as at once "the mind / And the mind's minister"; Christopher Salvesen drew attention to this passage in *The Landscape of Memory* (London, 1965), p. 70, a book to which I am indebted; see also, *Poetical Works of William Wordsworth*, ed. Ernest de Selincourt and Helen Darbishire, 5 vols. (Oxford), 5:343–44.

10. Colin Clarke in fact notes the frequency of an association of dreams with visionary insight in *Romantic Paradox*, pp. 76–77.

11. Kenneth Johnston also discusses this in "The Idiom of Vision"; the general parts of this essay form a kind of appendix to Clarke's book, but it includes two fine analyses of particular poems, "A Night Piece" and "St. Paul's."

12. In the final version, and in collected editions of Wordsworth's poems, the opening line runs "Dark and more dark the shades of evening fell."

13. In her journal entry relating to this vision, Dorothy wrote, "We had not wanted, however, fair prospects before us, as we drove along the flat plain of the high hill. Far far off us, in the Western sky, we saw shapes of castles, ruins among groves, a great spreading wood, rocks, and single trees, a minster with its tower unusually distinct, minarets in another quarter, and a round Grecian Temple also; the colours of the sky of a bright grey, and the forms of a sober grey, with a dome." (*Journals,* 1:178–79.)

14. See especially book 3, ll. 340 ff. and 496 ff.

15. This sonnet was subjected to various minor revisions, the most interesting being a revision of the last two lines to read: "Where these are not, 'twill stir about and roam / Feeling itself forlorn and insecure." This change makes better sense, but is rather limp, and is found only in a manuscript copy by Dorothy Wordsworth which Ernest de Selincourt and Helen Darbishire date March 1804; see *Poetical Works* 3:26, 418, and 428.

16. In chapter 12; 1:178 (Shawcross edition).

17. "The Idiom of Vision," p. 24.

18. *Biographia Literaria,* chapter 12; 1:186 (Shawcross edition). In *The Prelude* 1.237 ff. Wordsworth ascribes his inability to write a grand poem or "philosophic song" to a kind of selfishness, or egotism of anxiety,

> a more subtle selfishness, that now
> Doth lock my functions up in blank reverse,
> Now dupes me by an overanxious eye. . . .
> [247–49]

The visionary experience involves participation, which means a going out of the self.

19. "The Idiom of Vision," p. 25.

20. Cited from *The Prelude,* ed. by Ernest de Selincourt, rev. Helen Darbishire (Oxford, 1959), p. 525.

21. Mary Moorman comments on the passage in *William Wordsworth: The Early Years 1770–1803* (Oxford, 1957), pp. 584–85, and on the argument with Hazlitt and Coleridge, which is recorded in Coleridge's *Notebooks,* ed. Kathleen Coburn (London, 1957) 1:1616.

22. Hartman, *Wordsworth's Poetry,* p. 5.

23. *The Friend,* 4 January 1810; ed. Barbara Rooke (London and Princeton, 1969), 1:399 (and cf. 2:265).

DAVID YOUNG

"The Living World for Text":
Life and Art in *The Wild Swans at Coole*

Trying to understand why Yeats continues to mean so much to us, why his example still serves, or ought to serve, to guide poets of our own era away from some of the excesses that tempt them (for example, "confessional" poetry), involves, I think, a twofold and still uncompleted task: a full understanding of the importance that the ordering and organization of the *Collected Poems* achieve; and a greater comprehension of the means by which this poet attained a remarkable interaction between his art and his own life. While I shall be discussing only the latter achievement in this essay, it should be obvious to even the most casual reader of Yeats that the two matters are interconnected, and that a discussion of the one will inevitably have implications for the other.

Yeats' mastery of the life-art symbiosis was a slow and difficult process, and a part of the interest of the *Collected Poems* lies in the opportunity to watch its elaborate drama unfolding from poem to poem and volume to volume. I propose to discuss one of the crucial transition periods in this drama, that part of Yeats's life that was marked by his marriage, his purchase and restoration of the old tower at Ballylee near Coole, and of course by World War I and the death of Robert Gregory; or, to move from life to art, the period covered in part by the volume published in 1919, *The Wild Swans at Coole*.[1]

Wild Swans is an uneven collection, less impressive as a unit, perhaps, than *Responsibilities* (1914), with which it has elements of style and tone in common, or than the great collections it forecasts, among them *Michael Robartes and the Dancer* (1921) and *The Tower* (1928). But its very unevenness—as the whole design of the *Collected Poems,* by making order and truth out of change and growth, allows us to see— has a special interest in terms of the drama mentioned above. By being a sort of centaur, a compound of middle and late styles and attitudes, it tells us much about where Yeats had come from in using his life as a source for his art, at the same time that it clearly points the direction in which he was going.

The very title of the volume, compounded of an image that evokes Yeats's long-standing involvement with the Romantic and Symbolist traditions and a place name that suggests personal associations in a way not characteristic of previous volume titles (*In the Seven Woods* is the closest parallel, and the differences should be obvious), is indicative of its transitional nature, and the title poem, opening the volume, does nothing to contradict our sense of mixture and change. Its themes of human sorrow contrasted with the vitality of natural beauty are familiar from Yeats's earliest work, but its handling of setting and its relative absence of stylization give it a distinct newness. By stylization I refer to the ways in which Yeats had previously used mythology, Irish or Greek, to project his feelings about Maud Gonne and about his own life and times, or the elements of caricature—beggars, hermits, gods, witches, gypsies—that throng *Responsibilities*. Of course Yeats had written poems that were kindred in their simplicity and naturalness, though the best precedents, such as "Adam's Curse," have a less distinctive sense of place, a slighter dependency on the contemporaneity and reality of the setting. There is a kind of naturalness and an anchoring in the poet's own life and daily behavior that make the opening of this volume distinctive from all previous ones; a useful comparison would be the title (and opening) poem of *In the Seven Woods*, which begins naturally enough—"I have heard the pigeons of the Seven Woods / Make their faint thunder and the garden bees / Hum in the lime-tree flowers"—but drifts on to "Tara uprooted," to the allegory of "Quiet . . . laughing and eating her wild heart," and the apocalyptic "Great Archer / Who but awaits His hour to shoot," closing with a place name, "Pairc-na-lee," that has a different sort of ring from "Coole."[2]

The second poem of the volume, "In Memory of Major Robert Gregory," tells us even more about the way Yeats's use of his own life was changing, for it is an elegy unlike any that had yet been written in English. We can see its uniqueness more clearly when we place it next to Yeats's other attempt to write a full-scale elegy for Gregory, "Shepherd and Goatherd," a poem which, though he had written it earlier, Yeats chose to place less conspicuously, later in the volume.[3] "Shepherd and Goatherd" has some splendid moments (traditional

though it was in some ways, Yeats adapted it effectively to an Irish
setting and used it to test some of the ideas that would eventually be
aired in *A Vision*), but it falls short of total success by depending heavily on the form and manner of the pastoral elegy, a tradition with
which Yeats was evidently not fully comfortable; among other things,
it constrained him to talk about Gregory as if he had been a shepherd,
Lady Gregory as if she were an exceptionally dignified peasant, and
himself as if he were two characters, a lyrical young man and a visionary old goatherd. The poem deploys these artifices with bravura,
but Yeats's eventual discomfort with them was probably a factor in his
decision to try again.

"In Memory" is striking in its contrast to "Shepherd and Goatherd." Though its title suggests a formal expression of grief, and its
stanzaic regularity is immediately evident to the eye (Yeats used an
eight-line stanza, one of the favorite forms of his later poetry, this one
rhyming a-a-b-b-c-d-d-c), its manner is decidedly informal; we hear
the poet apparently rambling to himself or chatting with his wife, in a
domestic setting:

> Now that we're almost settled in our house
> I'll name the friends that cannot sup with us
> Beside a fire of turf in th' ancient tower,
> And having talked to some late hour
> Climb up the narrow winding stairs to bed: . . .
>   [130][4]

The elegiac design of the poem, anticipated in the "cannot" of the
second line, is soon clear to the reader. All the friends to whom Yeats
would like to show his tower are dead, and the first three he brings to
mind, Lionel Johnson, John Synge, and George Pollexfen, turn out
to represent qualities that were embodied in the recently killed and
immensely promising Gregory. As the poem nears its conclusion,
musing on what Gregory might have been and steering toward an
acceptance of his early death, Yeats draws on the domestic setting
sketched in the opening lines for a crucial metaphor:

> Some burn damp faggots, others may consume
> The entire combustible world in one small room
> As though dried straw, and if we turn about
> The bare chimney is gone black out
> Because the work is finished in that flare.
>   [133]

It is not simply that the poet is drawing on his own life and his recently acquired (and no doubt fickle) hearth, but that he is matching the simplicity and ordinariness of setting and metaphor with a similar design for the poem. Instead of public pronouncement, instead of the pitch of grief we might expect an elegy to open with, the poet seems to have backed into his subject, to have come accidentally upon the emotion aroused by loss.

I say "seems" because I think that readers do not forget that they are in the presence of an enjoyable fiction; the title itself ought to be enough to make them recognize the poet's guise—that he is sitting in his new home and thinking of nothing in particular—for the mask that it is. But the effect of informality and of participating with the poet in the process of allowing his mind to wander until it encounters powerful feelings persists, delighting us and preparing us for the paradoxical close:

> I had thought, seeing how bitter is that wind
> That shakes the shutter, to have brought to mind
> All those that manhood tried, or childhood loved
> Or boyish intellect approved,
> With some appropriate commentary on each;
> Until imagination brought
> A fitter welcome; but a thought
> Of that late death took all my heart for speech.
>   [133]

Apparent artlessness here reaches the height of art, as indeed it used to do in the pastoral. The poet confesses to failure while he simultaneously brings his poem to a successful close. One of the finest elegies in the language ends with its speaker claiming to be speechless. If Yeats was manipulating the trappings of pastoral in the earlier poem, he is here writing pastoral as we expect to find it in masters like Marvell and Shakespeare: an apparently simpler and more natural manner is simultaneously evidence of a greater degree of sophistication. "In Memory" is a triumph of invention and design that claims to be spontaneous and inadvertent; we enjoy the claim and recognize its validity even as we see through it. The validity consists in the fact that the artifice here does not, as in "Shepherd and Goatherd," muffle the emotion; it strengthens it. The managed spontaneity still succeeds in seeming, and being, spontaneous.

II

In addition to renewing the pastoral elegy by apparently neglecting it, and to strengthening the note of homely contemporaneity that *Wild Swans* has begun to sound, "In Memory of Major Robert Gregory" opens a number of interesting channels for speculation. I shall try to follow at least two of them in the remainder of this essay. The first concerns Yeats's conception of poetic form, which seems to have been changing dramatically in this period, and in a way that alters our perception of the relation of art to life; the second, more complicated, involves the poet's use of himself in his poems, his projection of his own habits, attitudes, emotions, and sense of self.

We can take up the first by contrasting the use of what may be called "outer" and "inner" form in the Gregory poem. That is a way of acknowledging that Yeats did not feel bound to traditional elements of design associated with the elegy, pastoral or otherwise; that he displaced them with a different and surprising poem that had a "natural" form of its own. Homely and domestic as it may be, "In Memory" also has strong elements of ritual. I refer not only to rituals of friendship, house-warming, and grieving, but to a lifelong preoccupation of this poet: spiritualism. In imagining visits from dead friends, Yeats is once again involved in summoning and conjuring, making contact with the supernatural. It is important, of course, that he is not doing it in a formal or literal fashion. The strategem works because it feels informal, even unconscious. The speaker summons not by means of a trance or seance, but by recollection and imagination, metaphorically. Nevertheless, it is worth noting how Yeats had integrated his interest in the rituals of spiritualism with the casual domestic circumstances out of which this unique elegy arises. His own life at this time must have been a curious mingling of supernatural research and home life, as he and his wife worked on discoveries that were to constitute the material of *A Vision*. And the basic formal principle worked out in the Gregory elegy, by which we move past an expected formality to an informality that has in turn elements of form drawn from habits and rituals familiar in the poet's own life, was to become a recurrent strategem for some of Yeats's greatest poems: "The Tower," "Among School Children," and "The Circus Animals' Desertion," to name but three. We can find it in a different, but no less impressive form, in one of the most original and successful poems in *The Wild Swans at Coole,* the sequence titled "Upon a Dying Lady."

Again the subject is death—that of Aubrey Beardsley's sister Mabel, whom Yeats visited in 1913 as she was dying of cancer—and again the treatment is more informal than we might have expected, a series of short, sketchy lyrics with a consistently light, almost carefree, manner. The reader is not quite sure whether to regard the group as one poem or as seven, an uncertainty Yeats himself felt at first.[5] The poems have, of course, a common subject, a shared vocabulary, and a consistency of tone. But they seem willing to be less formal or comprehensive in the face of a difficult subject, to fragment, to break off, to form tangential and overlapping relationships. We take such a procedure for granted these days, but it was unique in 1913. Yeats had written no poem of this kind before; he seems to have deliberately sought and found a looser, more casual sense of form for responding to such subjects as death and dying than had been the case in his own poetry before this—or, indeed, in anyone else's.[6]

As in the poem for Gregory, Yeats's apparent disregard for form (in this case his turning away from the temptation to write *the* poem that would sum up and portray the dying lady, contenting himself instead with a series of versions or sketches) is gradually revealed to mask a renewed regard: out of the casual manner of the poem there begins to rise an invigorating sense of certainty. We are aware first of multiplicity: as there are a number of poems, so there are many visits and visitors, much exchanging of presents, toys, and tokens, many small scenes and events. Then, through recurrence, this multiplicity is revealed to have a single, overwhelming meaning: life's frivolity as revealed when death looms close to it. Thus we have Mabel Beardsley's dolls in II and III after we have seen her as a doll herself, propped and rouged for display on her sickbed in I. We have her gaiety as an index of courageous recognition of the meaning of death in I, III, IV, and VII. From the image of the dolls and the dying woman's nonchalance come two natural extensions: the image of the child playing and being called home in IV, and the imagined afterlife with its dancing-place and tumultuous welcome in VI. The association of toys, play, festivity, and celebration are united in the final image, that of a Christmas tree her friends bring her in VII. As background we have a tradition that supports the lady's frivolity, ranging from the mock-serious art of her dead brother, of Pietro Longhi, and of Petronius, to a series of heroic characters from history and legend

"Who have lived in joy and laughed into the face of Death." The key word *face* recurs throughout the sequence, binding together the living, the dying, the dolls, the dead, and the "great enemy," death itself.

As we read, we watch the seven short poems knitting themselves into a common pattern whereby the serious and the frivolous are inextricably bound together. But the structure of the sequence allows room to move back and forth, so that there is a sense of leisure and play even as we watch associations intensify and apparent multiplicities close round a unity of purpose and recognition. The form of the poem, single and multiple, captures a duality in the subject and ultimately reflects a truth about the *Collected Poems* itself. And again, as in the Gregory elegy, we seem to be present at an acting out of the poet's own process of discovery; the poem stresses participation as an earlier one might have stressed completion.[7]

III

That last point will take us on to our second consideration, that of the poet's expanding mastery of effective ways in which to use his own life and self as a key to the order and meaning of his poems. I do not wish to imply that Yeats had consistently closed the reader out from participation in earlier poems. Nor do I claim that he was the first poet to explore the possibilities of re-enacting the process of discovery for the benfit of his readers: there are powerful precedents for what he was doing in, among others, Wordsworth. My point is that the openness and uniqueness of the new forms Yeats was finding his way to seem to have depended, at least in part, on a willingness to strike less formal poses, to allow the reader backstage, as it were. A good instance of this occurs in "Upon A Dying Lady." Yeats has for the most part merged himself with her other visitors, using the first person plural to characterize his reactions; we are aware that we are dealing with incidents the poet has experienced personally, and we know that he is treating a potentially solemn subject with apparent informality. In VI we are suddenly "face to face" with the poet because of an aside:

When her soul flies to the predestined dancing-place
(I have no speech but symbol, the pagan speech I made
Amid the dreams of Youth) let her come face to face, . . .
                                        [156–57]

I think this is an effective and refreshing way to be in touch with the poet. As in the elegy, it is a confession of shortcoming that in fact increases our confidence in Yeats's procedures; like an aside in a play, it strengthens a bond and furthers a complicity. Complaint had been the personal note most consistently struck in the earlier poems. This is not complaint, which soon grows tiresome, so much as a confidential modesty that matches the slippered ease of the Gregory elegy and the apparently informal assemblage that constitutes the whole design of the Mabel Beardsley sequence.

My students remark sometimes that it is a good thing Yeats married when he did, since it had the effect of cutting down on the number of Maud Gonne poems. Complaint, as I said, is tiresome. But I think that they, and other readers, are reacting to something other than the mere fact of Yeats's marriage and the new subjects it brought him. They are also responding to a shift of rhetoric in which the poet is more often present as a master of his art and life and less frequently portrayed as victimized lover or goaded public man. The drama of art versus life is gradually replaced by a sense of their interdependency and partnership that is finally more complex and more interesting. No doubt the displacement had its sources in his marriage, in the new materials that were coming in by means of Mrs. Yeats's automatic writing, and in the settling down in a neighborhood and home that combined immediacy with metaphoric potential. But the interest, I think, lies in the use to which Yeats was able to put these changes, in his handling of what had been an art-life dichotomy and was becoming a union that took him on to his finest poetry.

That *Wild Swans* is a good place to study this process in transition is confirmed by the fact that the volume contains, right at its center, a group of seven or eight Maud Gonne poems that Yeats wrote in 1915.[8] Some of them, like "A Thought from Propertius," belong to the manner of *Responsibilities*. Others, like "Broken Dreams" and "Presences," strike new notes but with mixed success. On the whole, these poems seem to me the least successful part of the volume; they make a reader look back toward "The Fisherman" and forward to "Upon A Dying Lady" for variety, nodding in agreement with the self-instruction in the short poem that immediately follows the group:

> Hands, do what you're bid:
> Bring the balloon of the mind

That bellies and drags in the wind
Into its narrow shed.

[153]

The image of being at the mercy of the elements and then choosing to exercise self-discipline and self-control is relevant, I think, to the way the group of Maud Gonne poems indulges the poet's sense of victimization by life versus the way in which most of the rest of the volume moves to assert his control of his life and emotions. It is not that the poems about Maud Gonne are one solid whine; they have what I take to be a delicate humor—"I will talk no more of books or the long war / But walk by the dry thorn until I have found / Some beggar sheltering from the wind, and there / Manage the talk until her name come round"(148)—and moments of intense loveliness—"She might, so noble from head / To great shapely knees / The long flowing line, / Have walked to the altar / Through the holy images / At Pallas Athene's side"(150). But their most persistent note, often through refrain, is that of being made helpless by love and the past:

She is foremost of those I would hear praised. . . .(148)
After nine years, I sink my head abashed. . . . (149)
I knew a phoenix in my youth, so let them have their day. . . . (149–50)
Vague memories, nothing but memories. . . . (150–51)

Again, as contrast to Yeats the artist / magician, summoning spirits to his side, we have the haunted man of "Presences," visited by ghosts who come unbidden and disrupt his work:

I have dreamed
That women laughing, or timid or wild,
In rustle of lace or silken stuff,
Climbed up my creaking stair. They had read
All I had rhymed of that monstrous thing
Returned and yet unrequited love.
They stood in the door and stood between
My great wood lectern and the fire
Till I could hear their hearts beating:
One is a harlot, and one a child
That never looked upon man with desire,
And one, it may be, a queen.

[152]

There is detachment here, and the domestic note discussed earlier as an anchoring device that makes the poem feel more real and vivid, but the issue of whether "that monstrous thing" will continue to come between the poet's lectern and the fire of inspiration, the hearth that is the source of such insight in the Gregory poem, remains unresolved, perhaps to good effect. Surely one justification for the group of poems in *Wild Swans* that deal with Maud Gonne is that they provide an interlude in which we wonder whether the unfolding drama of mastery and progress will falter or continue. There are such moments in later volumes and later poems, and they are rightly prized, but not, presumably, at the expense of the increasing mastery I have been describing. Its essential continuity can be demonstrated by reference to three more poems from the volume: "The Fisherman," "The Phases of the Moon," and "The Double Vision of Michael Robartes."

IV

"The Fisherman" might well be studied for its metric alone, which is handled with consummate skill, or in terms of its relation to Wordsworth. What I wish to stress about it is the way that it begins with an emotion common to *Responsibilities,* the frustration of the artist with the world he has hoped to make better—the first stanza contains a wonderful catalogue of wrongs—and then transcends it by an imaginative act in which the reader is allowed to participate:

> Maybe a twelvemonth since
> Suddenly I began
> In scorn of this audience,
> Imagining a man,
> And his sun-freckled face,
> And grey Connemara cloth,
> Climbing up to a place
> Where stone is dark under froth,
> And the down-turn of his wrist
> When the flies drop in the stream;
> A man who does not exist,
> A man who is but a dream;
> And cried, "Before I am old

I shall have written him one
Poem maybe as cold
And passionate as the dawn."
[146]

What is worth noting is not so much the apparent solipsism of this—
Yeats has anticipated that criticism ("A man who does not exist, / A
man who is but a dream") before plunging on—as the artist's triumphant manner of dealing with his difficulties. If his audience lets him
down, he will not lapse into complaint or despair; he will simply imagine the audience he needs so that he can resolve to write its ideal poem.
The marvelous thing about "The Fisherman," of course, is that it *is* the
poem it envisions, cold and passionate and inevitable as the dawn.
Again, the process and accomplishment coexist as they did in the Gregory elegy and the dying lady sequence, and the drama of the artist's
struggle with recalcitrant materials is counterpointed by his successful
demonstration of mastery over them.

This impressive synthesis, whereby one cannot tell where the
man's problems leave off and the artist's solutions begin, is to be found
in "The Phases of the Moon" in a still more interesting form. "Phases"
has so much in common with "Ego Dominus Tuus," which precedes
it (with "A Prayer on Going into my House" sandwiched between) in
the collection, that they must be considered together for a moment.
Both poems use dialogue, are set in the vicinity of the tower, and serve
to expound major Yeatsian concepts: "Ego" the notion of the antithet-
ical self as set forth in *Per Amica Silentia Lunae,* and "Phases" the wheel
of personality associated with the changes of the moon and fully discussed in *A Vision.*[9] The two poems also deal with the struggles of the
artist. In the somewhat loaded debate between Hic and Ille in "Ego
Dominus Tuus," Ille concludes the poem by imagining a situation in
which the act of summoning the anti-self can lead to artistic consummation:

I call to the mysterious one who yet
Shall walk the wet sands by the edge of the stream
And look most like me, being indeed my double,
And prove of all imaginable things
The most unlike, being my anti-self,
And, standing by these characters, disclose

All that I seek; and whisper it as though
He were afraid the birds, who cry aloud
Their momentary cries before it is dawn,
Would carry it away to blasphemous men.

[159]

This is one way of imagining a union of art and life. It may recall "The Fisherman" for a moment—the mysterious figure toward whom the poet's labors take him, the image of dawn, the poet searching "the wet sands by the edge of the stream." It is all invoked again when "The Phases of the Moon" opens with Michael Robartes and Owen Aherne, two characters who stand, as his fictional creations, for aspects of Yeats, but who also harbor mysterious knowledge he hopes to find. They are standing on a bridge, dressed in "Connemara cloth," and watching the light in the tower where the poet is reading late. Robartes enjoys the sardonic knowledge that he is withholding truths the poet is searching for:

He wrote of me in that extravagant style
He had learnt from Pater, and to round his tale
Said I was dead; and dead I choose to be.

[161]

Aherne, who plays a somewhat stilted sidekick in this little drama, then asks Robartes to "Sing me the changes of the moon once more," and they embark on the exposition which occupies the main body of the poem. When they have finished what remains, for me, the clearest explanation Yeats or anyone else had written of this subject, we return to the framing situation. This time it is Aherne who gloats over the poet's ignorance and imagines tantalizing him:

I'd stand and mutter there until he caught
"Hunchback and Saint and Fool," and that they came
Under the last three crescents of the moon,
And then I'd stagger out. He'd crack his wits
Day after day, yet never find the meaning.

[164]

This is a grotesque version of the meeting with the anti-self imagined by Ille in "Ego Dominus Tuus," and as such it serves to temper the visionary idealism of that poem. More important, however, is the irony of which Robartes and Aherne are necessarily unconscious; it is

the same irony that envelops Theseus in *A Midsummer Night's Dream*
when he speaks condescendingly of the poetic creativity that gives
him his very being and meaning, "a local habitation and a name."
Robartes and Aherne do not exist outside Yeats's imagination; their
mockery is at best his mockery of himself, but more than that it is an
assertion of mastery. Robartes scorns Yeats because "He has found,
after the manner of his kind, / Mere images." But Robartes is himself a
"mere image," a fictional character speaking in a poem, and his talk is
of "mere images" too, as in his account of the creatures of the full
moon whose minds' eyes are "fixed upon images . . . For separate,
perfect, and immovable / Images can break the solitude / Of lovely,
satisfied, indifferent eyes." If we are in touch with the ironies of the
situation, then we are ready for a full appreciation of the poem's close,
which follows on the lines of Aherne quoted above:

> And then he laughed to think that what seemed hard
> Should be so simple—a bat rose from the hazels
> And circled round him with its squeaky cry,
> The light in the tower window was put out.
>
> [164]

We will never quite know what to make of that bat. It reminds us
that the souls in the last phase have been described by Robartes as
"Crying to one another like the bats." It recalls the birds who are en-
visioned at the end of "Ego" as capable of overhearing and carrying
off the whispered mysteries. Its squeaky cry may also put us in mind of
Aherne's own *"aged, high pitched voice."* And the circle it describes is of
course a perfect complement to the cyclic view of human personality
Robartes and Aherne have just expounded, as well as to much else in
Yeats. At any rate, there is a neatness to it that calls attention to the
design of the poem, the "founding of the tale," as does the last line.
The putting out of the light coincides with the ending of the poem. To
Aherne and Robartes it may imply that the poor fellow has given up
for the night, but to us it implies that he has attained the knowledge
they mock him for studying toward, that he has in some way over-
heard them (the phrase "an old man cocked his ear" appears twice at
the beginning of the poem; the first time it refers to Robartes, the second time it may refer to Yeats), or, more simply, that he has finished
the poem he was writing, which was in fact "The Phases of the
Moon"! Again, at a moment of apparent failure, we have the trium-

phant completion of a poem that poses its own problems even as it goes about the business of resolving them, a pattern that even the little lyric about the balloon of the mind can be seen to follow.[10] And as it is getting difficult to tell failure from success, process from completion, so it has grown hard to tell art from life; far from constituting a sharp dichotomy, art and life, as they are perceived in a poem like "The Phases of the Moon," have such a complex interaction that it is difficult to tell where one leaves off and the other begins, just as it is next to impossible to separate Yeats the triumphant artist from Yeats the man of frustrations and constraints.[11]

V

Having brought us this far with intertwined dualities, Yeats takes us a step further in the poem which concludes *The Wild Swans at Coole,* "The Double Vision of Michael Robartes," perhaps the most distilled and difficult lyric in the volume. The setting is real but exalted: "Cormac's ruined house," the ruined, restored, and again ruined chapel "On the grey rock of Cashel" in County Tipperary. Robartes is the speaker. His previous appearance helps us both to connect him and to dissociate him from Yeats. His vision is indeed double, abounding in dualities. On the one hand he perceives forces that seem to rule out volition ("When had I my own will? / O not since life began") and depict man as a puppet: "Constrained, arraigned, baffled, bent and unbent / By those wire-joined jaws and limbs of wood" (167). On the other hand, he sees the dancer between the Sphinx and the Buddha as moving freely and beautifully, and is himself capable of the volition of making the song that is the poem. Love and knowledge constitute another duality, as represented by Buddha and Sphinx, and the movement of the dancer between them is paradoxical in its simultaneous stillness: "Mind moved yet seemed to stop / As 'twere a spinning top" (169). The three figures of the vision are both dead and alive, inside of time and beyond it:

> In contemplation had those three so wrought
> Upon a moment, and so stretched it out
> That they, time overthrown,
> Were dead yet flesh and bone.

> [169]

A double vision, indeed. But just as ordinary sight is the combination of two eyes, binocular vision, so there is something about Robartes's vision that brings the extraordinary and the ordinary together. He is "caught between the pull / Of the dark moon and the full," and so is everyone and everything. It is a "commonness of thought and images," and his response to it is what Yeats's response to experience has been throughout the volume: he makes it, by a three-part process, into a work of art:

> Thereon I made my moan,
> And after kissed a stone,
>
> And after that arranged it in a song
> Seeing that I, ignorant for so long,
> Had been rewarded thus
> In Cormac's ruined house.
> [169]

If vision is the reward of willful / will-less man, then art will be the consequence of vision. As long as the human imagination exists, houses that are ruined will be rebuilt, and "moans" will be rearranged into "songs." "The particular is pounded till it is man," and mind will in turn draw on "the minute particulars of mankind" in its search for tranquility and perfection. The process is endless; it encompasses both success and failure, ruin and rebuilding, and the more art allows us to experience it as a process in which we are simultaneously aware of dancer and dance, the more rewarding we will find it.

VI

This necessarily brief survey of *The Wild Swans at Coole* has left many poems undiscussed and, no doubt, many questions unanswered. I have not, for example, attempted to prove that its success in drawing a magic circle joining art and life can be attributed either to events in Yeats's own life, which was certainly taking on a new and reassuring coherence, or to solutions to artistic problems whereby he was able to settle differences that may have formerly impeded both life and art. I think that is a chicken and egg argument, or, to put it another way, I think the very success of the new union prevents us from tracking its sources or demarcating its boundaries. We should be glad simply to recognize the variety and excellence that ensued when Yeats, more or less simultaneously, began to project his own life and self in his poems with unprecedented effortlessness, and to employ new formal designs and rhetorical means that seemed to allow both for an impressive naturalness and an exhilarating complexity.[12] The amount of sheer artifice in *The Wild Swans at Coole* is probably higher than in any previous collection Yeats had written, but the effect is not to remove us from life but to bring us closer to it, so that even poems as arcane as "The Double Vision of Michael Robartes" seem different than they would in a less varied or less naturally based context. This is owing surely, to our sense of the degree to which the poetry is comprehensive, taking in life and death, failure and success, process and completion, self and anti-self, life and art.

I have drawn my title from a phrase in the Gregory elegy in which Yeats is praising Synge, for whom he reserves, I think, a greater admiration than is expressed for Lionel Johnson, the learned man who "dreamed" a "measureless consummation," or George Pollexfen, who combined worldly knowledge of horses and men with a mystic sense of reality when he had grown "sluggish and contemplative." With its image of Synge journeying to a place that would be an analogue to his own heart, and settling his attention as an artist squarely on this living world though he was a dying man (but this is yet another of those dichotomies that knit into a barrelhoop), Yeats outlines a program that seems to me not at all unlike the one that lies behind *The Wild Swans at Coole:*

> And that enquiring man John Synge comes next,
> That dying chose the living world for text
> And never could have rested in the tomb
> But that, long travelling he had come
> Towards nightfall upon certain set apart
> In a most desolate stony place,
> Towards nightfall upon a race
> Passionate and simple like his heart.
>
> [131]

The major difference here is that Yeats was by this time a settler rather than a traveller; as a master of magic, a conjuror, he can bring the living (and dead) world to himself, where he studies late in his tower and communes with spirits, fictions, dead friends, eternal mysteries. Sometimes he is haunted, sometimes he feels he has failed to summon successfully. But again and again, he, and we, are rewarded with poems that are consistent, original, comprehensive, and deeply beautiful.

NOTES

1. An earlier and much shorter (23 poems vs. 40, counting "Upon a Dying Lady" as one poem) version of *The Wild Swans at Coole* had appeared in 1917 from the Cuala Press. It did not, for example, contain the poems on Robert Gregory, "The Phases of the Moon," or "The Double Vision of Michael Robartes." Yeats had also published pamphlets—*Eight Poems* (London, 1916) and *Nine Poems* (London, 1918)—in which he experimented with different groupings and arrangements of the poems that he eventually brought together in the 1919 volume. For further details see *The Variorum Edition of the Poems of W.B. Yeats,* ed. Peter Allt and Russell K. Alspach (New York, 1975).

2. Pairc-na-Lee was one of the seven woods on the Gregory estate. My point is that the name will suggest to most readers the mythic Ireland of Yeats's early work, while Coole suggests an Ireland more historic than mythic, and a place and way of life more immediate and familiar to both Yeats and his readers.

3. Gregory was killed in action on 23 January 1918. Yeats wrote "Shepherd and Goatherd" in February and March, then turned to the writing of "In Memory" sometime in the spring. By 14 June he was writing his father that he had "just finished a long poem in memory of Robert Gregory, which is among my best works." See *The Letters of W.B. Yeats,* ed. Allen Wade (London, 1954), pp. 645–50, and A. Norman Jeffares, *A Commentary on the Collected Poems of W.B. Yeats* (Stanford, 1968), pp. 156 and 172.

4. Numbers following quotations refer to pages in the Standard Edition of the *Collected Poems* (New York, 1956).

5. When it was first printed in the *Little Review* in 1917, the series was titled "Seven Poems." Yeats had written to Lady Gregory (February, 1913): "I will send you the little series of poems when they are finished. One or two I think are very good." See Jeffares, *Commentary,* p. 192, and *Letters,* pp. 573–75.

6. If one looks to other poets for comparable experiments, there is Williams, with "January Morning," which he subtitles "A Suite" (*Al Que Quiere,* 1917), and Stevens, who was writing "Sunday Morning" in 1915 and "Thirteen Ways of Looking at a Blackbird" in 1917. Pound's *Mauberley,* meanwhile, belongs to 1920.

7. The nearest possible example of this contrast is the poem that immediately precedes "Dying Lady," "In Memory of Alfred Pollexfen," which Yeats actually wrote later, in 1916. It is scarcely a negligible poem, but the difference in the way it allows for a reader's response is instructive. Andrew Hoover, who read this essay in manuscript, has called to my attention a

passage in a letter written the same year as the Michael Robartes' poems: "Of recent years instead of 'vision,' meaning by vision the intense realization of a state of ecstatic emotion symbolized in a definite imagined region, I have tried for more self-portraiture. I have tried to make my work convincing with a speech so natural and dramatic that the hearer would feel the presence of a man thinking and feeling." *Letters*, p. 583.

8. Whether it is seven or eight depends on whether one includes "Memory." Jeffares, *Commentary*, p. 181, suggests that "the mountain hare" in this poem is Iseult Gonne. But I think it more likely to be Maud. Besides "Memory," this group includes "Her Praise," "The People," "His Phoenix," "A Thought from Propertius," "Broken Dreams," "A Deep-sworn Vow," and "Presences."

9. One curious fact: "Ego" is dated, by Yeats himself in *Per Amica*, as December 1915. He was, at that time, contemplating the purchase of the tower, but the actual transaction did not take place until 1917. If the lines suggesting that the poet is living and writing in the tower are as in the original draft, then Yeats had moved in imaginatively well in advance of his actual ownership and occupancy.

10. The paradoxical playfulness of the ending, and indeed of the whole framing situation, appears to have eluded most commentators. Thus Daniel A. Harris, in an often useful study (*Yeats: Coole Park and Ballylee* [Baltimore, 1973]), remarks that the end is "a most undignified end to the Romantic visionary tradition." He considers it a "crowning, brutal irony" that Robartes announces the cosmology *"out of Yeats's earshot"* (his italics) and feels that "the poem's philosophical bitterness runs deep" (p. 106). Harold Bloom (*Yeats* [Oxford, 1970]) gets closer, noting that "the irony is as much bent against the occult Robartes," but swerving then to a discussion of Blake. One wishes both these commentators had looked more carefully at Hugh Kenner's crucial essay "The Sacred Book of the Arts," first printed in *Gnomon* (1958) and included in John Unterecker's *Yeats* in the Twentieth Century Views series (Englewood Cliffs, 1963). Among its many insights is this one: "Aherne, Robartes, the doctrine of the phases, the baffled student, all of them, we are meant suddenly to realize, are components in a book, and so is the man who is supposed to be writing the book" (p. 22 in Unterecker).

11. It would be interesting, though exhausting, to enumerate the images in *Wild Swans* that constitute life-art interchanges. A few examples: Mabel Beardsley as a doll, human beings as puppets, the poet as "a weather-worn marble triton," an ordinary fisherman as the ideal audience for poetry, the collarbone of a hare as an instrument of vision.

12. For an essay that argues that the "autobiographical mode" of "The Wild Swans at Coole" and other poems of the period is closely related to the fact that Yeats was writing his own autobiography at this time and mastering the necessary conjunctions of fiction and fact, recollection and design, that go to make up successful autobiography, see Marjorie Perloff, " 'The Tradition of Myself': The Autobiographical Mode of Yeats," *Journal of Modern Literature* 4 (February 1975): 529–73.

Variations on the Theme

RICHARD S. SYLVESTER

Conscience and Consciousness: Thomas More

The role of "Conscience" in the life and works of Thomas More should need no emphasis for any student of sixteenth-century history. More's case achieved immediate fame in the aftermath of his trial and execution, and the twists and turns of his position have never failed to excite the interest of biographers from William Roper down to the most recent studies by R. W. Chambers, E. E. Reynolds, and others.[1] So strong has been the appeal of More's situation, to most ages and to most types of men, that it would not be incorrect to view his concern with the problem of conscience as the single most important fact of his entire career. One might even wish to suggest that, insofar as the question of conscience is concentrated in his trial, the case of Thomas More assumes a magnitude in sixteenth-century legal, political, and religious history that takes second place only to the world-shaking case of Martin Luther.

My own concern is not with these larger matters, which have been developed and will continue to be developed by scholars better qualified than myself as we come to learn more about the legal and political aspects of conscience in the sixteenth century.[2] I intend rather to focus on another side of More's personality—his literary ability—and to suggest how this kind of study can cast light on the broader moral and religious problems which his career presents. What should be emphasized at the outset, I believe, is More's own acute awareness of his situation when, on April 13, 1534, he was called upon to take the oath which would, in effect, have acknowledged the king to be the ultimate authority on earth in spiritual matters. More's own account of this scene, preserved for us in a letter of April 17 to his daughter Margaret, deserves to be quoted at length:

> When I was before the Lords at Lambeth, I was the first that was called in, albeit Master Doctor the Vicar of Croyden was come before me, and divers others. After the cause of my sending for, declared unto

me (whereof I somewhat marvelled in my mind, considering that they sent for no more temporal men but me), I desired the sight of the oath, which they showed me under the great seal. Then desired I the sight of the Act of Succession, which was delivered me in a printed roll. After which read secretly by myself, and the oath considered with the act, I showed unto them that my purpose was not to put any fault either in the act or any man that made it, or in the oath or any man that sware it, nor to condemn the conscience of any other man. But as for myself in good faith my conscience so moved me in the matter that though I would not deny to swear to the succession [i.e., of Anne Boleyn and her heirs], yet unto the oath that there was offered me I could not swear, without the jeoparding of my soul to perpetual damnation. And that if they doubted whether I did refuse the oath only for the grudge of my conscience, or for any other fantasy, I was ready therein to satisfy them by mine oath. Which if they trusted not, what should they be the better to give me any oath? And if they trusted that I would therein swear true, then trusted I that of their goodness they would not move me to swear the oath that they offered me, perceiving that for to swear it was against my conscience. . . . [After More's refusal of the oath] I was in conclusion commanded to go down into the garden, and thereupon I tarried in the old burned chamber, that looked into the garden and would not go down because of the heat. In that time saw I Master Doctor Latimer come into the garden, and there walked he with divers other doctors and chaplains of my Lord of Canterbury, and very merry I saw him, for he laughed, and took one or twain about the neck so handsomely, that if they had been women, I would have went [i.e., thought] he had been waxen wanton. . . . I heard also that Master Vicar of Croyden, and all the remnant of the priests of London that were sent for, were sworn, and that they were not lingered nor made to dance any long attendance to their travail and cost, as suitors were sometimes wont to be, but were sped apace to their great comfort so far forth that Master Vicar of Croyden, either for gladness or for dryness, or else that it might be seen (quod ille notus erat pontifici) went to my Lord's buttery bar and called for drink, and drank (valde familiariter).[3]

The little scene sets the tone and establishes the wry, ironic atmosphere for most of More's later letters from the Tower. The principles motivating his own act of conscience are firmly sketched; poised against them is the "merry wantonness" of those who take oaths very lightly indeed as they, in More's words, "play their pageant."[4] The view from the "old burned chamber" into the heat of the garden sun is cool and detached, a bemused perspective that becomes an habitual mode for More in the writings which he produced during his imprisonment.

More was to die, on July 6, 1535, "simply because," as Dom David Knowles has phrased it, "he would not admit that a lay ruler could have jurisdiction over the Church of Christ."[5] More's refusal of the oath during these fifteen months in the Tower took the form of an obstinate silence under lengthy interrogation, a silence that was to be broken officially only after he had been found guilty of high treason. The speech which he made then, as preserved for us by Roper,[6] is indeed impressive, but its grand finality does, I believe, conceal from us the fact that, for all his long silence on the question of his conscience, More had actually been revealing, in his letters and in the other works written during his imprisonment, precisely how he stood on the matter with which he was confronted. His official "silence," which could be construed, as it was by the government, to indicate denial, could also be taken, as More said at his trial,[7] to imply consent. But if the legal ambiguities involved here (so ably described in a recent article by R. J. Schoeck[8]) were not finally to serve More, he had nevertheless by no means been silent in the letters and papers which flowed from his pen while he remained a prisoner in the Tower. To see these final works in all their literary complexity is to appreciate to the full the care with which More constructed his case in all of its various ramifications.

What I am implying here, to put things in terms of the title I have chosen, is that Thomas More, in these last works, appears as a man of conscience in every viable sense of that much-debated term. A brief etymological note may help to clarify our perspectives. In Roper's *Life of More,* as I have tried to show elsewhere,[9] the word *conscience,* which dominates every page of the narrative, takes on a resonant double meaning. Both of the main sixteenth-century senses of the word emphasize the root *scientia,* knowledge in and of itself. *Conscience,* as the force of the prefix comes into play, is knowledge *within* oneself; but this knowledge can either relate to personal, and particularly moral, convictions (our own modern meaning), or it can be knowledge directed outward, a consciousness of the world and of others. The word *consciousness* itself does not appear in English until the late seventeenth century. In More's own day, as in both classical and medieval Latin and in modern French, *conscience* had for long meant both moral conviction *and* personal awareness. Thus when Roper depicts More as a "man of conscience," we are asked to respond not only to his hero's moral integrity but also to his finely articulated awareness, his consciousness, of the historical drama in which he was involved.

It is not difficult to establish these two different meanings of *conscience* as operative in More's works from the beginning of his literary career. I note here only a few instances, but further study may well turn up additional examples. Thus in *Richard III* the moral meaning of *conscience* dominates as More describes how the protector and his cohorts, to strengthen their case, "took of spiritual men such as had wit, and were in authority among the people for opinion of their learning, and had no scrupulous conscience,"[10] a situation not without its resemblance to the maneuvers in the 1530s of Henry VIII and his counsellors. *Utopia,* on the other hand, seems almost deliberately to eschew the word *conscientia* in its moral sense. When the term is used to describe the Utopians, it refers to their consciousness of their own good deeds ("et ipsa benefacti conscientia") or to their appreciation of the good life which results from the practice of the virtues ("ab exercitio virtutum bonaeque vitae conscientia," 174/31).[11] Given the peculiar ethos of the island, More seems to imply, a genuinely moral case of conscience could scarcely arise.

Throughout his career, More's own moral integrity seems rarely, if ever, to have been in doubt. However we define the problems which it was to raise for him and for others, his biographers assure us that we can safely take his basic honesty as a given in his character. Less often remarked on is the way in which, from a very early age, More demonstrated a remarkable consciousness of the world around him and of his own relationship to it. At one level, to be sure, to note this element in his personality is simply to affirm what no one has ever denied—that Thomas More was a remarkably intelligent human being. Yet what makes More so individual in his age is not just his intelligence, but rather the characteristic form in which that intelligence manifested itself. Erasmus struck the right chord when, in 1519, he agreed with John Colet that More was "England's only genius,"[12] emphasizing, I think, the artistic side of More's personality that revealed itself best of all in the imaginative insights of his literary work. More's "consciousness," in this respect, takes on a particularly dramatic cast, for it involves us, as we study both his art and his life, with his love of role playing and with his highly developed sense of humor that often proved so mystifying to his contemporaries.

This quality in him, though it may ultimately escape precise definition (as genius so often does), is evident enough from the moment

when, as a boy of fourteen, More "stepped in among the players" at
Cardinal Morton's House, making, as Roper tells us, "a part of his
own,"[13] improvising, experimenting with roles he might play, even if
they entailed a readjustment of the script which had already been accepted by the other actors. Throughout his life, and in many of his
literary works, More is constantly trying out roles for himself and
creating roles in his fictionalized dialogues. We also recall his playing
the part of the monk for four years at the London Charterhouse before
giving up this hard profession for another career—that of the law—
where his penchant for role playing might be viewed as better satisfied
insofar as he was always, as advocate, acting in the part of another. The
"putting of cases"—always a favorite metaphor of More's—was
never a merely legal exercise; it usually involved, never more so than
when he engaged in that activity with the soon-to-be-perjured
Richard Rich in the Tower,[14] an exercise of the literary and of the
moral imagination.

We remember too the bad actors of More's greatest works: his
Richard III missing his cue and thus spoiling the effect of the scene in
which he is to be hailed as king;[15] Hythlodaeus, in *Utopia,* who would
all too willingly turn a comedy into a tragedy, refusing to play the part
which the action demanded of a counsellor;[16] and Vincent, in *A
Dialogue of Comfort,* playing the part of a great lord at his uncle Antony's request ("take you his person upon you, and in this case answer
for him," says Antony),[17] but discovering, as he acts out this role, that
worldly greatness is incompatible with spiritual salvation.

Examples like these, which one could draw in great number from
both More's life and his works, establish quite clearly the most signal
quality of More's consciousness, namely his tendency to dramatize his
deepest convictions and, by means of this role playing, to analyze and
control the experience through which he is living. The paradoxes in
More's character which result from this tendency set him apart from
most of his contemporaries. Erasmus, in dedicating *The Praise of Folly*
to More, could take delight in the fact that his friend's name "came as
near to the word for folly [*Moria*] as More himself was far from the
meaning of it,"[18] but the more typical reaction of the age is no doubt
contained in the words of the messenger in the *Dialogue Concerning
Heresies,* who found that More "looked so sadly when he meant mer-
rily that many times men doubted whether he spoke in sport when he
meant good earnest."[19] Yet More's playfulness was seldom without
its serious side; and, in his Tower writings, his role playing never fails

to highlight the moral and religious problems with which his conscience had then to cope.

I do not intend here to illustrate this last point as fully as one might
like; but I do wish to propose that we can widen our understanding of
what conscience (and consciousness) meant to More by giving ourselves more completely to the rich language of the Tower works. Far
from being silent with regard to the innermost springs of his conscience, More speaks out here in a measured prose that does full justice
both to the strength of his commitment and to the process through
which it was developed. I quote, as a typical example, a letter to Margaret of 1534:

> And albeit (good daughter) that I think our Lord that hath the hearts of
> Kings in his hand would never suffer of his high goodness, so gracious a
> Prince, and so many honorable men, and so many good men as be in the
> Parliament to make such an unlawful law, as that should be if it so mis-
> happed, yet left I not that point unthought upon, but many times more
> than one revolved and cast in my mind before my coming hither, both that
> peril and all other that might put my body in peril of death by the refusing
> of this oath. In devising whereupon, albeit (mine own good daughter) that
> I found myself (I cry God mercy) very sensual and my flesh much more
> shrinking from pain and from death than methought it the part of a faithful
> Christian man, in such a case as my conscience gave me, that in the saving
> of my body should stand the loss of my soul, yet I thank our Lord, that in
> that conflict the Spirit had in conclusion the mastery, and reason with help
> of faith finally concluded that for to be put to death wrongfully for doing
> well (as I am very sure I do, in refusing to swear against mine own con-
> science, being such as I am not upon peril of my soul bounden to change
> whether my death should come without law, or by color of a law)—it is a
> case in which a man may lose his head and yet have none harm, but instead
> of harm inestimable good at the hand of God.[20]

What impresses one most about this passage (and there are several
others of similar effect which could be cited) is not so much its final
paradox, brilliant though that may be, nor even the ringing religious
faith that courses through More's words. What is really startling is
More's careful delineation of the way in which, long before he was
imprisoned, he had worked out his position, "revolving and casting in
his mind," almost as if he were casting himself in a series of dramatic
roles, just how he might play out his part.[21] More insists here that the
"framing of his conscience" was indeed a conscious act, a structured

and fully articulated comprehension of all the consequences to which his choice might lead him.

A little earlier in the correspondence, after More had made this same point to Margaret, telling her how he had spent "full surely many a restless night in devising"[22] upon what might happen to him, we find Margaret replying with the common-sense objection that this kind of "feigning in advance" can never be the same as the real thing: "No, father, it is not like to think upon a thing that may be, and to see a thing that shall be, as ye should (our Lord save you), if the chance should so fortune."[23] But More, in his answer, refuses to grant this point. God might perhaps allow him to "play the part" of Saint Peter; nevertheless, if such a fall should occur, "I trust that His goodness will cast upon me His tender, piteous eye, as He did upon St. Peter, and make me stand up again and confess the truth of my conscience afresh, and abide the shame and the harm here of mine own fault." "Nothing can come," More concludes, "but that that God will,"[24] but whatever comes—and here we touch upon the heart of his mystery—it will not involve the separation of his conscience from his consciousness.

The passages that I have just quoted come from the longest of More's Tower letters, the so-called Letter from Margaret Roper to Alice Alington,[25] which purports to be Margaret's account of a visit paid by her to her father in the Tower. The editors of More's 1557 *English Works* felt that the letter might well have been written by More himself, an opinion shared by many a later scholar. The letter is not really a letter at all, but rather a lengthy Platonic dialogue (Chambers[26] compares it to the *Crito*) in which More, very typically, gives free rein to his role-playing impulses at the same time that he offers his most detailed analysis of his case of conscience. The action takes place against the background of Alice Alington's (More's stepdaughter) account of her interview with Sir Thomas Audley, whom she had approached in the hope that he might plead for More now in the latter's hour of need. Far from being helpful, however, Audley (More's successor as Lord Chancellor) had brutally refused Alice's request, fobbing her off by telling her two simple fables that are supposed to illustrate what happens to men who are too scrupulous in their consciences.[27]

It is Alice's letter describing this "shameful" interview which Margaret takes to More—or so, at least, the stage directions run. More has, in fact, planned his dramatic dialogue with the utmost care; he will, apparently, play himself, but he casts Margaret, from beginning to end, in the role of Eve, the temptress who might persuade the man she loves most to forsake the principles by which he has lived. "What, mistress Eve, hath my daughter Alington played the serpent with you?" . . . "Mary, Marget, for the part that you play, you play it not much amiss." . . . "How now, daughter Marget? What now, mother Eve? Where is your new persuasion, to offer father Adam the apple yet once again?" . . . "That word was like Eve too, for she offered Adam no worse fruit than she had eaten herself."[28] The role assigned to Margaret is deeply paradoxical, not exactly a flattering part for one's best loved daughter to play. But More's "casting" here cannot be faulted; through it he wants Margaret to be reminded that she is not only Adam's daughter, created out of her father's flesh, but also the daughter of God, whose act was responsible for her creation as well as for Adam's. If Margaret's own consciousness is ever to approach her father's, then she must be coached to play a part in the drama which he has devised for himself.

More's strategy here sheds a good deal of light on what must have been one of the most painful aspects of his imprisonment—his acute mental anguish over what was happening to his beloved family now that it was deprived of its loving father. It is not so much that he worries about their material welfare (he can do little about this now in any event), but rather that he fears that they will not understand just why he is doing what he does—and if they do not understand, if they do not become fully conscious of what his conscience means, then their own spiritual welfare may well be in danger. Silence on this matter might be, for a time at least, a way of coping with the legal situation; it would not do for the family, however, and More does not use it, as he constructs these great letters, his only will and testament, in which he leaves all that means most to him to those whom he most deeply loves.

And what matters most here, as it does in *A Dialogue of Comfort,* is the actual process of the dialogue itself. Margaret must play her part in the drama, even if that part is a vile one; for it is only by acting out the role of Eve that she can become aware of the other roles that are open to her. More had trained this "dear daughter"[29] well and she would not have to play her part for long before she realized that, in Latin, to act (to play a part) and to do *(agere rem, agere causam, agere fabulam)* were one and the same word. If one judges in terms of the extant evidence, it seems clear 'that Margaret did indeed understand. In her last letter to her father, she no longer pleads with him to change his mind; instead, she prays "that our Lord of His infinite mercy give you His heavenly comfort, and so to assist you with His special grace that ye never in anything decline from His blessed will, but live and die His true, obedient servant," words which surely echo one of More's own most famous phrases—"the king's good servant, but God's first."[30]

Thus in the course of the letter to Alice Alington, and mainly through More's own masterly retelling of the two fables which Audley (as More deftly indicates) had so injudiciously misapplied, Margaret is brought to realize that conscience, as More understands it, is indeed worth dying for. This is (the phrase is put into Margaret's mouth) Thomas More's own "great matter," and the words used here are those which, since the first official mention of the divorce in 1527, had been applied solely and only, again and again, to the conscience of a king. There can be little doubt that More, both before and during these months in the Tower, saw his own "case of conscience" as standing in mighty opposition to the case which Henry had been presenting to the universities of Europe and before the papal courts. His Tower letters echo again and again with subtle suggestions of this conflict, as he quotes, no less than five times,[31] Proverbs 21:1 (cor regis est, et sicut diuisiones aquarum quocunque voluerit, impellit illud; "The King's heart is in the hand of the Lord, as the rivers of water: he turneth it whithersoever he will"), an aptly ambiguous passage that can be construed as either a blessing upon the king's actions or as a warning that Henry has responsibilities to a power greater than himself. So too, in the marginal notes which he entered in his Psalter, More writes "Pro rege" next to eight[32] different psalms. Some of these psalms are indeed "for the king," encomia designed to praise the royal power. But others (for example, Psalm 74) surely offer ironic contrasts between the "Rex pius et supplex"[33] of the Bible and the less than humble monarch whom More still believed himself to be serving.

Several times in the Roper-Alington letter More alludes to the "common council of Christendom" as the court in which his own conscience has been framed; he will make the point again in his great speech at his trial, but the affirmation is just as clearly uttered now within the context of this dramatic dialogue. Other men may think differently, believing like Audley that the conscience of a king is above the universal law, but More knows their minds and their motives even while he delicately, but with consummate irony, refrains from judging their actions:

> Yet, daughter . . . as for such things as some men would haply say, that I might with reason the less regard their change, for any sample [i.e., example] of them to be taken to the change of my conscience, because that the keeping of the prince's pleasure, and the avoiding of his indignation, the fear of losing of their worldly substance, with regard unto the discomfort of their kindred and their friends, might hap make some men either swear otherwise than they think, or frame their conscience afresh to think otherwise than they thought;—any such opinion as this is, will I not conceive of them. I have better hope of their goodness than to think them so.[34]

This man, Thomas More, more a counsellor to the king now than he ever was during his term of office, will never swear otherwise than he thinks; in him, and in those who could play his part with him, conscience and consciousness were one.

NOTES

1. William Roper, *The Lyfe of Sir Thomas More, knighte,* ed. E. V. Hitchcock, Early English Text Society (London, 1935); R. W. Chambers, *Thomas More* (London, 1935); E. E. Reynolds, *The Field is Won* (London, 1968). In quoting from sixteenth-century sources in this paper, I have modernized spelling and punctuation.

2. Among the contributions to this understanding, the conference on "The European Conscience from Erasmus to Pascal," organized by R. J. Schoeck and held at the Folger Shakespeare Library, November 16–17, 1973, should be noted. A considerably shorter version of this paper was read at this conference and I am much indebted to other participants for their lively interest and helpful suggestions. Among modern treatments of conscience I have found the following works most useful: *Conscience* [essays by Hans Zbinden, Eugen Böhler, R. J. Zwi Werblowsky, Hans Schäar, Josef Rudin, Ernst Blum, C. G. Jung], translated by R. F. C. Hull and Ruth Horine, edited by the Curatorium of the C. G. Jung Institute, Zurich (Evanston, 1970); Gertrud Jung, "ΣΥΝΕΙΔΗΣΙΣ, Conscientia, Bewusstsein," *Archiv für Gesamte Psychologie* (Leipzig, 1933), 89: 525–40 (on etymological developments); and Edward Engelberg, *The Unknown Distance: From Consciousness to Conscience* (Cambridge, Mass., 1972).

3. *St. Thomas More: Selected Letters,* ed. E. F. Rogers (New Haven, 1961), pp. 217–19.

4. Ibid., p. 219.

5. *English Historical Review* 76 (1961): 140–41.

6. Roper, *Lyfe,* pp. 92–95.

7. "Truly," quoth Sir Thomas More, "if the rule and maxim of the civil law be good, allowable and sufficient, that *Qui tacet, consentire videtur* (he that holdeth his peace seemeth to consent), this my silence implyeth and importeth rather a ratification and confirmation than any condemnation of your statute." Nicholas Harpsfield, *The Life and Death of Sir Thomas Moore,* ed. E. V. Hitchcock, Early English Text Society (London, 1932), pp. 185–86. Cited hereafter as *CW* 2.

11. *Utopia,* vol. 4 in the Yale Edition, ed. E. Surtz and J. H. Hexter (New Haven, 1964), pp. 164 and 174. Cited hereafter as *CW* 4.

9. See "Roper's *Life of More,*" *Moreana* 36 (1972): 47–60.

10. *The History of King Richard III,* vol. 2 in *The Yale Edition of the Complete Works of St. Thomas More,* ed. R. S. Sylvester (New Haven, 1963), p. 58. Cited hereafter as CW 2.

11. *Utopia,* vol. 4 in the Yale Edition, ed. E. Surtz and J. H. Hexter (New Haven, 1964), pp. 164 and 174. Cited hereafter as CW.

12. "Ioannes Coletus, vir acris exactique iudicii, in familiaribus colloquiis subinde, dicere solet Britanniae non nisi unicum esse ingenium: cum haec insula tot egregiis ingeniis floreat." The sentence occurs in Erasmus's 1519 biographical sketch of More, *Opus Epistolarum Des. Erasmi Roterodami,* ed. P. S. Allen et al., 12 vols. (Oxford, 1906–58), 4: 21.

13. Roper, *Lyfe,* p. 5.

14. Ibid., pp. 84–85.

15. *CW* 2, 66–68.

16. *CW* 4, 99. For a discussion of Hythlodoeus's "nunc sic uiuo ut uolo" and his refusal to enter into the service of princes (*CW* 4, 54–56), see my " 'Si Hthlodaeo Credimus': Vision and Revision in Thomas More's *Utopia,*" *Soundings* (formerly *The Christian Scholar*) 51 (1968): 272–89.

17. This beautifully played out scene occupies nine pages in the Yale Edition of the *Dialogue of Comfort.* See *The Yale Edition of the Complete Works of St. Thomas More,* vol. 12, ed. L. L. Martz and F. Manley (New Haven, 1976), pp. 229–37. Cited hereafter as *CW* 12.

18. Erasmus, *The Praise of Folly,* trans. H. Hudson (Princeton, 1941), p. 1.

19. *The Workes of Sir Thomas More . . . wrytten by him in the English Tonge* (London, 1557), sig. i₄. This dialogue was first published in 1529.

20. *Selected Letters,* p. 237.

21. According to the *Oxford English Dictionary,* the verb *cast* in the sense "to allot the parts of a play to the actors" does not occur before the early eighteenth century. But More's meaning here ("to revolve in one's mind, ponder, deliberate") shades easily into the dramatic meaning. Cf. *Richard III,* "For if she cast such fond doubts, that she fear his hurt, then will she fear that he shall be fet thence" (*CW* 2, 29).

22. *The Correspondence of Sir Thomas More,* ed. E. F. Rogers (Princeton, 1947), p. 530.

23. Ibid.

24. Ibid., p. 531.

25. Ibid., no. 206, pp. 514–32.

26. R. W. Chambers, "The Continuity of English Prose from Alfred to More and his School," in Harpsfield's *Life of More,* p. clxii.

27. Alice's letter is no. 205 in Rogers's *Correspondence.* For a full discussion of these fables, one of which More retells in *A Dialogue of Comfort,* see L. L. Martz's introduction to *CW* 12.

28. *Correspondence,* pp. 515, 524, 529.

29. Among More's gifts to the English language is the lovely adjective "daughterly," which he used, in his last letter to Margaret (*Correspondence,* p. 564), to describe the love she expressed for her father when she kissed him twice as he was led back to the Tower after his trial. See Roper, *Lyfe,* pp. 97–99.

30. *Correspondence,* p. 539. A further illustration of the intimate love and understanding between father and daughter during More's last months is the fact that More incorporated a complete sentence from one of Margaret's letters into his final English prayer, written in the Tower after July 1, 1535. Cf. *Correspondence,* p. 545, lines 29–34 and vol. 13 of the Yale Edition (*Treatise on the Passion, Treatise on the Blessed Body, Instructions and Prayers,* ed. G. Haupt [New Haven, 1976]), p. 229.

31. See *Selected Letters,* pp. 225, 233, 237, 239, and 244. More either quotes the verse in Latin or paraphrases part of it in English—almost as if a direct translation into English would make the undertones too strong.

32. See *Thomas More's Prayer Book,* ed. L. L. Martz and R. S. Sylvester (New Haven, 1969), pp. 47, 48, 104, 119, 125, 127, 147. The verses annotated are 19:10, 20:2, 60:7, 71:2, 74:2, 74:5, 75:5, 75:7, 88:23 (Vulgate numbers).

33. *Prayer Book,* p. 125, marginalia to Psalm 74:2. More intended to apply his annotation to the entire psalm. Note especially verses 7 and 10: "But God is the judge; he putteth down one, and setteth up another. . . . All the horns of the wicked also will I cut off; but the horns of the righteous shall be exalted."

34. *Correspondence,* p. 527.

ALVIN KERNAN

Shakespeare's Essays on Dramatic Poesy: The Nature and Function of Theater within the Sonnets and the Plays

Literature and the other fine arts, insofar as these concepts existed before the Renaissance, did not occupy the position of importance in ancient and medieval culture that they do in the modern world. The poet and painter did their work relatively unselfconsciously, and when an image of the artist or his work appeared within a work of art, the effect was most often to reiterate the subservience of writing or painting to the church, the palace, or the great house. Aeschylus and Euripides debate in *The Frogs* to show that plays are of value only insofar as they serve the state. The Muse inspires Hesiod, and Virgil leads Dante through Hell, not for the sake of art but for the sake of morality. Horace and Chaucer appear in their poems laughing modestly at any pretensions they or their works might have to high seriousness alongside the more important business of the world.

By the nineteenth century the situation had changed completely. The fine arts, including literature, had by then been identified as valuable in and of themselves because they had become the principal manifestations of such central values of the culture as creativity and beauty, and because they objectified that humanistic substitute for the soul, the transcendental power of imagination. Carrying such meanings and responsibilities as these, art and artists now became themselves heroic subjects worthy of full literary treatment. The subject of epic could now be "the growth of a poet's mind," of drama "six characters in search of an author," of the novel "the portrait of the artist as a young man," and of lyric poetry "notes toward a supreme fiction." The artist—poet, novelist, painter, sculptor, musician—now took his place as hero alongside more traditional figures such as the soldier, the king, and the lover, and the making of art became as central a literary subject as honor, war, or love.

It was during the Renaissance that this artistic self-consciousness first began to appear with sufficient insistence and emphasis as to suggest that the writers are using it not just as a quaint device, another "flower of rhetoric," but as an expression of fundamental values and concerns. *The Decameron* tells a story about how a group of young men and women from Florence escape the plague and avoid death by telling stories; *Don Quixote* is a romance which centers on the effects of reading romances and the relationship of mind-made fictions to reality; Ben Jonson's plays portray art as central to social life and persistently explore the harmful effects of the false artist and the wrong kind of art on society and on individuals; and the play-within-the-play, reflecting a continuing concern about what theater is and how it functions in society, is almost a standard feature of Renaissance English drama. These are only a few of the most obvious manifestations of a growing self-consciousness of all European writers after Petrarch about the proper role of the poet and the true nature of art. This new artistic self-consciousness is perfectly objectified in Velásquez's painting *Las Meninas*, done in 1653. The supposed subject is extremely traditional, the king and queen of Spain sitting for the royal portrait. The faces of the king and queen, however, appear only dimly in a small mirror hanging on the background wall. The center of the canvas, now vacated by the traditional subject, is filled by a group of spectators—a child, a dwarf, a servant—a group not altogether unlike the outcasts on the heath in *Lear*—looking out towards where the king and queen are presumably sitting, and where the viewer is standing. Alongside of the internal spectators stands the painter, Velásquez himself, at work painting the royal pair.[1] *Las Meninas* objectifies the modern conception that artists and the making of art may be more central to human life than kings and queens and affairs of state, and at the same time explains the shift in thought which has made such ways of thinking possible. The emphasis in the picture, and in the culture it reflects, has shifted from being to perceiving, from objectivity to subjectivity, from the thing known to the process of knowing, from the traditional outward social subject matter of kings to the inward psychological subject matter of the mind contemplating the world. And the perfect image of this intensified psychological conception of reality, of the mind as "its own place," is the artist creating art.

This artistic self-consciousness was associated with an extraordinary confidence in art and an extraordinary burst of artistic achievement in painting, sculpture, poetry, drama, architecture, music. The names of Petrarch, Leonardo, Erasmus, Michelangelo, Shakespeare, Rabelais, Bacon, and Cervantes justify the newly sensed power of art to reveal the secrets of nature and to create new realities imaged by the mind alone.[2] The English dramatists of the late Elizabethan and Jacobean years inherited the optimism of this humanistic poetic tradition, but their situation was enormously complicated by the peculiar conditions under which they wrote. On the one hand, they were educated men, university graduates for the most part, and this meant that they had been trained as humanists who saw themselves and their art as, ideally, the continuation of the great tradition of classical literature and the remarkable modern achievements of Italian art after Petrarch. Sidney was the ideal English figure. Just how seriously these writers took themselves and how traumatic writing for the theater could be for them can be seen in the instructive case of Robert Greene, who bought a groats worth of wit with a million of repentance. Those playwrights who did not have a university education seem to have very quickly acquired the fashionable, high aristocratic conception of poets and their art, somewhat ineptly in a case like Thomas Kyd, with rare success in the case of William Shakespeare, and with great effort and endless "advertisements for myself" in the case of Ben Jonson.

These writers all thought of themselves as poets, or at the very least as dramatic poets, but it was their fate to be forced to write for what was still very much a folk theater with acting companies organized along the lines of a guild and as the servants of a medieval household. Neither dramatic tradition nor literary criticism helped the poets to resolve the conflict between their humanistic aspirations and the crude realities of the actual English theater of the late sixteenth century. The traditions of the native drama, the mystery cycles, and the old moral allegories had already disappeared or were in the process of disappearing, and the playwrights were to a large degree writing for a new theater. The only critics available were Puritan polemicists like Gosson thundering that all stage plays were abominations, or an aristocratic neoclassical critic like Sidney who in his *Defence* chose the English theater as his example of debased art, and, not very helpfully, recommended its reform through strict observation of the neo-Aristotelian unities and limitation of the vast spread of time, space, and action characteristic of native plays.

Most importantly, the English playwrights were the first Western writers who as a group had to earn their livings by selling their work as a commodity in the marketplace. For, for all of its medieval method of organization and its inheritance from an older folk theater and traveling companies of popular entertainers, the Elizabethan theater was a business, one of the first to be organized in terms of venture capital. The professional actors who made up the playing companies bought plays outright from the playwrights, changed them at will in the theater, discarded or revamped them when they ceased to draw, and in general treated them as what they in fact were, property. And the value of the property was determined at the box office of the public theaters, that is, by the desire for entertainment of a broad cross-section of the London public.[3]

The playwrights, at least the better ones, were the first who had to write stretched between this powerful economic definition of their work as an entertainment commodity, and the high humanistic tradition of the true poet as a maker, in Sidney's words, of imaginary "golden" worlds which far outgo the "brazen" reality of mere nature.[4] In these circumstances, an authoritarian like Ben Jonson tried to resolve the problem by identifying his plays with the ancient tradition of stage comedy—Aristophanes, Menander, Terence, and Plautus—and by arguing continually, in his plays and elsewhere, that plays if written correctly could be true art, not mere entertainment. But most often the tension between the two views was not reflected so directly as in Jonson but found expression within the plays themselves in a subdued but very fundamental and tenacious uneasiness about playing and plays in general. That uneasiness is latent in Marlowe's *Doctor Faustus* where the magician commands all the magical powers of the playwright to transform the world, as if it were a stage, into the images of desire, producing grapes in winter or bringing Helen of Troy back to life, but finds in the end that he has sold his soul for mere trash, mere transitory and unsatisfactory images. The remarkable epigraph of the play, *Terminat hora diem, Terminat author opus,* seems to enforce this equation of the magician with the playwright. Artistic anxiety is openly present in Jonson's *Volpone,* where the enormous energy and power of playing take perverse form as the "great impostor" acts out his pretense of sickness on the curtained stage of his great bed in order to satisfy his lust, his greed, and his desire for power.[5] The protean ability of Shakespeare's Richard III to change shapes at will frees him from the limits imposed by his twisted body and a desperate time, but he uses his theatrical power to deceive, to kill, and nearly to destroy society.

It was Shakespeare of all the English dramatists who within his writings explored the question of the value and meaning of plays, and art in general, most thoroughly, most subtly, and with some real development in his critical point of view over a long period of time. Philip Edwards calls Shakespeare "the experimenter, engaged in a continuous battle, a quarter of a century long, against his own skepticism about the value of his art as a model of human experience,"[6] but the issues were not worked out in the abstract and philosophical terms of formal literary and dramatic criticism. Instead, they were imaged within the plays themselves where the conflicting points of view were dramatized as characters and theatrical situations and tested against one another in the plot. Few poets appear openly in Shakespeare's plays, and when they do they are marginal both in the plot and in their comprehension of what is going on: the sycophantic and faithless poet in *Timon,* the bumbling poet in *Julius Caesar* who intrudes with an irrelevant remark on the quarrel between Cassius and Brutus, Cinna the poet in the same play who is torn to pieces for his bad verses and his lack of any political sense, Old Gower the chorus in *Pericles,* and perhaps the satirist Jaques in *As You Like It*. The only playwrights among the dramatis personae are amateurs like Hamlet and Prospero, and perhaps Peter Quince.

But Shakespeare does give us in *The Sonnets* a full-length portrait of a poet trying to make the decaying system of patronage work by writing in the humanistic courtly tradition which had descended from Petrarch through du Bellay and Sidney to Spenser and Shakespeare. We get in *The Sonnets* a perfect image of what that older humanistic conception of poets and poetry had come to mean in England by the late 1590s. The subject matter is, at least at the first, elevated, tasteful, and social rather than private in its themes: the praise of beauty; compliments on the good looks and rare lineage of the spirited and noble young man to whom the older, deferential poet addresses his verses in all modesty; and good moral advice on that subject always of crucial interest to great houses, the necessity of marrying and begetting a male heir. But it is really the style that matters, not the subjects, and the real interest in *The Sonnets* is on the artful management of sound and language. The music is easy and smooth, though very complicated; the language is graceful, as elevated as the attitudes expressed, faintly exotic but not jarringly so, "rondure," "antique," "pyramids"; above all, the conceits and comparisons are witty and cleverly extended through ingenious length, for example, Sonnet 18's "Shall I compare thee to a summer's day?" It is wordcraft, skill, intricate devising, intelligence, and both social and linguistic good manners which the poet primarily offers his patron; and, he argues, so beautiful are his artifices that they will confer immortality on the person to whom they are dedicated: "Not marble nor the gilded monuments / Of princes shall outlive this pow'rful rhyme" (55).[7]

He was right, of course, but, ironically, the identity of Mr. W. H. has been lost and with it his promised immortality, and so it is the artist and his poems, not the patron, who live. But this historical accident is curiously right, for *The Sonnets* depict not the success but the breakdown of the poet-patron relationship, and this social overplot mirrors the failure on a psychological level of the conception of the humanistic poet and the kind of courtly poetry which patronage had created and supported. On the level of the overplot nothing goes right from the start. There are troublesome hints of possible homosexuality, which the poet is at pains to disclaim, and then the patron attracts the attention of other poets with newer and more arresting styles than those of his modest old-fashioned "house poet." Patron and poet quarrel and separate several times, and the patron seduces, or is seduced by, the poet's mistress, the "Dark Lady." The patron never really acquires a face or character—as if the relationship did not require either party, poet or patron, to assume any reality beyond the social role—and by the end of the sequence the poet has forgotten the patron altogether and is entirely absorbed in an extraordinarily complex relationship with the Dark Lady and an equally extraordinary awareness of the complexity of his own mind and attitudes:

> When my love swears that she is made of truth
> I do believe her though I know she lies,
> That she might think me some untutored youth,
> Unlearned in the world's false subtleties.
> Thus vainly thinking that she thinks me young,
> Although she knows my days are past the best,
> Simply I credit her false-speaking tongue;
> On both sides thus is simple truth suppressed.
> But wherefore says she not she is unjust?

And wherefore say not I that I am old?
O, love's best habit is in seeming trust,
And age in love loves not to have years told.
    Therefore I lie with her, and she with me
    And in our faults by lies we flattered be.
                            [138]

This is a long way in subject matter and in style from the easy compe-
tence and the graceful and relatively uncomplicated social attitudes
expressed in the opening sonnets. And the loss of a sure sense of identity or role is accompanied by a growing loss of certainty about the
effectiveness of the original sonnet style for imaging the new
psychological and social reality which emerges dramatically. At first
the doubts about the adequacy of style seem merely a rhetorical stance,
an expression of the required modesty, as in Sonnet 59 where the poet
humbly acknowledges that what he is saying has been said many times
before. But by Sonnet 76 he is talking more seriously about the sameness of his old-fashioned verse, and these feelings of inadequacy intensify (for example, Sonnet 108), until in Sonnet 130 the poet openly
mocks the tradition in which he began writing and praises the reality
which will not conform to the old poetic cliches: "My mistress' eyes
are nothing like the sun."

Perhaps the best way of summing up the change in poetics
dramatized in *The Sonnets* would be to say that the poet moves from
the lyrical to the dramatic mode—Sonnet 138 could be a scene from
Troilus or *Antony*—in order to deal with an increasingly difficult and
complex social and psychological reality. As Patrick Crutwell puts it,

> The simple, lyrical, undramatic appealed to, and wrote for, the courtly
> Renaissance world and the taste which grew from it, whose attraction, as
> we have seen, the young Shakespeare felt strongly; the multiple, critical,
> dramatic was alien to that world, its true home was the London theatre.[8]

Given this movement within *The Sonnets* towards an ironic awareness
of reality and the necessary development of a corresponding dramatic
style, it seems exactly right when we learn in Sonnet 111 that the poet,
his patron having failed him in the financial as well as other senses, does
in fact earn his living in the public theater:

O, for my sake do you with Fortune chide,
The guilty goddess of my harmful deeds,

That did not better for my life provide
Than public means which public manners breeds.
Thence comes it that my name receives a brand,
And almost thence my nature is subdued
To what it works in, like the dyer's hand.

The Sonnets enact a breakdown of the traditional patronage system for supporting poetry, and of the type of elegant poetry fostered by that tradition. In its place rises the professional dramatist, ironic, tough-minded, inquisitive, with enough of those "public manners" bred by "public means" to look directly at the complex motives and curious interactions of real psychological and social life under the pressure of intense passions. The theater is, then, justified by the professional actor and playwright in mimetic terms: it images reality better than the lyric mode. *The Sonnets* were presumably not finished until after 1600, and in his earlier plays Shakespeare had already offered more elaborate justifications for the theatrical medium in which he had to work.[9]

The Taming of the Shrew is a theatrical tour de force in the use of the play-within-the-play, consisting of plays set within plays and actors watching other actors acting, seemingly extending into infinity. In the outer play a drunken tinker, Christopher Sly, is picked out of the mud by a rich lord and transported, purely for amusement, to the lord's house. A little pretense is arranged, and when Sly awakes he finds himself in rich surroundings, addressed as a nobleman, obeyed in every wish, waited on by a beautiful wife. At this point a group of traveling players appears on stage and performs for Sly's delight *The Taming of the Shrew*. This inner play is in turn filled with other instances of playing. Young men disguise themselves in order to marry beautiful young girls and get their fathers' money, while servants play masters and masters play servants, all for pleasure and profit. Petruchio arrives "to wive it wealthily in Padua" and finds that theatrical methods alone will enable him to transform the beautiful and wealthy Kate from a cursed shrew, useless to herself and anyone else, into a loving and happy wife. Wooing as playing begins at once as Petruchio pretends that Kate is in all ways the very opposite of what in fact she is:

Say that she rail, why then I'll tell her plain
She sings as sweetly as a nightingale.

Say that she frown, I'll say she looks as clear
As morning roses newly washed with dew.
[2.1.170–74]

His acting intrigues Kate, at least to the extent that she agrees to marry him; and Petruchio's greatest play comes on his wedding day when he appears in a fantastic ragged costume, as if he were a figure from some strange fertility or initiation rite, and takes Kate on a wild ride through the rain and cold, falling and slipping about in the mud. The journey ends at an isolated country house where Petruchio forces Kate to fast, to remain awake, and to endure a number of frustrations to her will, all the time pretending that he is concerned only for her well-being. The point of all this playing and pretense is not only to show that Petruchio can dominate, make her play in his play, but to show Kate and make her feel the misery of a household and human relationships in which one selfish will is set absolutely against all others. Kate sees what shrewishness might become in the mirror of a play, and in reaction to this vision of misery she herself learns to become a player. At the end of the play we see a Kate who can cheerfully say that the sun is the moon or who can pretend to be absolutely subservient to a husband's will if domestic tranquility so requires. She has not been broken to her husband's will, nor even perhaps, if I understand the play properly, become more sweet-tempered, but she has learned that living and loving both require considerable pretense.

The inner play of the *Shrew* and the frame play of Christopher Sly arrive at the same place by reverse means, like two opposed mirrors. In both cases some troublesome and wasted portion of humanity has been transformed and redeemed by means of a play and acting, but Sly is shown what he might become in a positive sense, Kate in a negative. Kate expresses her understanding dramatically by pretending to believe everything Petruchio says, while Sly acknowledges the mysterious powers of art when he proclaims that he is no longer one of those ancient Slys who "came in with Richard Conqueror," but is rather something new and strange:

Am I a lord, and have I such a lady?
Or do I dream? Or have I dreamed till now?
I do not sleep: I see, I hear, I speak,

I smell sweet savors and I feel soft things.
Upon my life, I am a lord indeed
And not a tinker nor Christopher Sly.
                              [2.Ind. 68–73]

The *Shrew* restates dramatically the traditional Horatian view of the function of comedy as being both to please and to instruct, but it goes beyond this modest claim to suggest that the histrionic art is also capable of working absolute transformations, in the theater and in life. Restage the world and the life within it can be utterly changed! Art can make drunken tinkers and savage shrews into noble lords and loving spouses.

Love's Labor's Lost contains two internal plays, a "Masque of the Muscovites" danced ineffectively by the Prince of Navarre and his companions for the Princess of France and her attendants, and a disastrous bumbling attempt to stage a "Pageant of the Nine Worthies" by several pedants and local clowns. The actors in the "Pageant," hilariously unsuited for such heroic roles as Alexander or Pompey, forget their lines, mispronounce words, misplace their accents, stumble about the stage, and fail in general to create the needed theatrical illusion. Reality further mocks their attempts at pretense in the form of the jeering remarks of the Prince and his companions in the audience and then by an unwelcome voice announcing that the actor who is struggling to deliver himself of the role of Hector has gotten one of the local wenches with child. All this is done very lightly, and Shakespeare the professional dramatist in a London theater seems merely to be laughing at the performances of amateur players, perhaps also glancing somewhat apprehensively at the bombast and high heroic rant of some of his own plays performed in the public theaters of the city.

But even as the theater is mocked for the gap between its high pretensions and its moldy realities, for the inability of its illusion to transform a stubborn reality, its potential validity is slyly reaffirmed in an unexpected way. The young nobles who hoot and jeer in a most cruel way at the bumbling actors succeed in eventually calling attention to themselves and making us wonder if they are really entitled to act in such a superior way. Costard the "rational hind" speaks of one of his fellow players pretending to be Alexander the Great in the following way:

There, an't shall please you, a foolish mild
man; an honest man, look you, and soon dashed.
He is a marvelous good neighbor, faith, and a
very good bowler; but for Alisander—alas!
you see how 'tis—a little o'erparted.
                    [5.2.576–80]

As we listen, it begins to be impossible not to see that the Prince of
Navarre and his companions are also "a little o'erparted." Earlier in the
play they had set up an academy in which they planned to explore the
deep truths of philosophy and win undying fame by means of perpetual study, denying themselves food, sleep, and the company of
women. When the beautiful Princess of France and her ladies arrived,
the young men became lovers and poets as quickly, and with about as
much success, as they had earlier played the philosopher. The ironic
parallels between this kind of being "o'erparted" and that of the actors
in the Pageant become inescapable when the pretense of being lovers is
brought crashing down by the entrance of a messenger announcing
the death of the King of France. Reality brings Shakespeare's play to an
end in exactly the same way that it had interrupted the earlier "Pageant
of the Nine Worthies" with the announcement of Jaquenetta's preg-
nancy. *Love's Labor's Lost* yields more to reality than does *The Shrew*,
for at the end of *Love's Labor's Lost* the "wooing doth not end like an
old play; Jack hath not Jill" (5.2.872–73), as the lovers are separated and
the young men are forced to undergo a long and painful apprenticeship
to reality. Life has triumphed over art, and yet theater is not entirely
discredited, for even when its magical illusory powers are misused and
overwhelmed by a harsh reality, it can still reveal the not always recognized truth that what most men take for reality is only a badly played
pretense which will also in the end be overwhelmed by the unchanging
facts of natural existence.

This same extraordinary potency of theater, even when used jok-
ingly, appears again briefly in the little play scene in *1 Henry IV* where
that most versatile of Shakespearean actors, Falstaff, plays Henry IV
"in King Cambyses' vein," holding his countenance exactly right, and
doing it "as like one of those harlotry players," as ever Mistress
Quickly saw. With no more aids to illusion than a joint stool for a
throne, a lead dagger for a scepter, and a cushion for a crown, Falstaff
contrives a performance which exposes the great king in all his gravity

and power as more than a little of a fool, something of a pompous sham. Hal, seeing that Falstaff's performance, while true, does not reveal the full truth, pushes Falstaff aside, takes the role of king himself, and with no props at all delivers a stunning performance revealing what, underneath all the rhetoric, it really means to be a king, clever, hardheaded, looking always to the future, knowing far ahead of time what must needs be done, and tough enough to do it, "I do, I will." Here and elsewhere, Hal's strength comes in large part from his ability to pretend what needs to be, to make the role become his character.

In his first decade as a dramatist, Shakespeare, characteristically viewing the chief problem of the theater to be its relationship to reality, seems to have been on the whole optimistic about the power of playing to relate in various ways to the real world. He laughs at plays for their clumsiness and their exaggerations, but the laughter, while it acknowledges the dramatist's uneasiness about his trade, is still primarily only a modest disclaimer, the easy self-deprecation of an accomplished and self-assured professional dramatic poet who maintains the proud, humanistic tradition of the high value of art even on the stage of the public theater. Nowhere is the modesty so complete and at the same time the claim for playing so extensive as in *A Midsummer Night's Dream,* where Shakespeare dramatizes Sidney's boast that in place of nature's brazen world the poet alone produces a golden one, that imagination can perceive and art reveal an unseen reality beyond the range of the senses and of the rational mind. Art is no longer to be measured by its relationship to the given world but rather in terms of its ability to penetrate the screen and reveal truths that lie behind it.

No one could be more deficient in imagination, of course, than Nick Bottom the weaver and his mechanical friends who write and perform "Pyramus and Thisbe" to celebrate the marriage of Theseus in the hopes of winning a small pension, thereby parodying both the amateur players and the professional companies who played for the court of Elizabeth, or in aristocratic houses, on special occasions. Their literalness requires that the moon actually shine on the stage, that the wall through which Pyramus and Thisbe speak be solidly there, and that the actor who plays the lion assure the ladies in the audience, lest they be afraid, that he is only a pretend lion. The audience at the play, though socially superior, is not much more artistically imaginative than the players. Duke Theseus, his queen Hippolyta, and the young aristocratic lovers are merely whiling away a dull wait on their marriage night by watching the play. They amuse themselves with the ineptitude of the performers and, secure in an untroubled sense of their own solid, absolute reality, laugh at what unrealistic and trivial things are plays and players. (Their position is exactly that of the king and queen in *Las Meninas*.) Theseus, that champion of Athenian rationalism, has already publicly declared that the poet's imagination is no more trustworthy than the delusions of the lunatic or the lover's sense of the perfect beauty of his beloved:

> The poet's eye, in a fine frenzy rolling,
> Doth glance from heaven to earth, from earth to heaven;
> And as imagination bodies forth
> The forms of things unknown, the poet's pen
> Turns them to shapes, and gives to airy nothing
> A local habitation and a name.
>
> [5.1.12–17]

And yet, even as Theseus and his friends sit watching "Pyramus and Thisbe," laughing at poetry and plays and actors, they are themselves, seen from our vantage point in the audience, only "things unknown" which the imagination of William Shakespeare has bodied forth and given the habitation of Athens and such odd names as Helena and Hermia, Demetrius and Lysander.

The point is a subtle one, easily missed by an audience sharing in the stage laughter at the epic ineptitude and literal-mindedness of Bottom and his fellow players. Watching "Pyramus and Thisbe" how could anyone take plays seriously? And yet the point made by Shakespeare's perspective is finally inescapable. All the world *is* a stage, with players watching players watching players, as we watch Theseus watching Bottom pretend to be Pyramus. Perhaps, the logic of this endless dramatic perspective implies, the only reality finally lies in playing well and being aware that life is playing. If there is no escape from theater, and if playing is our only reality, then we have no reason to look down with Theseus and condemn as unreal any of those things that the imagination discovers and bodies forth for us onstage. A forest ruled over by a contentious fairy king and queen, a magical love potion which causes love at first sight, a comic trickster like Puck, all are at least as real as a duke who marries a queen of Amazons, rules over a city named Athens, and believes that a way of thinking called reason shows him the truth of things. And just to drive home the point, after Theseus

and Hippolyta and other couples, Bottom's play finished, make their
way to bed, thinking that reality reigns again, the stage fills with all
those fairies which Shakespeare's imagination has created to body
forth the beneficent but tricky forces at work in nature beyond the
range of the daylight eye. It is done very lightly, the claim half concealed and dismissed even as it is made, but reality is being heavily
discounted and a visionary power is being claimed for the dramatic
poet.

In *A Midsummer Night's Dream* Shakespeare claims for the dramatic
poet and for theater all the powers which humanism had conferred
upon art, but *Hamlet,* written a few years later, reveals a profound
skepticism about both the nature of theater and its importance in the
real world. *Hamlet* is of all Shakespeare's plays the most theatrically
self-conscious, providing a great deal of dramatic criticism and information about the English theater. The children's companies in London
are described, the various dramatic genres are catalogued, the reason
why players leave the city and travel is discussed, the necessity of limiting the clown's part in a play is emphasized, and the correctness of a
restrained style of acting is stressed. The play also contains the only
direct critical statement made by a Shakespearean character about the
proper

> purpose of playing, whose end, both at
> the first and now, was and is, to hold,
> as't were, the mirror up to nature;
> to show virtue her own feature,
> scorn her own image, and the very age
> and body of the time his form and pressure.
>
> [3.2.20–24]

The theory is unremarkable, stressing the conventional mimetic and
didactic functions of the drama. It conforms perfectly to the views
expressed in *The Defence of Poesie*—at least after the first section where
Sidney eulogizes the high mystery of the poet's calling—and indeed
Hamlet greatly resembles Sidney in his aristocratic disdain for the
opinions of the "groundlings," his dislike of the clown, his concern for
a play being "well digested in the scenes," and in his general principle
of the "temperance that may give it smoothness" in both the style of
playing and in the language of the play. But, as attractive as this aristocratic Sidnean aesthetic may be, it is not, like so many other theories in

Hamlet (as Maynard Mack was the first to point out in his seminal article "The World of *Hamlet*"), finally adequate to the experience it purports to explain and order.

There are two plays-within-the-play in *Hamlet,* both broken off before finished. For the first time in Shakespearean drama neither internal play is a parody, though both are definitely old-fashioned in style and form. The first internal play consists of lines from an old play, spoken by the leading tragedian of the company of touring professional players who have come to Elsinore, in which Aeneas tells the story of the fall of Troy and the death of Priam.

> The rugged Pyrrhus, he whose sable arms,
> Black as his purpose, did the night resemble
> When he lay couched in th' ominous horse,
> Hath now this dread and black complexion smeared
> With heraldry more dismal. Head to foot
> Now is he total gules, horridly tricked
> With blood of fathers, mothers, daughters, sons,
> Baked and impasted with the parching streets,
> That lend a tyrannous and a damned light
> To their lord's murder. Roasted in wrath and fire,
> And thus o'ersized with coagulate gore,
> With eyes like carbuncles, the hellish Pyrrhus
> Old grandsire Priam seeks.
>
> [2.2.459–71]

The old fashioned, rhetorical, but very moving lines provide at first sight an imaginative contrast to the events in Elsinore. In both Troy and Elsinore a great king was killed, a queen has survived, and a kingdom has been destroyed. But reality, if we take Elsinore for reality, falls sadly short of the idealized imaginative play world. In place of the scene of heroic death and epic sorrow in Troy, Elsinore offers a secret murder by poison, concealment of the crime, and the hasty remarriage of the queen, who scarcely remembers the old king, to the murderer. Where in the old play the pathetic fallacy operated to reveal that nature itself sympathized with the human disaster—"Then senseless Ilium, / Seeming to feel this blow, with flaming top / Stoops to his base" (2.2.481–83)—here the world goes calmly about its business, and, except for Hamlet, both man and nature seem unaware of the dreadful crime and its consequences. The effect of the play on the audience is not all that could be desired. Polonius can only remark on the diction—"That's good. 'Mobled queen' is good." But the chief spectator, Hamlet, does not miss the point and he contrasts his own inadequate reactions in Elsinore to the high style and the tears that the actor playing Aeneas weeps for Hecuba. Hamlet does seem to miss, however, what we might call the subtext of "The Death of Priam," for "the rugged Pyrrhus," object of horror though he may be with eyes flashing and covered with blood, *is* revenging the death of his father, Achilles, in the uncomplicated heroic style of an older age. He is the ideal revenger, then, who would be approved by warriors such as Achilles and Old Hamlet, and as such he is the model of what Hamlet feels he ought to be. But at the same time he is an image of such terror that he is a living argument against revenge. To put it in another way, Pyrrhus is at once an image of the murderer Claudius and the model for the revenger Hamlet. The mirror that "The Death of Priam" holds up to nature shows virtue her own feature and scorn her own image in a most ambiguous way, revealing both positive and negative aspects of revenge simultaneously in the same image.

The same kind of ambiguity is even more noticeable in that seemingly most effective of all moral plays, "The Mousetrap" or "The Murder of Gonzago," which Hamlet stages to catch the conscience of the king. Never, even in theory, has a play had more powerful effect on guilty creatures sitting at a play than here where after a dumb show, a few lines between the Player King and Player Queen about the difficulty of maintaining purpose in time, and a brief scene of murder in a garden, Claudius is stricken, rises from his seat and calls for light, making it perfectly clear to Hamlet and Horatio that he did indeed murder Old Hamlet. Murder *will* out and plays can, as Hamlet hoped, hold the mirror up to nature, not merely reflecting appearances but revealing what is hidden. But again the meaning of the play is uncertain, for the murderer of the Player King "is one Lucianus, *nephew* to the king." The play may be taken as either a re-enactment of the way in which Claudius killed Old Hamlet, or as an image of Hamlet the nephew taking his revenge on his uncle, who appears, even more confusingly, in the image of his father. Whatever the extent of the ambiguity, the consequences are again extremely anticlimatic. Claudius recognizes his sin for what it is and goes to the chapel to try to pray for his soul, but he discovers that he cannot give up his ill-gotten kingdom and queen, and so remains unreformed. Hamlet now knows for certain that his uncle is the murderer of his father, but instead of sweeping to his revenge, he fails to kill Claudius in the chapel, and the best he can

manage is a stormy scene in the bedroom with his mother and an accidental stabbing of old Polonius. The world that imagination envisions
and plays create has now become ambiguous in meaning and morally
murky. The effect such plays have on their audience is no longer very
clear or very positive. The "real" meaning of "The Mousetrap" seems
to be a statement of human helplessness, of men tied like actors to roles
they did not create, swept on in a plot where one can only be "ready"
for what must be. This despairing sense of theater, which goes apparently unnoticed by all the spectators, is voiced from somewhere near
the deep center of theatricality, from within the play-within-the-play
by the Player King, speaking to the Player Queen about the histrionic
existence which life imposes on mankind:

> Our wills and fates do so contrary run
> That our devices still are overthrown;
> Our thoughts are ours, their ends none of our own.
>   [3.2.215–17]

Hamlet does not seem to hear or understand these lines when they are
spoken, but the view of life which he finally is forced to accept—
"There's a divinity that shapes our ends, / Rough-hew them how we
will" (5.2.10–11)—is very close to what the Player King tried to tell the
Player Queen about human purposes and the shape they take in time.
The players still "tell all," but they now tell it in indirect and complex
ways, and though they reveal the truth, that truth is not likely to be
understood by the spectators or to affect the course of events.

  During the ten years after *Hamlet* Shakespeare did not use the device of a play-within-a-play. When theater is referred to the tone is
frequently negative. As Anne Righter says, "Shortly after the turn of
the century . . . the theatre and even the idea of imitation inexplicably
went dark for Shakespeare, and the actor, all his splendour gone, became a symbol of disorder, of futility, and pride."[10] In *Macbeth* the
ultimate image of the emptiness of life takes shape as a theater and a
bombastic actor:

> Life's but a walking shadow, a poor player
> That struts and frets his hour upon the stage
> And then is heard no more.
>   [5.5.24–26]

The boy actor who played Cleopatra discredits his own ability and that
of his crude theater, nominally Roman but Jacobean in its detail, to

present fully and faithfully that profound, complex, and remarkably ambiguous love which Antony and Cleopatra have lived out:

> The quick comedians
> Extemporally will stage us, and present
> Our Alexandrian revels: Antony
> Shall be brought drunken forth, and I shall see
> Some squeaking Cleopatra boy my greatness
> I' th' posture of a whore.
>
> [5.2.216–21]

But by now Shakespeare's view of theater is changing, and once again, even as the play seems to mock itself as a failure, it defends the value of the player's art. In Egypt, as in theater, it is the ability to play, to shift and change shapes like nature itself, which transforms the world. Cleopatra is as changeable as the river running through her land, and by her constant exploitation of different roles she defeats that stony Roman sameness which destroys everything of value by fixing it in a single immutable form. But only at the end of Shakespeare's career, chiefly in *The Tempest* (about 1610–12), does the play-within-the-play appear again in Shakespearean drama, and with its reappearance comes full statement of a renewed, though tempered, optimism about the importance of playing and theater in human life.

At the center of the ocean island on which the action of *The Tempest* takes place lies Prospero's cell, towards which all the major characters of the play are in movement. This geographical movement is the manifest form of a psychological movement from loss and suffering through acceptance to transformation and renewal, which is presented in symbolic terms in Ariel's song:

> Full fathom five thy father lies;
>   Of his bones are coral made;
> Those are pearls that were his eyes;
>   Nothing of him that doth fade
> But doth suffer a sea change
> Into something rich and strange.
>
> [1.2.399–404]

Years ago Prospero underwent this same physical and psychic journey when he was deposed as duke of Milan by his brother, set adrift on stormy seas with his infant daughter Miranda, and at last washed up on the savage island where he found and mastered Ariel and Caliban and became the ruler of the strange enchanted place. Out of these experiences and his studies he forged his magical arts, which in practice, like those of Faustus, take the form of theater. Prospero is a director-playwright, the master of illusion, who uses Ariel as an unlimited power of fancy to stage tempests, set scenes of rich banquets, sing songs, provide moral tableaux, and produce masques. The magus as dramatist uses his theatrical arts in every case to bring his visitors along toward the center of the island, to stage for them the inevitable life experience of suffering, loss, and renewal. But though these strange experiences on the island are very real to those who suffer them, they are never in physical danger: the clothes which the travelers wear in the shipwreck suffer no stain and lose no color. The dramatist by means of his art takes others, without real danger, to the very center of human experience, to a felt perception that the pattern of life is, as the final plays all tell us, loss, suffering, and recreation. To underscore the role that playing has had in providing this experience to the travelers, successful arrival at the center of the island culminates in an overt theatrical experience. Ferdinand and Miranda, having endured their loss and suffering, are rewarded with that "most majestic vision, and Harmonious charmingly" of the "Masque of Juno and Ceres" which makes visible the great gods themselves and through them reveals the energy and fruitfulness of the world in all its oppositions, spring and fall, male and female, land and sea, sower and reaper. When Alonso and his party arrive exhausted and despairing at the center of the island, they are renewed in turn with vision of a set scene in which Ferdinand and Miranda have been totally absorbed into art, the art of theater and the art of the game: Prospero like a stage manager pulls aside a curtain and "discovers Ferdinand and Miranda playing at chess."

The claim for theater could not be more absolute. It is both visionary and didactic for it creates an image of the central pattern of existence and then affects the imaginatively competent spectator in such a way as to allow him to experience and be transformed by the illusion without ever having to endure actually being drowned and reborn. "So potent art" as this, like the Shakespearean corpus itself, fully justifies the epic fashion in which Prospero now summarizes his, and Shakespeare's, theatrical magic:

> I have bedimmed
> The noontide sun, called forth the mutinous winds,
> And 'twixt the green sea and the azured vault
> Set roaring war; to the dread rattling thunder

Have I given fire and rifted Jove's stout oak
With his own bolt; the strong-based promontory
Have I made shake and by the spurs plucked up
The pine and cedar; graves at my command
Have waked their sleepers, oped, and let 'em forth
By my so potent art.

[5.1.41–50]

It is the most ringing assertion possible, as if the Renaissance itself
were through the person of its greatest poet speaking of all its full
confidence in the power of art. But even as the speech is delivered, the
magician-dramatist Prospero, like some medieval poet writing his
palinode, abjures his "rough magic," breaks and buries his staff, and
drowns his book "deeper than did ever plummet sound." As wonderful as plays may be, the old characteristic doubts about the ultimate
value of drama in relation to life still are not silenced. The great masque
is spoken of slightingly as only "some vanity of mine art"; the approach of those crude realists Stephano, Trinculo, and Caliban destroys theatrical illusion and breaks off the performance of the masque;
and, his play over, Prospero returns to Milan to take up his civil duties,
even as Shakespeare was preparing to return to Stratford, without any
plan for publishing his plays. Art can transform men but cannot ultimately change the world, life and death are larger and longer than art.
When the performance is over the actors and the play, however remarkable they may have been, simply melt into nothingness:

Our revels now are ended. These our actors,
As I foretold you, were all spirits and
Are melted into air, into thin air;
And, like the baseless fabric of this vision,
The solemn temples, the great globe itself,
Yea, all which it inherit, shall dissolve,
And, like this insubstantial pageant faded,
Leave not a rack behind. We are such stuff
As dreams are made on, and our little life
Is rounded with a sleep.

[4.1.148–58]

So, while the theatrical spectacle may be transitory, so too is the world
it images. Reality may endure longer than the insubstantial pageants of
art, but that reality is itself finally, at some vast remove in time, an
illusion too, and the great world will ultimately disappear, leaving not

even a puff of cloud behind to mark the space it once filled. A play, then, baseless fabric of a vision though it may be, is finally a true image of human life and the world, not so much in terms of its specific content as in the very conditions of pretense, its illusionary and momentary nature.

To have wrested this much affirmation, this much confidence in the power of the stage to image reality, from the London public theaters between 1590 and 1610—given the kind of plays produced most of the time in that fantastic world of make-believe—was an extraordinary achievement. But Shakespeare was not finally a Shelley, or a Joyce, or even a Wallace Stevens, believing in the power of art to create reality. He belongs to the Renaissance in his simultaneous delight in the power of art truly to reveal, not to make, reality, and in his medieval fear that it is finally only an illusion from which one must always return to Milan or to Stratford.

NOTES

1. See Leslie Epstein, "Beyond the Baroque: The Role of the Audience in the Modern Theater," *Tri-Quarterly* 12 (Spring 1968), for a full discussion of this painting and its importance in the development of the modern conception of art.

2. The best treatment of the pervasive sense of art in the Renaissance remains Jacob Burckhardt's *The Civilization of the Renaissance in Italy* (1860), which makes clear that art was thought to consist of not only the fine arts but all of the skills—government, manners, fortification, etc.—whereby men reshaped themselves, their society, and their world to more aesthetic and desirable forms.

3. J. F. Danby, *Elizabethan and Jacobean Poets* (London, 1952), works out in detail the wide range of adaptations made by poets and playwrights to the failure of patronage and the need to find new ways to support themselves. The difficult situation of professional writers in Renaissance London has recently been presented in full detail for the first time by G. E. Bentley, *The Profession of Dramatist in Shakespeare's Time* (Princeton, 1971).

4. Nature's "world is brasen, the Poets only deliver a golden." Sir Philip Sidney, *Defence of Poesie* (1595), in *The Prose Works of Sir Philip Sidney,* ed. Albert Feuillerat (Cambridge, 1963), 3:8.

5. Jonson's "persistent and at times vehement anti-theatricalism" is fully explored and explained by Jonas Barish, "Jonson and the Loathed Stage," in *A Celebration of Ben Jonson,* eds. William Blissett, Julian Patrick, and R. W. Van Fossen (Toronto, 1973), pp. 27–53.

6. *Shakespeare and the Confines of Art* (London, 1968), p. 10.

7. All Shakespeare citations are from *The Complete Signet Classic Shakespeare* (New York, 1972).

8. *The Shakespearean Moment* (New York, 1955), p. 26.

9. Two recent books, among a number of others, have undertaken to show that poetic and aesthetic questions are at the center of all Shakespearean drama, even when theatrical matters are not explicitly treated: James L. Calderwood, *Shakespearean Metadrama* (Minneapolis, 1971), and Lawrence Danson, *Tragic Alphabet* (New Haven, 1974).

10. *Shakespeare and the Idea of the Play* (London, 1964), pp. 155–56. Edwards notes, *Confines of Art* (p. 2), that "in Shakespeare's plays, most of the remarks about the nature of poetry are uncomplimentary," suggesting that the suspicion of all art, playing included, was characteristic from the beginning.

EUGENE M. WAITH

"Give Me Your Hands": Reflections on the Author's Agents in Comedy

It goes without saying: every author wants applause. More than that, by winning sympathy he wants to control and shape the responses of those he addresses. The strategy is well summed up in the phrase *captatio benevolentiae,* that courting of good will which the orator undertakes in his exordium. So direct an appeal is hardly possible in other genres of verbal art, though the teller of tales may, if he chooses, pause in his narration to lecture his readers, point to a moral, or tell them what to think about his characters. Not so the playwright, who is supposed to vanish into the thin air of negative capability. His way to the hearts of his audience must be devious, his appearances masked, his voice made to sound like another's.

When his play is printed, to be sure, he may publish over his own name an unashamed bid for sympathy in the form of a dedication, but in the theater, if he is to make anything like an overt appeal, he must deputize certain actors to address the audience on his behalf. The clearest case of such an appeal is the conventional ending of Roman comedy where, invariably, we find the request for applause: *Plaudite, Clare plausum date,* or some other variant of the formula. Prologues, inductions, choruses, and what used to be called "intermeans" give the author other opportunities to court the favor of his auditors in speeches made directly to them by actors. Then there are the less clearly defined cases where the words of a character may or may not convey the author's own opinions. Critics disagree about the role of the *raisonneur* in Molière's plays, for example, some of them warning us not to assume that his views are precisely those of his creator.[1] In some sense, of course, every character is the author's agent, instructed, so to speak, to create a certain impression at a certain moment. The concern of this paper, however, is exclusively with those agents who most clearly speak for the author and, on his behalf, seek to influence the response of the audience. I shall limit my examples to comedy, which seems both to allow and to require such appeals more than other kinds of drama. I propose to begin with the seemingly naive bid for applause in Roman comedy and proceed to some of the less direct ways in which comic agents ask for approval and tell us what to laugh at.

Plautus and Terence apparently took the concluding speech to the audience from the Greek writers of New Comedy. In *Dyscolus,* the one comedy by Menander to survive complete, the slave Getas says: "I hope that you have all enjoyed the way we won the bout with that old rascal. If you did, I'll ask you, gentlemen, both old and young, to give us your applause."[2] The last words of *Cistellaria,* probably one of the earliest Plautine comedies, show clearly how such endings were regarded by that time in Rome: "Now as to what is left, and left to you, spectators,—follow the old fashion and applaud our comedy at its conclusion."[3] Two centuries later Horace takes the custom for granted in some practical advice to the beginner in playwriting: "If you want an approving hearer, one who waits for the curtain, and will stay in his seat till the singer [*cantor*] cries 'Give me your applause,' . . . " (*Ars Poetica,* ll. 154–55).[4]

Horace's word *cantor* calls attention to some puzzling details. Who makes this appeal *ad spectatores,* an actor or a musician? Is he in any case no more than a stand-in for the author? Is he asking our applause for his performance or for the play? Inevitably the fortunes of the playwright are tied to those of the actors who present his characters, but when they speak to us directly the knot loosens enough to make us aware of the discrete identities of character, impersonator, and, behind them both, the author. In *Dyscolus* an actor playing the part of the tricky slave speaks the brief epilogue, and in Plautus, too, the speech is often made by an actor still in character. In *Cistellaria,* however, the speech heading is *Caterva,* and elsewhere it is *Grex,* both words for the acting company, and supposed by some translators to indicate a choric speech by several actors. Others assign such speeches to the head of the company. In Plautus's *Trinummus* and in all of the plays of Terence the speech heading is an omicron, a symbol for the *cantor* mentioned by Horace. Since, as W. Beare points out, actors had to sing and were called both *cantores* and *histriones,* the omicron probably indicates that one of the actors delivers the epilogue, though it is frequently translated as "stage musician."[5] There are instances, then, in which an actor *qua* actor (or perhaps more than one) makes the parting appeal, though possibly in the costume of the part he has been playing, and other instances in which he continues in his role even while speaking to the spectators.

Getas in *Dyscolus* seeks to capitalize on the pleasure they may have taken in his share in the discomfiture of "the bad-tempered man." In Plautus's *Mercator* the young lover's friend, Eutychus, stays even more firmly in character as he attempts to make a compact with the audience. He proposes that they join him in passing some laws to punish old men like those in the play, who interfere with the love affairs of their sons. And if such a law is pleasing to the young men in the audience, he begs for their applause—not for the general success of the comedy and the comedians, but explicitly for that flouting of Roman *pietas* and *gravitas* in which Erich Segal finds the essence of Plautine comedy.[6] The epilogue of the fortunate Eutychus serves the purposes of the author more obviously than most. When the fun is at the expense of the *senex amans* who foolishly rivals his own son, the point of view must be that of the young men, and the playwright must see to it that their cause is made attractive to spectators of any age. The conspiratorial bond proposed by young Eutychus and his special address to the *adulescentes* are the final touches in the author's design. In a sense, then, the voice we hear at this moment is not only more the character's than the actor's, but is also more nearly the author's. While the anonymous actor—*Cantor, Grex, Caterva*—in part seeks recognition for his performance, Eutychus urges us to recognize what Plautus has made ridiculous.

A variant reading in two Plautine manuscripts provides evidence that the words of the epilogue were sometimes understood to be those of the author *in propria persona;* for in MSS A and B the epilogue of *Epidicus* is assigned to *Poeta,* as if the author himself came onstage to say "plaudite et valete" and tell the spectators to rise and stretch their limbs. Though the other manuscripts assign these words to *Grex,* they may have been taken as the poet's even if spoken by one or more players.

A somewhat different sort of authorial intervention occurs in the prologues of Roman comedy. Many of them are at least in part expository, and to that extent have other objectives than *captatio benevolentiae.* Several aim at the most elementary control of a possibly unruly audience: "Don't make too much noise," "Pay attention to the

play," "Judge it fairly." In one case there is no doubt that the appeal is
to be understood as the author's: the speaker of the prologue to
Menaechmi, before making his plea, says: "I bring you Plautus, orally,
not corporally" (*Plautus,* 2:367). Terence makes the prologue even
more personal and uses it not simply to beg for good will but to defend
himself against ill will already expressed by rival playwrights and inat-
tentive spectators. At a performance of *Heautontimorumenos,* Lucius
Ambivius Turpio, by then an old actor, announced that Terence
wanted him to be not only the speaker of the prologue but also an
orator, to plead the author's case.[7] It was he who also spoke the second
prologue to *Hecyra,* explaining why the play had failed twice because
of interruptions and competing entertainment. He ended by urging
the audience to be swayed by him and to listen silently to Terence's
play. Here the dramatist's plea becomes forensic oratory with a famous actor as trial lawyer.

Roman comedy, somewhat like *Hamlet,* seems to be full of quotations. Full, that is, of characters, situations, and comic routines which
we have encountered in one or another European comedy from the
Renaissance to the present time. New Comedy, as Plautus and Terence practiced it, proved to be very fruitful. In the matter of authorial
intervention, too, the Romans laid down the broad outlines for their
successors. English writers of comedy in the sixteenth and seventeenth
centuries used and developed the various forms of this device glanced
at in the preceding pages: the parting appeal for applause, in which the
author is represented by an actor, sometimes still speaking in character; and the prologue, in which an actor begs a fair hearing for his
author and occasionally defends him against past misunderstanding.
Examples from a few comedies by some of the best practitioners of this
genre will show that the playwright's use of such agents was often a
comic technique of considerable subtlety.

When Puck begins his last speech, "If we shadows have offended,"
we know he is speaking for the actors. Soon he is saying:

> Gentles, do not reprehend:
> If you pardon, we will mend.
> Give me your hands, if we be friends,
> And Robin shall restore amends.
>   [5.1.425–26; 439–40][8]

He is playing a game with us like that of the actor or chorus at the end of
Cistellaria, who tells us that the bad actor will be thrashed while the

good one will get a drink. Presumably our applause may make the crucial difference (*Plautus,* 2: 183). Similarly, the spokesman for the company in *Captivi* says, "if you please, and if we have pleased you and have not been boring, intimate as much" (*Plautus,* 1:567). But Puck's is an epilogue in character: he is still a spirit who can reward us if we give him our hands—still the spirit who has alternately tormented and gratified the lovers in the play. As the chief trickster, and therefore a comic agent of great importance, he has made us laugh at his victims, and because of his superior powers he has had a special vantage point from which to look at human folly: "Lord, what fools these mortals be!" (3.2.115). Although he, too, makes stupid mistakes, he succeeds admirably in dramatizing for us the distance between the one who laughs and the object of laughter. For the moment, at least, we see through his eyes and achieve the comic perspective Shakespeare has designed.

In *A Midsummer Night's Dream* that comic perspective is inseparable from the theatrical metaphor which permeates the play. To see that the anguish of the lovers is a "pageant" for Puck and Oberon just as the star-crossed love of Pyramus and Thisbe as presented by Peter Quince's Men is "tragical mirth" for the stage audience is to see life as a comedy. In his epilogue Puck adds the further suggestion that we might think of the entire play as a dream. Puck's role in these manipulations of point of view makes him the author's agent in a way that no speaker of a classical epilogue is; yet in Shakespeare's more complicated contrivance the ancient one is embedded.

Rosalind, the most brilliant of Shakespeare's comic agents, questions the need for epilogues when she turns to address the audience at the end of *As You Like It.* But having called attention in this way to the gratuitous artifice of such speeches, she proceeds to give one, deciding to conjure rather than beg. Conjuring is what she has just been doing in the final scene, mysteriously producing Hymen to preside over the matches (including her own) which she has engineered. Has she magically produced a deity, as she hints that she can ("I can do strange things"—5.2.59), or has she arranged a *masque champêtre?* Is she moving the resolution of the story into the realm of the superhuman or into another layer of literary artifice? In any case she has established for the other characters a different kind of reality which, for the audience in the theater, seems to be at least half play, like her disguise and her games with Orlando. So when she begins to conjure in her epilogue we see her playing with the convention.

Although her strategy, somewhat like that of Eutychus in *Mercator,* is to bargain with various segments of the audience for applause, her appeal, first to the women, then to the men, is characteristic of her in its mockery and self-mockery. As she addresses each sex, but particularly as she addresses the men at the end, she exploits her own sexual ambiguity as Rosalind-Ganymede, and as the boy who plays this part:

> If I were a woman, I would kiss as many of you as had beards that pleased me, complexions that liked me, and breaths that I defied not; and I am sure, as many as have good beards, or good faces, or sweet breaths, will, for my kind offer, when I make curtsy, bid me farewell.

The compact is with an actor who asks for a vote of confidence as he pokes fun at himself and at what he is doing.

It is also, of course, a compact with the author. Shakespeare's choice of Rosalind as his chief agent, an enchantress mainly in the sense that she is a bewitching and flirtatious girl, tells us a good deal about the kind of comedy in which she appears. Though she has scheming and high spirits in common with Plautus's female trickster Phronesium in *Truculentus,* who plays her lovers off against each other—and asks for applause "for Venus' sake"—Rosalind is no *meretrix.* The values of medieval and Renaissance romance vested in her as the eponymous heroine of Lodge's narrative guarantee a kind of sympathy unlike that which the audience feels for the merely successful trickster. Rosalind is not only clever and desirable but, in the terminology of romance, adorable. Like other heroines of romance she embodies an ideal toward which she leads those who try to win her, and thus controls the action in more ways than Phronesium can be said to do.

Even more important is her contribution to the unity of the play. Combinations of the formulae of Plautine comedy with those of courtly romance are not rare, but few of them achieve the unity of tone found in *As You Like It.* The sudden jolts and outrageous juxtapositions of the *Celestina,* for instance, are utterly different. Largely through the agency of Rosalind the diverse elements of *As You Like It* are fused.

With some of Jaques's bent for satire and Touchstone's for the put-down abrupt, Rosalind does more than either of them to control the comic perspective; yet at certain moments she herself is vulnerable. As comic agent she makes lovers and the rituals of romantic love ridiculous, but as a woman in love she is the butt of Celia's jokes (3.2).[9]

It is the extraordinary balance of the impulses toward laughter, sympathy, and admiration which distinguishes *As You Like It,* and Rosalind, courting our approval, directing our responses long before she turns to beg for applause, holds the balance in her hands. In the famous wooing scenes, Silvius and Phoebe or Orlando and "Ganymede," she seems almost to hold for her author the strings which move the other characters.

If Rosalind can "do strange things," what Prospero can do is stranger. But when the magus at last speaks to the audience, his charms o'erthrown, he begs for the release which only the magic of applause can give him:

> Let me not,
> Since I have my dukedom got
> And pardoned the deceiver, dwell
> In this bare island by your spell;
> But release me from my bands
> With the help of your good hands.
> [Epilogue, ll. 5–10]

While the metaphor of magic for the art of the writer is common, it is unusual to apply it to the reception of that art, and hence, though it is easy to think of Prospero as the surrogate that he partly is for the magician, Shakespeare, it is more surprising to be asked to think of our part in this transaction as a matching magical procedure. Yet the applause, the approval, the response demanded of us do in fact depend on an answering exercise of imagination, to which Prospero's *jeu d'esprit* calls attention. Actors are only too aware of the dependence of their "act" on the reception they are getting. Without the desired response they cannot fully transform themselves into their roles. And if they fail, the author also fails. The magic succeeds only when it produces a countermagic.

Prospero is quite unlike most comic agents, though on occasion he can be the familiar *eiron* who deflates another character as he does by his reply to Miranda's best remembered lines:

> O, wonder!
> How many goodly creatures are there here!
> How beauteous mankind is! O brave new world
> That has such people in't!
> *Prospero.* 'Tis new to thee.
> [5.1. 181–84]

He is also, as Bernard Knox has pointed out, a direct descendant of the irascible *senex* of Roman comedy,[10] but his influence on the effect of the play depends more on his awesome powers and on his renunciation of them. By his magic he brings about the resolution demanded by comedy; by his final abnegation he gives a special significance to the happy ending. By means of both he helps to push romantic comedy toward romance.

The *mythos* which Northrop Frye abstracts from New Comedy of young lovers triumphing over blocking characters to establish a new society[11] is not in itself far removed from romance. The character of the comedy, as he shows, depends entirely on what is emphasized. The infinite horizons of romance are suggested both by what Prospero has taught himself to do and by his benignity of purpose when he says:

> Their understanding
> Begins to swell, and the approaching tide
> Will shortly fill the reasonable shore,
> That now lies foul and muddy.
> [5.1. 79–82]

He refers specifically to the dissolving of his charm and the return to normal functioning of minds bewitched, but his words, spoken after he has given up the idea of vengeance, imply hope for the spiritual growth of his enemies. The compelling image of the tide sweeping in to make a "reasonable shore" of what "now lies foul and muddy" is a fine emblem for the fulfilment of a humanist dream. In the epilogue, where he reminds us of his own growth into forgiveness, he offers a final testimony of his renunciation of power by throwing himself on our mercy. Though the ending of *The Tempest* does not assure us that all the characters have "found themselves" in the favorable sense implied by Gonzalo (5.1.208–13)—Caliban at best will be more prudent; Antonio and Sebastian are suspiciously silent—the emphasis on growth, greatness of spirit, and reconciliation is precisely that of romance.

One of the most persuasive and rewarding of Northrop Frye's schemata is that which situates comedy between romance and satire.[12] The distance between comedies pushed toward these two extremes may be measured by comparing two speeches—Miranda's, quoted above, and Edward Knowell's in *Every Man in his Humor:* "Oh, manners! That this age should bring forth such creatures! / That Nature should be at leisure to make 'em!" (4.7.130–32).[13] Even though Miranda's enthusiasm is undercut by her father's reply, wonder is rooted in the play. Edward Knowell's attitude, as he amuses himself and his friend Wellbred with the antics of acquaintances whom he encourages to perform like trained animals, is characteristic of the satirist, at once fascinated and contemptuous. He would agree with Puck that mortals—most mortals, at least—are fools, but he is both more concerned and more malicious; after all, he has to live with these creatures.

Jonson assigns to many of his agents the task of making this view prevail. Sometimes he uses a prologue, induction, or "intermean" to tell the audience what a proper comedy should do. Occasionally, like Terence, he defends himself against critics. His concern, especially in the "comicall satyres," with precisely the right satirical attitude, neither too bitter nor too complaisant, was noted and discussed at length by O. J. Campbell.[14] It appears clearly in the first of these plays, *Every Man out of his Humor,* in which the author's agent is a character named Asper. In the induction, after giving the stage audience an often-quoted definition of "humor," he promises to scourge those who have succumbed to humors and affectations, and to hold up a mirror in which "the times deformitie" can be seen.[15] His plan is that of the professional satirist but it also embraces the standard program of comedy, complete with Ciceronian mirror, as found in many a Renaissance treatise. When the action of the play begins, Asper assumes the role of a less admirable satirist, Macilente, whose view of the world is discolored by envy. One persona serves as a foil for the other.

Jonson's elaboration of the ancient device may be overingenious, but the very complexity adds something to the experience of the epilogue. There Macilente says:

> Wel, gentlemen, I should haue gone in, and return'd to you, as I was ASPER at the first: but (by reason the shift would haue beene somewhat long, and we are loth to draw your patience farder) wee'le intreat you to imagine it. And now (that you may see I will be out of humour for companie) I stand wholly to your kind approbation, and (indeed) am nothing so peremptorie as I was in the beginning: Mary, I will not doe as PLAUTUS, in his *Amphytrio,* for all this (*Summi Iouis causa, Plaudite:*) begge a *Plaudite,* for gods sake; but if you (out of the bountie of your good liking) will bestow it; why you may (in time) make leane MACILENTE as fat, as Sir IOHN FAL-STAFFE.
>
> (5.11.75–87)

The speech is a deliberate challenge to the audience's awareness of the device, of dramatic tradition, of contemporary drama, and hence of the well-read author who stands behind the actor playing Asper-Macilente.

Jonson's tour de force in this line is the induction to *Bartholomew Fair,* where his Terentian self-defense against the criticism of the unknowing is ironically presented in the conversation between the Stagekeeper and the Book-holder. About half of the induction is given over to the "Articles of Agreement" between the author and his spectators, who are made to promise that they will judge fairly and not expect too much—especially not expect "Tales, Tempests, and such like drolleries" (ll. 115–16). It is as if Jonson, threatening and cajoling, were just the other side of the tiring-house wall, and likely to emerge at any minute. Above all, he seems determined that the spectators recognize the world of the play as their own world and yet as a fair in which many extravagant and absurd objects are presented. The comic point of view to be attained is very close to that proposed in *Every Man out of his Humor,* but the device of the later induction is immeasurably superior.

In the three plays which stand with *Bartholomew Fair* as his best he keeps a more circumspect distance. His agents are at work, however, seeing to it that the audience takes pleasure in the discomfiture of fools and impostors. Long before Volpone, Truewit, or Face demands applause each one has established his credentials as a trickster whose cleverness merits, as in Roman comedy, a certain kind of admiration. The fact that Volpone and Face are themselves impostors hardly diminishes the admiration, though it results, of course, in feelings very different from those inspired by Rosalind or Prospero.

Truewit may arouse a kind of admiration reminiscent of Rosalind. His diatribes are highly entertaining, as are the thrust and parry of his conversations with his friends Clerimont and Dauphine Eugenie. All three become more interesting as characters than the *adulescentes* of Roman comedy, whose places they occupy in the plot, and more directly the occasion for laughter than the trickster who mainly makes others look ridiculous. The wit does this, of course, but like the clown he is also a funny man. His way of putting things is at least as amusing as the objects of his ridicule.

Truewit and his friends may have established another bond with their audience. In the "private house" where *Epicoene* was first performed they may have had, as Michael Shapiro suggests, a special appeal as representatives of polite society[16]—brilliant youths in whose wit and urbanity many of the young men present would have liked to see reflections of their own. As seventeenth-century English comedy turns in the direction of what came to be called the "comedy of wit" this appeal becomes more marked, and the shift of setting to the rooms of gentlemen and the gathering places of fashionable people brings about a change of tone. What is ridiculous is not simply the failure to achieve a balance of humors or a reasonable outlook but the failure to behave "like us." The exclusive point of view is that of the arbiters of elegance. To some extent this is already the case in *Epicoene*. Morose is absurd by anyone's standards, but Truewit's first comments on him—"I met that stiff piece of formality, his uncle, yesterday, with a huge turbant of nightcaps on his head, buckled over his ears" (1.1. 129–31)—emphasize grotesquerie, rigidity, a lack of *savoir faire.*

The effect of the comedy clearly depends on seeing the action from the point of view of the three young men, and especially of Truewit, who, "like Jonson," as Jonas Barish remarks, "speaks from a higher altitude of perception than his friends."[17] Any inclination to sympathize with Morose dilutes somewhat one's relish of the comedy. Even Barish, in his excellent discussion of the play, worries about "Dauphine's heartless dismissal of the old man," but Truewit shows how the denouement is to be viewed when he says: "Spectators, if you like this comedy, rise cheerfully, and now Morose is gone in, clap your hands. It may be that noise will cure him, at least please him" (5.4. 222–24). Somewhat heartless he may be, but not bitter. Only detached enough to continue to see Morose as a laughable monster. Since Truewit moves in what the play assumes to be the right circles there is some snob-appeal in Jonson's technique of encouraging the audience to see through Truewit's eyes.

One final example will show how this sort of appeal was managed in the heyday of the comedy of wit. Although Sir George Etherege introduces only the briefest and most perfunctory request for applause at the end of *The Man of Mode,* and that delivered by the foolish Old Bellair, his bid for the approval of a group he knew well is a central feature of the play. It is built into his characterization of Dorimant, who, though he never directly addresses the audience, has special claims to being considered as an agent similar to those I have already discussed.

It is a matter of record that contemporary audiences believed that Dorimant, his friend Medley, and the egregious Sir Fopling Flutter were portraits of living people, but they disagreed in their identifications. Dennis held the majority opinion that Dorimant was most like Rochester, while Lockier told Spence that Etherege "was exactly his own Sir Fopling Flutter, and yet he designed Dorimant, the genteel rake of wit, for his own picture!"[18] In any case Dorimant and his friends were thought to represent that select group, "the court wits," to which Etherege belonged.

The stage mirror, as it usually appears in Ciceronian definitions of comedy, reflects ridiculous creatures familiar to the audience from daily contact, and it is often suggested that the spectator will recognize and laugh at his own follies. (Just how often this salutary effect is achieved we need not pause to ask.) Thus, the prologue to *The Man of Mode,* written by Sir Car Scroope, another of the court wits, rallies the audience with the announcement that it is about to see it own follies:

> Then, for your own sakes, be not too severe,
> Nor what you all admire at home, damn here.
> Since each is fond of his own ugly face,
> Why should you, when we hold it, break the glass?
>   [ll. 36–39]

The epilogue by Dryden goes further. Sir Fopling is "knight o' th' shire and represents ye all" (1. 16). These insults are amusing in themselves, but another kind of reflection in the stage mirror is more important for the working of this comedy. In a better-known epilogue (to the second part of *The Conquest of Granada*) Dryden says that the wit which makes the comedy of his day superior to Jonson's is imitated from the conversation of the ladies and gentlemen in the audience. The wits would have been pleased to think that Dorimant and Medley were reflections of themselves, for these characters—especially Dorimant —are flattering portraits. As John Harold Wilson says: "Here is no question of realism; Etherege seized upon and embodied in his play not the real, day by day life of Whitehall, but the life which Whitehall was pleased to imagine it led."[19] In the 1707 edition of Rochester it was said that "Sir *George Etherege* wrote *Dorimant* in Compliment to him, as drawing his Lordship's Character, and burnishing all the Foibles of it, to make them shine like Perfections."[20]

It is easy to imagine that any playwright would have sought the approval of such influential spectators as Rochester and his fellow wits, but Etherege's portrayal of an "ideal" wit in Dorimant is specifically a means of ensuring that his play be seen from the proper point of vantage. While Sir Fopling looks foolish from any angle, episodes such as Dorimant's break with Loveit (2.2) must be seen from his point of view if they are to be comic. Sympathy with Loveit would be more disastrous than sympathy with Morose and yet easier to justify by ordinary standards of ethics, since she has not given such provocation as Morose. What makes her ludicrous is her loss of the self-possession which is one of Dorimant's chief social accomplishments. To the extent that the audience can be led to adopt, temporarily at least, the criteria of this witty libertine, making, if necessary, a willing suspension of disapproval, to that extent it will relish what happens and what is said. Not that Dorimant himself is invulnerable. Medley laughs at him when one of his schemes fails (3.3. 300–05), but he is ridiculous here by his own standards: for the moment he has lost control of the situation. There are similar moments in *Epicoene* when Truewit is laughable, but even when these wits falter they do not sink to the depths of absurdity of pretenders like Sir Fopling Flutter and Sir Amorous La Foole, or outsiders like Old Bellair.

The audience in 1676 was not, of course, entirely composed of courtiers and their ladies,[21] but they were the most important spectators. An analogy with the princely theaters of Renaissance Italy may not be extravagant. There the perspective of the scenery was often such that it appeared exactly right from only one place—the ducal box. Figuratively speaking, the Restoration wits occupied the one place from which the comic perspective of *The Man of Mode* was exactly right, and we who are not Restoration wits are obliged to imagine ourselves in their position. Etherege's strategy is to make it seem desirable.

However remote the Forest of Arden may seem from the Mall and Lady Townley's house, both worlds are indebted to the conventions of romance. Not only is Dorimant in his way as idealized a character as Rosalind, but the concern with refinement of manners and speech which underlies the behavior of all the sympathetic characters in *The Man of Mode* is a conspicuous part of the tradition from Chrétien de Troyes to Madeleine de Scudéry. Though it is a very special sort of refinement, which Richard Steele and many others after him found singularly repellent, it can be seen as one answer to the persistent demand, voiced by Sidney, Jonson, and Dryden, for comedy which avoids the crudities of farce and offers what Dryden called "a pleasure which is more noble."[22]

This sort of pleasure Dorimant encourages us to take in Sir Fopling's performance at Lady Townley's. "Soothe him up in his extravagance," says Dorimant to Medley. "He will show the better" (3.2. 132–33). As Dryden saw, Sir Fopling is not a "monstrous fool" nor a "nauseous harlequin" (Epilogue, ll. 1, 3), but a fool sufficiently like a wit so that he might even be taken for one. The distinction is clear but delicate. Like Dorimant, he is interested in clothes, but a little *too* interested. His affectation of a few too many French phrases makes his conversation more silly than fashionable. To observe him Dorimant draws us into the circle with Medley, Emilia, and Lady Townley. In this way, on his author's behalf, Dorimant solicits our approval for his standards and places us where we should stand. If his efforts are successful it is likely that, at the end, we shall applaud the comedy.

Dorimant is at the outermost fringe of the group of comic agents who, in one way or another, admit that they are working for the playwright. Unlike most of them, he gives this information only by signals which the right kind of audience will understand. Beyond him are the undercover agents who may work as hard and as efficiently, but will never admit it.

Notes

1. See W. G. Moore, *Molière,* rev. ed. (Oxford, 1962), p. 73.

2. *Menander's Dyscolus,* ed. and trans. Warren E. Blake (New York, 1966), p. 112.

3. *Plautus,* ed. and trans. Paul Nixon, The Loeb Classical Library, 5 vols., 2 (Cambridge, Mass., 1917, rpt. 1965), 183.

4. *Satires, Epistles, Ars Poetica,* ed. and trans. H. Rushton Fairclough, The Loeb Classical Library, rev. ed. (Cambridge, Mass., 1929), p. 463.

5. W. Beare, *The Roman Stage* (1951; rpt. New York, 1965), pp. 166–69.

6. *Roman Laughter: The Comedy of Plautus* (1968; rpt. New York, 1971), pp. 1–41 and passim.

7. *Terence,* ed. and trans. John Sargeaunt, The Loeb Classical Library, 2 vols., 1 (Cambridge, Mass., 1912; rpt. 1964), 119.

8. All quotations from Shakespeare are taken from the *Complete Signet Classic Shakespeare,* ed. Sylvan Barnet (New York, 1972).

9. As the scholar to whom this volume is dedicated wrote in a well-known essay, "What is really high in Shakespearean comedy is to be Rosalind, who both indulges love and schools it" ("Engagement and Detachment in Shakespeare's Plays," *Essays on Shakespeare and Elizabethan Drama,* ed. Richard Hosley [Columbia, Mo., 1962], p. 287).

10. "*The Tempest* and the Ancient Comic Tradition," *English Stage Comedy,* ed. W.K. Wimsatt, Jr. (New York, 1955), p. 65.

11. *Anatomy of Criticism* (Princeton, 1957) pp. 163–71.

12. Ibid., p. 177.

13. Unless otherwise indicated, all quotations from Ben Jonson are taken from volumes in *The Yale Ben Jonson,* ed. Alvin B. Kernan and Richard Young (New Haven, 1962–74).

14. *Comicall Satyre and Shakespeare's Troilus and Cressida* (San Marino, Calif., 1938). See also Alvin Kernan, *The Cankered Muse* (New Haven, 1959), esp. pp. 150 ff.

15. Induction, ll. 88–122; *Ben Jonson,* ed. C. H. Herford and Percy Simpson, 3 (Oxford, 1927), 432. References to *Every Man Out* are to this edition.

16. "*Audience vs. Dramatist: Jonson's Epicoene . . . .*" *English Literary Renaissance* 3 (1973): 411.

17. *Ben Jonson and the Language of Prose Comedy* (Cambridge, Mass., 1960), p. 177, p. 185.

18. Joseph Spence, *Observations, Anecdotes, and Characters of Books and Men,* ed. James M. Osborn, 2 vols. (Oxford, 1966), 1:281; 3:638–40. See also *The Dramatic Works of Sir George Etherege,* ed. H. F. B. Brett-Smith, 2 vols. (Oxford, 1927), 1:xxiii–xxv; and John Harold Wilson, *The Court Wits of the Restoration* (Princeton, 1948), pp. 163–64.

19. *The Man of Mode,* ed. W. B. Carnochan (Lincoln, Neb., 1966). All quotations from the play are taken from this edition.

20. In a memoir falsely attributed to St. Evremond. See Osborn, *Spence,* 2: 639.

21. *The London Stage: 1660–1800,* ed. W. Van Lennep, 5 vols., 1 (Carbondale, Ill., 1965), clxii–clxxi.

22. *Preface to an Evening's Love: Essays of John Dryden,* ed. W.P. Ker, 2 vols. (Oxford, 1926), 1:143.

JAMES M. OSBORN

Thomas Traherne: Revelations in Meditation

The manuscript pages of Thomas Traherne's "Meditations," written for private purposes and for the eyes of his intimate friends, abound with autobiographical passages. Paradoxically, these passages supply meager biographical details, for Traherne concerned himself primarily with the relationship between God and man. His trim prose conveys clearly his ideas on his ethical and philosophical system. He describes feelingly how the soul of an individual may merge with the Divine Spirit and be led into the state of felicity. Traherne's positive affirmations are often inspiring, but few concrete details emerge about his own life.

Fortunately the outline of his biography has been established from external evidence. Because Traherne qualified as an Oxford author, a brief sketch of his life appeared in volume 2 of Anthony Wood's *Athenae Oxoniensis* in 1692, only eighteen years after Traherne's death. Born the son of a shoemaker in Hereford in 1637,[1] he matriculated at Brasenose College, Oxford, on March 1, 1652. After taking the B.A. degree in October 1656, Traherne "left the house for a time [and] entered into the sacred function." Following the Restoration, in November 1661, Traherne "was actually created Master of Arts," an event which Wood seemed to regard as unusual.[2] Wood added: "About that time he became rector of Credenhill commonly called Crednel near the city of Hereford." Ecclesiastical records show that Traherne's appointment to this small parish became official in December 1657, three years before the Church of England benefited from the restoration of Charles II. Credenhill, about four miles west of Hereford in the valley of the river Wye, contained approximately thirty families. Strung along a section of the old Roman road, Watling Street, it nestled under a steep hill topped by the remains of a Roman campsite.

Traherne's duties in the Credenhill parish were slight enough to allow him time for long contemplation on religious subjects. The literary form in which he cast his thinking was the meditation, the unit of potential prayer in prose or verse which, as Louis Martz has shown, became a popular form for devotional writing, structured according to handbooks developed on the European continent.[3] For Traherne, as for many other men dedicated to spiritual life, meditation served as an exercise essential to the attainment of mystical relationship with the Deity. These exercises of meditation attempted to follow the three steps or "degrees of truth" recommended by Saint Bernard:

> We rise to the first by humble effort, to the second by loving sympathy, to the third by enraptured vision. In the first truth is revealed in severity, in the third in purity. Reason, by which we analyze ourselves, guides us to the first, feeling which enables us to pity others conducts us to the second; purity by which we are raised to the level of the unseen, carries us up to the third.[4]

Although most of Traherne's single meditations are attractive in themselves, their impact derives chiefly from the structure within the "centuries," or groups of one hundred meditations, into which he organized these highly personal "mental prayers."

Most lovers of seventeenth-century literature remember the remarkable story of the discovery of the manuscript of Traherne's *Centuries of Meditations,* but for the benefit of any others a brief summary may be useful.[5] In the winter of 1896–97, while rummaging through a sidewalk bookstall, William T. Brooke, a snapper-up of ill-considered trifles, encountered two seventeenth-century manuscript volumes. They were, he perceived, in the same handwriting. Brooke was well read in seventeenth-century literature, with a special knowledge of sacred poetry and hymnology. This interest prompted him to pay the few pennies asked for the volumes, which he carried home for further study.

At once he recognized the admirable qualities of the verse and prose, and concluded that they must be the work of some known author. After study he decided they were unpublished writings of Henry Vaughan. Brooke revealed his discovery to that querulous Presbyterian clergyman Dr. Alexander Grosart, then in the twilight of his life, which had been just as busy outside the church as in it. Grosart had published reprints of rare Elizabethan and Jacobean literature extending to more than ninety volumes, plus another sixteen volumes edited from manuscript sources. Since Grosart was then engaged on a new edition of Vaughan's poems, he persuaded Brooke to sell the two new manuscript volumes to him. But Grosart did not live to publish his edition. After his death in March 1899, the bulk of his library was acquired by Charles Higham, a bookseller on Farrington Street.

Here the name of Bertram Dobell enters the story. Animated by a strong love of poetry, Dobell had built up a successful bookshop on Charing Cross Road, but devoted his off-hours to the study of literature, including the writing of verse, at which he acquired commendable skill, especially as a sonneteer. He had also published the *Poetical Works* of his friend James Thomson, and editions of several of Shelley's writings. Brooke was one of Dobell's friends, and so he had heard about the supposed manuscripts of Henry Vaughan. Higham allowed Dobell to study the manuscripts, and eventually to purchase them.

Dobell's study convinced him that the poems were not by Vaughan, for despite superficial resemblances, they differed notably in style, thought, and temperament from Vaughan's known writings. How, then, was he to determine the genuine author? Here Dobell's friend Brooke again provided a key. Brooke pointed out, in an obscure anonymous theological book, a poem which he considered similar in style to the poems in the anonymous manuscript. With this slender clue they went to work. The style of the theological work and that of the prose and verse in the manuscript were so much alike that Dobell became convinced they were products of the same mind. Though the printed book was anonymous, the "Address to the Reader" stated that the author served as Private Chaplain to Sir Orlando Bridgeman. Brooke then dug out from Wood's *Athenae Oxoniensis* the information that one Thomas Traherne had held this position. Wood listed two theological books by Traherne titled *Roman Forgeries* and *Christian Ethics*.

Dobell then examined these books carefully and was rewarded by finding evidence which unlocked the mystery, for one poem tucked into *Christian Ethics* proved to be a variant version of one in the manuscript of "Meditations." Here was positive proof that the manuscripts were by Thomas Traherne. Dobell happily announced his discovery to the learned world and in 1903 published *The Poetical Works of Thomas Traherne*. In 1908 Dobell published the other manuscript under the title *Centuries of Meditations*.[6]

Written about 1671, in the last years of Traherne's short life, the
Centuries of Meditations demonstrated his vivid memory of childhood
experiences and attitudes which passed through successive stages as
Traherne grew into maturity. To this material a highly significant new
manuscript was added in 1964 when I acquired and identified a
hitherto unknown volume titled *Select Meditations,* written by
Traherne about 1661, during his early days of religious and
philosophical development.[7] This was the period of Traherne's pastoral service at Credenhill.

Though there are many parallels, the 376 new meditations differ
from the later *Centuries,* especially in Traherne's religious sentiments
and attitudes.[8] The title *Select Meditations* is pregnant with implications about Traherne's early thinking on theology and philosophy. It
implies that he had already adopted meditation as an instrument of
expression, and that he had selected groupings of a hundred meditations as organizational structures.[9] The *Select Meditations* belong to the
period immediately following the Restoration of the monarchy and
the reestablishment of the Church of England. Indeed, the earliest
complete meditation in the manuscript (forty-three leaves having
been torn out), number 82 of the First Century, asks God to "Save this
Nation, Spare th[y] People . . . let Thy Cities prosper, our vilages
flourish, our children Grow up in fear of thy Name, like Oliv plants
about thy Table. Soften our Kings Heart, Teach our Senators Wisdom." By Senators, of course, Traherne means members of the recon-
stituted Houses of Parliament.

Similarly, in the subsequent pages of the *Select Meditations* we read,
"Thou hast brought in the Gospel of thy Son into our land Converted
our Kings Senators and Nobles. . . . Established thy word and worship by Laws, Builded thy Selfe Temples, and Apoynt[ed] Revenues
for thy Church and Ministers, Greatly are the Bishops [of] our
Saviour Dignified, & our Cittys Beautified with those thy Most
Glorious and Beautifull Houses [Churches]" (1.85). In contrast,
Traherne points to the activities of the Puritan clerics: "But O the
wickedness of Ignorant zealots! who contemn thy Mercies and De-
spise the union the Beautifull union of thy Nationall church!" (1.85). In
this stirring passage he beseeches God not to pursue revenge on the
Puritans: "O profane not the Throne of thy Glory. let not the Heathen
Trample it under foot. Much less let Christians Defile it with their
Bloud!" (1.85).

That these meditations were written before the outbreak of the second Dutch War in 1665 seems established by 1.86: "As long as our Nation continueth in peace under the wings of Magistrates & christian Laws thy people in peace may Celebrat Thee." Similarly, in 1.88 Traherne contrasts the Cromwellian church's tendency to "Throw a way the peace and welfare of a Nation upon every Trifle. Invade her liberties, Lay waste her Laws, Rejoyce in her Confusion, contemn her Magistrates, Trample her Peace and flourishing Estate." Again in 2.42 Traherne recalls conditions during the recent civil wars when orthodoxy had to be practiced in privacy: "When all other Comforts fail, when the Sword hath wasted our land, when Cittys are Destroyed, when our Assemblies are fled, when nothing is near but woefull Solitariness, the soul that can Liv in communion with Him shall sing His praises."

Book 3 of *Select Meditations* continues the praise of the royal function of "A king, a freind, a sovereign. . . . Then did Citties need a Governor, Societies a Gardiner, Kingdoms a Phisitian . . . so that the office of Kings is exceeding Glorious" (3.11). "Drunkards & whoremongers & revilers with all covetous men and Lyars, see not those Joyes for the sake of which Temples are erected: Ingratefull Pharisies, and Lofty Hypocrites, Disobedient Hereticks & self conceited Holy ones; that make Devisions, and are Despisers of union, peace and External flourishing" (3.23). These contrast with the blessings of the reestablished Church of England: "A flourishing church, converted Citties, Religion Established by Laws, Kings and Magistrates turned from Paganisme. the freedom of the Gospel, & the Shining Light which a Golden candlestick giveth in a National church" (3.23). The function of the revived national church receives continued praise: "The Government of a church Established by Laws is a Great fortress in which the welfare of Millions is concerned" (3.24). The Church of England is equated with "the vineyard of God"(3.25).

Evidence that Traherne wrote *Select Meditations* in the rural setting of Credenhill is found in his reflections on the parish church in 3.83: "When I see a Little church Environed with Trees, how many Things are there which mine Eye discerneth not The Labor of them which in Ancient Ages Builded it; the conversion of a kingdom to God from Paganism, its protection by Laws, its subjection to kings, its Relation to Bishops. . . . The Divine Service, office of the ministery, solemn

Assemblies Prayses & Thanksgivings, for the sake of which it was permitted, is Governed, standeth & flourisheth. perhaps when I Look upon it, it is Desolate & Empty almost Like a heap of Stones: non of these things appearing to the Eye, which nevertheless are the Spirituall Beauties which adorn & clothe it." The benefits of bucolic life at Credenhill appear briefly in a subsequent meditation where gold and silver are counted as rubbish in contrast to the wealth of agriculture. "I eat not the Grass that Groweth for my cattle, yet it is mine, and soe are all the corn feilds upon the whole Earth: becaus it sustaineth a more Noble Breed: Gold & Silver is Shining Grass: unto which they have imputed a fained value, but less than Corn & Grass in Eden"(3.85).

That Traherne's country parishioners found his use of the first person singular objectionable he confesses in meditation 54 of book 3, while recognizing his own fault of loquacity:

> Profound Inspection, Reservation & silence; are my Desires. O that I could attain them. Too much openness & proneness to Speak are my Diseas. Too easy & complying a Nature. Speaking too much and too Long in the Best Things. Mans nature is Nauseating & weary. Redundanc is Apprehended even in those Things of which there can be never Enough . . . The Ignorance of man maketh those Things obscure that are Infinitly Easy those things ugly that are in themselves Beautifull, those Things inconvenient that are in themselves Blessed. Here I am censured for speaking in the singular number, & saying I . . . Felicity is a Bird of Pardice so strang that it is Impossible to flie a mong men without Loseing som feathers were She not Imortal. There it shall be our Glory and the Joy of all to Acknowledge. I am the Lords, & He is mine. Every one shall speak in the first person, & it shall be Gods Glory that He is the Joy of all. can the freind of GOD, & the Heir of all Thing[s] in Heaven & Earth for bear to say, I . . . It is Inconvenient here to [be] Exposed unto many. Bright be & Humble: that is Divine & Heavenly on the Inside.

Joan Webber has commented perceptively on this passage in her study *The Eloquent I.* For Traherne, she believes, that "I" fulfills itself in becoming one with God, one with other souls, thereby becoming infinite. "In Traherne we have the most explicit representation of the cosmic personality that is afforded by seventeenth-century literature. Startling enough on paper, this mode of speaking must have been difficult indeed for his parishioners to appreciate if he tried to practice it face to face. And in all probability he did."[10] Carol Marks has pointed out that in Hebrew the same word signifies *Eye* and a fountain."[11]

Miss Webber finds in this likely word-play "the central image of the fountain-'I'. To ask him [Traherne] to limit his enthusiasm would have been to ask a fountain to flow less copiously."[12] Yet the memory of his parishioners' negative response may have been behind Traherne's complaint a decade later in *Centuries of Meditations,* where he wrote of "the Reproaches, Mockings and Derisions . . . while they scoffed at me, for pretending to be the only man, that had a Book from Heaven" (3.34).

Many of the autobiographical details in the new manuscript dovetail with those in the *Centuries,* especially with the memories of infancy which occupy book 3 of the *Centuries.* Already in the *Select Meditations* we find Traherne's central theme of infancy as the state of an unfallen Adam, the child who lives in an inner paradise of innocence until corrupted. Such corruption can later be overcome by a life of devotion, which, if rationally and properly pursued, can attain felicity through mystical relationship with the Deity.

For example, 3.29 of *Select Meditations* describes Traherne's infancy in Hereford and anticipates the familiar autobiographical passages of book 3 of *Centuries of Meditations:*

> Gods kingdom, His Subjects & Laws are Divine Things. when I Look upon them in the Light of the Citty wherein I Lived. I remember the time when its Gates were Amiable, its Streets Beautifull, its Inhabitants immortall, its Temple Glorious. its Inward Roomes & chambers Innocent and all Misterious, soe they appeared to the little stranger, when I first came into the world. As sweet every thing as paradice could make it. for I saw them all in the light of Heaven. And they were all mine, Temple streets skies houses Gates and people. I had not learned to appropriat any thing other way. The people were my Living joyes and moving Jewells sweet Amazments walking Miracles: And all the place a Grand Hive, & Repositary of Delights. But little did I imagine there was a-nother kingdom (then) to be enjoyd. I was as far from conceiving that as I was from apprehending any other way of appropriating Riches than Sight and Love. That was the way of Angels, and that was mine. All I Saw was Still mine own. They in Heaven have no clossets tills nor cabinets to hide Treasures and more precious than to be called Jewels. They most enjoy them while they see them all the Delight and joy of other persons. Those Gates & those wals did then confine seeming the Limits surely of the world, if not of my desires. And when I place my selfe now in that Citty, and see Ages all mine! and Divine Laws & Gods wayes in many kingdoms. And my Soul a Temple of that Day! exalted to be the Image of

allmighty God among them all, A companion of kings & of the Holy Angels: me thinks those are very Glorious things. New and wonderfull yet more High Divine and Great than New and wonderfull. that city being in the midst of all my Divine Treasuries so surmounted. which once seemed it self Divine & Glorious & yet in that city all enjoyd.

In the following decades Traherne's recollections of these celestial visions became elevated into the heightened descriptions which begin the third book of the *Centuries*.

Will you see the Infancy of this sublime and celestial Greatness? These Pure and Virgin Apprehensions I had from the Womb, and that Divine Light wherewith I was born, are the Best unto this Day, wherin I can see the Universe. . . . They are unattainable by Book, and therfore I will teach them by Experience. Pray for them earnestly; for they will make you Angelical, and wholy Celestial. Certainly Adam in Paradice had not more sweet and Curious Apprehensions of the World, then I when I was a child.

Here and elsewhere Traherne has adopted Saint Augustine's example of exploring personal memories for signs of grace as a method of praising God for creating the glories of the universe. Thus Traherne "may be seen as Augustinian in theme, in his style and in the method of meditation."[13]

Traherne's meditations reveal him as man of his environment. The fact that Traherne was born into poverty haunted his memories of childhood. He wrote poignantly of feeling bound by his father's impoverishment and concluded, "it is not our Parents Loyns, so much as our Parents lives, that Enthrals and Blinds us" (*CM* 3.8). Traherne held vivid memories of these early years: "once I remember (I think I was about 4 yeer old, when) I thus reasoned with my self. sitting in a little Obscure Room in my Fathers poor house. If there be a God, certainly he must be infinite in Goodness . . . how comes it to pass therfore that I am so poor?" (*CM* 3.16). This same question recurred in several forms: "How can I believ that He gave his Son to die for me, who having Power to do otherwise gave me nothing but rags and Cottages" (*CM* 2.6). The environment of his early childhood sometimes depressed his spirits: "Another time, in a Lowering and sad Evening, being alone in the field, when all things were dead and quiet, a certain Want and Horror fell upon me, beyond imagination. The unprofitableness and Silence of the Place dissatisfied me, its Wideness terrified me, from the utmost Ends of the Earth fears surrounded me" (*CM* 3.23).

Some of these fears may have originated in the death of Traherne's mother and his cobbler father during his early childhood. Thomas and his older brother Philip appear to have been reared by their uncle, Philip Traherne, an innkeeper in Hereford. Philip was a staunch royalist who served as mayor of the city in 1622, and again in 1645 when Thomas was eight years old. Traherne's poem "Solitude" in his *Poems of Felicity* mentions "the Mayor's Gown" among the paraphernalia of city life. But, more important, "Solitude" echoes the loneliness of the "sad Evening, being alone in a field."

> How desolate!
> Ah! how forlorn, how sadly did I stand
> When in the field my woful State
> I felt! Not all the Land,
> Not all the Skies,
> Tho Heven shin'd before mine Eys,
> Could Comfort yield in any Field to me,
> Nor could my Mind Contentment find or see.

Memories of the same years in his uncle's tavern also may be seen behind Traherne's poem on "Poverty" preserved in the same manuscript.

> As in the House I sate
> Alone and desolate,
> No Creature but the Fire and I,
> The Chimney and the Stool, I lift mine Ey
> Up to the Wall,
> And in the silent Hall
> Saw nothing mine
> But som few Cups and Dishes shine
> The Table and the wooden Stools
> Where Peeple us'd to dine:
> A painted Cloth there was
> Wherein some ancient Story wrought
> A little entertain'd my Thought
> Which Light discover'd throu the Glass.

The decade or so when Traherne lived at his uncle's inn coincided with his school years in Hereford. There his celestial visions were rudely interrupted both by the rough talk and the materialism of the tavern customers. Apparently he now had to endure "the Songs and

Mockings of the Drunkards" (*CM* 3.93). At school he encountered skepticism among his schoolmates and teachers.

> Being Swallowed up therfore in the Miserable Gulph of idle talk and worthless vanities, thenceforth I lived among Shadows, like a Prodigal Son feeding upon Husks with Swine. A Comfortless Wilderness full of Thorns and Troubles the World was, or wors: a Waste Place covered with Idleness and Play, and Shops and Markets and Taverns. As for Churches they were things I did not understand. And Scholes were a Burden: so that there was nothing in the World worth the having, or Enjoying, but my Game and Sport, which also was a Dream and being passed wholy forgotten. So that I had utterly forgotten all Goodness Bounty Comfort and Glory: which things are the very Brightness of the Glory of GOD: for lack of which therfore He was unknown. [*CM* 3.14]

This mundane attitude contrasted with the glow in which the city first appeared to his childhood eyes. Yet neither the swaggering skeptics in the tavern nor the pedantry of his classes in Latin and rhetoric dimmed his higher visions.

> When I come from the scholes, haveing there heard them dispute De Ente De forma materiali, D Quid-ditate, and such like Drie and Empty Theames: when I came from the Heathen poets, having seen their vanities Dreames & fables. or else from the market haveing there seen a great deal of chattering about cloth and money, & things more Drie than Haeccieties & fables. yea when I come from Taverns haveing there seen Roaring Boys that can swear & swagger & wallow in their vomitt: O what a Glorious thing is that kingdom which in the Temple I behold! [*SM* 3.30]

The "heathen poets" filled Traherne's head with passages from Cicero (*SM* 4.21) or about Apollo's oracle (*SM* 4.6) or Troy and Pyramus (*SM* 4.30).

In contrast to these "Roaring Boys" of the tavern, Traherne felt solace in the enlightened members of the populace who continued to lead pious lives, despite the depravity surrounding them. "Wheras now there are thousands in the World, of whom I being a Poor Child was Ignorant, that in Temples, Universities and Secret Closets enjoy felicity. whom I saw not in Shops, or Scholes or Trades; whom I found not in Streets, or at feasts, or Taverns: and therfore thought not to be in the World: who enjoy Communion with God, and hav fellowship with Angels evry Day. And these I discerned to be a Great Help unto me" (*CM* 3.28). Although the city familiar to Traherne consisted largely of "Dirt, Streets and Gutters," yet he became curious about how other social classes lived: "for as for the Pleasures that were in Great Mens Houses I had not seen them: and it was my real Happiness they were unknown. for becaus Nothing Deluded me, I was the more Inquisitive" (*CM* 3.15).

Ultimately his inquiring mind received the satisfaction of witnessing "that Bliss which Nature Whispered and Suggested to me. Evry New Thing Quickened my Curiosity and raised my Expectation. I remember once, the first time I came into a Magnificent or Noble Dining Room, and was left there alone, I rejoyced to see the Gold and State and Carved Imagery. but when all was Dead, and there was no Motion, I was weary of it, and departed Dissatisfied" (*CM* 3.22). Traherne's response altered favorably, however, once he saw the local gentry in active social swing. "But afterwards, when I saw it full of Lords and Ladies and Musick and Dancing, the Place which once seemed not to differ from Solitary Den, had now Entertainment and nothing of Tediousness but pleasure in it. By which I perceived (upon a Reflexion made long after) That Men and Women are when well understood a Principal Part of our True felicity"(ibid.).[14]

The cumulative effect of these encounters with the outside world of schoolmasters, tavern habitués, and gaiety within great houses seems to have produced the portion of a prayer written in *Select Meditations* 1.92. "Surmount therefore O my Soul thy fathers hous, by way of Eminence Enclude thy family, exceed the Citty wherein thou wast born, fill the Ages, Salute the Angels, Inherit Kingdoms, penetrat the Earth, Encompass Heaven, Reign, Triumph, prais, Adore, O Life and Love Sing forever." The progress of Traherne's career from humble beginnings in Hereford to spiritual tranquility in an all-embracing euphoria of universal love is well summarized in the penultimate poem in book 3 of *Select Meditations:*

> My Growth is strange! at first, I onely knew
> The Gates & Streets mine Infancy Did veiw
> In those first walls, But Thence my nimble Ey
> In Speedy Sort did to the Mountaines flie
> command the feilds and make the Eden Mine
> which round about those Citty Walls did shine
> Then other Citties at a Distance found
> In unexpected sort my powers crownd.

Then Seas, & Lands that were beyond the Seas
New kingdoms Distant did my Spirit pleas
Yea all the nations of the Peopled Earth
Became my joy my Melodie and Mirth
My Light my wealth, The Skies those Higher Things
The Sun the Stars the Holy Angels wings
All these Adornd at once my Heavenly Sphere
And round about me did my Joys appear.
Can any more than these my Riches be!
can any more Adorne Infinitie!
yes other Worlds! whose Ages stord with Joys
Kings Sages Queens, new Hosts of Girls & Boys
That standing in misterious sort behind
Each other, ravish and Delight the mind,
nor ceas I yet, but in each Spirit See
All These, the world, my God, again to be
As in a Sphere of Light, And these as mine
In every Soul with new Delight did Shine.
At this I stopt; & Thought no other store
could move my Soul his Glory to Adore
But when I these at once began to see
In every Soul more plesant far to be
Then in them selves, Lands Ages Kingdoms there
More Rich more Bright more Glorious to appear
Being clad in thoughts. I scarsly could beleive
The splendor of the wealth my God did give
A Greatness then my soul did seeme to gaine
That wholy was Divine & did remaine
Inlayd with Depths of Pleasure & Delight
That made the Greatness much more Infinit.

This eloquent prayer near the end of *Select Meditations* serves as a bridge to the *Centuries of Meditations,* written about ten years later. The beginning of the *Centuries* discloses that Traherne's discovery of the euphoric state of universal love coincided with the growth of his special friendship with a devout female. This lady had actually given him an "Empty Book" to be filled with meditations. In return, Traherne promised to assist her advancement to Glory by "the Gentle Ways of Peace and Lov" (*CM* 1.4). Indeed, her reward would "be so Glorious, that Angels durst not hope for so Great a One till they had seen it" (ibid.).

This special friend of Traherne's, "the lady of the *Centuries,*" was

first identified by Gladys Wade in 1944.[15] She established that
Traherne's friend was Mrs. Susanna Hopton, a devotional writer who
lived in nearby Kington, Herefordshire. A passage on friendship early
in *Select Meditations* (number 38 of the Second Century) proves
that their friendship had already reached a special status around 1661:
"And cannot I here on earth so Lov my freinds! O my T. G. O my S. H.
O my Brother! the wise & Holy Sages! that see a little, & understand
your Glory. ye are Treasures unto me Greater than the world!"[16]

The brother was, of course, Philip, whose devotion to Thomas
included his misguided habit of trying to "improve" Thomas's
poems. "T. G." probably refers to Thomas Good, rector of Coreley,
Shropshire, who had recently become prebendary of Hereford
Cathedral, and in 1672 was elected to the mastership of Balliol College, Oxford.

The third friend and treasure, "my S. H.," clearly alludes to
Susanna Hopton. Miss Wade and H. M. Margoliouth have shown that
Traherne gave Mrs. Hopton a number of his manuscript works besides the *Centuries of Meditations*.[17] It is quite possible that the volume
of *Select Meditations* was once among them. But wherever the
manuscript volume slumbered for three hundred years, Traherne's
reference to "my S. H." proves that Susanna Hopton was counted as a
"treasured friend" around 1661, ten years or more before she gave him
the book of blank paper in which Traherne wrote the sequence now
entitled *Centuries of Meditations*.

The earlier manuscript, *Select Meditations,* also shows that during
Traherne's Credenhill residence his religious mysticism had already
reached an advanced state. The climax of religious meditation which
he sought consisted of entering the presence of the Deity, of speaking to God and having God reply to him. In *Select Meditations*
3.69 Traherne reports,

> In my close Retirements I was some years as if no Body but I had been in
> the world. Al the Heavens and the Earth are mine: mine a Lone. And I had
> nothing to do but walk with God, as if there had been non other but He & I.
> when I came a-mong men I found them to be superaded Treasures, & I am
> alone still: The Enjoyer of all. But have Greater work: To Glorifie God. O
> that I could do it, wisely, as I ought.

This newly achieved intimacy with the Deity Traherne celebrates in
other passages, for example in *Select Meditations* 4.4:

It proceeding from the perfection of the Nature of God that I am made his Son & united to Him. This very Thing is the Divine Light that Shews me to be his Bride, that maketh me his Image [,] Advanceth me to his Throne [,] giveth me Ability [,] to Inherit all Things, maketh me his freind, enableth me to Live in communion with Him.

In the next decade, when Traherne composed the *Centuries of Meditations,* he wrote with confident assurance of the mystical relation between him and his creator. Especially in the most autobiographical section of the *Centuries,* the meditations of book 3, Traherne reveals happiness in his familiar relationship with the All Highest. For example, 3.59 ends: "[I] knew there was a Dietie, becaus I was satisfied. For Exerting Himself wholy in atchieving thus an infinite felicity He was infinitely Delightful Great and Glorious, and my Desires so August and Insatiable that nothing less than a Deity could satisfy the." In 3.60 Traherne continues, "This Spectacle once seen, will never be forgotten"; this he follows with the statement, "The Image of God is the most perfect Creature" (3.61). A few meditations later Traherne announces, "Little did I imagine that, while I was thinking these Things, I was Conversing with GOD" (3.66). The revelation produced an extended vision. In these inspired passages Traherne describes his personal relationship with God, and through God, his relationship with the greatest characters in biblical history. "There I saw Moses blessing the Lord for the Precious things in Heaven. . . . There I saw Jacob, with Awfull Apprehensions Admiring the Glory of the World . . . . There I saw GOD leading forth Abraham, and shewing him the Stars of Heaven." There Traherne enjoyed "communion with the Diety" (3.67).

In his *Meditations,* both the *Select* series of about 1661 and the *Centuries* a decade later, Traherne reveals himself as a true mystic, one who has been in the presence of the Deity, one who rejoices to describe the experience. As Benjamin Jowett observed, "Many are the wand bearers, but few are the mystics."[18]

This is not the place to trace the origins of Traherne's mysticism, nor to relate his version with the writings of Augustine, nor with Neo-Platonists on the Continent, or the Cambridge School, or other philosophers and theologians. Instead, my purpose has been to show how naturally Traherne has revealed details of his autobiography, of his personal relationships and the intimate mysticism of his relationship with his creator. Indeed, these glimpses of "the author in his work" give Traherne's meditations a special interest for modern readers. The revelations in his meditations bring us close to the devout, learned, and truly holy human being who created these long-hidden pages.

NOTES

1. Traherne's date of birth was established by H. M. Margoliouth. See the introduction to his definitive edition, *Thomas Traherne: Centuries, Poems, and Thanksgivings* (Oxford, 1958), p. xxxviii.

2. As quoted by Bertram Dobell in the introduction to *The Poetical Works of Thomas Traherne B.D.*, ed. Dobell (London, 1903), p. xxxiv.

3. Louis L. Martz, *The Poetry of Meditation: A Study of English Literature of the Seventeenth Century* (New Haven, 1954).

4. St. Bernard, *The Twelve Degrees of Humility and Pride*, trans. B.R.V. Mills (London, 1929), p. 40.

5. For a full account, see Dobell's introduction to *Poetical Works*.

6. See also the account of another discovery in the introduction to *Traherne's Poems of Felicity*, ed. H. I. Bell (Oxford, 1910).

7. Announced in "A Meditation Upon Traherne," a paper delivered at a meeting of the fellows of the Pierpont Morgan Library on October 7, 1964. The *Times Literary Supplement* published excerpts under the title "A New Traherne Manuscript," October 8, 1964, p. 928.

8. When published these *Select Meditations* will appear as a third volume of the *Oxford Traherne*. For allusions to *Select Meditations* in recent scholarship, see: Louis L. Martz, *The Paradise Within, Studies in Vaughan, Traherne, and Milton* (New Haven, 1964), especially the appendix "Traherne's 'Select Meditations,' The Osborn Manuscript"; Anne Ridler, ed., *Thomas Traherne, Poems Centuries, and Three Thanksgivings* (Oxford, 1966), introduction; Joan Webber, *The Eloquent "I": Self and Style in Seventeenth Century Prose* (Madison, 1968), pp. 219, 220, 223, 224, 225, 266; Carol L. Marks and G. R. Guffey, eds., *Christian Ethics* (Ithaca, 1968), introduction; A. L. Clements, *The Mystical Poetry of Thomas Traherne* (Cambridge, Mass., 1969), pp. 9, 44, 98, 111, 154, 175–77, 180; Stanley Stewart, *The Expanded Voice: The Art of Thomas Traherne* (San Marino, Cal., 1970), pp. 15, 121, 123, 125, 140, 210, 223–24; Richard D. Jordan, *The Temple of Eternity: Thomas Traherne's Philosophy of Time* (Port Washington, N.Y., 1972), pp. 47, 68, 72.

9. This new evidence controverts Margoliouth's conjecture that in 1671 Traherne "started writing his paragraphs . . . and numbering them" (*Thomas Traherne*, pp. x–xi). See also Martz, *The Paradise Within*, p. 211.

10. *The Eloquent "I"*, p. 223.

11. "Thomas Traherne and Cambridge Platonism," *PMLA* 81 (1966): 533.

12. *The Eloquent "I,"* p. 224.

13. Martz, *The Paradise Within,* p. 54.

14. Margoliouth suggests that this incident occurred when Philip, the innkeeper, catered for an entertainment at a local great house, and took his nephew with him (*Thomas Traherne,* 2: 274).

15. See Gladys Wade's *Thomas Traherne: A Critical Biography* (Princeton, 1944), pp. 80–88.

16. See also Martz's appendix to *The Paradise Within.*

17. Wade, *Thomas Traherne,* pp. 85–86; Margoliouth, *Thomas Traherne,* pp. xxxiv–xxxv.

18. Jowett's *Plato* (1871), 1: 381.

WILLIAM K. WIMSATT

Rhetoric and Poems: The Example of Swift

I

"Cousin Swift, you will never be a poet." Words supposedly uttered by Dryden on the occasion of Swift's first publication, his Pindaric *Ode to the Athenian Society* (1692). If the story is an invention, we may well think it a happy one.

We have the four ungainly Odes, written to the sober norm of his patron and Covering Cherub Sir William Temple, and the two pentameter couplet poems: *To Congreve* and *On Temple's Illness*. The *To Congreve* is especially instructive—a creaky adulatory buttonholing, a supposed love affair with the encomiastic muse, a savage presumptive fancy of his own power and calling as a satirist. *Saeva indignatio* without much evidence that it has been earned. "How easy it is to call rogue and villain," Dryden was saying in this very year, 1693, "and that wittily! But how hard to make a man appear a fool, a blockhead, or a knave, without using any of those opprobrious terms!" Swift all his life would be a rebel to this rule, but he had not yet found an idiom which could make the defiance interesting.

We entertain the image of an obscure young country versifier, who, except for the external testimonies of authorship, we might well hesitate to identify with the man-about-town and political writer, aged about forty-six in 1713, who could produce, in tetrameter couplets, the darkly lustrous myth of dalliance *Cadenus and Vanessa,* or, in his later years and bereavement at Dublin, could contrive *Verses on the Death of Dr. Swift* (1731) and *On Poetry: A Rapsody* (1733).

II

Much earlier he had demonstrated, if only for a moment, a successful way of writing even the pentameter couplet, in his two London poems of 1709 and 1710, *A Description of the Morning* and *A Description of a City Shower*. These are witty burlesque poems, but it is worth saying that they are not written in witty couplets, not like Pope or Dryden.

> The Slipshod Prentice from his Masters Door,
> Had par'd the Dirt, and Sprinkled round the Floor.
> Now *Moll* had whirl'd her Mop with dext'rous Airs,
> Prepar'd to Scrub the Entry and the Stairs.
>
> [5–8][1]

The sentences avoid rhetorical pointing. The structure is studiously flat—a sort of soft-mat photo texture. This is the quiet anti-poetic, the bathetic. This ineloquent mock-pastoral-aubade, as Claude Rawson[2] points out, invites definition by contrast with the vibratory ethos or personal projection of such romantic city poets as Baudelaire and Eliot. *Morning* is the flatter of the two poems. It is a *very* flat poem, and hence short. This style could not be sustained long. The *Shower* is more rhetorical.

> Here various Kinds by various Fortunes led,
> Commence Acquaintance underneath a Shed.
> Triumphant Tories, and desponding Whigs,
> Forget their Fewds, and join to save their Wigs.
>
> [39–42]

They said it was the best thing Swift "ever writ," and he too thought so. This city rainstorm, so elaborately derived from Dryden's Virgil, the First *Georgic* and the Second and Fourth *Aeneids,* is described ingeniously by Brendan O Hehir as "an oblique denunciation of cathartic doom upon the corruption of the city."[3] The closing triplet and alexandrine are *not* low burlesque, not a mere travesty of Dryden's style, despite Swift's much later note on the passage (1735) and his letter to a friend. As there is really nothing wrong with either a triplet or an alexandrine, nothing prevents us from reading these as the climax of the poem's high burlesque or mock-georgic-heroic, raising low matter to a focus of ample and pregnant realization.

> Sweepings from Butchers Stalls, Dung, Guts, and Blood,
> Drown'd Puppies, stinking Sprats, all drench'd in Mud,
> Dead Cats and Turnip-Tops come tumbling down the Flood.
>
> [61–63]

All the life of the farm, says Irvin Ehrenpreis, appears as decayed garbage, yet still in action.

III

But even earlier Swift had made another and even better discovery. If it was an accident that he found his true idiom, the tetrameter or short couplet, during his *Wanderjahre,* the ten years of his unsettlement, from 1699, shuttling between England and Ireland, yet it may be seen as an emblematic accident. The immediate and chief antecedent of Swift's anti-sublime and anti-pathetic idiom is usually and correctly enough placed in the short, harsh couplets in stringy sequences and the absurdly manufactured rhymes of Samuel Butler's *Hudibras* (a very long poem which Swift is *said* to have known by heart and which indeed is present here and there in his *Tale of a Tub*).[4] This spavined mock epic, however, has its own antecedents, in English and continental literature, and difficult as they may be to trace, we can say something about the overall view.

The long couplet as perfected by Dryden and Pope came from the classical Roman hexameter and elegiac couplet,[5] and its basic theoretical formula can be found in the figures of parallel, antithesis, metaphor, and turn described in book 3, chapters 9–11 of Aristotle's *Rhetoric.* Add only such refinements as zeugma (described with the other figures in Puttenham's *Arte of Poesie,* 1589), chiasmus, and the vernacular figures of accentual meter and rhyme. The Popean couplet, in which Swift was always to experience a relative discomfort, was Ovid with the impasto of rhyme. Marvell's short couplet, as in the *Coy Mistress* and *The Garden,* may be described in the same mainly classical terms. But the short couplet in its laughing mode was something broader and coarser, distinctly late Latin, vernacular, and anti-classical. It was a revolt against and a vagabond swerve away from the ancient decorum. Its genius may be illustrated characteristically, at one of its peaks, in the deviant Latin poets of the high Middle Ages—the *vagantes* (*vagi clerici*), refugees from Parisian discipline, irreverent, scoffers, ribalds, ironist, parodists: Golias, Primate, Bishop, Archpoet. We know that these poets, having flourished for their brief heyday, lay long out of sight, beneath the horizon for some six centuries. Even by Chaucer's time a Goliardeys was no better than a coarse jester, a jangler, the quarrelsome Miller of the Canterbury prologue. In the Victorian mid-nineteenth century, the antiquarians Thomas Wright and Andreas Schmeller were performing acts of resurrection when they brought out their editions of the poems ascribed to Walter Map (1841) and of the Benedictbeuern manuscript, *Carmina Burana* (1847). During Swift's lifetime, it is true, we find the *Historia Poetarum et Poematum Medii Aevi,* edited by the Helmstadt scholar Polycarp Leyser at Halle in 1721. And Pope in a satiric squib alludes to Blackmore as an ArchPoet. The tradition was no doubt carried all along in student drinking songs, such as the *Gaudeamus igitur,* which emerges in Germany during the later eighteenth century. But there is no likelihood that either Swift or Pope knew any Goliardic poetry.

I am speaking synchronically of poetic affinities. "Deep within I seethe with anger," confessed the twelfth-century Archpoet to his patron the Archchancellor of the Empire. "In my bitter mind I'm talking. . . . I'm like a dead leaf on the wind."

> Aestuans intrinsecus ira vehementi
> in amaritudine loquar meae menti:
> factus de materia levis elementi
> folio sum similis de quo ludunt venti.

The four-plus-three medieval Latin septenary and the trochaic tetrameter (*Dives eram et dilectus*) were contemporaries of the French octosyllabic, and the French was the model for the English. The Goliardic rhyming was the last expressive burst of Latin as a spoken language.[6] It is Latin hovering on the verge of vernacular: a verse written in clanging contrast to the quantitative measure of the classical tradition, and revelling in a verbal chime that is a barbaric opposite to the logical homoioteleuton of classical prose. Rhyme in the Goliardic-Skeltonic-Scarronian-Hudibrastic tradition is all that Gothic, rude, and beggarly jingle deplored by such civilized theorists as Campion, Milton, and Roscommon. In that short-couplet tradition Swift found his own voice, his characteristic freedom and crashing energy. Thwarted *Episcopus,* actual *Decanus,* Swift was an Augustan *Archipoeta Redivivus*—not a libertine singer of wine, woman, and song, nevertheless exuberant in the license of rhyming irreverence, "the sin of Wit, no venial crime."

> The Language *Billingsgate* excel
> The Sentiments resemble *Hell*.
>
> [*A Panegyric* (1729–30), ll. 108–09]

It is a familiar enough idea that Swift made poetry out of anti-poetic materials, or simply that he made poetry that was anti-poetry. I myself might prefer to say that the anti-poetry of that age was only the anti-classical, and that the paradox of the anti-poetic, in our own age of postexpressionism, has lost most of its force. After the cruelty, the blackness, the obscenity, the absurdity, the suicide, the zero level of our modern comic experience, Swift is no longer a radical instance of inversion as such. I proceed to some rhetorical observations, moving, perhaps unadventurously, within the established demonic frame of reference. Details, I believe, are likely to win against outline in any account of the episodic, spotty, staccato career of Swift in verse. Nevertheless, I have a central and fairly simple aim in this paper. That is, to show some of the main ways in which the short couplet, rather than the long, emerged as his appointed expressive instrument.

IV

The long couplet in the classical tradition, and especially that couplet as it is refined by Swift's friend Alexander Pope, is a structure composed of *processed words,* words manipulated into new, momentary phrases—ellipses, compressions, inversions, zeugmas, extraordinary junctures, suspensions:

> Where Wigs with Wigs, with Sword-knots Sword-knots strive.
> Where *Nature moves,* and *Rapture warms* the Mind.
> A hero perish, or a sparrow fall.
> And now a bubble burst, and now a world.
> The sot a hero, lunatic a king.

Pope's unit of wit is the half-line. His rhymes depend very much on the very special syntactic mechanism which brings them into conjunction. "Each Atom by some other struck," Swift himself wrote in a poem to Pope, "All Turns and Motion tries; Till in a Lump together stuck, Behold a *Poem* rise!" (*Dr. Sw——to Mr. P——e,* 1727). Even in Pope's use of the starkest everyday language, he arranges with atomic care; he maximizes in very exact, if excited and unusual, sequences.

> Shut, shut the door, good *John!* fatigu'd I said,
> Tye up the knocker, say I'm sick, I'm dead.
> > [*An Epistle to Dr. Arbuthnot,* 1–2]

The short couplet, a release and freedom for Swift, was a hobble for Pope. Swift did not think Pope imitated his couplet very well. He disparaged Pope's imitation of his style in supplying the episode of the town mouse and the country mouse to fill out the Horatian *Satire* 2. 6. Probably we could not always, under any circumstances (that is, if not told the authorship in advance), be sure of seeing in Pope's lines something essentially different from the plainer and in a sense heavier phrasing of Swift. Lines 9–28 of this poem are debated, the external evidence failing. But from line 133 on we are certain about Pope. And thus:

> O charming Noons! and Nights divine!
> Or when I sup, or when I dine,
> My Friends above, my Folks below,
> Chatting and laughing all-a-row,
> The Beans and Bacon set before 'em,
> The Grace-cup serv'd with all decorum:
> And even the very Dogs at ease!
> Which is the happier, or the wiser,
> A man of Merit, or a Miser?
> Whether we ought to chuse our Friends,
> For their own Worth, or our own Ends?
>   [*Satire* 2. 6. 133–50]

The half-line chiming units and with them a certain buoyancy and sprightliness, a graceful soaring, fit conveniently with our knowledge on external evidence that these lines were written by Pope.[8]

V

The earliest surviving short-couplet poem by Swift, the *Verses Wrote in a Lady's Ivory Table Book* (1698?), is a sharp example of his peculiar love for what we can best, I think, call live *whole* phrases.

> Here you may read (*Dear Charming Saint*)
> Beneath (*A new Receit for Paint*)
> Here in Beau-spelling (*tru til deth*)
> There in her own (*far an el breth*)
> Here (*lovely Nymph pronounce my doom*)
> There (*A safe way to use Perfume*)
> Here, a Page fill'd with Billet Doux;
> On t'other side (*laid out for Shoes*)
> (*Madam, I dye without your Grace*)
> (Item, *for half a Yard of Lace.*)
>   [7–16]

Add the following from the Horatian *Epistle* 1.7, to Lord Oxford, purporting to narrate Swift's first encounter with him:

> Swift, who could neither fly nor hide,
> Came sneaking to the Chariot-side,
> And offer'd many a lame Excuse;
> He never meant the least Abuse—
> *My Lord—The Honour you design'd—*
> *Extremely proud—but I had din'd—*
> *I'm sure I never shou'd neglect—*
> *No Man alive has more Respect—.*
>   [*To Lord Oxford* (1713), ll. 63–70]

Swift's short couplets are composed, characteristically, of ready-made phrases, from the colloquial and stereotype repertory, pieces of stock language laid together in bundles, clattering parallels. He rattles the literal commonplaces, brandishes the living speech. We are close to the specimens of fatuity which he collected so lovingly in his *Polite Conversation* (in modern American parlance, *The Cliché Expert Takes the Stand*). The lines largely lack internal figural structure. The wit may come in the contrast between phrases drawn from different fonts, as that of the beau and that of the lady so systematically rhymed in the *Ivory Table Book*. Johnson said of Swift's prose (*The Conduct of the Allies*), "He had to count ten, and he has counted it right." Of Swift's verses, Johnson said, "there is not much upon which the critic can exercise his powers."

One may have felt the same kind of literalism, or fidelity to real speech, in the hexameter couplets of the greatest French comic writer, Molière. It is tempting to draw this proportion: as Pope, especially in his Homer, is to Racine, so Swift, in his short couplets, is to Molière.

VI

Swift found Berkeley's *Alciphron* "too speculative."[9] Swift was anti-metaphysical, anti-speculative. His orientation toward *things*— hard objects, such as can be set on a shelf, put in a box, or carried in pocket or hand (a "rhyming and chiming" universe, yet how unlike the dappled cosmic vision of the poet Hopkins)—reminds us of the philosophers in the Grand Academy of Lagado who conceived the

notion of carrying *things* about with them, to use instead of words. One
of Swift's most reliable poetic devices (as we might expect in general
from the author of *Gulliver*) is the catalogue or "inventory" of miscellaneous physical things or of verbal things: the *Furniture of a Woman's
Mind* ("A Set of Phrases learnt by Rote; A Passion for a Scarlet
Coat"—[1727], 2. 415); the key literal items of millinery concern, *lace,
stuff, yard, fan,* (in rhyming positions), the samples of card-table talk,
the cheats, complaints, and accusations, all the splattering enu-
merations of a cluttered life that make the *Journal of a Modern Lady* ("I
but transcribe, for not a Line / Of all the Satyre shall be
mine. . . . Unwilling Muse begin thy Lay, / The Annals of a Female
Day"—[1729], 11.28–29, 34–35); the verbal trash that composes the
cliché mind of a *Grisette* (1730); the list of false parts removed by *A
Beautiful Young Nymph Going to Bed* (1731); the disgusting clutter of a
Lady's Dressing Room (1730): "Of all the Litter as it lay; . . . An Inventory follows here."

> The various Combs for various Uses,
> Fill'd up with Dirt so closely fixt,
> No Brush could force a way betwixt.
> A Paste of Composition rare,
> Sweat, Dandriff, Powder, Lead and Hair.
> [8, 10, 20–24]

The imputation of slovenly vice or, at the mildest, of helter-skelter
frivolity conveyed in these catalogues represents a juncture of couplet
rhetoric and a certain kind of sexism which I am not concerned to
develop in this paper.

   Such verbalized and inventoried objects are most conspicuous
when they occur as rhymes. Rhyme is the most brillantly attractive
feature of Swift's verse. "Rhyme," says Butler in *Hudibras,* "the rud-
der is of verses" (1.1.403). So much of Swift's line, says Martin Price,
"is absorbed into the rhyme."

   In a cunning blend of prudence and artistry, Swift sometimes
teases us with a rhyme word left blank—either a scatological word
("Celia, Celia, Celia——") or the name of some dangerous political
target.

> How the Helm is rul'd by——
> At whose Oars, like Slaves, they all pull.
> [*To a Lady* (1733), ll. 159–60]

If we have any doubt how the music of that rhyme goes, we can consult its complement in another poem of about the same date.

> But why wou'd he, except he *slobber'd,*
>   Offend our Patriot, Great Sir R——?
>   [*The Life and Character of Dean Swift* (1733), ll. 107–08]

The first poem quoted just now, the *Epistle to a Lady, Who desired the Author to make Verses on Her, in the Heroick Stile,* exhibits, I believe, the most sustained instance of this unheroic device that Swift ever achieved.

> I, WHO love to have a Fling,
> Both at Senate-House, and——   King
> . . . .
> If I treat you like——   a crown'd Head
> You have cheap enough compounded.
> Can you put in higher Claims,
> Than the Owners of *St. J*——*s.*   James
> You are not so great a Grievance
> As the Hirelings of *St. St*——*s.*   Stephens
> You are of a lower Class
> Than my Friend Sir *R*—— *Br*——*s.*   Robert Brass
>   [221–22, 239–46]

That kind of rhyming is the complementary opposite of a French diversion described by Addison in *Spectator* 60, the game of *bouts-rimés* —where only the rhyme words are given, and the player is challenged to fill in the blank lines to his fancy. Swift's extraordinary rhymes sometimes seem to invite being extracted from his verse for use in that way too. A few of his most bravura passages might make almost manageable parlor games. What might we not make, for instance, of such a series of expressions as:

> dupes us
> *Peri Hupsous,*
> *Longinus,*
> outshine us.
> over-run ye,
> for love or money,
> translation,
> *Quotation.*

Words combined into makeshift rhymes play a large part here. In many, perhaps in most, of Swift's comic two-syllable rhymes, we find one makeshift (sometimes with forced accent, and better if the first of the couplet) combined with one ready-made, the excuse or occasion for the couplet. In the passage I have just dismembered, we note, along with the excellent *Peri Hupsous* and *Longinus*, the no less ready-made cliché or tag phrase "for love or money." The closing couplet, formed on the Latinate *translation* and *Quotation,* may be said to take advantage of a very easy linguistic opportunity.

> A forward critic often dupes us
> With sham quotations *Peri Hupsous*
> And if we have not read *Longinus,*
> Will magisterially outshine us.
> Then, lest with Greek he over-run ye,
> Procure the book for love or money,
> Translated from Boileau's translation,
> And quote *Quotation* on *Quotation.*
>   [*On Poetry: A Rapsody*
>   (1733), ll. 255–62]

A more minute rhetorical examination of this passage might choose for special remark such a word as *magisterially,* unrolling itself so magisterially that, although only one word of four, it manages to usurp three of the line's four metrical ictuses; it illustrates what we might have been suspecting, that Swift's apparently flat and plain bundles of simple phrases are susceptible of very nice tilting within the metrical frame. The last couplet, with its easy rhyme of *translation* and *quotation,* is fortified internally in each line by an anagnorisis or "turn" upon the rhyming word.

It is difficult to make significant statistical statements about Swift's rhyme. The most florid passages stand out in the memory and color the whole. Broaden the base for a moment and think of the English tradition, most notably Butler, Swift, and Byron. Swift, said Byron, "beats us all hollow, his rhymes are wonderful."[10] Byron shows himself a true Swiftian when he joins Aristotle with Longinus via the word *bottle.*

> —"Longinus o'er a Bottle,"
> Or, "Every Poet his *own* Aristotle."
>   [*Don Juan,* 1. 204]

The English comic rhymes are poetic *objets trouvés,* a flotsam and jetsam, jumble and tumble, of miscellaneous prefabricated linguistic objects, conspicuous curiosities, bric-a-brac, trophies hauled in, a polyglot litter, gravels, seaweed, driftwood, of a language and culture—classical adjuncts, history, proper names, tags, quotation on quotation, a world of partial assimilations to the native English stock, a collage of newspaper scraps, a Table Book of the real and the verbal world, where the poet finds scrawled his heterogeneous chiming vocabulary. Think of Stephen Dedalus on the beach at Sandymount, meditating the "ineluctable modality of the visible." "Signatures of all things I am here to read. . . . Seaspawn and seawrack, the nearing tide, that rusty boat."

The homonyms of a language sometimes offer each other so much mutual support as hardly to be realized for the different words which they actually are. Thus *light* in weight and *light* in color. Or they clash and compete, and one of a pair may win, the other surviving only in some formalized and redundant phrase ("without *let* or hindrance") or in a classic quotation ("By heaven, I'll make a ghost of him that *lets* me"). The feat of rhyming verse is to find and focus a context where a clash of partially homonymous expressions is rendered harmonious—in illustration of the Jakobsonian rule that in poetry the axis of selection (the range of equivalence which is put to one side in straight prose) is projected onto the axis of combination, which in poetry is an axis of analogy. Swift's short-couplet rhymes are a maximum demonstration of this feat, not verbal music but paronomastic meaning. "Longinus" becomes a new signature; it reveals a latent aspect of its meaning as it evokes "outshine us." *Peri Hupsous* gives up a secret through its affinity for "dupes us."

VII

Swift persisted in experiment with varied verse forms throughout his career. He returned often enough to the pentameter couplet. He wrote anapests. He tried ballad stanzas, songs, Skeltonic dimeters. He scored such successes as the breathless gabble meter of *The Humble Petition of Frances Harris* and *Mary the Cook Maid's Letter to Dr. Sheridan,* or the squalid stanzas of the *Pastoral Dialogue* of Dermot and Sheelah. But it is fair to say that the poetic virtues which I am trying to celebrate are

exerted at their maximum in the jabbing four-stress couplet (sometimes trochaic, more often iambic) which Swift made so specially his
own voice.

One of the conveniences which he discovered through the use of
his couplet was speed. The extraordinary speed of which this idiom
was capable appears perhaps most strikingly in some of his shorter
narrative poems. *The Progress of Marriage* (1721–22), for instance: how
to begin a story.

> Aetatis suae fifty two
> A rich Divine began to woo
> A handsome young imperious *Girl*
> Nearly related to an Earl.
> [1–4]

Or *The Progress of Love* (1719): how to execute a turn in the middle of a
story.

> Suppose all Partyes now agreed,
> The Writings drawn, the Lawyer fee'd,
> The Vicar and the Ring bespoke:
> Guess how could such a Match be broke.
> (Guess how! She had run off with John the butler.).
> For truly John was missing too:
> The Horse and Pillion both were gone
> Phillis, it seems, was fled with John.
> [21–24, 40–42]

Or the principle of metamorphosis. Parallels (or similars) in general
make for similitude, analogies, puns, metaphors, even metamorphoses—and even the latter a speedy operation in the short couplet. In an early couplet poem, *Baucis and Philemon* (1708–09), the
metamorphosis, as Ehrenpreis observes, is like a "series of answers to
riddles. How is a cottage like a church? How is a kettle like a bell?"[11]

> The chimny widen'd and grew high'r,
> Became a Steeple with a Spire:
> The Kettle to the top was hoist
> And there stood fastn'd to a Joyst. . . .
> [95–98]

Or the disappearing trick. How to make two trees disappear, gradually
yet completely, in six lines.

Here *Baucis,* there *Philemon* grew.
Till once, a Parson of our Town,
To mend his Barn, cut *Baucis* down;
At which, 'tis hard to be believ'd,
How much the other Tree was griev'd,
Grew Scrubby, dy'd a-top, was stunted:
So, the next Parson stub'd and burnt it.

[172–78]

One hazard of the short line, the short, straight syntax, is that this structure may produce too many antithetic reversals, parentheses that get out of hand, digressions, loquacity—a sort of scrappiness. Swift's lesser poems are often enough notable as paragraphic assortments rather than as continuous movements. But segmentation can also produce the radiantly disjunct concentrations, the movement as of a series of shrapnel bursts, in such passages of Swift as the opening paragraphs of the *Verses on the Death of Dr. Swift* (1731).

Dear Honest *Ned* is in the Gout,
Lies rackt with Pain, and you without:
How patiently you hear him groan!
How glad the Case is not your own!

What Poet would not grieve to see,
His brethren write as well as he?
But rather than they should excel,
He'd wish his Rivals all in Hell.

[27–34]

A term used very frequently by appreciators of Swift—whether of his verse or of his prose—is "energy." Energy—in his short verse a kind of direct insistence, an urgent announcement, a raw shock. The diapason of disgusting energy, for instance, that permeates the group of poems in which Cassinus and Peter and Strephon and Chloe and Corinna and Celia pursue their malodorous adventures. Or the energy of smiling outrage, the art of "obliging Ridicule," as he himself termed it (*Poems,* 1. 216), which he found so congenial in his poems of compliment to the other sex.

WHY, *Stella,* should you knit your Brow,
If I compare you to the Cow?

[21–22][12]

Another term which the critics have favored and which applies very well to a somewhat different range of energy in Swift is "exuberance." A nearly equivalent word might be "bumptiousness." Under this head I present a concluding contrast between Swift and his kindred spirit Pope. *On Poetry: A Rapsody,* from which we have already quoted, shows Swift in a maximum parallel to Pope—to Pope in the Horatian *Epistle to Augustus,* of course, an apology for poetry, with satire on the contemporary scene and salute to a reigning dunce. Swift did not, like Pope, write a close imitation of Horace, but he clearly had the classic model in mind (*Poems,* 2. 658). Swift's poem anticipated Pope's by four years (1733). Consider the end of each poem. Pope's so remarkable for innuendo and subtlety:

> But Verse alas! your Majesty disdains;
> And I'm not us'd to Panegyric strains:
> The Zeal of Fools offends at any time,
> But most of all, the Zeal of Fools in ryme.
> Besides, a fate attends on all I write,
> That when I aim at praise, they say I bite.
> A vile Encominum doubly ridicules;
> There's nothing blackens like the ink of fools.
>   [*Epistle to Augustus,* 2. 404–11]

(The poem, we know, was mistaken by some for a panegyric upon the administration.) Add a certain kind of literalness in Pope which invites special illustration from another poem: "Three thousand Suns went down on *Welsted's* Lye" (*Epistle to Arbuthnot,* l. 375). Not exuberance! Pope means that more than ten years had passed before he answered Welsted in *The Dunciad.*

How different all that from the cheerfully over-obvious ironies of Swift! (The *Rapsody* on poetry deceived Queen Caroline. But several printers and publishers of the poem at Dublin were taken into custody; *Poems,* 2.640.)

> Say, Poet, in what other Nation,
> Shone ever such a Constellation.
> Attend ye *Popes,* and *Youngs,* and *Gays,*
> And tune your Harps, and strow your Bays.
> Your Panegyricks here provide,
> You cannot err on Flatt'ry's Side.
> Above the Stars exalt your Stile,
> You still are low ten thousand Mile.

On *Lewis* all his Bards bestow'd
Of Incense many a thousand Load;
But *Europe* mortify'd his Pride,
And swore the fawning Rascals ly'd:
Yet what the World refus'd to *Lewis,*
Apply'd to *George* exactly true is:
Exactly true! Invidious Poet!
'Tis fifty thousand Times below it.[13]
       [2.656–57, ll. 465–80]

"Overshooting the mark," said Longinus, "ruins the hyperbole."[14] "Those hyperboles are best, in which the very fact that they are hyperboles escapes attention." But Swift's way was to invert all those rules enunciated by classical authorities on the heroic or the sublime. His finesses came by extravagance—inventive extravagance. It takes a genius to go so joyfully wrong. This is the open door into the sunlight of laughter which Swift discovered when he moved from the murky constraints of his pentameter metaphysics on the illness of Temple into the abandoned fun of the *Lady's Ivory Table Book.*

NOTES

1. Swift's verse is quoted throughout my essay from *Swift's Poems,* ed. Harold Williams (Oxford, 1958), vols. 1, 2, 3.

2. It is a pleasure to acknowledge the kindness of Professor Rawson in allowing me to study an eloquent chapter on the poems, from his forthcoming book on Swift.

3. Brendan O Hehir, "Meaning of Swift's 'Description of a City Shower,' " *ELH* 27 (1960): 194–207. Cf. David M. Vieth, "*Fiat Lux:* Logos versus Chaos in Swift's 'A Description of the Morning,' " *Papers on Language and Literature* 8 (1972): 302–07.

4. Laetitia Pilkington, *Memoirs* (London, 1748), 1:136; Harold Williams, *Dean Swift's Library* (Cambridge, 1932), pp. 87–88.

5. William Bowman Piper, *The Heroic Couplet* (Cleveland, 1969), chaps. 2–3.

6. Jakob Schipper, *A History of English Versification* (Oxford, 1918), pp. 126, 182, 192; F. A. Wright and T. A. Sinclair, *A History of Later Latin Literature* (London, 1931), pp. 234, 296, 305–06, 319, 323, 324, 330; F. J. E. Raby, *A History of Secular Latin Poetry in the Middle Ages* (Oxford, 1957), 2:173, 183, 278, 362; *The Oxford Book of Medieval Latin Verse,* ed. F. J. E. Raby (Oxford, 1959), pp. 251, 485, 486; *Psalterium Profanum, Weltliche Gedichte des lateinischen Mittelalters,* ed. Josef Eterle (Zurich, 1962), pp. 534–36, 579–81.

7. Pope is quoted from *The Twickenham Edition of The Poems of Alexander Pope* (London, 1939–69), vols. 1–11.

8. Pope's Horatian *Epistle* 1.7, "Imitated in the Manner of Dr. Swift," seems to betray his hand far less clearly. On the other hand, Pope, adding only ten scraps from another poem by Swift, transformed the conclusion of the *Verses on the Death of Dr. Swift* from a curiously straight and inflated (if in part ironic) panegyric of the Doctor to what has been described as a "rapid-fire" antithetic dialogue, on the Horatian and Popean model. See Arthur H. Scouten and Robert D. Hume, "Pope and Swift: Text and Interpretation of Swift's Verses on His Death," *PQ* 52 (April 1973): 207–08, 215.

9. *The Correspondence of Jonathan Swift,* ed. Harold Williams (Oxford, 1965), 1:16.

10. E. J. Trelawney, *Recollections of the Last Days of Shelley and Byron* (Boston, 1858), 1:37.

11. Another early poem, *Van Brug's House* (1703–06), executes some remarkable metamorphoses of poetry and heraldry into architecture.

12. With a burst of laughter, and in the presence of his victim (Lady Acheson, an "agreeable young Lady, but extremely lean"), Swift once boasted: "That Lady had rather be a *Daphne* drawn by me, than a *Sacharissa* by any other pencil" (*Poems,* 3: 902). His awareness of another possible sensibility is expressed in an earlier poem censuring some freedom in raillery taken by his crony Sheridan.

> If what You said, I wish unspoke,
> 'Twill not suffice, it was a Joke.
> [*To Mr. Delany,*
> 1718, ll. 65–66]

13. Other examples of hyperbolic number in Swift: *On Censure* (1727), l. 27; *Journal of a Modern Lady* (1729), l. 139; *Strephon and Chloe* (1731), l. 99; *Apollo* (1731), l. 20.

14. *Peri Hupsous,* chap. 38. Translation of W. Rhys Roberts.

DAVID M. VIETH

The Mystery of Personal Identity: Swift's Verses on His Own Death

I

Jonathan Swift's poem *Verses on the Death of Dr. Swift* holds a peculiar fascination for readers, as is shown by an avalanche of recent publications. It is by far the most popular of Swift's approximately 250 authentic poems and is generally regarded as his greatest. Since the contents fulfill the promise of the tantalizing title, the *Verses* would seem an ideal subject for a commemorative volume whose theme is "The Author in His Work." In a recent article, for instance, Arthur H. Scouten and Robert D. Hume jointly conclude, "Probably the key to response to the poem lies in our sense of the poet's presence in his poem," "in an awareness of the author in his poem."[1]

The truth, unfortunately, is less simple, as the discussion by Scouten and Hume illustrates. They complain, with justice, of "the current critical muddle" resulting because "critics are at present in radical disagreement about how to read the *Verses*." They themselves, however, fail to distinguish between the "poet" or "author" and a real-life Jonathan Swift who delighted in expressing himself through assumed identities. Moreover, in their comment that the poem "is organized to juxtapose and contrast the clashing views of a variety of speakers," Scouten and Hume barely recognize one of its major features, its multiplication of identities. Each of these, they say, "including Swift in the first person," projects "an *artificial* point of view."[2] Logically, therefore, if we seek the real Jonathan Swift, or "poet" or "author," just about the last place to look would be "in his poem"!

Three problems posed by the *Verses* can be discerned in the Scouten-Hume discussion. First, the poem's hypnotic appeal to readers, together with their inability to agree about its purpose, points to the need for an *affective* approach—that is, an approach less in terms of intrinsic "meaning" than in terms of reader response. The "current critical muddle" can scarcely be traced to deficiencies in the critics, for some of them are quite distinguished, and others, less widely known, are equally perceptive. Second, any new approach to the poem must take into account its most neglected aspect: its multiplication of identities. Several of these identities can be called "Jonathan Swift," many of them are fictions created by each other, and they are not even all alive at the same time. Third, multiplication of identities raises the question of identity itself. This is particular, personal identity, exemplified by the identity of Jonathan Swift. The critics, to judge from their "radical disagreement," find it very much a mystery.

II

First, then, an affective treatment of the *Verses* is called for by the astonishing diversity of recent interpretations. Swift's "last voyage" threatens to become as puzzling as Gulliver's.

Thus, over the past twenty years, we have been told that the concluding lines of the *Verses* are an unqualified self-eulogy that is "disgusting," or that these lines should be taken ironically, or that the self-eulogy is not ironic and is *not* disgusting. The idealized portrait of Swift may be a satiric *exemplum* of vanity, or—on the other hand—it may be an ethical or religious *exemplum* (however qualified) of right attitudes and actions.[3] The poem may be primarily, or partially, or not at all, a Horatian *apologia pro vita sua*.[4] It may be a "parody of obituary verse," or a true elegy combined with satire, or a "traditional meditation on death." Thematically, the poem may be a Platonic treatment of the relationship between flesh and spirit, or an affirmation of "the ideal of art as a defense against time."[5] Its portrayal of human nature has been called optimistic or (more commonly) pessimistic. Or the *Verses* may be political propaganda.[6]

The best comments on the *Verses* have, to my mind, been those of Gareth Jones, Robert W. Uphaus, and Edward W. Said. Rejecting critical efforts to reduce the "particularities" of Swift's poetry to some simplistic "positive" or "generalising abstraction," Jones experiences the *Verses* as an "enactment," a "personal statement," "an exploration which we ourselves must share and live through."[7] Uphaus, emphasing Swift's "biographical presence" in his poetry, maintains that in the *Verses* Swift "confidently affirms his own identity and convictions, his own sense of self."[8] Said, in the most brilliant analysis thus far, describes the poem as Swift's endeavor to transform his "presence" into an event in history.[9]

A recurring question in these discussions is what relationship exists between the panegyric at the end of the poem and the maxim from La Rochefoucauld with which it begins. Some readers find the two integrally related; others feel the self-eulogy contradicts, contrasts with, or rebuts the maxim; still others recognize a problem but evade it. In Maurice Johnson's view, "Exaggerated praise for the 'dead' Dean, in [the poem's] latter part, has the structural function of balancing the exaggerated weakness of character Swift imputes to himself in early lines."[10] Scouten and Hume claim that "the poem does possess a basic structural coherence" centering upon La Rochefoucauld's maxim, but their idea of "the theme of the poem" disintegrates, in the manner objected to by Gareth Jones, into the list of abstract vices in lines 39–42 ("Self-love, Ambition, Envy, Pride").

Like the bewilderment of twentieth-century readers, the ambiguous responses of Swift's contemporaries require an affective explanation of the *Verses*. The poem was enormously popular, passing through at least nine editions in 1739, the year of its first publication.[11] At the same time, Swift's friends, notably Alexander Pope, were distressed by what they considered to be the vanity of his self-praise. So fascinated was Pope with the poem, yet so disapproving of the apparent vanity (almost as if it were his *own* vanity), that he took upon himself a drastic revision of Swift's manuscript, evidently excising as many as 165 lines and adding 62 new lines from Swift's earlier poem *The Life and Genuine Character of Doctor Swift, 1733*.[12]

Behind these varied responses to *Verses on the Death of Dr. Swift* lies our second concern, its dazzling multiplication of identities. Several of these represent Swift himself. To begin with, there is the "real-life" Swift—Jonathan Swift #1, we may call him—who wrote the poem. He creates a second "Swift," Jonathan Swift #2, who is the poem's principal identity up to the concluding eulogy and its principal speaker throughout. That he is a fiction is emphasized by his ignorance, prior to line 73, that he is writing a poem: "Thus much may serve by way of Proem, / Proceed we therefore to our Poem" (71–72).[13] This second "Swift" creates the host of friends, enemies, and mere

acquaintances—some, like Pope, Gay, and Arbuthnot, corresponding
to real people, yet all in a sense fictitious—who populate the middle of
the poem and are imagined commenting upon the Dean's death. Out
of this group comes the unnamed speaker at the Rose Tavern who
creates the idealized "Swift" portrayed in the concluding panegyric—
Jonathan Swift #3. The footnotes, with their curmudgeonly tone, belong to still a further "Swift," Jonathan Swift #4, who speaks of the
other three "Swifts" in the third person.

Hence the reader is constrained to ask, in the words of the American television show *To Tell the Truth*, "Will the *real* Jonathan Swift
please stand up?" Evidently the answer, deliberately paradoxical and
absurd, is that Jonathan Swift #1, the factual, flesh-and-blood "Swift,"
is imaginatively least "real," whereas the most "real" is Jonathan Swift
#3, the blatantly fictitious identity of the concluding panegyric.[14]

III

Our third concern, the mystery of personal identity, unfolds as we
examine, in turn, each of the multiple identities of Swift generated by
the *Verses*.

The first "Jonathan Swift"—Swift #1—consists of the minimal
human agency needed to write the poem. This identity, the flesh-
and-blood Swift, ceased existence finally and completely on October
19, 1745, and in that sense is no longer "real." Inside the poem, he exists
only at second hand through the other personae of Swift. Outside the
poem, he can be found, though never at first hand, in other works by
Swift, in remarks by Swift's contemporaries, and in the life-records
generally. Thus limited is Swift's own conception of "the author in his
work."[15]

Questions of identity become more insistent with Swift #2, the
half-fictitious principal speaker of the *Verses*.[16] Significantly, his cue
for entrance, in the poem's first line, is La Rochefoucauld's maxim,
"Dans l'adversité de nos meilleurs amis nous trouvons quelque chose,
qui ne nous deplaist pas," translated in the epigraph itself as "In the
Adversity of our best Friends, we find something that doth not dis-
please us." The juxtaposition of maxim and persona implies that the
maxim is to be understood through the persona and in light of the
poem's multiplication of identities. In terms of the maxim, as "Reason
and Experience prove," friends are more useful than enemies for defin-

ing one's sense of personal identity because the relationship is closer. With enemies, the relationship is more distant, straightforward, and standardized. If an enemy suffers adversity, we can rationalize that he got what he deserved; if he prospers, we can uncritically blame the baseness of human nature, the corruption of society, or the injustice of the universe.

The closer relationship with a friend, however, is ambivalent and far more complex. Since we are expected to have benign feelings toward friends, any secret satisfaction at their misfortune, or envy of their success, will produce an inner psychological friction that intensifies our sense of being, our unique identity; as Marshall Waingrow has said, it "sharpens the separation of selves."[17] For this purpose, "No Enemy can match a Friend" (120). Guilt feelings increase the sense of identity. This sense can come through self-gratification, as in feeling one is less ill than "honest Ned . . . in the Gout," or through envy, as in wishing that a friend who has performed some "heroick Action" in battle will have "his Lawrels cropt" or that rival poets who "excel" were "all in Hell." The climax of the "proem" summarizes:

> To all my Foes, dear Fortune, send
> Thy Gifts, but never to my Friend:
> I tamely can endure the first,
> But, this with Envy makes me burst.
> [67–70][18]

Additional aspects of personal identity are dramatized in the most titillating lines in the "proem," involving Pope, Gay, and Arbuthnot (also St. John and Pulteney in succeeding lines):

> In POPE, I cannot read a Line,
> But with a Sigh, I wish it mine:
> When he can in one Couplet fix
> More Sense than I can do in Six:
> It gives me such a jealous Fit,
> I cry, Pox take him, and his Wit.
>
> Why must I be outdone by GAY,
> In my own hum'rous biting Way?
>
> ARBUTHNOT is no more my Friend,
> Who dares to Irony pretend;
> Which I was born to introduce,
> Refin'd it first, and shew'd its Use.
> [47–58]

Several conclusions about the technique and meaning of Swift's *Verses* can be drawn from this passage. First, it shows how the poem functions *affectively* to entrap the reader. We empathize with the speaker because we are embarrassed that Swift would say such things about himself; embarrassment for him becomes embarrassment for ourselves. The emotions of envy and spite being expressed are, by most people, "thought too base for human Breast"; but even if, like the speaker, we "believe 'em true" to human nature, our social context or "frame" would prevent us from publicly owning up to such motives.[19] Alexander Pope was so embarrassed that, as we have seen, he cut out one-third of the poem (although not this passage, perhaps because he felt its special reference to him would disarm criticism).

Second, the quoted lines illustrate the *relativity* of human consciousness and identity. Initially they seem like an embarrassing confession of despicable motives on "Swift's" part. Paradoxically, however, as many readers have noticed, they convey a deft compliment to the talents of Pope, Gay, and Arbuthnot. In a further paradox, as John Irwin Fischer remarks, the fact that "these lines are handsome praise" means that they also represent "an act of true magnanimity" by Swift.[20] Human consciousness depends disconcertingly upon one's point of view.

A third conclusion, really a corollary of the second, is that consciousness is *solipsistic.* Each human identity is unique, and, in a very important sense, can be experienced only from the inside. Swift, dramatizing the mystery of human identity in the manner he chose in the *Verses,* necessarily had to write about his *own* death, for he could not possess interior knowledge of anyone else's identity. Nor could he have achieved the same effect with a generalized *Verses on the Death of John Doe,* for human identity exists only *in particular,* not in general— even though this rule is, paradoxically, a general truth. In its exploration and enactment of human identity from the inside, including the "particularities" stressed by Gareth Jones, Swift's poem differs fundamentally from Pope's *Epistle to Dr. Arbuthnot,* to which it is often compared. Although "Pope" in the *Epistle* is partly the real-life Alexander Pope, he is equally a succession of outward-oriented, generalized stances by an ideal poet in relation to his public.[21]

This third conclusion, however, underscores a logical contradiction in the *Verses.* Since we, the readers, are not Swift, how can we experience *his* identity from within—get inside his skin, so to speak?

The problem and its rhetorical solution are illustrated by a later couplet that matches the earlier passage about Pope, Gay, and Arbuthnot (St. John appears in the next couplet, Pulteney together with St. John a few lines before): "Poor POPE will grieve a Month; and GAY/A Week; and ARBUTHNOTT a day" (207–08). As Maurice Johnson adroitly demonstrated years ago, the couplet would lose its edge if it occurred in a poem entitled "Verses on the Death of Dr. Shift" and read like this: "Poor Polk will grieve a month; and Jay / A week; and Higglesby a day."[22] The effect depends upon our previous knowledge of Swift, Pope, Gay, and Arbuthnot. By a rhetorical trick, we can seem to enter Swift's consciousness, seem to empathize with him, to the degree that we have some preconceived notion of his identity—for instance, his love-hate feelings toward Ireland, his *saeva indignatio,* his relationships with Vanessa and Stella, or his skill as ironist and satirist.

A fourth conclusion is that human identity, for Swift in the *Verses,* is defined *socially.* Hence Swift #1 is never a real identity in the poem, merely a logical postulate. The inner psychological frictions needed to define personal identity must come through close ties with other people, particularly friends. Waingrow (approved by Fischer) observes, "Ironically, what appear to be the most self-regarding of emotions are shown in fact to be utterly dependent upon the condition of others."[23] Conspicuous in the middle section of the *Verses,* after the "proem," is the sheer number of other people utilized to define the identity of the speaker, Jonathan Swift #2. Also conspicuous is the exaggerated realism of their behavior, which places the speaker firmly in the "real" world, even if through relationships of covert or open hostility. The gadabout of the central portion of the poem resembles the Swift we see in the second volume of the Ehrenpreis biography, who must have known thousands of people personally.

Although Swift #2 remains the central identity, the transition at line 73 from "proem" to "poem" entails a radical reversal of perspective. The speaker's envy of Pope, Gay, and Arbuthnot (47–58) is balanced by the brevity of their mourning for him (207–08). Against his selfish concern for "honest Ned . . . in the Gout" (27–30) is set that of "some Neighbour" who feels "a Pain, / Just in the Parts, where I complain" (135–42). In general, the human selfishness of La Rochefoucauld's maxim, previously displayed by the speaker, now is illustrated through the behavior of other people. Nevertheless, the focus continues to be on the speaker, whose identity is located at second hand by a kind of theatrical triangulation. This literary sleight of hand is performed through the stunning fantasy, introduced just after the "proem" and dominating the rest of the *Verses,* of Swift witnessing the events surrounding his own death. One is reminded of the common juvenile fantasy in which a child daydreams his own funeral, usually imagining the remorse felt by various adults who have (he thinks) mistreated him. In Swift's *Verses,* amusingly, people respond in the exact opposite way.[24]

This indirect definition of identity becomes highly complex in passages like the famous card-game, located just before the poem's time-scheme moves to the year following "Swift's" death. Several frames of reference interact to produce humor, irony, and satire:

> My female Friends, whose tender Hearts
> Have better learn'd to act their Parts[,]
> Receive the News in *doleful Dumps,*
> "The Dean is dead, (*and what is Trumps?*)
> "Then Lord have Mercy on his Soul.
> "(Ladies I'll venture for the *Vole.*)
> "Six Deans they say must bear the Pall.
> "(I wish I knew what *King* to call.)
> "Madam, your Husband will attend
> "The Funeral of so good a Friend.
> "No Madam, 'tis a shocking Sight,
> "And he's engag'd To-morrow Night!
> "My Lady *Club* wou'd take it ill,
> "If he shou'd fail her at *Quadrill.*
> "He lov'd the Dean. (*I lead a Heart.*)
> "But dearest Friends, they say, must part.
> "His Time was come, he ran his Race;
> "We hope he's in a better Place."
>
> [225–42]

One "frame" is the card game itself, while a second comprises the everyday social relationships among the card players. Two further frames, closely linked to the second, consist of the attitudes of these people, expected and actual, toward the supposedly absent (because deceased) Dean. A fifth frame, "containing" the others, is the fantasy in which the Dean, instead of being absent, becomes a silent and invisible auditor. Still another frame consists of the religious references. Humor results from incongruous interaction between frames:

"Trumps" as cards or the trumpet of the Last Judgment; "Heart" as a card or a token that "He lov'd the Dean"; six deans as pallbearers versus a king in cards; "Lord have mercy on his Soul" rhymed with "Vole," meaning "all" (the tricks in quadrille).[25]

The switch from "proem" to "poem" at line 73 marks one stage in an intricate opening-out of perspectives designed to focus upon Jonathan Swift #3, in the panegyric, as paradoxically the most "real" Swift. We progress from smaller to larger social contexts: from "Swift" individually to "Swift" in relation to friends and acquaintances, and then as seen by public figures in England, such as Walpole and the queen. We proceed from an inward to an outside view, from subjective to objective, with ever-increased distancing of judgments. Starting with the characterless Swift #1, we move to the self-revealing Swift #2 of the "proem" and then to the externalized judgments of onlookers in Dublin and London. In this process of distancing, "Swift" as identity recedes nearly to the vanishing point, as "if he never did exist" (248). In the last thirty lines of "Lintot's" monologue, just preceding the scene at the Rose Tavern, Swift is not once mentioned. At a further remove, however, he is resurrected in the "Character impartial" delivered in the tavern by "One quite indiff'rent in the Cause."[26] The distancing process hints that this is the most "impartial" or objective view of Jonathan Swift we can expect to get.

Several supplemental time-schemes move the *Verses* toward the concluding panegyric. The poem's middle section follows the conventional chronology of a funeral: the Dean fatally ill (73–142) and then dead (143–244), with news of these events spreading and eventually diminishing a year later (245–98). In historical time, we have "Swift" still alive, judged by himself (1–72); then dying and dead, judged by contemporaries (73–298); and finally memorialized in the future by all mankind—by, one might say, Prince Posterity.[27]

IV

Thus the *Verses* project into the future an idealized image of "Swift," Jonathan Swift #3, that is somehow more "real" than his other identities. It also seems clear, from the case assembled by Barry Slepian and accepted, even augmented, by most of his successors (including Scouten and Hume), that this panegyric is tinged with more than a little irony. What has not been acceptable is Slepian's conclusion about the purpose of this irony, namely that Swift is satirizing himself, along with other people, for vanity. Nevertheless, the irony is there, and it implies something false as well as true about the idealized image. Like any other myth, Swift #3 is fictitious in some details although true and "real" in more profound ways.

Specific details, in addition to the pervasive hyperbolic tone of the panegyric, confirm the presence of irony. We are told that in Swift's satire, "Malice never was his Aim; / He lash'd the Vice but spar'd the Name." Not only is this plainly untrue of most of Swift's satires, but, as Slepian observes, "he had just finished attacking thirteen people by name" in this very poem.[28] The claim that "His Satyr points at no Defect, / But what all Mortals may correct" would scarcely satisfy any reader who has winced at the incorrigible human failings portrayed in Gulliver and the Yahoos. "Power was never in his Thought," "He never Courted Men in Station," and "He never thought an Honour done him, / Because a Duke was proud to own him" describe inaccurately either the younger Swift of 1699–1714 or the embittered older man still wishing to become a bishop.[29] At the beginning of the panegyric, in the couplet alleging that Swift "To steal a Hint was never known, / But what he writ was all his own" (317–18), the second line is itself stolen from Denham's elegy on Cowley: "To him no Author was unknown, / Yet what he wrote was all his own."

Irony is evident in the sentimentalized, melodramatic diction of the panegyric: "all our golden Dreams," "save their sinking Country," "sacrifice old *England*'s Glory," "the dire destructive Scene," "Heav'n his Innocence defends." Most striking is the exaggerated parallelism of these lines (so striking that the first line supplied a recent book title):[30]

> Fair LIBERTY was all his Cry;
> For her he stood prepar'd to die;
> For her he boldly stood alone;
> For her he oft expos'd his own.
>   [351–54]

The fictional quality of Swift #3, and also of Swift #4, the author of the footnotes, is emphasized by the repeated use of superlatives and absolutes. Slepian comments,

Throughout the poem, both in the verses proper and in Swift's own foot-notes, the sources of the comedy are irony and exaggeration. The amazing total of 122 words are superlatives or absolutes. *Ever, universal, univer-sally, without the least, numberless, greatest, utmost, alone, still, mere, absolute,* and *any* occur once; *not one, not a, utterly,* and *nothing* occur twice; *the most, always,* and *only* occur four times. *Every* occurs six times; *never,* twenty times; *no,* twenty-three times; and *all*—perhaps the key word in the poem—forty-one times.[31]

The quaintly cantankerous exaggerations of Swift #4 are illustrated by his first footnote (italics mine):

> The Author imagines, that the Scriblers of the prevailing Party, which he *always* opposed, will libel him after his Death; but that others will re-member him with Gratitude, who consider the Service he had done to Ireland, under the Name of M. B. Drapier, by *utterly* defeating the destruc-tive Project of Wood's Half-pence, in five Letters to the People of Ireland, at that Time read *universally,* and convincing *every* Reader.

Further, Swift's *Verses* are noteworthy both for what they are *not,* generically speaking, and for the important features of Swift's career they exclude. Most critics accept the poem as only secondarily a Hora-tian apologia; a few virtually deny it this status. Nor are the *Verses* primarily a religious poem or a "meditation on death." Even Fischer, the chief proponent of this view, concedes: "Surprisingly, however, Swift's reflections on death have little of either the fear or horror one would naturally expect in thoughts stemming from painful physical disabilities. Neither did Swift's imagination dwell upon vivid death-bed scenes or upon the circumstances of final corruption."[32] Swift's speaker expresses no fear of death and comes no closer to a deathbed scene than his swipe at "all the Sniv'llers round my Bed" (142). Death figures in the poem only as the necessary precondition of human iden-tity and the final seal upon it (as in the death of a tragic protagonist). Also, unlike Pope's *Epistle to Dr. Arbuthnot,* Swift's *Verses* include re-markably little autobiography. In contrast to Pope's idealized por-trayal of his father and mother at the end of the *Epistle,* Swift says nothing specific about his parents or any other relatives, nothing about Stella or Vanessa, nothing about Sir William Temple. There is no ac-count of Swift's childhood comparable to Pope's "I lisp'd in Num-bers, for the Numbers came." There is, in fact, no reference to any specific event in Swift's life prior to 1713, when he was already forty-five years old.

As Peter Schakel points out,[33] the *Verses* make no reference, outside the footnotes, to any individual literary work by Swift. Even the footnotes do not mention *A Tale of a Tub, Gulliver's Travels,* or *A Modest Proposal.* Refraining from aesthetic judgments, the panegyric begins by stressing that Swift's works were ironical, satirical, moral, and popular:

> As for his Works in Verse and Prose,
> I own my self no Judge of those:
> Nor, can I tell what Criticks thought 'em;
> But, this I know, all People bought 'em;
> As with a moral View design'd
> To cure the Vices of Mankind:
> His Vein, ironically grave,
> Expos'd the Fool, and lash'd the Knave.
>   [309–16]

There is no reference to Swift's more than forty years of efforts in behalf of the church. Emphasis falls, instead, partly on Swift's relationship with his friends, but mostly on his public moral character, especially as this was exhibited in two areas of his activity, the English Tory ministry of 1710–14 and Ireland after 1714—representing, respectively, Swift in power and Swift out of power. His stances in these two areas are not merely idealized but frozen in time.[34] In one passage,

> Two Kingdoms, just as Faction led,
> Had set a Price upon his Head;
> But, not a Traytor cou'd be found,
> To sell him for Six Hundred Pound,
>   [355–58]

Swift actually telescopes two episodes, each involving a reward of £300, that occurred ten years apart (1714 and 1724). The composition of the *Verses* is likewise frozen in time, one footnote specifying that "this Poem still preserves the Scene and Time it was writ in" and another referring pointedly to "this present third Day of May, 1732."

We need to remind ourselves how fully the success of the *Verses* derives from our affective response. The half-ironic, highly selective panegyric gains our assent so far as it fits our preconceived notions of Swift's identity. Above all, this is Swift the Irish national hero, the

"Swift" of Yeats, Joyce, and Beckett. We can gauge the risk Swift took if we recall how many aspects of our standard image he chose to omit: for example, his relationships with Stella and Vanessa, his alleged misanthropy, his position as the greatest prose writer of all time. Guessing astutely, Swift managed to predict, project, and even predetermine the kind of official image that would make the *Verses* come alive for posterity. His success in thus imposing his semi-fictitious self-image on the future resembles that of other historical and literary figures such as Alexander the Great, Cleopatra, Thomas Jefferson, Lord Byron, Abraham Lincoln, or Winston Churchill.

V

I shall conclude by suggesting that *Verses on the Death of Dr. Swift* can be seen as yet another instance of Swift's uncanny skill in perpetrating hoaxes, as with the Bickerstaff Papers and the Drapier's Letters. In these hoaxes, Swift typically generates a fantasy which, by drawing in other people voluntarily or involuntarily, not only competes with "reality" but maneuvers it aside and takes its place. The situation becomes one in which Swift is writing the entire script.

Early in 1708, as is well known, Swift exposed the nonconformist astrologer and almanac-maker John Partridge by bringing out, in the fictitious persona Isaac Bickerstaff, a rival almanac predicting that Partridge would die on March 29 (just before April Fools' Day). As the expected day arrived, Swift published anonymously a fictitious account of Partridge's death, followed by a mock elegy and epitaph, a faked prophecy by Merlin, and a *Vindication* of Bickerstaff. Others gleefully joined in with pamphlets of their own, one result being that the Company of Stationers apparently struck Partridge's name from its rolls, the equivalent of being declared legally dead. Partridge protested in vain. Swift's fantasy, with the collusion of other people, had replaced "reality."

A more serious hoax, but a hoax nonetheless, is the episode of the Drapier's Letters in 1724–25. Fantasy entered with the very first letter, in which the fictitious M. B., Drapier, denounced Wood's copper halfpence as debased coinage and called for a boycott. When the Fourth Letter appeared, orders were issued to prosecute the printer, John Harding, and to offer a reward for a discovery of the author—who was never arrested, although Swift's authorship was an open secret. To the Grand Jury Swift addressed his broadside *Seasonable Advice,* arguing that the case against the printer should be dismissed. When the Grand Jury, urged to make a presentment (that is, indictment) of this broadside, refused to do so, they were discharged by Whitshed, the Lord Chief Justice. Swift, increasingly manipulating events while remaining free himself, may have been a visible but untouchable presence in the courtroom on this very day; observing the motto on Whitshed's coach, he penned the lines beginning, *"Libertas & natale Solum;* / Fine Words; I wonder where you stole 'um." Swift next published *An Extract* contending that Whitshed's action in discharging the Grand Jury had been arbitrary and illegal. When the new Grand Jury was urged by Whitshed to make a presentment of Swift's libels, they instead made a presentment, composed by Swift himself, of those persons who were trying to impose Wood's halfpence on Ireland! Earlier, public support mounted in the form of petitions and declarations, while the Dublin populace repeated these Bible verses (1 Samuel 14:45):

> And the people said unto Saul, Shall Jonathan die, who hath wrought this great salvation in Israel? God forbid: as the Lord liveth, there shall not one hair of his head fall to the ground; for he hath wrought with God this day. So the people rescued Jonathan, that he died not.

Wood's patent was withdrawn. Incredibly, Swift had forced all participants, including the English government, to follow his script—this in the face of the probability that Wood's halfpence was honest coinage, as reported in Sir Isaac Newton's assay.

Like the affairs of Partridge and Wood's halfpence, *Verses on the Death of Dr. Swift* is a hoax that concerns a serious issue, utilizes a fictitious or semi-fictitious speaker, and is designed to "make things happen." Unlike Bickerstaff and the Drapier, however, Swift in the *Verses* is himself at once the issue, the central figure, and the outcome of the affair. The concluding panegyric freezes historical events into a tableau with Swift as its focus, like the central figure in Emanuel Leutze's sentimentalized but unforgettable painting *Washington Crossing the Delaware.* As Edward Said remarks, most of Swift's writing was conceived "neither as art in our sense of the word, nor as craftsmanship for its own sake," but was "planned in some way to change" historical events.[35] The absurdly presumptuous intention of the *Verses*—more or less successful, as the poem's popularity attests—is to transform the image of Jonathan Swift into a teleological fulfillment of history.

NOTES

1. "Pope and Swift: Text and Interpretation of Swift's Verses on His Death," *Philological Quarterly* 52 (1973): 205–31.

2. Ibid., pp. 205, 222, 225 (italics theirs).

3. John Middleton Murry, *Jonathan Swift: A Critical Biography* (London, 1954; New York, 1955), pp. 454–60. Barry Slepian, "The Ironic Intention of Swift's Verses on His Own Death," *Review of English Studies* n.s. 14 (1963): 249–56. Marshall Waingrow, *"Verses on the Death of Dr. Swift,"* *Studies in English Literature* 5 (1965): 513–18. John Irwin Fischer, "How to Die: *Verses on the Death of Dr. Swift,"* *Review of English Studies* n.s. 21 (1970): 422–41. Also Irvin Ehrenpreis, *Literary Meaning and Augustan Values* (Charlottesville, 1974), pp. 33–37.

4. Robert C. Steensma, "Swift's Apologia: 'Verses on the Death of Dr. Swift,' " *Proceedings of the Utah Academy of Sciences, Arts, and Letters* 42 (1965): 23–28. Julie B. Klein, "The Art of Apology: 'An Epistle to Dr. Arbuthnot' and 'Verses on the Death of Dr. Swift,' " *Costerus* 8 (1973): 77–87. See also Mary Claire Randolph, "The Structural Design of the Formal Verse Satire," *Philological Quarterly* 21 (1942): 376; P. K. Elkin, *The Augustan Defence of Satire* (Oxford, 1973), pp. 111–14; and Joseph Horrell, ed., *Collected Poems of Jonathan Swift,* Muses' Library, 2 vols. (Cambridge, Mass., 1958), introduction, 1:xxxiii.

5. Herbert Davis, "Swift's Character," in *Jonathan Swift 1667–1967: A Dublin Tercentenary Tribute,* ed. Roger McHugh and Philip Edwards (Dublin, 1967), pp. 7–15. Ronald Paulson, "Swift, Stella, and Permanence," *ELH* 27 (1960): 298–314, and *The Fictions of Satire* (Baltimore, 1967), pp. 189–206. Donald C. Mell, "Elegiac Design and Satiric Intention in 'Verses on the Death of Dr. Swift,' " *Concerning Poetry,* vol. 6, no. 2 (Fall 1973): 15–24, and *A Poetics of Augustan Elegy* (Amsterdam, 1974), pp. 53–62.

6. Hugo M. Reichard, "The Self-Praise Abounding in Swift's *Verses,"* *Tennessee Studies in Literature* 18 (1973): 105–12. James L. Tyne, S.J., "Gulliver's Maker and Gullibility," *Criticism* 7 (1965): 161–66. Peter J. Schakel, "The Politics of Opposition in 'Verses on the Death of Dr. Swift,' " *Modern Language Quarterly* 35 (1974): 246–56.

7. "Swift's *Cadenus and Vanessa:* A Question of 'Positives,' " *Essays in Criticism* 20 (1970): 424–40.

8. "Swift's 'Whole Character': The Delany Poems and 'Verses on the Death of Dr. Swift,' " *Modern Language Quarterly* 34 (1973): 406–16. Uphaus draws upon Maurice Johnson, "Swift's Poetry Reconsidered," in *English Writers of the Eighteenth Century,* ed. John H. Middendorf (New York and London, 1971), pp. 233–48. See also Wayne C. Booth, *A Rhetoric of Irony* (Chicago and London, 1974), pp. 120–23.

9. "Swift's Tory Anarchy," *Eighteenth-Century Studies* 3 (1969): 48–66. Said's interpretation is nearly ignored by Scouten and Hume, who direct their most virulent criticism against the most thoroughgoing Christian interpretation, that of Fischer.

10. " 'Verses on the Death of Dr. Swift,' " *Notes and Queries* 199 (1954): 474.

11. According to William King, one of Swift's friends in England to whom he entrusted the publication of the *Verses,* "I do not remember anything published in my time that hath been so universally well received as the Dean's last poem. Two editions have been already sold off, though two thousand were printed at first. In short, all people read it, all agree to commend it; and I have been well assured, the greatest enemies the Dean has in this country, allow it to be a just and a beautiful satire. . . . I have had the greatest pleasure in observing the success and general approbation which this poem hath met with" (*The Correspondence of Jonathan Swift,* ed. Harold Williams, 5 vols. [Oxford, 1963–65], 5:139).

12. The figures are taken arbitrarily from Scouten and Hume, "Pope and Swift," p. 207. For King's and Pope's uneasiness about the vanity of Swift's self-panegyric, see Swift's *Correspondence,* ed. Williams, 5:139, and *The Correspondence of Alexander Pope,* ed. George Sherburn, 5 vols. (Oxford, 1956), 4:130.

13. All quotations from the *Verses* are taken from *Swift: Poetical Works,* ed. Herbert Davis (London, 1967), pp. 496–513.

14. This appears to be the technique of the "reversible meaning" discussed briefly in my article "Toward an Anti-Aristotelian Poetic: Rochester's *Satyr against Mankind* and *Artemisia to Chloe,* with Notes on Swift's *Tale of a Tub* and *Gulliver's Travels,*" *Language and Style* 5 (1972): 123–45, especially p. 134. For a more extended discussion, see my essay "Divided Consciousness: The Trauma and Triumph of Restoration Culture," *Tennessee Studies in Literature* 22 (1977): 46–62.

15. A useful analogy is Jorge Luis Borges's well-known story "Borges and Myself."

16. Swift #2 functions something like the speaker of a prologue or epilogue in the contemporary theater—for example, Dryden's famous epilogue to *Tyrannick Love,* spoken by the "dead" Nell Gwyn. See my article "The Art of the Prologue and Epilogue: A New Approach Based on Dryden's Practice," *Genre* 5 (1972): 271–92, and also Mell, "Elegiac Design," p. 22–23.

17. "Verses," p. 515.

18. The earlier verse rendering of La Rochefoucauld's maxim is less precise:

In all Distresses of our Friends
We first consult our private Ends,
While Nature kindly bent to ease us,
Points out some Circumstance to please us.
[7–10]

Indeed, the second couplet, Christopher Ricks suggests, may conflate La Rochefoucauld with a song by George Granville ("Notes on Swift and Johnson," *Review of English Studies* n.s. 11 [1960]: 412–13). In the first couplet, the rhyme "Friends / private Ends" may be introduced here and repeated three times later (75–76, 331–32, 407–08) to question whether "Friends" are really motivated by conscious, deliberate "private Ends" or by less conscious, unformulated longings for a sense of "self." Thus, with the "Friends" who find satisfaction in the Dean's fatal illness and death, "it is hardly understood, / Which way my Death can do them good" (77–78). The Verses, as Waingrow says, "convey a subtle critique of friendship" (p. 515), a burlesque of the classical ideal of amicitia which was still widespread in early eighteenth-century England and which held special importance for Swift's friend Pope; see Maynard Mack, The Garden and the City: Retirement and Politics in the Later Poetry of Pope 1731–1743 (Toronto, 1969), pp. 30–32. The words friend, friends, and friendship occur 22 times in the Verses (exclusive of the motto), more than in any other poem by Swift.

19. Illuminating in this connection is Erving Goffman, Frame Analysis: An Essay on the Organization of Experience (Cambridge, Mass., 1974). The normal expectations surrounding friendship, dramatized in the Verses, are a good example of a Goffmanesque "frame," context, system of reference, or social matrix. Swift's peculiarity is that, for him, "identity" is defined through friction with a "frame" rather than by achieving harmony within it. At the end of the Verses, of course, the identity of Swift #3 expands absurdly to engross the entire "frame." Goffman's "frame analysis" seems to me peculiarly adaptable to other works by Swift such as Cadenus and Vanessa and A Modest Proposal.

20. "How to Die," p. 431.

21. These stances, I take it, include the deservedly successful poet pestered by favor-seekers (ll. 1–124), the naïf or ingénu (ll. 125 ff.), the vir bonus (ll. 261 ff.), and the satirist as hero (ll. 334 ff.). For my terminology I am indebted to Maynard Mack's well-known essay "The Muse of Satire," Yale Review 41 (1951): 80–92.

22. The Sin of Wit: Jonathan Swift as a Poet (Syracuse, N.Y., 1950), pp. 59–60.

23. "Verses," p. 514.

24. The fantasy framework operates in still another way to maintain focus upon the identity of the speaker, Swift #2. Although the onlookers feel they are duping "Swift" by making malicious remarks that he cannot hear, his fantasy dupes them instead by monitoring their compromising behavior, almost as if he had electronic "bugging" devices planted in appropriate locations in Dublin and London. His frame "contains" theirs. Also, just as "Swift's" envy of Pope, Gay, and Arbuthnot turned into a compliment to them, so now the nasty gossip of his friends, as Waingrow observes, turns into a compliment to him ("Verses," p. 516).

25. Technically there is further Goffmanesque "framing." A transcription of an actual conversation during a bridge game is given in Goffman, Frame Analysis, pp. 548–49.

26. The reminder that "Swift" is now "Remote from St. John, Pope, and Gay" (438; italics mine) contrasts with earlier references to Swift's close friendships with Pope, Gay, Arbuthnot, St. John, and Pulteney.

27. Other aspects of the chronology partake of absurdity. For example,

Swift #3 comes into being, like a butterfly out of a chrysalis, only after the "death" of Swift #2. Similarly, Swift #4 compiles his footnotes after the "death" of Swift #2 and in assumed independence of Swift #1.

28. "The Ironic Intention," p. 255.

29. Similarly ironical are the claims that Swift "Was never ill receiv'd at Court"; that (in spite of his faith in the Tory ministry under Queen Anne, described later in the *Verses*) "He follow'd *David*'s Lesson just, / *In Princes never put thy Trust*"; and that he "kept the Tenor of his Mind," endured "Exile with a steady Heart," and "Was chearful to his dying Day." In view of the universal selfishness associated elsewhere with the rhyme "Friends / private Ends," it is unconvincing that "Without regarding private Ends," Swift #3 "Spent all his Credit for his Friends."

30. *Fair Liberty Was All His Cry: A Tercentenary Tribute to Jonathan Swift 1667–1745,* ed. A. Norman Jeffares (London and New York, 1967).

31. "The Ironic Intention," p. 254.

32. "How to Die," p. 425.

33. "The Politics of Opposition," p. 248.

34. Terms denoting temporal finality are most prominent in the lines on the Tory ministry: "finding vain was *all* his Care," "Here ended *all* our golden Dreams," "Was *all* destroy'd by one Event," and (referring to Queen Anne's death) "Too soon that precious Life was ended, / On which *alone,* our Weal depended" (italics mine).

35. "Swift's Tory Anarchy," p. 51.

LILLIAN D. BLOOM

Addison's Popular Aesthetic:
The Rhetoric of the *Paradise Lost* Papers

Addison thought of his spectatorial aesthetic not as a science or system but as a judgmental whole. Yet this integrity has been fragmented by scholarly specialization. Within the last two generations the papers on wit and the "Essay on the Pleasures of the Imagination" have been almost isolated from their journalistic context and his other critical statements. Both have been written about and their sources traced: his study of the imagination has been especially applauded for its portent of a new literary sensibility. But the commentary on *Paradise Lost,* which precedes the "Essay" by only seven weeks, is often described as something apart, an impressionistic series of exclamations or the tag-end of baroque criticism.[1]

The sacrifice of the whole for the piece has uncovered details of truth, large and small, that contribute to our understanding of Addison the critic. What is overlooked through such sacrifice is that he wrote of taste, of literature and its affective delights in a periodical where the philosopher and wit sometimes turned good-natured gossip and more rarely a newsmonger. Here, in the *Spectator,* he achieved "a peculiar intimacy" with his more than three thousand daily readers.[2] As individuals, they fell short of an intellectual ideal; they had no deep understanding of the classical poets or knowledge that went beyond French and Italian critics to include those "Ancient and Modern who have written in either of the learned Languages" (S 291). His was, as he admitted, a popular audience, one fascinated by the jargon of literary trends and a literature of meteoric flash. Still he intimated confidence that he could rouse their artistic consciousness and quicken their expectancy of self. Some day, consequently, they would chat with profit about the best poetry and prose "in Clubs and Assemblies, at Tea-Tables, and in Coffee-Houses" (S 10). He had no other aim than to create men and women of "Polite Imagination."

Vicariously he knew all those who bought or borrowed the *Spectator*. They were busy members of the middle station who read on the run and, like the archetypal merchant Sir Andrew, blithely attributed an Ovidian quotation to Horace or Virgil. Others came from "the fashionable End of Town"—the moles, embryos, idols, and blanks of society—who fretted away their energy in a ditto of days without ideas or "right judgment." Whatever their class, they tended to be "Mob-Readers" self-victimized by a taste that was "extremely *Gothick.*" When they read, they looked to "nothing but the Husk and Rind of Wit, prefer[red] a Quibble, a Conceit, an Epigram, before solid Sense and elegant Expression" (*S* 62). These words are Dryden's, quoted by Addison not only to argue his position from authority but to shift the onus of responsibility if the scolding seemed too harsh for some. Still he never ignored the unreliability of an audience that scanned the miscellanies for poems like William Dingley's "Upon a Bee Entomb'd in Amber," a hodge-podge of nineteen metaphors, which smothered reason with imagistic exuberance and had "no manner of Influence, either for the bettering or enlarging the Mind of him who reads them."[3]

Confronted by this cultural opacity, Addison became a tutor of public taste who had to efface his didactic identity. His aesthetic could not be delivered as if from a schoolmaster's desk. It had to provoke "literary curiosity by gentle and unsuspected conveyance" and then to present its standards "in the most alluring form, not lofty and austere, but accessible and familiar." Despite its publication in separate sheets, his theory of art had a coherence consistent with the journal's thematic oneness and his own perspective. That is, he had "ingrafted into the *Spectator* many pieces that had laid by him in little hints and minutes, which he collected from time to time, ranged in order, and moulded into the form, in which they now appear: particularly the *Essays on Wit; The Pleasures of the Imagination; The Critique upon Milton;* and some others."[4] He himself was less concerned with when his aesthetic was formulated than with the possibility that its unity might not be realized. He therefore risked pointing it out as if through an act of shared memory. Just before he introduced his analysis of what delighted the imagination, he thought back to the week when as an *entertainer* he "endeavoured to detect several of those false kinds [of wit] which have been admir'd in the different Ages of the World; and . . . to shew wherein the nature of true wit consists." He reminded his readers that as an exercise in critical method he had shortly thereafter tested two ballads by epic rules to prove the imaginative strength "in a natural Simplicity of Thought" (*S* 409).

In that same essay he implied that such investigation became a lead-in to the center of his aesthetic, a lengthy perusal of *Paradise Lost* in which he had illustrated the poem's "just" sublimity and "particularized" most of those "rational and manly Beauties" characteristic of "that Divine Work." His public, to whose discernment he flatteringly appealed, could appreciate that once he had examined the individual accomplishment he was prepared to draw generalizations from it and follow the "Subject at large." The "Essay on the Pleasures of the Imagination" extended the papers on the epic, widened their focus, and predicated concepts that gave "a Beauty to many Passages of the finest Writers both in Prose and Verse." Before he concluded the "Essay," he likened the Miltonic poem to majestic architecture, "that particular Art, which has a more immediate Tendency, than any other, to produce those Primary Pleasures of the Imagination." He acknowledged the poet as one who, in mastering the genius of fancy, drew upon a gift that neared divine creativity. And in a series of rhetorical questions the essayist of the imagination set forth the vision of the fabulous storyteller: "What can be conceiv'd greater than the Battel of Angels, the Majesty of Messiah, the Stature and Behaviour of Satan and his Peers? What more beautiful than *Pandaemonium,* Paradise, Heaven, Angels, *Adam* and *Eve*? What more strange, than the Creation of the World, the several Metamorphoses of the fallen Angels, and the surprising Adventures their Leader meets with in his Search after Paradise?"[5]

Addison's aesthetic is threaded on a single string with both ends knotted together. And why not, he had earlier hinted, for as one idea fostered another, it became "very hard for the Mind to disengage it self from a Subject in which it has been long employed" (*S* 63). Even while he reacted strongly against literary shoddiness, he was moved by a counterimpulse to literary greatness. He thus undertook his study of Milton's epic, which since its publication had sold more than twelve thousand copies and was judged magnificent by such modish critics as Roscommon and Dryden—even by "sower undistinguishing" Dennis.[6] Through foresight or serendipity Addison placed the eighteen Saturday essays on *Paradise Lost* about midway through the *Spectator.* And on eighteen Saturdays he proved that the artistic experience paral-

leled a humane quest for excellence. Never before or after did he ex-
pend so much time and space on a literary theme. Yet he was neither
quixotic nor profligate of his own effort and interests. He knew that
the poem had provoked consistent admiration often quite separate
from understanding. In 1699, for instance, John Hopkins did a rhymed
imitation of several books as a gloss for ladies who found the poem too
arduous for concentrated reading. More significantly, Addison was
sensitive to the successful gamble of his friend-publisher Jacob Tonson, the elder. After printing three folio editions of the heroic poem for
the gentry and nobility between 1688 and 1695, the bookseller determined to make the work accessible in relatively inexpensive and
ever-diminishing formats, to open a new market for it. The 1711 edition appeared in duodecimo, precisely the little book handily stored in
pocket or reticule and ready for scrutiny in random moments. With no
feeling of risk, then, Addison wagered modestly with himself that
anyone of common sense and good nature could respond pleasurably
to the narrative or the "plain literal" meaning of *Paradise Lost*.[7]

He therefore planned an approach to the poem that, while often
using familiar critical language and authority, skirted intellectual rigor
and instead elicited the delights of the imagination, which "have this
Advantage above those of the Understanding, that they are more obvious, and more easie to be acquired." He and his audience mutually
benefited from such an approach: for the imagination, when once
stimulated by the poet's "Invention" and the journalist's muted coach-
ing, had a momentum of its own, as inevitable as life and in fact de-
veloping from it. Addison intended that each should react to the poem
according to his capacity, sketch for himself scene and picture, form
new worlds wherein charms and terrors not visible in the universe
excited aesthetic satisfaction as well as moral security. An antidote to
the pleasures of vice and folly, those of the imagination were happy
therapy, "like a gentle Exercise to the Faculties, awaken[ing] them
from Sloth and Idleness, without putting them upon any Labour or
Difficulty" (*S* 411). Few of the spectatorial faithful could withstand
such enticement, the lure of joy and wholesomeness without effort.

Not only did Addison have an approach that worked and eased his
task, but time was on his side. A seasoned empiricist, he believed that
"Delight in any particular Study" increased proportionately to the
"Application" given it. As week after week he described the worth of
Paradise Lost, he expected an appreciation of enduring literature to in-

crease, even to become habitual for some. Aware that the first few papers might grate as a lesson, he was also convinced that successive numbers would satisfy as an "Entertainment" (*S* 447). He was right. Not many papers on the Miltonic epic had been printed before beaux and coquettes, merchants or their wives, country squires visiting in town, were buying the Saturday issues with agreeable regularity. What is more to the point, he helped them and subsequent generations to enjoy the poem. As early as 1714 it was conceded sardonically that "Mr. A——n has discovered a Multitude of Beauties in *Milton's* Paradise lost, several of which might perhaps have been undiscovered for many ages." By 1753, according to Theophilus Cibber, "it had become unfashionable not to have read" the poem, and Addison had played not a singular but a major role in this community of taste. For one who had immediate deadlines to meet, he was probably indifferent to what lay beyond the *Spectator's* here and now. The fact remains that some twenty-five years after Cibber, Johnson praised the essayist who "by the blandishments of gentleness and facility . . . has made Milton an universal favourite, with whom readers of every class think it necessary to be pleased."[8]

Certainly unspoiled by pedantry, Addison's learning was ordered and honed by journalistic utility. His critical arguments were consciously provocative; his standards—flexible in spirit and practice—were clarified as much through illustrative and anecdotal material as through seemingly casual explanation. There was never an invisible speaker or unidentifiable magisterial presence in the papers on *Paradise Lost;* the tone was personal. Sometimes he wrote in the familiar first person singular; at other times he used the pronoun *we* with the expansiveness of a confidant. Whichever the pronoun, he hoped for a dialogue. "I shall not . . . presume," he declared, "to impose upon others my own particular Judgment on this Author, but only deliver it as my private opinion" (*S* 262). He was willing to take on predecessors from Aristotle to Dryden, who discoursed on the epic as a genre. And to heighten the immediacy of any debate, he invited challenge from his readers.[9] No matter what the quarrel, however, or who the opponent, he managed always to intimate his modesty and Milton's accomplishment. He thus conceded that his commentary on *Paradise Lost* was not definitive and he "question[ed] not, but any Writer, who shall treat of this Subject after me, may find several Beauties in [it], which I have not taken notice of" (*S* 321). A part of the rhetorician's art, his humility was nonetheless restrained and hence credible. It provided everyone with a momentary delusion of equality; each had a right to hold critical opinions and to have them heard.

The essays on *Paradise Lost* are panegyrical, Addison making sure that the quality of praise was supported by a long poetic tradition and less expectedly by pertinent discoveries of "the most common and ordinary Systems of Arts and Sciences" (*S* 291). It never occurred to him to camouflage his eclecticism, for unless he was wide-ranging in what he borrowed he could never have fulfilled his editorial function. Had he settled on a single critical or philosophical scheme, he would have thwarted his "Enquiry after Truth" and negated his promise to set forth an image of a world in which the imagination goaded the intelligence and sensory impression led to the "fixt and immutable" ideal. His was a drive "to Cultivate and Polish Human Life, by promoting Virtue and Knowledge, and by recommending whatsoever may be Useful or Ornamental to Society."[10] And he deemed it an irreversible truth that *whatsoever* could be discussed only when *whosoever* and their work were absorbed into one's intellectual being. If a few contradictions surfaced in his nonsystem, so be it. They were not overly important to him or even apparent to those who followed his comments over weeks and months.

His syncretism also sprang from a definition of the "judicious and formidable Critick." If his prototype were suddenly deprived of generosity and discretion, of a "good Insight into all the Parts of Learning," he would at that instant be metamorphosed into "an Illiterate heavy Writer" and a hobby-horsical dogmatist. But, as Addison conceded, all critics were fated to err, even Aristotle, whose remarks were trapped by time and unable "to square exactly with the Heroic Poems" written since his death. In his appreciation of Milton he tried to escape some of the barriers of self and historical identity through the use of a multiple voice. "I . . . have taken the Liberty sometimes to join with one [critic]," he wrote, "and sometimes with another, and sometimes to differ from all of them, when I have thought that the Reason of the Thing was on my Side." His papers "irradiated" a paradoxical sense of assurance and engaging hesitation but above all a curiosity that defied resistance. "The Mind of Man naturally hates every thing that looks like a Restraint upon it," and Addison was sure that no honest search could end in nothing. The Keatsian confession that "there is not a fiercer hell than the failure in a great object" would have been alien to his ethos.[11]

II

Addison wrote about *Paradise Lost* for many reasons. It had long been admired by his patron, Lord Somers, who sought its popularity almost as a cause; it had become virtually a Tonson publication and it was well on the way to being regarded as a Whig document.[12] The spectatorial critic would not have belittled these practicalities. Ultimately, however, he wrote about the poem because it moved him deeply. And like any epic, it virtually taught itself. Its many episodes and allegories built upon biblical account "insinuated" their devotional meaning "imperceptibly." This is the way he would have it. Tempted as he admittedly was to explicate Milton's "infinite Allusions to places of Scripture," he disciplined his religious bent and noted only "such as are of a Poetical Nature, and which are Woven with great Beauty into the Body of his Fable" (*S* 357). Had he done otherwise, he might have estranged those who resented being sermonized. He might have left himself open to offenses he identified: to the charge of blue-nosed condescension or the guilt "of Presumption and Impertinence." He therefore encouraged his readers to study the poem—possibly a book a week—and share in the discussion, for "the Mind is never so much pleased, as when she exerts her self in any Action that gives her an Idea of her own Perfections and Abilities" (*S* 512). Whatever else his examination of the Miltonic epic accomplished, it would persuade his readers of their sensitivity and good taste.

That he was always responsive to them is a journalistic fact. If he appeared reticent about the way in which his critical method worked, he did disclose its essential details in carefully scattered essays. He seemed able to intuit just how many abstract ideas could be handled and when. From an overview of the *Spectator* we now know that his aesthetic depended upon a process of both partition and reconstitution. Momentarily, that is, the ethical tenor was isolated from structure, but only momentarily, for the ethical was in fact organically bound to the poetic design. He allowed no substantive division between the fictional-imaginative and the didactic-moralistic. When, for example, he interpreted the end of *Paradise Lost,* he pointed out that the dialogue of Adam and the Arch-Angel was "full of Moral and Instructive Sentiments." He did not enumerate them; most were evident in the lines he quoted that described Eve's sleep "and the effects it had in quieting the Disorders of her Mind." Because he had long urged a sympathetic association with the fallen Adam and Eve, he converted the portrait of the "Mother of Mankind," her misery eased by resignation and hope, not into a series of maxims but into a statement of the human predicament from which all drew "the same kind of Consolation." Each reader gained a further reward as soon as he imaged Eve's beauty and translated an artistic emotion into a "Secret Pleasure and Satisfaction" (S 369).

Addison's sense of an audience also meant that he had to second-guess, to move and be moved by shifting preferences and fickle loyalties. Intermittently over a period of four and a half months he promoted *Paradise Lost* as a poem that provided an affective experience of near-infinite variety. Alert to the possibility of overstating his enthusiasm for the poem and so dissipating his persuasive energy, he agreed that like any work of art it was not perfect and he had no choice but to "remark the several Defects which appear in the Fable, the Characters, the Sentiments, and the Language." Even as he promised candor, he asked for "pardon" and permission to "alledge at the same time whatever may be said for the Extenuation of such Defects" (S 297). There is throughout the Milton papers a running series of debates on several levels of rhetorical intensity: Addison in argument with other critics, Addison with himself, Addison with his audience. The give-and-take of discourse shaped his commentary.

Occasionally he assumed a John Bullish stance, invoked both God and country, extolled *Paradise Lost* as an epic "look'd upon, by the best Judges, as the greatest Production, or at least the noblest Work of Genius in our Language, and therefore deserves to be set before an English *Reader in its full Beauty"* (S 321). And its author, happily born in the right country, was also a Christian whose ideas and language were culled from "the Books of the most Orthodox Divines" and the Bible. Because Addison considered other biographical details irrelevant to his exegesis and potentially abrasive, he suppressed them. Almost by way of compensation he turned the poem's religious exaltation into an aesthetic good. Moreover, he deferred to the vogue of the Christian epic in England and the popularity of declamations like Dr. Felton's that Milton "oweth his Superiority over *Homer* and *Virgil* . . . to the Scriptures."[13] In endorsing the commonplace whenever and wherever it appeared, Addison moderated its assertiveness, added his usual politeness, and then avowed "without derogating from those wonderful Performances [of the Greek and Roman poets], that there is an

Indisputable and Unquestioned Magnificence in every part of *Paradise Lost,* and indeed a much greater than could have been formed upon any Pagan System" (*S* 267).

Such appeals, as he knew, guaranteed only temporary allegiance. His arguments, those on which he depended, had to do several things at once: they had to clarify elementary difficulties and illustrate the poem's greatness, its novelty and beauty, all those qualities that aroused one's passion and imagination; they had to correct the well-known misinterpretations of Dryden and Dennis, who had fallen into the Satanist fallacy; they had to give perspective to the description of Milton as one "quite upon the Wings," a hyperbolic image that overemphasized—at least for the unsophisticated—the poet's rapture and minimized his control.[14] When Addison began *Spectator* 267, the first of the *Paradise Lost* essays, he immediately set the poem's importance where the poet had set it, as an epic that dramatized the story of redemptive hope for fallen man. His task as *amicus poetae* was never easy; it was to prove more painful, certainly longer lasting than he had anticipated. To satisfy its demands, particularly in the first six essays, he often drew lightly upon authority; that is, he gave the English epic a patina of its own by measuring it against classical models and bolstered his judgments with those of critics beyond usual reproach.

Authority was his synonym for the rules that he treated with tough-minded discrimination. They came to him in part from the critics on heroic poetry: Aristotle and Longinus, Le Bossu, Chapelain, and the two Daciers, Dryden and Dennis. But more compelling to Addison than any dicta-maker was the classical epic—especially the *Aeneid*—"from [which] the justest Rules of this Art are rather to be taken, then from the Dry Precepts of the Critics."[15] He never denied the validity of the rules, deeming them a tribute to the long chain of artistic endeavor and man's rational evaluation of that effort. Within their ambience, the essayist nevertheless granted himself the right of freedom judiciously if emphatically exercised. By the fifth of the *Paradise Lost* sheets, he concluded with "*Longinus,* that the Productions of a great Genius, with many Lapses and Inadvertencies, are infinitely preferable to the Works of an inferior kind of Author, which are scrupulously exact and conformable to all the Rules of correct Writing" (*S* 291).

He sometimes challenged authority, involved himself in controversies that he chose to highlight. Those on the periphery of battle—his public—were attracted to verbal skirmishes and became participants fearless of defeat. He further enjoyed performing as a debater who exhibited insouciance and gentlemanly verve. He initiated his study of Milton with Dryden unnamed but pinned to the paper by a sharpened quill.[16] "I shall wave the Discussion of that Point which was started some Years since, Whether . . . *Paradise Lost* may be called an *Heroick Poem*. Those who will not give it that Title, may call it (if they please) a *Divine Poem*" (S 267). He won a debate with a single phrase that first defined the action of the English epic and then carried his audience from a stock term connoting superiority to one suggesting the superlative. Irritated by arguments "that turn chiefly upon Words," he beat Dryden at his own quibble.

In the same essay Addison again evinced his derring-do. Many of the French critics had quarrelled among themselves over the duration of a heroic action. Even in its time the fatuity of the debate was apparent to some: Dryden, for example, found it "of no more concernment to the common reader, than it is to a ploughman, whether February this year had 28 or 29 days in it." More tactful than Dryden, Addison did not dismiss the debate. He argued instead that Milton's poem had a series of settings lying "out of the reach of the Sun and the Sphere of Day," that any attempt therefore to calculate time had to be "more curious than instructive."[17] Ridiculing pedantic addiction to trifles, he smiled the quarrel into oblivion. And his audience, still suspicious of spectatorial intention in the *Paradise Lost* papers, had to admit that a point was scored against every schoolmaster under whose fussiness they once squirmed.

There were other quarrels of varying consequence. He handled them all with a decorous mixture of dispatch and mild seriousness. But those that seemed to threaten—or to hamstring—his interpretation he saved for the last essay on the heroic poem. Of the two problems at issue, he refuted Le Bossu's assumption that the "Epic Writer first of all pitches upon a certain Moral, as the Groundwork and Foundation of his Poem, and afterwards finds out a Story to it." Had Addison tried to moderate this statement, he would have become entangled in hairsplitting over priorities and authorial purpose; his work for eighteen weeks would have ended irresolutely. Nor did he accept the Frenchman's related proposition that the epic was built on a single moral precept. Addison spoke directly to the constant readers of the *Spectator* and again apologized for "not find[ing] out the particular Moral which is inculcated in *Paradise Lost.*"[18] After so many months of analysis both he and they refused to attribute anything simplistic to the poem. While he underscored the theme of obedience to divine order—a theme applicable to social conduct—he implied that this was perhaps special pleading. With easy grace he conceded that no heroic poem could survive unless it possessed a "Soul," a core of moral values that had gained universal consent.

His attitude toward most debates spanned rhetorical polarities: at times the debate itself became a device, encouraging involvement in the poem as a poem; at other times it hinted a need to stay free of scholarly cruces external to the literary achievement. It was not that he thought these problems unimportant; he simply preferred to put first things first. He checked his own interest in recondite detail—a listing of Milton's literal translations from classical poetry—because he "would not break the Thread of these Speculations" to introduce "such Reflections as would be of no use but to the Learned" (*S* 321). And while he namedropped, he curtailed his dependence upon another's critical opinion. Throughout his commentary—and with visible assurance after the sixth essay—he urged the enjoyment of a creative experience in which the unfamiliar was made known and the familiar sustained new depths of meaning. Impelled by a controlled idealism, he believed that such an experience transformed not merely the person but reality as well. Specifically, when one reacted with "Pleasure" to "the Perusal of noble Work," then "something" happened. The "something" gave "Greatness of Mind to the Reader," who then moved step by step to a percipience of divinity. Through such movement, inseparable from desire, the individual and his world are forever altered: his spirit is refined by altruistic ambition, nourished by hope of eternity, and brought to its "last, adequate, and proper Happiness."[19]

III

Addison's hope for his audience was adjusted to who they were and what they wanted. If they did not enjoy their reading, then his efforts and even their casual good will were wasted. He therefore demonstrated *Paradise Lost*'s many pleasures by concentrating on its fiction. He knew the delight of hearing a story retold, particularly one whose scriptural starkness was now clothed in language and metaphor "both Perspicuous and Sublime." He also recognized the relish of meeting characters, motivated and active, who before had been names only. He understood the attraction of an emotional treat, one that evoked as many feelings as the psyche comfortably afforded. The pleasures of the imagination would appear largely through the fiction, for the fancy "takes the Hint" and leads it to unexpected places of joy and passion (S 417). His followers would respond because they had little alternative, and he would delicately attune their reactions to the epic's "Matter."

He often mentioned the term *fiction* but stopped short of definition, which, he sensed, would become a trap of convoluted hypotheses, a strain on patience, and an interruption of his own narrative that paced itself with the poem's. He related the word to Milton's power of imagination that conceived anew "the whole System of the intellectual World; the *Chaos,* and the Creation; Heaven, Earth and Hell," and all the warring inhabitants thereof.[20] But Addison saved this description of epic sweep for the halfway point in his series of essays. At that time he assumed his audience was able to envision a vastness beyond sight and to derive satisfaction from a fancy that extended itself "by Degrees" from the individual mind of which it was a part to the world itself and then to "the Infinite Space that is every where diffused about it" (S 420). Indeed, Addison understood that *greatness,* whether as a metaphor or a concept, often escaped ordinary perception; he therefore presented the word and various of its connotations slowly, by hint and uncomplicated statement. In his first paper on *Paradise Lost,* he acknowledged the sublimity of the poem's subject but rendered it manageable through reduction: by virtue of journalistic license it became an exciting conflict, an action of cosmic violence that remained plausible.

Even so, in this same crucial essay, he guarded against losing any partisans reluctant to venture far, even imaginatively. He promised them that the epic's plot, uncluttered by troublesome minutiae, provided an entertainment "of the greatest Simplicity; uniform in its Nature, tho' diversified in the Execution." As if he questioned his own argument, he again appealed to them, this time as devotees of the theater. Eager to give the heroic poem a structural parallel that was at once familiar and presumptive evidence of dramatic flair, he likened it to *The Spanish Friar.* Just as Dryden in his tragedy had "two different

Plots look like Counterparts and Copies of one another," so Milton complemented the theme of man's fall with "the Fall of those Angels who are his Professed Enemies." Addison became a Pied Piper, his stragglers lured forward not by music but by a pledge to share with them the best "Story [he] ever met with."

In almost every paper he introduced allusions to Milton's inventive power. Often he elaborated on them; sometimes he left them as mere intimations. Whatever the method, he gradually unfolded the intricacies of the fiction, invited popular participation in its action, and whipped up admiration and astonishment. The poet, he early emphasized, was fenced in by a paucity of scriptural information and a concomitant need to exercise "Caution in every thing he added" to material sanctified by religious tradition. Against all predictable odds he triumphed, filling "his Story with so many surprising Incidents, which bear so close Analogy with what is delivered in Holy Writ, that it is capable of pleasing the most delicate Reader, without giving Offense to the most scrupulous" (S 267). With a single sentence Addison flattered those who assumed literary sensibility even as he salved the worries of both Anglican enthusiast and professional doubter. Just three papers before the end of his study, he explained the effect of the narrative on an audience now so caught up in it that they wished neither to find fault nor disbelieve. More than a "Comment upon sacred Writ," the action appeared to be "a full and compleat Relation of what the other is only an Epitome" (S 351). The *Spectator*'s pronouncement, which meant to set up a startling contrast, nevertheless served rational belief and vindicated a literary truth. Through talismanic invention Milton had made "probable" a biblical account of miracles, had converted myth or articles of faith into acceptable piety, and brought reader, Christian, scoffer, or any combination thereof—each in his own way and at his own pace—to a sense of divine presence.

In the introductory essays to *Paradise Lost,* Addison wrote first of action and then of characterization, basing his order overtly on Aristotelian precedent and tacitly on a journalistic cunning that acknowledged the interest of people in people. He could not contradict the truth that the actors in the English epic were fewer in number and variety than those in the *Iliad* and the *Aeneid.* He therefore did what he was customarily to do whenever he found a Miltonic deficiency. He sought an "Extenuation" and asserted a dimension in the poet's portraiture absent in classical models. His "Characters, most of them, lie

out of Nature, and were to be formed purely by his own Invention."
But Addison offered no clue to the meaning of this statement, one
whose aesthetic idea was innovative and perhaps open to controversy.
Instead he invoked unimpeachable native authority for analogical
proof. "It shews a greater Genius in *Shakespear* to have drawn his *Caly-
ban*, than his *Hotspur* or *Julius Caesar*"; the first was a creature of dramatic imagination, "whereas the other might have been formed upon
Tradition, History, and Observation" (*S* 279). Within the cir-
cumscribed space of three "distinct Sheets," the essayist had his public
appreciate that Milton's images of Satan and the Christ, of Adam and
Eve before the Fall, were poetically elusive, their bodies and voices
derived from no visible or existent materials. Yet there they were
within the poem, at once believable and exalted, testifying to a creative
genius that rivalled Shakespeare's. The achievement was Milton's; the
amalgam of rhetoric and critical intelligence Addison's; the sudden
wonder belonged to those who read *Paradise Lost* and its spectatorial
appreciation.

Addison relied on a process of foreshortening to fix his disciples'
relationship to the four dominant characters in the poem. The process
was analytically sound, dangerous only in its view of Satan. The critic
knew that his difficulties were compounded by the poem itself, that the
first two books alone dramatized Satan at the height of his new
majesty and in the guise of a leader who seemed morally invincible
even in defeat. Because anyone might well be ensnared by such magnificence, Addison with simple directness drew the most fallen of
angels as an antagonist involved in a futile struggle against omnipotence and a humanity capable of admitting that anguish "for Truth's
sake / is fortitude to highest victory." Within so direct a presentation
there was yet room to emphasize the contradictions in the satanic personality. By virtue of his angelic heritage and the scope of his destructive design, he was both sublime and "big with absurdity." He possessed "a superior Greatness" counterbalanced by a "Mock-Majesty."[21]
His very spirituality was his depravity. Out of the *Spectator*'s canvas of
words there emerged a figure rapt in thought yet encumbered by absolute ignorance, immersed in activity while figuratively held in a vise.

Intrigued by these paradoxes that formed the portrait, Addison
nevertheless yielded to the exigency of time and space. He therefore
limited his enthusiasm, brushed on the strokes cleanly and lightly. The
spectatorial interpretation, at one with the poet's, was unmistakable:

there was beauty that enticed with evil just as there was radiant vitality that gloried in malevolence and a wanton refusal to obey. Satan's whole role was "very apt to raise and terrifie the Reader's Imagination." That is, the Addisonian assembly dared not blink away their sinfulness and its secret cause. At the same time, however, their terror was mitigated by delight, for the primary emotion was built on the expected defeat of the villain seen "chewing Ashes, groveling in the Dust, and loaden with Supernumerary Pains and Torments" (S 369). With this last ironic picture of demonic energy "miserable in the height of [its] Triumphs," the Christian critic joined his readers to gloat over the serpent's loathesomeness, and together they experienced joy from their disgust.[22]

If Addison lingered as long as he could over the details that animated the satanic figure, he condensed his discussion of the Christ. He had to establish him as the hero of *Paradise Lost* while conceding the inadequacy of the term *hero* to delineate messianic behavior. He therefore focused on his role as savior, his love and creative sociability, at once equatable with the best in man and far surpassing it. Apparently as awed as the poet by the divine character, Addison could do little to describe him as an actor until the sixth book, where "the Author's Imagination was so inflamed with this great Scene of Action, that wherever he speaks of it, he rises, if possible, above himself" (S 333). This statement said little; it merely supposed that any image of the war in heaven, when it came, would happen beyond the sound or sight of the critic's words. What the statement did provide was a signal to those who had followed the Saturday issues of the *Spectator* for twelve weeks. They could now feel justly liberated from all that was "little or trivial." Ready for a multitude of pleasures, they read Milton's similes of bellicose horror, participated in his many "uncommon" inventions, and replied with emotions that ran a course from astonishment to fear. Still their reactions required a control no more heard than a whisper, and so their guide casually mentioned those kaleidoscopic events for which they were to watch: the varied contests on succeeding days; angelic force rendered maniacal; and finally the arrival of the Messiah who chose not to win a war but to end it.

Respecting the near-mystical intensity of these battle descriptions, Addison was more intimately engaged by Milton's portrayal of the Christ as the agent of creation and stunned by a poetic talent that evolved the seventh book from such hints as the Pauline "By Him were all things created . . . visible and invisible." Always the journalist, he fretted about his explication of this book, if only because he was unable to predict how his readers would take to "Loftiness in Sentiments," where there is no passion, no "Tumult or Agitation." He therefore button-holed each of them in a dialogue about greatness that aroused a sense of transcendent serenity. He called upon Longinus, whom he cited, and he used the metaphor of the ocean, its vastness in contrary states of storm and tranquillity. The dialogue, however, soon became a judgment pronounced by one voice, which asserted that there was nothing "in the whole Poem more Sublime than the Description" of the Messiah "drawing the first Outline of the Creation" (S 339). But once again, authority, imagery, and assertion could carry Addison just so far. Ultimately he had to rely upon the individual imagination for any visualization of emergent harmony and a subsequent quiet that suffused the soul.

Of all the figures in *Paradise Lost,* Adam and Eve came closest to reflecting an ethic—domestic and spiritual—that was identifiable in human terms. Addison, for example, made the ancestral claim that the pair were real and symbolic, the "Progenitors" and "Representatives" of all mankind. Their spectatorial descendants were to see "four distinct Characters in these two Persons": man and woman "in the highest Innocence and Perfection, and in the most abject State of Guilt and Infirmity" (S 273). With this *peripeteia* in mind, Addison began very early to direct the emotions of a theater-oriented society. He pressed their enjoyment of a dramatic spectacle, the newness and splendor of the edenic Adam and Eve. Simultaneously he foreshadowed their weakness and fall. He was nonetheless conscious that two long generations and a revolution of values separated the poet from the commentator, severe "Presbytery" from Latitudinarian Anglicanism. Deliberately or not, he eased the rigor of Milton's judgment that the man and woman "manifold in sin deserv'd to fall."[24] He thus interpreted them as household characters in a tragedy that appealed not to stern intellectuality but to the heartstrings. In the periodical Adam became a too-loving husband who, finding his wife "irrecoverably lost," wished "to perish with her, rather than to live without her" (S 351). Adam's was a gallant sin and thereby Addison rationalized the mood of his audience. "Every one," he agreed, "is apt to excuse a Fault which he himself might have fallen into" (S 357).

His exoneration of the repentant Adam arose less from Milton's poem than from his vision of a world wherein people are morally feeble, behavior unpredictable, and happiness a fugitive possibility beyond general expectation. It arose too from his communion with a group of people who needed to undergo "the most melting Passions of Humanity and Commiseration" for the afflicted couple (*S* 357). Having participated in the Fall through poetry and commentary, they had earned the right to indulge in pity with all its restorative pleasures. For this emotion, as the journal had hinted and would later explain, was a "pleasing Anguish, as well as generous Sympathy, that knits Mankind together, and blends them in the same common Lot" (*S* 397). In fact, their pity became tinged with selfless love when through an act of imagination they pictured themselves alongside the new "*Adam* triumphant in the height of Misery" (*S* 369).

Inevitably the *Paradise Lost* papers became not merely a literary entertainment but an unvoiced call to piety; "the curious . . . [were] to Devotion happily betray'd."[25] Such was Addison's private intention for eighteen Saturdays, the day on which he usually wrote of man linked one to another by charity and redeemed from viciousness through industry and God's grace.

NOTES

1. The tradition—early expressed by Samuel Monk and H. T. Swedenberg—is reaffirmed by Ernest Tuveson in *The Imagination as a Means of Grace* (Berkeley and Los Angeles, 1960), p. 92. Others, however, have argued for or illustrated coherence in Addison's criticism: Clarence D. Thorpe, "Addison's Contribution to Criticism," in *The Seventeenth Century: Studies in the History of English Thought from Bacon to Pope, by Richard Foster Jones and Others Writing in his Honor* (Stanford, 1951), pp. 321, et passim; Jean Wilkinson, "Some Aspects of Addison's Philosophy of Art," *Huntington Library Quarterly* 28 (Nov. 1964): 31–44; John Timmerman, "Divinity and Creativity: The Aesthetic Framework of Joseph Addison," *University of Dayton Review* 8 (Fall 1971): 17–28.

2. Leigh Hunt, "The Literary and Philosophical Examiner," in *The Examiner* (10 Jan. 1808); William Hazlitt, "On the Periodical Essayists," in *Lectures on the English Comic Writers* (London, 1841). For the circulation figures of the *Spectator,* see Donald F. Bond's edition (Oxford, 1965), 1: xxv–xxix. (All references to the *Spectator* are from this edition.)

3. For Sir Andrew on the authorship of classical aphorisms, see *S* 549, and for Addison once more on Gothic taste, *S* 409. "Dedication of the *Aeneis,*" in *Essays of John Dryden,* ed. W. P. Ker (Oxford, 1900), 2:223. (All Dryden references are from this edition.)

4. The description of Addison's talent to pique literary curiosity is Johnson's in *Lives of the English Poets,* ed. George Birkbeck Hill (Oxford, 1905), 2:146. For the premise that these critical essays were roughed out prior to the composition of the *Spectator,* see, e.g., "The Life of Joseph Addison," in *A General Dictionary, Historical and Critical* (London, 1734), 1:249; N. Ogle's biographical preface to the periodical (London, 1827), pp. xxxv–xxxvi; and Henry Montgomery, *Memoirs of the Life and Writings of Sir R. Steele* (Edinburgh, 1865), 1, pt. 2, 299.

5. *S* 415, 417. For the God-like nature of poetic imagination and the talent of "that one Man," see *S* 421 and a holograph fragment of the "Essay," Houghton Library, Harvard University, Eng. Mss. 772, ff. 21–23. Addison's essays on wit comprise nos. 58–63; on ballads, nos. 70, 74; on the imagination, nos. 411–21.

6. Wentworth Dillon, Earl of Roscommon, *An Essay on Translated Verse* (1684). Dryden, "The Author's Apology for Heroic Poetry and Poetic Licence" (1677), 1: 178 ff.; and "A Discourse concerning the Original and Progress of Satire" (1693), 2: 28–30. John Dennis, "The Grounds of Criticism in Poetry" (1704), in *The Critical Works of John Dennis,* ed. E. N. Hooker (Baltimore, 1939), 1: 333–34, et passim. (Addison's allusion to Dennis appears in *S* 291.) For Milton criticism prior to Addison, see *Milton, The Critical Heritage,* ed. John T. Shawcross (London, 1970), vol. 1.

7. By 1762 the publishing world knew what Addison (probably at Tonson's urging) had planned, i.e., a series of papers directed at those whose pocket was "so agreeably filled" with the "smaller editions of *Milton's* Works" (*A Familiar Explanation of the Poetical Works of Milton to which is prefixed Mr. Addison's Criticism on Paradise Lost.* With a Preface by the Rev. Mr. Dodd, pp. iii–iv).

8. Richard Fiddes, *A Prefatory Epistle concerning some Remarks to be published on Homer's Iliad* (London, 1714), pp. 12, 13; Cibber's *Lives of the Poets* (London, 1753), 5:196n.; Johnson, *Lives,* 2:147.

9. He wished to have his readers question his evaluation of the Sin-Death episodes (*S* 273) and the propriety of Milton's language (*S* 285).

10. See his dedication to Lord Somers, in the *Spectator,* 5: 174.

11. *S* 273, 291, 321, 412; "Preface" to *Endymion* (1818).

12. Thomas Newton in the "Dedication" to his three-volume edition of *Paradise Lost* (1749) described "Lord Sommers, as a great admirer and encourager of this work." The seventh, eighth, and ninth editions of the epic were dedicated by Tonson to Lord Somers who had pushed for and subscribed to the publication of the expensive fourth. Newton, again in his "Dedication," indicated that the poem had always been associated with those who act "upon the true Whig principles."

13. Henry Felton, *A Dissertation on Reading the Classics, and Forming a Just*

Style ([1709], 1713), 2d ed. (London, 1715), p. 113; also Dennis, *Critical Works,* 1:363–73. For the popularity of the Christian epic in England, see H. T. Swedenberg, *The Theory of the Epic in England 1650–1800* (Berkeley and Los Angeles, 1944), pp. 24–25, 63–64.

14. *S* 333; Dennis, *Critical Works,* 1: 342. For Dryden on Milton's hero, see "Dedication of the *Aeneis,*" 2: 165; Dennis, 1: 334.

15. *A Dissertation upon the Roman Poets,* trans. Christopher Hayes (London, 1718), p. 27.

16. "A Discourse . . . of Satire," 2: 29.

17. Addison restated his position in *S* 369; Dryden, "Dedication of the *Aeneis,*" 2: 204. For a summary of the French position, see René Le Bossu, *Treatise of the Epick Poem,* trans. W. J. (London, 1695), bk. 2, chap. 18; bk. 3, chap. 12.

18. *S* 369; Le Bossu, *Treatise,* bk. 1, chap. 7.

19. *S* 409, 413.

20. *S* 315.

21. *Paradise Lost,* 12: 569–70; *S* 303, 309.

22. *S* 412; for the satanic role, see *S* 303.

23. *S* 580.

24. *Paradise Lost,* 10: 16.

25. Edward Cobden, *A Poem on the Death of the Right Honourable Joseph Addison, Esq* (London, 1720), p. 17.

ARTHUR W. HOFFMAN

Allusions and the Definition of Themes in Congreve's *Love for Love*

Examining the themes of a Congreve play and pursuing the allusions which give range and definition to the themes, one can approach an understanding of where this author's locus of values is and something of how he arrived at that place. The biographical image of Congreve is, of course, important, and that image has been revised and sharpened over the past several decades. The major features of this image still need to be more widely known, as do some incidental features which contribute to an index of the man: the range of his reading and the caliber of his knowledge of Greek and Roman literature; the pain and patience of his unusually early and protracted struggle with cataracts and blindness; the true intent and meaning of his carefully drawn will. Beyond biography, however, Congreve has expressed himself in and committed his ethos to his works.

The reader of *Love for Love* may expect to find the annotation at times defective or inaccurate, largely, one supposes, because the play has not been pored over by legions of editors. It is a relief that there is not a commentary of biblical dimensions to deal with, but, on the other hand, obvious errors remain enshrined, awaiting only an editor who will read the text of the play attentively for their surgical and definitive removal. In the second act, for example, Sir Sampson delivers himself of a Latin maxim, and all editors who annotate the passage concur in an erroneous translation which misrepresents Sir Sampson as reverentially submissive to astrological lore and to the disposition of stars and planets. Actually Sir Sampson's Latin tag asserts that the wise man will rule over the stars.

Critics do not seem to have misread the plot of *Love for Love* as many of them have the much more intricate plot of *The Way of the World,* but they do seem to have slipped into a curious distortion of emphasis in talking about the structure and major motifs of the play. Among other things, the play is about Valentine Legend's courtship of Angelica and the terms on which he finally wins her, but the proportions of the story are cast very differently from the proportions assigned to Mirabell's pursuit of Millamant in *The Way of the World*. The two plays *are* alike in act 1; Angelica is not onstage nor is Millamant. In act 2, Angelica does appear, but Valentine comes on after she has left. There is no encounter between the two until the third act. Valentine and Angelica come onstage together in the third act. Scandal enters with them and has an important part of the conversation that ensues. When Valentine's brother Ben appears, Valentine leaves. Valentine is onstage for two-sevenths of the act and Angelica for three-sevenths of the act. In act 4, Valentine, to avoid signing a document resigning his rights to his father's estate, is feigning madness. An attempt is made to impose on Angelica the idea that Valentine has lost his wits because he has despaired of success in his love for her, but Angelica sees through the design, and once again there is no encounter. At the end of the act, Angelica returns; she does exchange a few words with Valentine, but the exchange is severely limited by Angelica's deliberately insisting that Valentine is indeed mad and that there is not much to be gained by talking to him. She torments him in this vein until close to the end of the act; other characters take up some of Valentine's attention during this encounter, which lasts for two-sevenths of the act. The fifth act is largely devoted to Angelica's maneuvers with Valentine's father. Valentine enters late in the act; the settling of the final terms of his relationship to Angelica occupies slightly more than one-fifth of the act. Without adding all of this up to define some mathematically precise part of the play as a whole that belongs to Valentine and Angelica together, one can say that clearly in this play the hero and heroine are defined much more by their relations with other characters than they are by encounters in which we see them relate to each other. Accordingly, one of Northrop Frye's comments applies more satisfactorily to this play than it does to *The Way of the World*:

> There are two ways of developing the form of comedy: one is to throw the main emphasis on the blocking characters; the other is to throw it forward on the scenes of discovery and reconciliation. One is the general tendency of comic irony, satire, realism, and studies of manners; the other is the tendency of Shakespeare and other types of roman-

tic comedy. In the comedy of manners the main ethical interest falls as a rule on the blocking characters. The technical hero and heroine are not often very interesting people.[1]

Valentine and Angelica are not such interesting people as Mirabell and Millamant, partly because far less time is spent on direct encounters to develop them as characters in relation to one another. Nevertheless, Norman Holland says:

> It is to the education of Valentine that the title *Love for Love* refers: Valentine learns to substitute real love for showy love. In return Angelica gives him real love for real love, a response not possible for love merely social; viz., Tattle and Frail or Scandal and Mrs. Foresight.[2]

Since the direct focus on Valentine and Angelica is quite limited, the possibility that the title encompasses a wider range needs to be kept in mind. For example, to say that "love for love" refers to the education of Valentine neglects the fact that Valentine and Angelica have roles as mentors with respect to love for love, Valentine in relation to his father, and Angelica in relation to Foresight, Sir Sampson, and Scandal.

It is well to look at some of the characters, other than the hero and heroine, and consider what they are doing in the play; important among them are Valentine's father, Sir Sampson, Valentine's younger brother, Ben, the sailor, as well as Angelica's uncle, old Foresight, the astrologer. To a significant degree, these characters reflect familiar types: Sir Sampson, the heavy father, the *senex;* Ben, the outsider, the intruder upon society, the natural man; and Foresight, the humorous, pretentious, and phony astrologer. Some critics have thought that these characters exist in and for themselves as humorous portrayals—Lamb, for example, saw Ben in that way—or that Foresight is in the play mainly as foil for Sir Sampson, or that each of these characters appears mainly to allow Congreve to exhibit his stylistic virtuosity. The case for their being more nearly integral to the play might be made along these lines: from the beginning of the play Valentine works at trying to hold his right as eldest son and to get his father to express anew his paternal identity in terms other than those of sheer authority; Sir Sampson insists on Valentine's resigning his right and, when appealed to for his blessing, rudely retorts that Valentine already has his blessing in the form of money to pay his debts. The abrupt conversion from one order of value to another is a blunt instance of the failure of an attempted relationship. Ben, the sailor son, to whom Sir Sampson proposes to divert the estate, is, it turns out, incapable of relating to anybody, including eventually his father. Ben's incapacity is underscored when he first comes onstage:

> *Sir Sampson.* Thou hast been many a weary League *Ben,* since I
>   saw thee.
> *Ben.* Ey, ey, been! Been far enough, an that be all—well
>   Father, and how do all at home? How do's Brother *Dick,* and
>   Brother *Val?*
> *Sir Sampson. Dick,* body o' me, *Dick* has been dead these two
>   Years; I writ you word, when you were at *Legorne.*
> *Ben.* Mess, and that's true: marry I had forgot. *Dick's* dead as
>   you say. . . .   [3.1.287–95][3]

Foresight, directly upon his introduction, is shown isolated from all the members of his household, trying and failing to keep his niece at home and mocked for the failure of his relationship to his wife. His gaze is fixed Laputian-fashion on the stars, and, like the Laputian wife, Mrs. Foresight keeps running off to the continent down below for a good physical tumble with the coachman. These relationships, however, are swiftly obliterated. She spends a night with Scandal, and in the morning astonishes him with her bland ignorance of any such episode.

Among the secondary characters, relationships are established and disestablished with bewildering but managed rapidity. Miss Prue, Foresight's daughter by his first wife—or, to be strict about the evidence, by a former wife—is brought on from the country by Foresight, with Sir Sampson's encouragement, as a prospective bride for Ben. Miss Frail, Mrs. Foresight's sister, learning that Ben is to be designated the heir to his father's estate, engineers a diversion that engages Miss Prue with Tattle. Tattle teaches the country girl the way of the town, a way which her innocence learns with excited facility and finds fascinating. The way of the town is to arrive at physical intimacy by successive disavowals of the words, gestures, and acts which constitute intimacy—disavowing them while performing them. Swiftly perfected in this catechism of deceit—Prue is an anagram or twist on "pure"—Miss Prue is diverted from a prospective relationship to Ben by a nonrelation to Tattle, and even the nonrelation is not quite consummated. The field is thereby cleared for Miss Frail who, consigning to quick oblivion her myriad and notorious casual relationships, takes dead aim at achieving another nonrelation, since it is Ben's estate and not Ben that she wants. When it becomes clear that Ben will not inherit the estate, Miss Frail bluntly rejects Ben. The final paradigm of nonrelationship is ludicrously extreme and absurdly just: Tattle, disguised as a friar, marries Miss Frail, disguised as a nun, he believing that he is marrying Angelica and Miss Frail believing that she is marrying Valentine. The friar-nun marriage, besides being an apogee of the nonfeasible relationship, alludes to a pornographic friar-nun exhibit popular at least as early as Ben Jonson's day, as well as to a dimension of religious devotion realized in the culmination of love between the true Valentine and Angelica. And in the midst of all this activity, Miss Prue is left isolated, rejecting a dildo and howling for a man.

One way of pressing the point that these characters and actions relate to a consideration of serious themes is to move to the neglected dimension of allusion in Congreve. Shakespearean reference, in one form or another, has been at least glancingly recognized and sometimes also deprecated by critics. Hazlitt, for example, writes:

> The peremptory bluntness and exaggerated descriptions of Sir Sampson Legend are in a vein truly oriental, with a Shakespearean cast of language, and form a striking contrast to the quaint credulity and senseless superstitions of Foresight.[4]

Hazlitt, at any rate, hears well enough. Our contemporary critic, John Wain, writing of Congreve, Etherege, and Wycherley together, says:

> It hardly needs to be argued that these writers were conscious of Shakespeare; his achievement was tangibly present to their minds, so that they were forever introducing random scraps of his material into their work.[5]

The only fair way to respond to this in the case of *Love for Love* is to cite not isolated examples but a series of instances of Shakespearean allusion. Take Valentine's mad scene in act 4, in which Holland recognizes some general reference to *Hamlet,* and in which editors have identified but not commented on one specific reference to *Hamlet.* In this scene, Valentine is feigning madness so that he will not be legally competent to sign over his right of inheritance; his father comes in, accompanied by a lawyer, and makes soothing speeches to the boy whom he had, just a little while ago, disavowed as his son, called a rogue and a dog, and prophesied would meet his end by hanging. Before Sir Sampson enters, Angelica has been interrogating Jeremy, Valentine's servant, about his master's madness:

> *Jeremy.* No strange matter, Madam; my Master's mad, that's all:
>   I suppose your Ladyship has thought him so a great while.
> *Angelica.* How d'ye mean, mad?
> *Jeremy.* Why faith, Madam, he's mad for want of his Wits. . . .
>   [4.1.29–33]

The first gravedigger has a similar exchange with Hamlet:

> *Hamlet.* How came he mad?
> *First Clown.* Very strangely, they say.
> *Hamlet.* How "strangely"?
> *First Clown.* Faith, e'en with losing his wits.
>   [5.1.160–63]

Later on in Congreve's mad scene, the following exchange takes place between Valentine and his father:

> *Valentine.* . . . The two greatest Monsters in the World are a Man
>   and a Woman; what's thy Opinion?
> *Sir Sampson.* Why, my Opinion is, that those two Monsters join'd
>   together, make yet a greater, that's a Man and his Wife.
> *Valentine.* A ha! Old Truepenny, say'st thou so? thou hast nick'd
>   it—But its wonderful strange, *Jeremy!*
> *Jeremy.* What is, Sir?
> *Valentine.* That Gray Hairs shou'd cover a Green Head—and I
>   make a Fool of my Father.
>   [4.1.262–72]

The clearest Shakespearean reference here is to Hamlet and the ghost of his father. When Hamlet calls upon Horatio and Marcellus to bind themselves to secrecy by swearing an oath upon his sword, the Ghost's voice from below cries "Swear," to which Hamlet responds: "Ah, ha, boy! Say'st thou so? Art thou there, truepenny?" (1.5.149–50). In Congreve's scene, this scrap of Shakespeare is not "random" but relevant in a number of ways. First of all, Valentine is talking to the "ghost" of his father, a man who has disavowed his paternity and is putting on a great show of affection solely in order to get his son to act contrary to his own interest. "Truepenny" carries the implication of honest value, and is, in Congreve's context, thoroughly ironic, since honest value is exactly what the father is not trying to offer, no matter

how often he calls his son "honest Val." What the father says about the
monstrosity of marriage, however, strikes Valentine as "honest,"
largely, one supposes, because of parental failures in relation to children, and Valentine, for his own mixture of reasons, shares something
of the Hamletian revulsion from marriage. Valentine's final speech
about gray hairs covering a green head is closer to speeches in *Lear* in
which an old father is being urged to see his folly. Probably the most
devastating allusion in the whole scene is to *King Lear*. A violent out-
burst of feigned madness by Valentine has driven the lawyer from the
room. Valentine's father is dismayed by the lawyer's departure, but
when Valentine becomes calmer, he enters into dialogue with his son:

> Sir Sampson. He recovers—bless thee, *Val*—How do'st thou
>   do, Boy?
> Valentine. Thank you, Sir, pretty well—I have been a little
>   out of Order; won't you please to sit, Sir?
> Sir Sampson. Ay boy—Come, thou shalt sit down by me.
> Valentine. Sir, 'tis my Duty to wait.
> Sir Sampson. No, no, come, come, sit you down, honest *Val:* How
>   do'st thou do?
>
> > [4.1.194–201]

There may be references to types of dutiful and orderly service and
fidelity as represented by Milton and in Bishop King's "The Exequy";
the scene alluded to in *Lear* is between Lear and the Fool on the heath:

> Lear. My wits begin to turn. Come on, my boy. How dost, my boy?
>   Art cold? I am cold myself.
>
> > [3.2.67–69]

Sir Sampson, with his lawyer on call in the next room, feigns tender
concern for his son in the language that Lear uses when, on the verge of
madness, he begins to understand his kinship with all mankind.
Angelica judges Sir Sampson severely at the end of the play, but no
judgment of Sir Sampson is more severe than that produced by the
juxtaposition of Lear's madness and Sampson's sanity. Again, the
Shakespearean scrap is far from random. One more instance from the
mad scene—Scandal, observing Sir Sampson's show of affection for
his son in the lines just cited, comments: "Miracle! the Monster grows
loving" [4.1.205]. The allusion is to Caliban, the monster in *The
Tempest*. Sir Sampson, by the extremity of his conduct as a father, has
lost his title not only to that role but to his general humanity. As Van

Voris has noticed, monstrosity is a theme of this play[6]—as it is of *Lear,*
one might add—worked out by Congreve in the dimensions of comedy. The motif of nonrelation that has been outlined leads into the
symbol of monstrosity.

Scandal's allusion to Caliban applied to Sir Sampson is actually
anomalous, but it does serve to associate Sir Sampson with Ben; Ben is
the figure who is heavily characterized by references to Caliban. It may
even be that his name is intended to recall the brutishly shortened form
of Caliban (" 'Ban, 'Ban, Cacaliban," 2.2.188), but there are plenty of
other references. Miss Prue, sophisticated by her encounter with Tattle, rejects Ben immediately and calls him "a great Sea-calf" (3.1.418).
In the fourth act, Miss Frail, having learned that Ben is not to be Sir
Sampson's heir, abruptly reverses her attitude of fondness in these
terms:

> O see me no more,—for thou wert born amongst Rocks, suckl'd by
> Whales, Cradled in a Tempest, and whistled to by Winds; and thou art
> come forth with Finns and Scales, and three rows of Teeth, a most
> outragious Fish of prey.
>
> [4.1.398–402]

Astonished by her abrupt change of attitude, Ben naively supposes
that vehement love has driven the lady mad, in return for which charitable assumption she rounds upon him with the epithet "Monster."
Like monstrosity, madness is a pervasive symbol in the play, centered
of course in Valentine's play-acting of madness, but liberally and frequently imputed to other characters in the play, often in connection
with one or another form of love.

If the fact that Congreve is an allusive dramatist has been overlooked or not taken very seriously, the symbolic dimensions of his
plays have been, in varying degrees, recognized. The allusions that
Congreve employs, however, both expand and help to define the
symbolic side of characters and situations. Connecting Ben with Caliban, for example, tends to prevent one from misreading his role in a
late seventeenth-century play. It stamps him—no matter what his virtues by contrast with characters sophisticated in fraud, habituated and
polished in deceit—as the unassimilable outsider, the figure who cannot respond to nurture in society, the creature whose element is not
land but water, the son whom only a madman or a fool would choose
as the inheritor of his estate and continuator of the family.

Legend is the family name, and a variety of legends flicker and play over the course of the drama—a "Valentine" legend, a "Sampson" legend, a "Caliban" legend, and, from outside the family, a form of angelic legend. Indeed, though nomenclature is clearly significant in all of Congreve's plays, in *Love for Love* the names and careers of characters seem to invoke a kind of myth making that is not so overtly suggested in the other comedies. Valentine, the young man in love, is associated with books, with poetry, with poverty, with the prodigal son appealing for the blessing of his father. He is truth speaking through madness, and finally a martyr for love. An *elemental* symbolism is suggested by the naming, disposition, profession, and verbal habits of the characters. Sir Sampson is associated with the earth almost as fully and clearly as Ben is with water. When Sampson meets with Foresight he ridicules astrology and expresses his sense of experience thus:

> I tell you, I have travel'd old *Fircu,* and know the Globe. I have seen the *Antipodes,* where the Sun rises at Midnight, and sets at Noon-day. . . . I know the length of the Emperour of *China's* Foot; have kiss'd the Great *Mogul's* Slipper, and rid a Hunting upon an Elephant with the Cham of *Tartary*—Body o' me, I have made a Cuckold of a King, and the present Majesty of *Bantam* is the Issue of these Loyns.
>
> [2.1.206–09, 219–23]

"Body o' me" is Sampson's characteristic oath, reiterated throughout the play, and in this speech directed to Foresight he exuberantly flaunts his knowledge of the earth and boasts of having scattered his image through the world. The negative side of his promiscuity is probably suggested by the reference to "the present Majesty of *Bantam.*" On the evidence of an ambassadorial visit to London, the inhabitants of Bantam were, in Congreve's day, regarded as far from majestic. Diminutive fowl were thought to be native to Bantam. The literary allusion, furthering the definition of Sir Sampson and devastating in effect, is to Ben Jonson's *The Alchemist,* and specifically to Sir Epicure Mammon, who expected to be made King of Bantam. Greedy, inflated, globe-girdling wishes and fantasies are summed up and judged in the Mammon allusion, and under this rubric the earth symbolism takes on the cast of gaping physical lust and materialism.

Foresight, on the other hand, whose sexual prowess is nil, is associated with the element of air, and with power exercised not sexually but in terms of an arcane knowledge. In reply to Sir Sampson, Foresight says:

> But I tell you, I have travell'd, and travell'd in the Coelestial *Spheres,* know the *Signs* and the *Planets,* and their Houses. Can judge of Motions Direct and Retrograde, of *Sextiles, Quadrates, Trines* and *Oppositions,* Fiery *Trigons* and Aquatical *Trigons.* Know whether Life shall be long or short, Happy or Unhappy; whether Diseases are Cureable or Incureable. If Journeys shall be prosperous, Undertakings successful; or Goods stoll'n recover'd, I know—
>
> [2.2.210–18]

Foresight, of course, has no special or effective knowledge of the celestial spheres, and is as little able to find meaningful and responsive order in them as Sir Sampson, exerting the strength of his authority in the earth, is able to bring order to the house of Legend. Sampson is rather, as Angelica warns him, like another of his name, perilously close to pulling an old house down on his head at last. Foresight and Sampson are linked also by the cant of Puritanism; they regularly call one another "brother" even when most contemptuous of one another. They are linked temporarily by mercenary interest, but basically their making so free with the term "brother" is the severe ironic signature of another nonrelation, this time within the older generation.

Valentine, the true heir to the house of Legend, and Angelica, Foresight's niece and the member of the Foresight family who has a clear and penetrating mind, as angels are supposed to have—these are the figures who are to be united at the end of the play in a marriage of fire and air. It is useful to consider what the play's epigraph may suggest about central themes. If Shakespeare had affixed epigraphs to his plays, no doubt they would by now have been very thoroughly treated. Congreve's epigraphs have often been ignored, or, what Karl Shapiro suggests is the characteristic fate of the poet, mistranslated. The epigraph of the play is taken from the *Third Satire of the Second Book of Horace.* It is unusual in that Congreve has taken lines from two separate locations in this satire[7] (l. 184 and l. 271), adjusted and slightly modified them, run them together and punctuated as a continuous quotation. The Latin lines are: "Nudus agris, nudus nummis, insane, paternis" (184) and "Insanire paret certa ratione modoque" (271). A close translation of each would be: "Stripped of his fields, stripped, O madman, of any patrimony" (184) and "As if he should prepare to run mad by fixed rule and method" (271).

Congreve's alteration of the lines removes *insane* from line 184, presumably because, in his combination of the lines, *insanire* in line 271 will carry that idea. He alters the conditional *paret* of Horace's line 271 to *parat* in order to make a continuous statement in the indicative mode. The fact that Congreve tinkers in this way to manufacture an epigraph constitutes, one would think, sufficient reason for those who translate to be scrupulous. Yet Herbert Davis, in the best modern textual edition of the plays, was content to resort to a loose seventeenth-century version of Horace, adjusted to couplet form, taking no account of Congreve's modifications, and deliberately separating once more what Congreve had joined together. Davis is not alone. Other modern editors, when they bother with the epigraph at all, translate either loosely, or very close to the separate Horatian lines. Only Gamini Salgado, in the Penguin edition, respects Congreve's Latin, and he translates it this way: "Bereft of land and patrimony, the fool is ready to be mad by rule and regulation."[8] This is, at least, a consecutive statement, but when both Congreve and Horace say *nudus* in an emphatic repetition, one is bound to feel rather cheated when left simply with "bereft." Since Congreve's play does have something to do with divestiture, this small matter may be of some importance. Under the circumstances, the repeated "naked" or "stripped bare" should not be obscured. Nor should the consecutiveness of the statement Congreve has shaped be overlooked. The preparing to run deliberately mad is, as Congreve formulates it, a consequence of the divestiture. The image of nakedness is prominent on Congreve's title page. Translators of the epigraph should let the image stand.

The first line Congreve had adapted from Horace follows a story illustrating avarice (in one son) and prodigality (in a second son). The several lines leading into the second line taken over by Congreve may also be pertinent:

> "My Master, a thing that admits of neither method nor sense cannot be handled by rule and method. In love inhere these evils—first war, then peace: things almost as fickle as the weather, shifting about by blind chance, and if one were to try to reduce them to fixed rule for himself, he would no more set them right than if he aimed at going mad by fixed rule and method."[9]

Notice that in Horace the subject is *love*—love cannot be reduced to fixed rule and method any more than madness can. But Congreve's allusions to *Hamlet* remind us of a madness that had method in it and, as a matter of fact, Valentine's madness is quite effective tactically in his contest with his father. On its more serious side, Valentine's madness is not merely a method of defense, but a voice adjacent to Lear, though emerging from comedy, freed by feigned madness from some of the limits of comedy, speaking both the anguish and the recognitions of divestiture and laying bare the hypocrisy of society's vestments and investitures.

In the Horatian satire, Damasippus, a man whom financial disaster has made a convert to Stoicism, is the speaker during much of the poem; Damasippus denounces a number of forms of madness, including avarice and prodigality, ambition and self-indulgence, and superstition. The madness attacked under self-indulgence is the madness of love. Damasippus has the role of *adversarius* or satiric interlocutor, to use the terms of John Aden's analysis of these satires. Horace makes Damasippus speak at length in order that both the zeal and the duration of the discourse will undercut the Stoicism of which he is the advocate. At the end of the satire Horace moves to establish the distance between himself and Damasippus; the essence of the exchange is:

> *Horace.* Well, what is my madness?
> *Damasippus.* You write verses, you have a bad temper, you live beyond your means, you are always falling in love.
> *Horace.* You greater madman, spare the lesser!

Clearly Horace regards love, like poetry, as a venial madness.

Finally, a word about the title of the play. There are a number of likely proximate sources for the title. Van Voris mentions Fletcher's play, *The Elder Brother.* Nobody mentions Dryden's translation of Theocritus's *Twenty-Third Idyl* (published 1685, subtitled "The Despairing Lover") where the phrase "love for love" appears in the final line of the poem, a prominent position, and in a poem, moreover, published in a miscellany volume to which Congreve contributed. The ultimate source, Van Voris suggests, though he does not elaborate, is Plato's *Phaedrus.* This dialogue is devoted to the subject of love and contains the famous myth of the charioteer and his two horses. Less well remembered are other features of the dialogue: (1) An opening disquisition in which a fine, specious, rhetorical argument is made for the superiority of the nonlover—that is to say, the calculating lover—to the lover. (2) Socrates, in response to this speech, presents an argument for the lover, urging that " 'No truth is in that tale' which says that, when a lover may be had, one ought to accept the non-lover, rather than the lover, because the lover is mad, the non-lover in his senses. It would be right enough, if to be mad were simply and solely an evil. But in reality the greatest blessings come to us through madness, for there is a madness that is given from on high." (3) In the course of Socrates' speech the myth of Anteros is alluded to in direct connection with the phrase "love for love": "When he is with the lover, both cease from their pain, but when he is away then he longs as he is longed for, and has love's image, love for love (Anteros) lodging in his breast. . . ."[10]

Quite briefly, the pertinence of these features of the *Phaedrus* to Congreve's play may be suggested along the following lines: (1) Congreve thoroughly expresses a full spectrum of nonloving relationships, most of which he seems completely to reject. (2) Congreve touches in several ways on the theme of the lover's madness. When Tattle offers to make love to Angelica, he begins by asserting his complete mental and physical soundness, and Angelica retorts:

> O fie for shame, hold your Tongue. A passionate Lover, and five Senses in perfection! when you are as Mad as *Valentine,* I'll believe you love me, and the maddest shall take me.
>
> [4.1.585–88]

(3) Congreve seems to express a validation of excess, even of madness, in Valentine's final act of renunciation which Angelica takes as ultimate proof of love. Convinced that Angelica is about to marry his father, Valentine is now ready to sign over his rights. He is now prepared willingly to offer and accept complete divestiture. There are two reactions to this, one from Scandal: "S'death, you are not mad indeed, to ruine your self?" (5.1.541–42). Angelica's reaction is, first, in an aside, the exclamation: "Generous *Valentine!*" (5.1.550). And then, after she tears up the pledge that obligates Valentine to sign, she says directly to him: "Had I the World to give you, it cou'd not make me worthy of so generous and faithful a Passion." (5.1.560–62). (4) The somewhat unfamiliar myth of Anteros, alluded to by Plato, seems very congenial to Congreve's play. According to Lemprière, the myth runs as follows:

> Anteros, a son of Mars and Venus . . . was the god of mutual love and of mutual tenderness. Venus had complained to Themis that her son Cupid always continued a child, and was told that, if he had another brother, he

would grow up in a short space of time. As soon as Anteros was born, Cupid felt his strength increase and his wings enlarge; but if ever his brother was at a distance from him, he found himself reduced to his ancient shape. From this circumstance it is seen that return of passion gives vigour to love.[11]

Eros, conceived as boundless desire, is differently appreciated by the Augustans than by the Romantics, but Eros-Anteros together would have, for the Augustan writer, a great attraction as imaginative truth.

NOTES

1. Northrop Frye, *Anatomy of Criticism* (New York, 1968), pp. 166–67.

2. Norman Holland, *The First Modern Comedies* (Cambridge, Mass., 1959), p. 172.

3. All references to the text of *Love for Love* are to the edition by Herbert Davis, *The Complete Plays of William Congreve* (Chicago, 1967).

4. William Hazlitt, *Lectures on the English Comic Writers,* Lecture IV, p. 72, cited from *The Complete Works of William Hazlitt,* ed. P. P. Howe, vol. 6 (London and Toronto, 1931).

5. John Wain, "Restoration Comedy and Its Modern Critics," in *Preliminary Essays* (London and New York, 1957), p. 23.

6. W. H. Van Voris, *The Cultivated Stance: The Designs of Congreve's Plays* (Dublin, 1965), pp. 91–92.

7. Horace (Quintus Horatius Flaccus), *Satires, Epistles and Ars Poetica,* with an English translation by H. Rushton Fairclough (London and New York, 1929), p. 168 and p. 174.

8. Gamini Salgado, ed., *Three Restoration Comedies* (London, 1968).

9. Fairclough's translation, p. 175.

10. Plato, *Phaedrus.* The two passages in this paragraph are cited, respectively, from Lane Cooper's edition and translation, *Plato: Phaedrus, Ion, Gorgias, and Symposium, with passages from the Republic and Laws* (London and New York, 1938), p. 26, and from the translation and edition by Benjamin Jowett, *The Dialogues of Plato* (New York, 1914), vol. 3, p. 416.

11. John Lemprière, ed. (rev. by F. A. Wright), *Classical Dictionary* (New York, 1949), p. 50.

PETER HUGHES

Allusion and Expression
in Eighteenth-Century Literature

Once an angry man dragged his father along the ground through his own
orchard. "Stop!" cried the groaning old man at last, "Stop! I did not
drag my father beyond this tree."[1]

We might begin our discussion of allusion by considering a neglected
alternative to our usual way of playing certain kinds of games. Consider the way we play darts or shoot arrows at a target. Our usual
way—aiming at an agreed mark and judging our success according to
whether or where we hit it—may blind us to a less inhibiting alternative: shooting our darts or arrows first, then drawing or shaping the
target around them.

   Previous discussions of allusion have assumed, for the most part
silently, the first game model, which is based upon reference to a prior
and ascertainable goal. The allusion hits or misses an identifiable reference. If the hit is palpable, as in Pope's "What Lady's Face is not a
whited Wall?", we find what Maynard Mack has described as "the
way allusion can construct a cogent metaphor without intruding on a
casual surface."[2] But this rarely happens, and the constructed identities
we call metaphors result from referential allusions only when they
reach the explicit level of quotation; when one text strikes or glances
off another. Allusion generally follows the neglected second game
model. By seeming to repeat something, a text creates a context for
itself, and since we are usually not sure what it repeats, we draw or
twist the context to suit the text. We continually draw the target
around the dart; we falsify for the sake of meaning; we hunt out references to explain repetitions.

   The importance of allusive recurrence in eighteenth-century literature has been neglected by previous studies of allusion, which have defined allusion almost entirely in terms of reference. Surprisingly little has ever been written on the meaning of allusion, and one must infer definitions from what are for the most part unexplained examples or passing remarks. Although it was part of his title, the late Reuben Brower nowhere explained what he meant by calling Pope's work "the poetry of allusion."[3] It is clear, however, that like Mack in the study referred to earlier, Brower and other critics of the period emphasize allusive reference. So too do critics of other periods and literatures, like Herman Meyer, whose *The Poetics of Quotation in the European Novel*[4] treats at length the aesthetic and stylistic aspects of the subject; it also includes a valuable study of *Tristram Shandy*. One of the few modern critical discussions that recaptures the eighteenth-century sense that allusion involves historical recurrence and the problem of modernity is that by I.A. Richards in *Principles of Literary Criticism*. In his comments on "allusiveness in modern poetry" he recognizes its relations to shifts of historical and psychological perspective, but closes by condemning allusion as a "trap," a "shibboleth," and an invitation to "insincerity."[5] Yet at the end of this same work, in an appendix entitled "The Poetry of T.S. Eliot," what had earlier been condemned as "recondite reference" and allowed only a small place in literature is praised as "a technical device for compression."[6] We are all as a result indebted to Irvin Ehrenpreis, who has recently examined and outlined the referential aspects of allusion, casting light on the obscurity in which earlier criticism had left the subject—and more than a little heat on those who have praised eighteenth-century literature for the dunciadic qualities of vagueness and suggestive muddle.[7] His categories for referential allusion (echoes and allusions, general allusion, and parallel poetry) are helpful, and his skeptical comments on allegory and irony are excellent. But Ehrenpreis stops short of a crucial distinction by limiting his discussion to matters of reference.

We must go beyond these limits to include repetition, which with the Renaissance became a way of reading a text, just as in earlier times it had been a way of listening to or telling a story. This obsessive practice of readers was well established by the eighteenth century. By tracing allusions in this way, they renewed the allusive game through foul play, the text through misreading. Pope often grappled with this problem in justifying his own satires, and toward the end admitted that it had something to do with his own scandalous success. In the second dialogue of his *Epilogue to the Satires* we learn how much his work depends upon expressive repetition, how little upon mimetic reference:

> Vice with such Giant-strides comes on amain,
> Invention strives to be before in vain;
> Feign what I will, and paint it e'er so strong,
> Some rising Genius sins up to my Song.
>   [6–9]

This view of literature, which as I shall suggest is implicit in much eighteenth-century writing, is alien to that "representation of reality" offered by Auerbach. But it is native to the expressive strategies of Pope and his contemporaries, for whom allusion offered a language in which the play of wit could be turned into a forbidden game. Parody and imitation, those allusive tactics, allow the game to continue by breaking the rules, thereby satisfying a deep-seated need for continuity, for a literary history that allows the modern writer to remember the ancients without being trapped in the past.

There is about allusion, as a classical scholar has shrewdly noted, so strong an element of "contravention of idiom"[8] that the primacy and authenticity of a given text can be ascertained by the existence of another text that contravenes the more usual idiom or syntax of the first. As we move from textual to interpretive criticism, this contravention of idiom can seem more like a violation. The allusion in "Each does but hate his neighbour as himself"—to take another example from Pope—plays blasphemous games with scripture.[9] So too do many allusions to those other privileged fictions of the period, classical texts, sacred and secular decrees, providential histories, and even such examples as operatic libretti and tunes. This is true even of some allusions in which the quoted reference is exact. There it is the context of the later occurrence that contravenes, as in *Tristram Shandy's* abuse of a formal anathema, which in itself is quoted exactly and without parody, or the highwayman's travesty of the grand march from Handel's *Rinaldo* in *The Beggar's Opera*. Like Tartuffe when he confesses himself "un méchant, un coupable" (3.6), such allusions contravene the truth even as they tell it.

What is at issue in these twisted references is not formalist irony or ambiguity, which have been overpraised and misapplied to eighteenth-century texts, but something closer to the recurrence *(ricorso)* of

Viconian irony, which is the rediscovery of our present selves through
reading and writing about past texts; a rediscovery that prefigures T.S.
Eliot's sense of the individual talent's relations with literary tradition.
Vico spoke for his European contemporaries and described their way
of renewing the past when he said "Irony could certainly not have
begun until these times of reflection, because it is shaped from falsehood through a reflective power that puts on the mask of truth."[10]
Vico recognized that the past could no longer be understood through
allegory and metaphor, and that history could no longer be accepted or
experienced as a providential narrative. The last historian to attempt
this in English was Clarendon, whose *History of the Rebellion* tries to
unite divine and human agency in a narrative that presents historical
events as finally mysterious. The fall of the Commonwealth had in
Milton's eyes robbed England's history of its mysterious coherence,
and *Paradise Lost* deserves one critic's description of it as an "epitaph on
history."[11] The last poet to retain this belief and interest in history was
Dryden, and the allegorical defects of *The Hind and the Panther* and
Absalom and Achitophel, which too many critics have tried to paper over
in their readings, show how shaky and skeptical the poet's sense of
providence had become. Attempts to perpetuate providential history
without the authority of scripture to justify and clarify allusions to the
past, attempts such as Denham's in *Cooper's Hill*, come unstuck right
before the reader's eyes and even, if we recall its various versions, in the
poet's own hands.

The growth throughout Europe of a new critical sense of history,
whose theory appears in Vico's *New Science* and whose practice could
already be seen in Paolo Sarpi's *History of the Council of Trent* (1619), a
favorite work of Swift's; Richard Simon's *Critical History of the Old
Testament* (1678), which Dryden deals with in *Religio Laici;* and Pietro
Giannone's *Civil History of the Kingdom of Naples* (1723), from which
Gibbon took lessons in irony, led not only to a widening split between
the City of God and the civil society of men, but also to a separation
between past and present. Past events become victims of constant rereadings. Allusion, the central technique in such rereadings, robs the
past of its mystery, turning it into mock-epic and anti-heroic, but it
also confers on the past an increasingly literary modernity, turning the
sacred books of the ancients into the mock-books of the Scriblerians.
The history of events *(res gestae)* turns into allusive history. It becomes
in fact literary history, which properly considered is a narrative of the

changing values of words and verbal patterns *expressed as the events they once merely recorded or referred to.*

This great change, which filtered downward and inward during the eighteenth century, gave the writer a greater power but a new poignancy. The burden it placed upon him was not the burden of the past, as W.J. Bate has argued,[12] but the burden of his verbal power. The great talents of the period did not feel burdened by the genius or grandeur of the past. The past had been lightened and distanced into allusion, turned into oracular paper blown by the wind. Cut off from the ideal past by the latterday "Flood" of the civil war and by pervasive Cartesian doubts about the scientific truth of historical accounts, they were pushed forward, often resisting, by the period's theory of progress. The two parts of this theory combined to increase the value and necessity of allusion; for while those who held it exalted a modern ability to recall and reconstruct the past (in ways reflected in cultural activities as different as classical scholarship and Palladian architecture), they also denied that this past could or should be repeated or transmitted into the present and future. The plight of the talented writer, and the appeal of allusion, forecast both the problem and the solution of modern alluders and quoters like Eliot, Borges, and Benjamin. As Hannah Arendt has described this predicament,

> Insofar as the past has been transmitted as tradition, it possesses authority; insofar as authority presents itself historically, it becomes tradition. Walter Benjamin knew that the break in tradition and the loss of authority which occurred in his lifetime were irreparable, and he concluded that he had to discover new ways of dealing with the past. In this he became a master when he discovered that the transmissibility of the past had been replaced by its citability and that in place of its authority there had arisen a strange power to settle down, piecemeal, in the present and to deprive it of "peace of mind," the mindless peace of complacency.[13]

That last description of the writer nicely evokes Pope's Horatian manner and exiled retirement at Twickenham: it also evokes the self-concerned and unpious attitude of the eighteenth-century talent toward the citable past.

Far from approving pious borrowings from classical and English authors, the Scriblerians condemned it as plagiarism, as a cultural death that imposes on the present a decomposing mound of paper. In *The Art of Sinking in Poetry* we find a scathing view of that kind of allusion, "As *Virgil* is said to have read *Ennius,* out of his Dunghil to draw Gold; so may our Author read *Shakespear, Milton,* and *Dryden,* for the contrary End, to bury their Gold in his own Dunghil."[14] When practiced by dunces, allusion does indeed become a burden, but it is a burden of the present. Like the paper that clogs the way in *MacFlecknoe,* the works of mediocre contemporaries stifle and defile the imagination of the true poet. The sharpest distinction drawn between the Scriblerians and Grub Street is the distinction, at once social and literary, between those who converse and live and those who scribble and publish. In their distaste for the printed word, for the word as sign, as opposed to the word as speech, the great writers of the period turn against the mechanical replication that published allusion and quotation become. In this preference for speech over sign, *logos* over *verbum,* they shared the views of many others. Perhaps the plainest expression of this approach, which reappeared later in Rousseau's *Essay on the Origin of Languages,* is that of the French priest and theoretician of language Bernard Lamy: "The words on a page are like a dead body stretched out on the ground. In the mouth of the one who advances them, they are effective; on paper they are lifeless, incapable of producing the same effects."[15] Lamy's contrast could serve as a description of *Tristram Shandy's* brilliance, which lies in playing off these two extremes. Printer's signs are played off against speech, mechanical quotation against endless talk.

The dead weight of their scribbling and hostile contemporaries, which we can still feel in the *Dunciad* and the *Tale of a Tub,* forced the great talents of the age to see in printed words and wooden allusion the great threat to their creative lives. The attempt made in those two satires to counter that threat is what makes them such self-destructive works. Swift's *Tale* is in the end consumed by its own vertigo and madness. Pope's *Dunciad* makes of its insistent allusion an anti-world of words and in the end unmakes it. To free themselves from this stifling weight became their great task, but they could not do it through the willed forgetting practiced by extreme moderns in their own day and later by Nietzsche,[16] who suffered under the even greater weight of German classical scholarship. Their education and their sense of exile from the past led them into Vico's recurrence, into remembering themselves as creative speech and making that their future. Pope does this in his *Epistle to Arbuthnot,* and Sterne makes it the structuring principle of *A Sentimental Journey.* In her introduction to an edition of Sterne's book, Virginia Woolf caught exactly what he and his contemporaries were up to, and up against: ". . . though the writer is always haunted by the belief that somehow it must be possible to brush aside the ceremonies and conventions of writing and to speak to the reader directly as by word of mouth, any one who has tried the experiment has either been struck dumb by the difficulty, or waylaid into disorder and diffusity unutterable."[17] Because they saw their writing contemporaries as the enemy, the conventional and increasingly debased allusive language of the time bored and repelled them. This put them in a strange situation; for as Geoffrey Hartman has observed, "Words commonly help to 'present' us, and should we feel that they are defective, or else that we are defective vis-à-vis them (words then becoming the 'other', as is not unusual in poets who have a magnified regard for a great precursor or tradition), a complex psychological situation arises."[18] Given their regard for those who had gone before, the solution found by eighteenth-century writers had to lie in making of the way back a new way forward.

In trying to understand their psychological situation we have a burden of our own to lay aside: the Freudian obsession with parricide. The most subtle treatments we have of relations between desire and creative act, and of the "other" that separates them, continually overlook the kind of impulse that dominated so many eighteenth-century talents, because Freud "seems to have been deaf to the importance in myth of both sororicide and fratricide."[19] By comparison with their hateful contemporaries, their figurative brothers and sisters, the fathers and ancestors of the writers who concern us were almost beloved. The chief defect of these paternal figures was that they had squandered the legacy they should have left to their natural or literary offspring. The parable of the age was that of the Prodigal Father. "We acknowledge them our fathers in wit:" says Dryden of the dramatists of the last age, "but they have ruined their estates themselves, before they came to their children's hands."[20] Seen from a psychological viewpoint, the literary history of the eighteenth-century in England was an attempt to renew through allusive recurrence what Burke at the century's end called inheritance—"the image of a relation in blood."[21]

This sense of inheritance and descent was deeply felt. In the poetry of Dryden and Pope it is more intensely expressed than any other kind of psychic or personal relation. Think of Dryden's lines to Congreve, "The Father had descended for the Son: / For only You are lineal to the

Throne" or by parodied contrast, the grotesque will and testament of
MacFlecknoe. Think too of the way Pope joins filial piety and poetic
filiation in the *Epistle to Arbuthnot*. In his interpretation of this poem,
and at greater length in *The Garden and the City*,[22] Maynard Mack
touches on the essential and neglected power of allusion: its ability to
give a life-history to a poet who would otherwise stand accused of
fratricidal satire. The extraliterary allusions of Pope's life that Mack
also considers (his garden, grotto, house, portraits) confirm a search
for friendship and for his own *genius loci,* to balance, we might say, the
isolation and inner exile he increasingly felt. A certain kind of allusion,
in ways we are about to consider, spares the poet the fearful task of
self-invention; a plight of the Moderns the Ancients ridiculed but that
we no longer find so ridiculous. As a poet who is one of our contemporaries has said,

> Our problem is not
> to find who remembers our parents—our problem is
> to find who remembers ourselves. I love our problem,
> it becomes our solution: unbecoming, it dissolves.[23]

The remembrance of self soon becomes inseparable from the projection of self and the allusive recurrence of the past.

The other face of allusion, the dark side of the moon whose
reflected light we see in explicit references, is repetition. Unlike referential allusion, which requires an identifiable source, repetition needs
only recurrence to create its aesthetic effect. In musical terms, reference
is thematic variation, repetition is rhythm. And while the making and
reading of allusive references depends upon memory and recollected
texts, repetition carries memory with it, freeing us from recollection
and projecting us into an aesthetic present and future. If eighteenth-
century texts depended solely or even chiefly upon referential allusion
they would all have slipped into oblivion; methods of reading and
teaching them that emphasize reference only hasten that fate. In asserting the importance of repetition to such texts, we should recall what
Swift wrote to Pope after the *Epistle to Bathurst* first appeared in
Dublin:

> Your poem on the Use of Riches hath been just printed here, and we have
> no objection but the obscurity of several passages by our ignorance in facts
> and persons, which make us lose abundance of the Satyr. Had the printer
> given me notice, I would have honestly printed the names at length, where

I happened to know them; and writ explanatory notes, which however would have been but few, for my long absence hath made me ignorant of what passes out of the scene where I am.[24]

Such topical allusions defeated even Swift; we should not be surprised that they defeat us. We should notice at once, however, that Swift did not find this an insuperable problem; he describes the obscurity of these references, which we would have to extend outward from the names of persons and hints of scandal to include most of its referential allusion, as an exceptional objection to an otherwise satisfying poem. We shall see why that was so when we consider the *Epistle* as one of our texts for comment, but let us for now note the fact: one of the most knowing and judicious readers in the poem's first audience missed many of its most topical allusive references, and yet he did not think he had missed its meaning or value.

What satisfied Swift was not recollection, but the aesthetic repetition that both raised and gratified his expectations as a reader. Kierkegaard, who treats psychologically the recurrence that Vico describes as historical, distinguishes both processes involved in allusion: "Repetition and recollection are the same movement, only in opposite directions; for what is recollected has been, is repeated backwards, whereas repetition properly so called is recollected forwards."[25] By repetition the writer *rehearses* his text, which becomes both a process and a performance. It also becomes, in that other sense of process, a trial directed toward a future verdict. The respect for origins that is both a cause and a result of primitivism has led us to describe as recollection and backward reference what should be thought of as repetition and forward projection. We continue to describe as myths or revivals what are for modern readers ideologies or reforms. Like Aeneas at his most pious, we persist in remembering our future.

But in the eighteenth-century the whole activity of writing (and reading) texts was based upon the stylistic and psychic patterns of repetition. It is surely clear, even at first reading, that the recurrence of metric patterns is characteristic of the verse (with Pindaric exceptions proving the rule), and that the question of rhyme, the recurrence of sound to create (or simulate) sense has depths that swallow up any simple notions of single or explicit meaning. Within that structuring impulse of repetition we find a gothic excess of rhetorical figures, from anaphora to zeugma, all of which gratify or switch our expectations of recurrence. The period's prose writers remove the magical elements of rhyme and printer's hieroglyphs, but from Congreve to Johnson writers clearly found the temptation to create repetitive patterns hard to resist. Only the impulse to mimic conversational speech, to rehearse talk, set limits to this patterning. Even the characterizing of wit as "What oft was thought but ne'er so well express't," a notion so often translated into intellectual history, could and should be seen as the enactment of repetition itself.

Just as referential allusion has its kinds of characteristics, so too does repetitive allusion. Apart from the general category of those that inhere in the prosodic elements of a text—of which we may see many examples in our texts for comment—there are others that we can name according to known aesthetic and verbal categories. The most striking of these in eighteenth-century texts is that of pseudo-aphorism or proverb, in which the universal and memorable effect of such expressions is feigned by the writer. A second is that of the grotesque or perverse, in which we recognize an original text chiefly through the distortion we have before us. A third is what might be called ventriloquism, in which the writer repeats himself. A fourth might be called that of *reflux,* similar to an individual Viconian *ricorso,* in which obsessive responses of the writer transform external and apparently unconnected events into a repetitive narrative. There are undoubtedly other kinds of repetitive allusion, which I hope will emerge from further study. To that end, and to illustrate the modes of repetition I have just mentioned, we shall now turn to passages taken from three quite different kinds of works. In each of these texts, we shall see much else besides allusion, but I shall concentrate in my remarks on the interpretive questions raised by their allusive patterns. And finally, I shall suggest in each case the direct or oblique relations that exist between reference and repetition.

In discussing with a class Congreve's *The Way of the World,* I was recently struck by a resemblance between Lady Wishfort's diatribe against Foible at the start of the fifth act and the clash between Subtle and Face that opens Ben Jonson's *The Alchemist.* One notices in these texts (Example I) that the verbal echoes are accompanied by a striking repetition of dramatic motives. One enraged character tells another, against whom the rage is directed, that only charitable patronage brought him (or her) up from the gutter and into a position of comfort and trust, that this trust has been abused, and that the guttersnipe must now get out. The sequence in both passages follows a sumptuary pattern from former hunger and nakedness to what the audience is meant to notice—sleek prosperity—and part of the force of Congreve's repetition is the street language used by Lady Wishfort (who was earlier unwilling, we may recall, to "unbend the severity of *Decorum*") to lash out at her servant. This exchange evokes Face's gibes at Subtle, but beyond the evocation is the trap this catches Lady Wishfort in. She reveals a peculiarly close and grotty acquaintance with low life, and in so doing she exposes herself. The switch from one class of speaker to another, from a pair of confidence tricksters to a well-born lady of a certain age, creates in addition what Harold Bloom has called a "discontinuity"[26] and rightly described as one of the marks of this kind of repetition.

The scene-to-scene repetition apparently involves *recurrence* to an earlier and identifiable text, but not, I think, a *reference*. The allusion is one that does not seem to have been noticed by any of the several editors and critics whose commentary on the play I have consulted, and it is not mentioned in the one general study of the afterlife or *Nachleben* of Jonson in Restoration theater.[27] One might note in passing that Congreve may well have seen *The Alchemist* performed at Dublin's Smock Alley theater, and that for Restoration playwrights Jonson was perhaps the most admired ancestor. But having said that, we must recognize that the repetition is more important that what is repeated. The untypical and sleazy precision of Lady Wishfort's insults leaves the impression that she has heard them somewhere before. *Where* we need not know. But this kind of grotesque repetition, which does not require a reference, can nonetheless be clarified by one—not specifically to a text, but to the context or enactment that a theatrical scene provides.

Such a repetition may however demand a more involved and affective approach to reading than we usually expect. My own sense of this allusion, for example, is based upon an earlier production of *The Alchemist* in which I had myself played the part of Subtle. My sequence of recall began with the explosive start to Congreve's scene—so like Jonson's opening—the kinetic violence that is felt before any meaning has emerged from the text. The next thing that struck me was the oddly archaic flavour of Lady Wishfort's language, not only in the sense that the terms seemed a little dated—she is after all getting old—but in the more precise and historical sense that her diatribe seemed a social ana-

chronism, its fullness of language a breach of Restoration style, a
throwback to a less stratified mode of social encounter. When put to a
verbal test these passages appear to bear out my impression. David
Mann's concordance to Congreve's plays[28] makes it possible to establish that nearly all of the compound and simple nouns in her harangue
occur only here. There is then a root sense in which this passage belongs somewhere else. It has been taken out of its context, *torn out,* like
one of Benjamin's quotations, but unlike them it does not need to be
identified. We know it to be *other,* alien, a grotesque in the original
sense that there is a conflict between material and subject, structure and
function, context and text; just as there is in grotesque carvings of vines
and branches that twist under their weight of wood or stone.

When we turn forward—and back—to Pope's *Epistle to Bathurst*
(Example II) we find those repetitions that gave Swift a sense of the
poem's texture that he could not gain from unknown references. We
find in particular the kind of repetition I have called pseudo-aphorism,
a type we find frequently in the poetry of Pope and Johnson. The
anecdote introduced in this passage, and annotated by the poet (who
declares it to be a true story from the reign of William III), takes on
through repetition the force of secret history. Two characteristic
grammatical elements bring about this effect. First, the insistent pointing of memory through the use of the definite article: placed five times
in the first three lines to persuade us that we have heard this before and
that what we have heard is true. The second element is that of verb
metaphor: the *dropping, gingling* Guinea *spoke* and *told.* In her valuable
book on metaphor, Christine Brooke-Rose records analyses that
show how heavily Pope depends upon metaphor created through
verbs rather than nouns. Such metaphors are more frequent and important in his work than in that of any other major English poet.[29]
Verb metaphors, which are steeped in temporal and local significance,
are the characteristic tropes of such historical and recurrent allusions.
By contrast noun metaphors, fused into identity, are typical of symbolic and allegorical modes. Both of these elements lead to the fashioning of the quasi-proverbial "Old Cato is as great a Rogue as you."

The entrance of Cato into this homemade history is entirely Pope's
doing. It does not appear in any of the anecdote's earlier versions, and it
lifts the passage to the level of folk wisdom, an honest and proverbial
account at odds with Old Cato's conduct. But it does not limit or direct
the reader to one proverb rather than another: we are dealing here with

aphoristic repetition rather than with reference. In discounting reference I am not offering an arbitrary notion of repetition. I should argue instead that this text shows how fully recurrence expresses the psychological needs of the poet's life. Pope's own curdled sense of independence, which has points in common with Swift's tory anarchism, shares with it a focus on figures of Roman virtue. His doubts about the figure of his own time can be traced in the use of Cato's name, from the admiring "While Cato gives his little senate laws" from his prologue to Addison's *Cato* to the contemptuous "Like Cato, give his little senate laws," significantly part of the Addison / Atticus portrait from the *Epistle to Arbuthnot*. The merging of Cato and true patriotism had earlier led Ben Jonson to write "The Voice of Cato is the voice of Rome," a secular parody of *vox populi vox dei*. Pope's naming of Cato as "the Patriot" may well have been further linked to Pope's obsessive idea that he and his friends were the happy few, those who had upheld the defeated cause of honor. This was a position traditionally ascribed to Cato, as in Lucan's saying, *Victrix causa deis placuit, sed victa Catoni*.

Pope's continuing insistence upon the proverbial and aphoristic, of which this is one example, deserves further study. The full extent of this stylistic compulsion, which appears in several other major eighteenth-century writers, will only appear after we complete a study of the developmental role in seventeenth- and eighteenth-century prose and verse of the commonplace books, collections of proverbs, and grammars that use axioms and aphorisms as examples.[30] I suspect that their appearance, out of context but everywhere in contemporary education, their abbreviated recurrence—*verb. sap.* floating in a void—had the effect of creating allusion without reference, repetition without difference, a *revenant* rising out of every schoolbook.

Even in Pope's satirical recourse to the classical world the value of the source, the primacy of the prior, remains unquestioned. Addison or a corrupt politician may be mocked through Cato, but Cato remains inviolate. This shows in practice how allusive repetition draws the target around the arrow, since two almost identical allusions, repetitions by the poet of his own words, could drastically alter their meanings in different contexts. But that classical order, in which circular recurrence was a historical limit and cultural repetition was an imaginative necessity to ensure the survival of those names and ideals that might otherwise slip out of memory and into oblivion, was also per-

ceived in the eighteenth century in a different and colder light; as a
pagan cult that had become, in a Christian and bourgeois society, an
instrument of social control and moral corruption. In our text from
Richardson's *Clarissa* (Example III) we find a revealing but not untypical example of that subversive perception. In stylistic terms, we find
the use of allusion to contradict both its classical source and the Lucretian notion of repetition as an unredeemed cycle of instinctual life.

Clarissa's loutish brother writes to tell her to submit to her family's
wishes and marry Solmes. But he twists this proposal by quoting *Amor
omnibus idem* from Virgil's third Georgic, which he urges her to read in
Dryden's translation. She is outraged by "this insolent letter," and by
much more than the suggestion that women have no Latin. What
prompts her angry repudiation of his "allusion or reference to the
Georgic" is the Lucretian doctrine of that allusion, its levelling suggestion that love is the same for all, for man and beast, and that love is no
more than a repetitive cycle of copulation. Dryden, the source Clarissa
is sent to, softens the harshness of the Virgilian epithets that cluster
around *amor* in the Georgic (e.g., *durus amor* 259), but he gives a sweat-
ing urgency to Virgil's descriptions of female sexuality that Clarissa
seems to have perceived and been offended by. Mares, according to
Virgil, should be kept lean before coupling; Dryden translates that
passage as follows:

> For fear the rankness of the swelling Womb
> Shou'd scant the passage, and confine the room.
> Lest the fat Furrows shou'd the sense destroy
> Of Genial Lust; and dull the Seat of Joy.
> But let 'em suck the Seed with greedy force;
> And close involve the Vigour of the Horse.
>
> [218–23]

But Clarissa refuses to be reduced to animality by classical texts and
training—hence her jabs at her brother's education and her complex
word-play on *humanity*. The final effect of this allusive repetition is
grotesque, but the perversion or twisting has shifted, and in a most
disturbing way, from the allusion to its source. Clarissa's revulsion
from the georgic world evokes a larger aspect of her character and
response to others, an aspect that reveals the central horror in
Richardson's novel. Clarissa repeatedly describes those who surround
her as animals. Solmes, for example, is described as a sloth or badger, a

"bent and broad shouldered creature" who "stalks" and "squats." Throughout the novel Clarissa imagines herself threatened by night creatures like the monsters that crouch on and around the sleeping woman in Fuseli's drawing *The Nightmare*. And her fantasy, of course, came true. The degrading allusion repeated itself as a tragic event.

This transformation of allusion into event, with which I shall close, becomes in the later eighteenth-century a striking effect of allusive recurrence. It also becomes, in the Gothic novel and the political writings provoked by the French Revolution, a link with the visionary allusions of the English Romantics. It could even be expressed as a general principle and as a tentative conclusion. Insofar as allusion is referential it is explosive, soon reduced to paper fragments. Insofar as it is repetitive it is implosive, concentrating words, speech-acts, and fantasies into events.

EXAMPLES

I. (a) Congreve: *The Way of the World*, 5.1.

Lady Wishfort. Out of my house, out of my house, thou *Viper*,
  thou *Serpent,* that I have foster'd, thou bosome traytress, that
  I rais'd from nothing—begon, begon, begon, go, go,—that I took
  from Washing of old Gause and Weaving of dead Hair, with a
  bleak blew Nose, over a Chafeing-dish of starv'd Embers and
  Dining behind a Traverse Rag, in a shop no bigger than a Bird-
  cage,——go, go, starve again, do, do.
Foible. Dear Madam, I'll beg pardon on my knees.
Lady Wishfort. Away, out, out, go set up for your self again
  ——do, drive a Trade, do, with your three penny-worth of
  small Ware, flaunting upon a Packthread, under a Brandy-sellers
  Bulk, or against a dead Wall by a Balladmonger. Go hang out an
  old *Frisoneer-gorget,* with a yard of Yellow *Colberteen* again;
  do; an old gnaw'd *Mask,* two rowes of *Pins* and a *Childs Fiddle;*
  A *Glass Necklace* with the Beads broken, and a *Quilted Night-cap*
  with one Ear. Go, go, drive a trade,——these were your *Commodities*
  you treacherous Trull, this was your *Merchandize* you dealt in
  when I took you into my house, plac'd you next my self, and made
  you Governante of my whole Family. You have forgot this, have
  you, now you have feather'd your Nest?

(b) Jonson: *The Alchemist,* 1.1.

Face. Why, I pray you, have I
  Been countenanc'd by You? Or you, by me?
  Do but collect sir, where I met you first.
Sub. I do not hear well.
Face. Not of this, I think it.
  But I shall put you in mind, sir, at Pie Corner,
  Taking your meal of steam in, from cooks' stalls,
  Where, like the father of hunger, you did walk
  Piteously costive, with your pinch'd-horn nose,
  and your complexion, of the Roman wash,
  Stuck full of black and melancholic worms,
  Like powder corns, shot, at th' artillery yard.
Sub. I wish you could advance your voice a little.
Face. When you went pinn'd up, in the several rags
  Y' had rak'd and pick'd from dunghills, before day,
  Your feet in mouldy slippers, for your kibes,
  A felt of rug, and a thin threaden cloak,
  That scarce would cover your no-buttocks—
Sub. So, sir!

II. Pope: *Epistle to Bathurst,* 65–78

> Once, we confess, beneath the Patriot's cloak,
> From the crack'd bag the dropping Guinea spoke.
> And gingling down the back-stairs, told the crew,
> 'Old Cato is as great a Rogue as you.'
> Blest paper-credit! last and best supply!
> That lends Corruption lighter wings to fly!
> Gold imp'd by thee, can compass hardest things,
> Can pocket States, can fetch or carry Kings;
> A single leaf shall waft an Army o'er,
> Or ship off Senates to a distant Shore;
> A leaf, like Sibyl's, scatter to and fro
> Our fates and fortunes, as the winds shall blow:
> Pregnant with thousands flits the Scraps unseen,
> And silent sells a King, or buys a Queen.

III (a) Richardson: *Clarissa,* 1: 256–57 (Everyman's Library edition).

> If after one fortnight's conversation with Mr. Solmes, and
> after you have heard what your friends shall further urge in
> his behalf, unhardened by clandestine correspondencies, you
> shall convince them that Virgil's *Amor omnibus idem* (for
> the application of which I refer you to the Georgic, as trans-
> lated by Dryden) is verified in you, as well as in the rest of
> the animal creation; and that you cannot, or will *not,* forego
> your prepossession in favour of the *moral,* the *virtuous,* the *pious*
> Lovelace [I would please you if I could!] it will then be
> considered, whether to humour you, or to renounce you for ever. . . .

> Late as it was when I received this insolent letter, I wrote an
> answer to it directly, that it might be ready for the writer's
> time of rising. I enclose the rough draft of it. You will see
> by it how much his vile hint from the Georgic, and his rude one
> of my *whining vocatives,* have set me up. . . .

> You might have told me, brother, in three lines, what the
> determination of my friends was; only, that then you would not
> have had room to display your pedantry by so detestable an allusion
> or reference to the Georgic. Give me leave to tell you, sir, that
> if *humanity* were a branch of your studies at the university
> it has not found a genius in you for mastering it. Nor is either
> my sex or myself, though a sister, I see, entitled to the least
> decency from a brother who has studied, as it seems, rather to
> cultivate the malevolence of his natural temper, than any tendency
> which one would have hoped his parentage, if not his education,
> might have given him to a tolerable politeness.

(b) Virgil: *Georgicon,* 3. 242–44

> Omne adeo genus in terris hominumque ferarumque,
> Et genus æquoreum, pecudes, pictæque volucres,
> In furias ignemque ruunt: amor omnibus idem.

(c) Dryden: Virgil's *Georgics,* 3. 375–80

> Thus every Creature, and of every Kind,
> The Secret Joys of sweet Coition find:
> Not only Man's Imperial Race; but they
> That wing the liquid Air, or swim the Sea,
> Or haunt the Desart, rush into the flame:
> For Love is Lord of all; and is in all the same.

NOTES

1. Gertrude Stein, *The Making of Americans* (New York, 1937), p. 3.

2. "Wit and Poetry and Pope," in *Pope and his Contemporaries: Essays Presented to George Sherburn* (Oxford, 1949), p. 30.

3. *Alexander Pope: The Poetry of Allusion* (Oxford, 1959).

4. Translated by Theodore and Yetta Ziolkowski (Princeton, 1968).

5. New York, n.d., p. 218.

6. *Principles,* pp. 290–91.

7. *Literary Meaning and Augustan Values* (Charlottesville, 1974), esp. pp. 1–48.

8. Guy Lee, *Allusion, Parody and Imitation* (Hull, 1971), p. 7.

9. Sanford Budick has considered the importance of blasphemy in Pope's poetry in his *Poetry of Civilization: Mythopoetic Displacement in the Verse of Milton, Dryden, Pope, and Johnson* (New Haven and London, 1974), pp. 111–55.

10. My translation of "L'ironia certamente non pote cominciare che da'tempi della riflessione, perch'ella è formata dal falso in forza d'una riflessione che prende maschera di verità" (*Scienza nuova* 1744, para. 408, in Giambattista Vico, *Opere,* ed. Fausto Nicolini [Milan and Naples, n.d.], p. 521). All further references to Vico are from this edition.

11. Malcolm Ross, *Poetry and Dogma: The Transfiguration of Eucharistic Symbols in Seventeenth Century English Poetry* (New Brunswick, 1954), chap. 4, "History and Poetry: The Decline of the Historical Concrete," pp. 88–112.

12. In *The Burden of the Past and the English Poet* (New York, 1972).

13. Introduction to Benjamin's *Illuminations,* trans. Harry Zohn (New York, 1968), p. 38.

14. Edited by Edna Leake Steeves (New York, 1952), p. 39.

15. My translation of "Les paroles sur un papier sont comme un corps mort qui est étendu par terre. Dans la bouche de celui qui les profère, elles sont efficaces; sur le papier elles sont sans vie, incapables de produire les mêmes effets" (quoted by Jacques Derrida, "Le Cercle linguistique de Genève," *Marges de la Philosophie* [Paris, 1972], p. 174 n.).

16. In his "Of the Use and Misuse of History for Life," whose significance Paul de Man has explored in "Literary History and Literary Modernity," *Blindness and Insight: Essays in the Rhetoric of Contemporary Criticism* (New York, 1971), pp. 142–65.

17. Introduction to *A Sentimental Journey* (London, n.d.), pp. vii–viii.

18. "The Dream of Communication," in *I.A. Richards: Essays in his Honor,* ed. R. Brower, H. Vendler, and J. Hollander (New York, 1973), pp. 173–74.

19. Philip Rieff, "Freud and the Authority of the Past," in *Explorations in Psychohistory,* ed. Robert Jay Lifton (New York, 1975), p. 87.

20. "An Essay of Dramatic Poesy," in *Essays of John Dryden,* ed. W.P. Ker, 2 vols. (Oxford, Clarendon Press, 1900), 1:99. I am grateful to Christopher Ricks for letting me read his forthcoming article "Allusion: the Poet as Heir," which shows, with particular reference to Dryden, the importance of these attitudes of descent and legacy.

21. *Reflections on the Revolution in France . . .* (Garden City, 1973), p. 47.

22. Toronto, 1969.

23. Richard Howard, "Decades," in *American Review,* ed. Theodore Solotaroff (New York, 1975), p. 28.

24. Letter of 1732–33 in *Correspondence of Alexander Pope,* ed. George Sherburn (Oxford, 1956), 3:343.

25. *Repetition: An Essay in Experimental Psychology* (New York, 1964), p. 33. Barbara Lauren has pointed out to me that this kind of repetition creates a *contextual* allusion that may be opposed to the *textual* allusion of reference.

26. *The Anxiety of Influence* (New York, 1973), pp. 77–92.

27. Among the editors of Congreve and Jonson who have not noticed any allusion are Summers and Mares, and Egon Tiedje does not mention any in his *Die Tradition Ben Jonsons in der Restaurationskomödie* (Hamburg, 1963).

28. *A Concordance to the Plays of William Congreve* (Ithaca, 1973).

29. *A Grammar of Metaphor* (London, 1958), pp. 303–05.

30. I am indebted to Lisa Jardine for her comments on this subject, and to Franz H. Mautner for directing me to his important studies of aphorism, especially "Der Aphorismus als Literatur," in his book of collected essays *Wort und Wesen: Kleinere Schriften zur Literatur und Sprache* (Frankfurt am Main, 1974), pp. 279–99. Brian Vickers has also suggested that Pope's practice here is comparable to Swift's use of Bacon.

GEORGES MAY

Autobiography and the Eighteenth Century

Only a few years ago literary scholars could still be heard complaining—and with some justification—that autobiography was not receiving its fair share of the attention of contemporary criticism.[1] The situation is now radically different: in the last decade or so, and on both sides of the Atlantic, theoretical writings on the subject have appeared at an unprecedented rate.[2] The bulk of them justify retrospectively the prophetic assertion made by one of the complainers, to the effect that literary theorists had been wrong in neglecting for so long a type of writing seemingly incompatible with the contemporary vogue for methodology, for in effect autobiography "is a mode of art complex enough to delight the heart of the most mechanical textual engineer."[3] As a result, a theory of autobiography has clearly been for some time in the process of being constructed. Judging, however, from the fundamental contradictions still reflected in the writings of contemporary students of the subject, no consensus is about to be reached.

One of the reasons for the deadlock was perceptively analyzed over twenty years ago by one of the chief pioneers in the field. In the opening pages of his influential book *English Autobiography*, Wayne Shumaker pointed out that, on the one hand, a sound working definition of autobiography could not be agreed upon in the absence of what he called "a trustworthy history" of autobiographical texts, and that, on the other, the writing of such a history would first require a sound working definition, enabling the historian to steer an intelligent course through the maze of literary works which could all claim to be autobiographical. "Accordingly," wrote Shumaker, "the critic and the historian are like men who stand outside a doorway inviting each other, by gestures and smiles of encouragement, to go first to the buffet supper within, while the bread and ham and cheese lie undisturbed on the table."[4] Regardless of the mass of critical writings on autobiography of the last few years, and regardless of the ingenuity displayed by their authors, we are still in the same impasse. The two men are still outside the doorway, and it would be hazardous to predict which will eat his sandwich first.

If, therefore, the present essay attempts to build what is primarily an historical argument, it is less out of conviction that history has a better chance than theory of breaking out of the vicious circle than because of personal preferences. But it is also because of the fact that, while scholars of autobiography still appear to disagree on almost every proposition of a theoretical nature, they often echo each other in observing that modern autobiography had its origins in the eighteenth century with the writings of such masters as Rousseau, Gibbon, Franklin, and Goethe.[5]

The initial purpose of this essay is to probe the legitimacy of this consensus: did modern autobiography indeed have its start in the eighteenth century? And, since the question will be answered in the affirmative, its ulterior purpose is to try to understand the reasons behind this historical fact, with the ultimate hope that a better appreciation of the nature of autobiography may perhaps also be gained in the process.

I

One of the reasons why contemporary theorists have been unable so far to agree on a definition of autobiography—and why, therefore, this essay will not, as it should, begin with a definition—probably has to do with the fact that the term "autobiography" constitutes a label of an essentially different nature from the other ones commonly used to docket works of literature. Autobiography is neither a genre, nor a form, nor a style, nor even a language, as has been argued—often with considerable skill—by one or the other of the chief contemporary theorists of this kind of literature. Rather it is something much vaguer and more general: a literary attitude, which we have come readily to recognize because we have all read so much autobiographical literature, but which simply does not lend itself to the would-be scientific approaches featured in most trends of contemporary literary theory.

To be sure this attitude can be observed long before the eighteenth century, in the works of authors as varied as Saint Augustine, Cardano, Cellini, Montaigne, or Bunyan, to mention only a few of the better-known writers whose works are often viewed as early prototypes by students of autobiography. Nevertheless, certain aspects of this attitude, and especially certain of their literary consequences, probably cannot be observed, and surely not all simultaneously, before the eighteenth century. Let us now examine briefly three of these aspects.

First, it is doubtful that, prior, say, to Jean-Jacques Rousseau, any autobiographer harbored the rather outrageous pretension of attracting the interest of a reading public—albeit posthumously—to the biography of a given individual—himself—by virtue of the simple fact that he was a human being. Among the early prototypes we find writers who assumed the public might be interested in their life histories, but for some specific reason or reasons on which their reputations were based, quite independent of their eventual fame as autobiographers. Such a case clearly would be that of Benvenuto Cellini, who states at the very beginning of his *Life:* "All men of whatsoever quality they be, who have done anything of excellence, or which may properly resemble excellence, ought, if they are persons of truth and honesty, to describe their life with their own hands."[6] Others, especially Montaigne, seemingly believed that the public would be interested in them merely because they were fellow-members of the human race, but they did not write full-fledged autobiographies: in this respect, the *Essays* offer at best a collection of disconnected self-portraits. Indeed one should perhaps, at this point, ask the rhetorical question whether the reading public can ever be interested in the life story of any individual whose only claim to fame is precisely his autobiography. Granted that attics the world over are presumably full of unpublished autobiographies by quite unknown men and women, few responsible publishers would deem it a worthwhile business to print them, regardless of the seemingly insatiable hunger of today's reading public for "private lives."

Yet there appear to be, beginning with the eighteenth century, exceptions or near exceptions to this rule—if indeed it is one. Take, for instance, Casanova's *Memoirs*. Although perhaps not an out-and-out nobody, their author surely was in no way a public figure. Indeed Casanova himself was the first to acknowledge this, as he stated in his "preface": "Dear reader, examine the spirit of this preface, and you will at once guess at my purpose. I have written a preface because I wish you to know me thoroughly before you begin the reading of my

Memoirs. It is only in a coffee-room or at a *table d'hôte* that we like to converse with strangers."[7] Casanova's fame rests, therefore, exclusively on his *Memoirs,* as does also that of his anonymous follower, a century later, the Victorian author of the celebrated *My Secret Life,* whose reputation cannot result from anything but his autobiography, since we are not even sure who he was. If this is so, then must we not acknowledge the novelty in the eighteenth century, not only of the attitude of the autobiographer who assumes his private life to be of potential interest to the public, but—perhaps more important—of the attitude of the public itself ratifying this assumption?

To be sure, as we speculate on eighteenth-century attitudes, we should not be blind to the danger of doing so from a distortingly modern viewpoint: what captures our interest today may well be merely a reflection of our modern cultural prejudices and may have left the average eighteenth-century reader indifferent. The fact is, for instance, that most of the men and women of the period who undertook to write stories of their lives did so, as had almost all of their predecessors in the seventeenth century, primarily in an effort to bear witness to what they had seen and heard, and eventually also done, rather than out of the urge to express their intimate personalities. In other words, they were motivated as memoir-writers, even if they often—and here lies the novelty—wrote also as autobiographers.

In this respect Donald Greene was entirely correct when he attempted to build a case for the reading of eighteenth-century autobiographies on the basis of their unique documentary value.[8] Nevertheless, his viewpoint, faithful as it is to that of the eighteenth century, is nowadays largely an obsolete one. As the average eighteenth-century autobiographer attempted—consciously and conscientiously—to fulfill his duty as a privileged witness, it happens that in the process of so doing he also—wittingly or unwittingly—wrote self-revelatory statements, which, in our post-Romantic and voyeuristic age, have now become the real source of the continuing interest of the reading public.

James Boswell, for instance, may well have felt that he personally had little claim to the curiosity and interest of his reader, aside from his privileged relationship with his illustrious friend Samuel Johnson. In the same way, Marguerite Cordier (Madame de Staal-Delaunay) was moved in the 1740s to write her *Memoirs* essentially because she believed she had been a privileged witness to the life of a highly influential public figure of her time, the Duchesse du Maine. Whereas nowadays, as we know, Boswell's diaries have found their own faithful public, quite apart from what they may occasionally have to say about Dr. Johnson or other noteworthy contemporaries. As for Mme de Staal, most of the readers she still has today are entirely indifferent to and oblivious of her haughty mistress Mme du Maine.

While this shift admittedly reflects a great deal on ourselves, it also reflects on the nature of these eighteenth-century texts. If we should think, for instance, of so prestigious a predecessor of Mme de Staal as Joinville, writing in the early fourteenth century his *Memoirs* on the life of Louis IX, what still holds our interest in them today is primarily the record of what Joinville saw and heard, occasionally of what he said or did, but not of what he was, about which the *Memoirs* tell us nearly nothing. Although Joinville may well have been quite as interesting an individual as Boswell or Mme de Staal, we can read him only as we do a reporter, because his book does not readily lend itself to a more personal approach.

Concluding now on this first and original aspect of eighteenth-century autobiography—which could be viewed as a new emphasis on "private lives"—one can postulate that, beginning toward the middle of the eighteenth century, even memoir-writers (as distinguished from autobiographers) could not fail to write about themselves, even when their conscious intention was not to do so. As for the distinction between memoirs and autobiographies, it is only a theoretical one: the fact is that there is a continuous spectrum from one to the other, say from Joinville to Rousseau, or from Caesar to Gibbon. In most works of this nature the two elements—testimony and self-revelation—are present: only their dosage varies. The hypothesis which has just been discussed is that, some time toward the middle of the eighteenth century, the scale began to tip toward self-revelation, and, in so doing, contributed to the advent of modern autobiography.

In order to move on now to the second original aspect of eighteenth-century autobiography, we must backtrack briefly to the distinction made earlier and *en passant* between autobiography and self-portrait.[9] Entries in a diary, or, as was suggested above, texts of the kind of Montaigne's disconnected, probing looks at himself, are more akin to self-portraits than to autobiography. The reason for this statement is that, in order fully to deserve its name, autobiography must, like biography, encompass an entire life, or at least a good part of a life.

Short of this, a crucial element is missing, namely the experience of the passing of time.

A consequence of this is that an authentic autobiographer can rarely—and perhaps never—escape the need at some point to strive at reconstructing his own past to show its unity and continuity. In so doing he may either recreate this continuity by discovering it himself retrospectively, or, more often, he may introduce it *ex post facto* into the blocks of his life already completed. The point at issue is not, therefore, whether the autobiographer is truthful, but whether, in disposing his facts in some kind of order, he is or not following the inner urge to achieve a meaningful pattern. While this particular phenomenon has been observed and discussed by a number of previous critics,[10] it is so central to the present argument that it ought perhaps to be briefly illustrated with a few examples.

The case of Rousseau immediately comes to mind, for his entire autobiographical endeavor, whether in the *Confessions* (written in the 1760s) or in the *Dialogues* (written in the late 1770s), clearly was to demonstrate that the inconsistencies and contradictions which his enemies were gloating over were not in fact present in his life. Whether he meant to convince himself or his readers of this proposition is a moot point; but, again, it is less the historical veracity which is here at issue than the intention. In Rousseau's case it is so well-known that it probably is unnecessary to insist on his capital example. Moreover, since Rousseau is still too often regarded nowadays as a paranoiac, his approach to autobiography may be judged by some readers to be aberrant, whereas, at least on this particular point, it is in fact exemplary. A quick look at some of his followers will confirm this judgment.

The first one chronologically is Benjamin Franklin, a man as famous for his common sense as Rousseau is for his idiosyncrasies. The second part of his *Autobiography* was "begun at Passy 1784," less than two years after the posthumous publication of the first six books of Rousseau's *Confessions*. Therein Franklin discusses his allegedly lifelong method aimed at achieving what he calls "moral perfection." Throughout the passage on this subject the old man's effort at remolding his early life to the image of his later one is noticeable, but perhaps nowhere more so than in the concluding part: ". . . it may be my Posterity should be informed, that to this little Artifice, with the Blessing of God, their Ancestor ow'd the constant Felicity of Life down to his 79th Year in which this is written. What Reverses may attend the Remainder is in the Hand of Providence: But if they arrive the Reflection on past Happiness enjoy'd ought to help the Bearing them with more Resignation."[11]

Equally as symptomatic as Franklin's use of the adjective *constant* of the urge to emphasize the cohesive pattern of one's life is Gibbon's choice of image when, in his *Memoirs of My Life,* he comes to the crucial passage from adolescence to adulthood which took place during his first stay in Switzerland: "Such as I am, in Genius or learning or manners, I owe my creation to Lausanne: it was in that school, that the statue was discovered in the block of marble."[12] As a recent and perceptive commentator on this particular aspect of Gibbon's autobiography puts it: "Gibbon became an autobiographer for the same reason he became a historian—to see a pattern or plan in what might appear to be, from a distance, a welter of haphazard, chaotic, or contradictory experiences."[13]

When it comes now to the harmonious and majestic development of Goethe's life, as it smoothly unfolds to the readers of *Dichtung und Wahrheit,* it also quite clearly is a deliberate creation of the autobiographer himself, whose choice of a title, as has been observed more than once, makes his intention transparent. For the second part of his autobiography Goethe chose as an epigraph a quotation from one of his own earlier works, thus subtly underscoring his consistency, quite apart from the claim to continuity contained in the quotation itself: "Was man in der Jugend wünscht, hat man im Alter die Fülle" ("What youth desires, old age brings in abundance"). The practical application of this surprising and reassuring axiom is spelled out at least twice to the reader of *Dichtung und Wahrheit:*

> Our wishes are presentiments of the capabilities which lie within us, and harbingers of that which we shall be in a condition to perform. Whatever we are able and would like to do, presents itself to our imagination, as without us and in the future. We feel a longing after that which we already possess in secret. Thus a passionate anticipating grasp changes the truly possible into a dream of reality.
>
> There are few biographies which can present a pure, quiet, steady progress of the individual. Our life, as well as that whole in which we are contained, is, in an incomprehensible manner, composed of freedom and necessity. That which we would do is a prediction of what we shall do, under all circumstances.[14]

Although all these quotations beg for comment and discussion, perhaps they will suffice as they stand to support the contention that these autobiographers' efforts at reconstructing, retrospectively and in an orderly manner, lives which in all probability had been lived with more abandon and less fear of inconsistency, are a characteristic feature of eighteenth-century autobiography. One could retort, of course, pointing especially to Saint Augustine's *Confessions,* that this feature can be detected long before the eighteenth century. But it is a well-known fact that, in literary history, it is nearly always possible to find isolated precedents for any given aspect of literature; whereas, beginning in the latter half of the eighteenth century, examples, far from being isolated, appear in large numbers. Indeed it is on this third original aspect of eighteenth-century autobiographies that we should now concentrate briefly: the sudden concentration of autobiographical vocations and talents.

To begin with, this historical phenomenon should not simply be dismissed as accidental by ascribing it wholly to the admittedly enormous influence of Rousseau's *Confessions,* posthumously published between 1782 and 1789. While it is quite true that the model they provided was almost instantaneously and overtly imitated, not only in France by Restif de la Bretonne, Madame Roland, Marmontel, and a few others, harbingers of the tidal wave which was to follow, but on the other side of the Channel as well, notably by Gibbon, we should not forget that, regardless of their prodigious impact, Rousseau's *Confessions* did not create the fashion out of whole cloth. No single work is ever sufficient to create a fashion; else, one might ask, why did the famous works of some of Rousseau's predecessors—Saint Augustine, Cellini, Montaigne—not give birth to an earlier autobiographical tradition?

As we know, the suggestion for Rousseau to write the story of his life came, not so much from an inner and irresistible impulse, as from the very clear- and commercially-minded publisher Marc-Michel Rey of Amsterdam, who had the extraordinary critical insight to sense both that the public of the 1760s had an interest in autobiography and that Rousseau had an innate talent for it. Even without Rousseau the eighteenth century would have witnessed the onset of modern autobiography, although admittedly things would not have been quite the same.

Another illusion against which we should guard as we look at these first few major achievements in modern autobiography is to think that they differ much in intent and perhaps even in nature from many other less outstanding contemporary attempts. Far from it: the autobiographies of Rousseau, Franklin, Gibbon, and Goethe have this important feature in common with quite a few less universally known ones of their age, that they were written with the intention to crown, in one way or another, large and famous literary productions. In other words, they were premised on already existing reputations, much in the way that Cellini's *Life* was premised on its author's achievements as an artist. The examples of three more or less contemporary playwrights—chosen among many others which could serve as well—will perhaps help clarify the argument. Colley Cibber in England, Jean-François Marmontel in France, and Carlo Gozzi in Italy were all three successful authors of many plays which—justly or wrongly—have suffered severe devaluation subsequently, while their reputations as autobiographers have survived to the point that their autobiographies are nowadays just about the only works of theirs still to attract readers. By virtue of a remarkable paradox, whereas their autobiographies deserved according to them to be read because of their other achievements as writers, the judgment of posterity is that, although they now are all but forgotten as playwrights, nevertheless their autobiographies remain worth reading. On the one hand, this makes their case analogous in a way to that of Casanova. On the other, it adds force to the argument that the time in which they lived marked the beginning of the golden age of autobiography.

II

As we think back upon the brilliant quartet of outstanding men—Rousseau, Franklin, Gibbon, and Goethe—whose names presumably would appear on anyone's list of major autobiographers of all times, we observe that, despite Rousseau's and Gibbon's short-lived flirtation with Catholicism, they were all Protestants. In view of the importance of the role of confession in Catholic life, and of the frequently heard opinion that autobiography is in some ways linked to confession, this fact may first strike some as unexpected. Could the title chosen by Rousseau in the wake of Saint Augustine be misleading? The answer has to be yes for at least two reasons. The first is that there is so little common ground between confessing to God, which is Saint Augustine's purpose, and confessing to man, which is, only in part,

Rousseau's, that it is regrettable that Rousseau did not choose another title for his first autobiography. The second reason is that, as has just been suggested, the confession of some of his misdeeds is only one of Rousseau's several motivations as an autobiographer, and almost surely not the most important. If we were to use the classification suggested by a recent critic of autobiography, we would certainly say that Rousseau's *Confessions*—as well as his *Dialogues*—deserve more the label "Apology" than "Confession."[15] One way or the other the false homonymy between the two famous titles has unfortunately contributed to obscuring the fact that there is very little in common between Rousseau's attitude toward autobiography and Saint Augustine's. In the interval, and especially toward the end of it, had taken place that critical cultural change: secularization.

This basic shift in attitude and in values probably constitutes the first major factor accounting for the timing of the birth of modern autobiography. Frequently analyzed and discussed by scholars, it requires little elaboration at this point. Georges Gusdorf among others has devoted an unusually pertinent and impressive section of one of his books to showing how individualism constituted, especially in the Renaissance, a "modern" attitude falling outside the Christian tradition. Although his analysis deals in part with periods other than the eighteenth century, it remains highly relevant to our concerns here. Indeed it includes a number of penetrating remarks regarding the difference between Saint Augustine's *Confessions* and Rousseau's.[16]

At the opposite pole, other scholars, notably William Matthews,[17] appear prepared to include religiously inspired memoirs in the autobiographical tradition. As a result and on the basis of the distinguished English group of seventeenth-century Christian writers (John Bunyan, Richard Baxter, Margaret Cavendish, and others), a case has been made for rolling back the starting point of modern autobiography all the way to the mid-seventeenth century. The reason, however, why in the present essay this group of writers is disqualified from membership in the modern autobiographical tradition is precisely because the onset of this tradition would appear inexplicable outside of its historical connection with the trend toward growing secularization.

Essential though it is, however, secularization does not suffice to explain everything. As we know, major swerves in the history of human culture result most often, not from single causes, but from clusters of interrelated causal forces. Next in importance to the power-

ful trend toward secularization is probably that other shift which
Wayne Shumaker had in mind when, singling out what he thought
was the most significant cause "for the emergence of an interest in
'truthful' life histories," he mentioned "the substitution of inductive
thought habits for deductive. . . . The view that Truth, instead of
being already known in its essentials, could be discovered only by the
slow accumulation of particulars."[18]

That this factor, which could be described also as a growing preference for the concrete over the abstract, has in other respects been identified as a hallmark of the eighteenth century could be confirmed in
many widely different ways. For instance, in the first chapter of his
Philosophy of the Enlightenment, Ernst Cassirer identified as a basic feature of the European Enlightenment what he called "a shifting of emphasis. This emphasis is constantly moving from the general to the
particular, from principles to phenomena."[19]

One could seek another confirmation simply by glancing at the
contemporary development of the novel. The favorite model of the
eighteenth century, as we know, was the novel, frequently written in
the first person, that related the story of an individual character. The
greatest fictional heroes and heroines of the time all pour forth themselves the stories of their lives: Moll Flanders and Pamela, Marianne
and Des Grieux, Tristram Shandy and Werther. Indeed a French scholar has recently defended the striking hypothesis that the rise of
memoir writing in the late seventeenth century was made possible in
France by the strength of literary fashions present in the contemporary
development of the novel,[20] whereas one tended to believe that the
reverse had taken place. One way or the other, the conclusion would
be the same, in pointing to a causal factor clearly connected with the
trend toward secularization: instead of being known because of accepted universal principles, the truth about man had from then on to be
achieved slowly, problematically, and indirectly through the study of
selected individuals, imaginary or authentic, depending on whether
one read novels or autobiographies.

Oddly enough this interest in a multiplicity of different models of
humanity did in no way detract from the belief—which was to remain
pretty much unchallenged until the twentieth century—that there was
also such an entity as Man. The shift in sensibility between the preceding age and the eighteenth century simply oriented the curiosity of the
public less toward the universal attributes which made men all alike

than toward the more picturesque, and eventually exotic, factors which made them outwardly different from each other. In this respect, the eighteenth-century taste for what eventually came to be known as anthropology ought probably to be explained by reasons quite different from those which lie behind the current vogue of anthropology. Structuralism, which is one of the intellectual temptations of our own age, although originally connected with anthropology through the works of Claude Lévi-Strauss, rests in effect on assumptions radically different from those of the eighteenth century. Based on a faith in a scientific method of approach, it consists first in establishing universal principles on the basis of an observation of various cultural data, and then in applying these principles in a primarily deductive manner. If we go back to Cassirer's analysis of eighteenth-century philosophy, this method may well appear to proceed from a step back to pre-eighteenth-century attitudes of the mind, associated with the philosophical systems of Descartes or Leibnitz.

These conjectures lead to a third consideration which may help us to understand why modern autobiography had its first heyday in the late eighteenth century. It has to do with another well-known problem: that of the relationship between science and art. A recent book by an American historian discusses among other topics the issue of whether history is an art or a science, and reminds us that the pervasive attitude of the eighteenth century, especially although not exclusively in France, was that the dominion of art, or at the very least of literary art, was much broader than is nowadays held to be the case.[21] According to the prevailing taste of the time astronomy, geology, zoology, as well as what we now call, begging the question, political science, and several other sciences and pseudo-sciences, all lent themselves to sophisticated literary presentation, under the pen of gifted stylists such as Fontenelle, Montesquieu, Voltaire, Buffon, Swift, Hume, Gibbon, Franklin and many other literary artists. Behind this phenomenon, which also accounts for the fact that the autobiographies of the time are works of art in their own rights, may lie the hypothesis or the belief that truth is perhaps a subjective, rather than an objective, concept.

If this is so, then it follows that this third consideration is linked with the previous one. In order to find some support for this rather tempting hypothesis, let us recall Rousseau's famous discussion of the question of historical truth—in this case of autobiographical truth—as he conducts it in the fourth Promenade of the *Rêveries* (1777). In an effort to defend his own truthfulness in the *Confessions,* Rousseau writes:

> I never said less; at times I said more, not where facts, but where circumstances surrounding them were concerned; and this kind of lie resulted more from an excess of imagination than from an act of the will. Indeed I am wrong to call this a lie, for none of these additions was one. When writing my *Confessions,* I was already old and felt a distaste for the hollow pleasures of life, which I had barely sampled and of which my heart had fully felt the vanity. I was writing from memory; memory often failed me, or offered me but incomplete remembrances; and I filled in the gaps with details with which my imagination supplemented these remembrances, but which never contradicted them. I loved to tarry on the happy moments of my life, and occasionally I embellished them with ornaments suggested to me by nostalgia. I said things which I had forgotten as they seemed to me to have probably been, as they perhaps had indeed been, never at variance with what I remembered them to have been.[22]

While this may strike us as an unusual way in which to establish one's truthfulness, we should remember that it was by no means exclusive to Rousseau. Even though he thought of himself as different from all others—a belief still shared by some of his readers—the difference, in this case as in many others, was one of degree rather than of kind. The same attitude precisely can be detected among many of his followers. Here again the title chosen by Goethe for his autobiography comes to mind, as well as the explanation given of it by the author at the end of his preface, where he cites "the half-poetic, half-historical treatment employed."

If autobiographical truth is indeed different from historical or scientific truth, then perhaps we can understand why would-be scientific critical methods of approach have not yet succeeded in producing an acceptable theory of autobiography. Again the difficulty is a familiar one: how could a rational analysis be adequate to what often is admittedly the record of irrational experiences? This question leads to a final consideration in this rapid survey of the possible causes accounting for the birth of modern autobiography in the eighteenth century. An example will help formulate it: it is the story of Goethe's betrothal to Lilli Schönemann as he recounts it in the seventeenth book of *Dichtung und Wahrheit.* After the two lovers have heeded the command uttered by Mlle Delf—"Take each other by the hand!"—they fall into each other's arms, an experience which the autobiographer recalls as "the most agreeable of all recollections." Whereupon he comments, "It is pleasant to recall those feelings, which are with difficulty expressed and are hardly to be explained."[23]

The charm held for the older Goethe by this episode of his youthful years still operates on today's readers of his autobiography, as does that of several other similar events recorded in the book. The text invites us to wonder at this point whether the reason for this fascination has to do with the fact that the incident is felt by the young man to be inexplicable, or rather—for it strikes us as perhaps less mysterious than Goethe states it to be—with the fact that it does not result from entirely rational causes. Analogous passages could easily be found in other autobiographies of the eighteenth century: Gibbon's conversion to the Catholic faith, or Rousseau's vision on the road to Vincennes. They all have this feature in common, that a crucial experience of the past is vividly remembered by the autobiographer who finds himself all the more fascinated by it that he cannot account for it rationally.

Thus the journey back to one's past can be seen as opening a window onto another world, a world lying beyond the oppressively rationalistic atmosphere which one breathed at the time, and which, to a very large extent, we are still breathing today. For, despite what has been recalled above regarding the shift from deduction to induction, or from principles to phenomena, the despotic dominion of reason had not yet been shaken. In spite of this—or rather, perhaps, because of it—the yearning for something else, something more fulfilling and more exalting, took during the latter part of the eighteenth century several strikingly irrational forms, notably the taste for the esoteric and the occult. Perhaps it is appropriate at this point simply to recall that Mesmer was born only nine years after Kant, and Saint-Martin ten years after him.[24]

In line with this final hypothesis, then, the turn toward autobiography would appear to fit within the general movement of ideas in the period as it is known to us. The autobiographical urge experienced, roughly at the same time, by a number of the most distinguished minds of the time, especially with its stress on childhood, on obscure instincts, and on the mysterious recesses of the psyche, may well have been part of a spontaneous search for an antidote to the excessively rational side of the Enlightenment. And, in turn, perhaps this consideration may also help us understand why autobiography, regardless of the pronouncements of its overeager gravediggers,[25] still holds such a powerful appeal for today's reading public. For, if the previous argument has any merit, then it may strike us that the historicocultural factors which contributed to the birth of modern autobiography two centuries ago are strikingly akin to those which are observable in our own contemporary culture. Our age, too, has witnessed a sharp move toward secularization, an increasingly ambiguous attitude vis-a-vis the powers of reason and of scientific thinking, and the temptation of the irrational. And our age, too, is still witnessing—regardless of the fact that the printed word is supposed to have been superseded several years ago by the other so-called media—a relentless outpouring of autobiographies for which the thirst of the public is seemingly unabated. Both observations may be deemed reassuring to those of us, devotees of the eighteenth century, who find it heartening to identify common grounds between that bygone age and our own.

NOTES

1. "Autobiography has been unjustifiably ignored by contemporary literary critics," wrote, for instance, Stephen A. Shapiro at the beginning of the abstract of his "The Dark Continent of Literature: Autobiography," *Comparative Literature Studies* 5 (Dec. 1968): 421.

2. Here are a few titles, beginning in 1968, aside from the essay mentioned in the previous note: Barrett John Mandel, "The Autobiographer's Art," *The Journal of Aesthetics and Art Criticism* 27 (1968): 215–26; Francis R. Hart, "Notes for an Anatomy of Modern Autobiography," *New Literary History* 1 (1969–70): 485–511; Jean Starobinski, "Le style de l'autobiographie," in *La relation critique* (Paris, 1970), pp. 83–98 (previously published in *Poétique,* 1970); Michel Lejeune, *L'autobiographie en France* (Paris, 1971); James Olney, *Metaphors of the Self: The Meaning of Autobiography* (Princeton, 1972); *Genre* (two special issues on autobiography) 6 (March–June 1973): 1–249; Michel Lejeune, "Le pacte autobiographique," *Poétique,* No. 14 (April 1973): 137–62; Elisabeth W. Bruss, "L'autobiographie considérée comme acte littéraire," *Poétique,* No. 17 (1974): 14–26; William L. Howarth, "Some Principles of Autobiography," *New Literary History* 5 (Winter 1974): 363–81; Roger J. Porter and Howard R. Wolf, *The Voice Within: Reading and Writing Autobiography* (New York, 1973); Jeffrey Mehlman, *A Structural Study of Autobiography: Proust, Leiris, Sartre, Lévi-Strauss* (Ithaca, 1974); Karl J. Weintraub, "Autobiography and Historical Consciousness," *Critical Inquiry* 1 (1974–75): 821–48; seven papers of the symposium on autobiography held in December 1974 at the Collège de France (*Revue d'Histoire littéraire de la France* 75 [1975]: 899–

1066); PhilippeLejeune,*LePacteautobiographique* (Paris, 1975); and Elizabeth Bruss, *Autobiographical Acts: The Changing Situation of a Literary Genre* (Baltimore, 1976).

3. Shapiro, "The Dark Continent of Literature," p. 424.

4. Wayne Shumaker, *English Autobiography: Its Emergence, Materials and Form* (Berkeley and Los Angeles, 1954), p. 1.

5. See, for instance, Shumaker, *English Autobiography,* pp. 20 ff.; Roy Pascal, *Design and Truth in Autobiography* (Cambridge, Mass., 1960), chapter 3, "The Classical Age of Autobiography"; Shapiro, "The Dark Continent of Literature," p. 422; and Francis R. Hart, "Notes for an Anatomy," p. 492.

6. *The Autobiography of Benvenuto Cellini,* trans. John Addington Symonds (New York, 1927), p. 3.

7. *The Memoirs of Jacques Casanova de Seingalt,* trans. Arthur Machen, 6 vols. (New York, n.d.), 1: xl. Some time after the present article was sent in, René Démoris, in the introduction of his edition of Casanova's *Mémoires* (Paris, 1977), p. xxix, discussed the feature which makes this autobiography "an original departure in the development of the genre, in that for the first time the non-historical individual comes into his own *as a non-historical individual*" (author's italics; my translation).

8. Donald Greene, "The Uses of Autobiography in the Eighteenth Century," in *Essays in Eighteenth-Century Biography,* ed. Philip B. Daghlian (Bloomington, 1968), pp. 43–66.

9. For a discussion of this frequently made distinction, see, for instance, Shumaker, *English Autobiography,* p. 103; and Georges Gusdorf, "Conditions et limites de l'autobiographie," in *Formen der Selbstdarstellung: Analekten zu einer Geschichte des literarischen Selbstportraits,* ed. Günter Reichenkron and Erich Haase (Berlin, 1956), p. 111. This distinction, on the other hand, is blurred throughout by William L. Howarth's essay (cited above).

10. See, for instance, Pascal, *Design and Truth,* pp. 184–85; and Mandel, "The Autobiographer's Art," pp. 220–21.

11. *The Autobiography of Benjamin Franklin,* ed. Leonard W. Labaree et al. (New Haven, 1964), p. 157.

12. Edward Gibbon, *Memoirs of my Life,* ed. Georges A. Bonnard (London, 1966), p. 86.

13. Roger J. Porter, "Gibbon's Autobiography: Filling up the Silent Vacancy," *Eighteenth-Century Studies* 8 (Fall 1974): 5–6.

14. Johann Wolfgang von Goethe, *Dichtung und Wahrheit,* trans. John Oxenford (New York, 1969); or see the University of Chicago Press's edition, 2 vols. (1974), 1:420–21, and 2:95. The first quotation appears near the end of book 9; the second toward the middle of book 11.

15. " 'Confession' is personal history that seeks to communicate or express the essential nature, the truth, of the self. 'Apology' is personal history that seeks to demonstrate or realize the integrity of the self. 'Memoir' is personal history that seeks to articulate or repossess the historicity of the self" (Hart, "Notes for an Anatomy," p. 491). Rousseau himself protested by anticipation against the possible interpretation that his *Confessions* were

an "apologie." See, for instance, the earlier version of his introductory statement to the *Confessions,* in *Œuvres complètes,* "Bibliothèque de la Pléiade" (Paris, 1959), vol. 1, p. 1149.

16. Georges Gusdorf, *La Découverte de soi* (Paris, 1948): "L'attitude dogmatique."

17. William Matthews, "Seventeenth-Century Autobiography," in William Matthews and Ralph W. Rader, *Autobiography, Biography and the Novel* (Los Angeles, 1973), pp. 1–26. See also Paul Delany, *British Autobiography in the Seventeenth Century* (London, 1969).

18. Shumaker, *English Autobiography,* p. 29.

19. Ernst Cassirer, *The Philosophy of the Enlightenment* (Boston, 1955), p. 22.

20. René Démoris, *Le Roman à la première personne; du classicisme aux Lumières* (Paris, 1975), pp. 99, 125.

21. Peter Gay, *Style in History* (New York, 1974), pp. 185 ff.

22. Rousseau, *Œuvres complètes,* p. 1035. My translation.

23. Goethe, *Dichtung und Wahrheit,* 2:345.

24. An interesting witness of the late eighteenth century, the Baroness d'Oberkirch, observes several times in her *Memoirs* the contrast between the rational philosophy of her age and the fascination of her contemporaries for the esoteric. To wit this entry, datelined 1784 and suggested by the success of Saint-Martin's *Tableau naturel des rapports qui existent entre Dieu, l'homme et l'univers:* "This century the most immoral ever, the most unbelieving, the most philosophically boastful, is switching, as it nears its end, not toward faith, but toward gullibility, superstition, devotion to the supernatural. Would it be because, like an old sinner afraid of hell, it judges its fear to be tantamount to repentance? As we look around, we see nothing but sorcerers, initiates, necromancers and prophets. What will the last years be like of a century which began so flashingly, which used up so much paper to prove its materialistic utopias, and which is now only concerned with the soul and its sovereignty over the body and its instincts?" (*Mémoires,* 2 vols. [Paris, n.d.], 2:87). My translation.

25. See, for instance, the opening pages of André Malraux's *Antimémoires* (Paris, 1968).

FRANK H. ELLIS

Johnson and Savage: Two Failed Tragedies and a Failed Tragic Hero

Two failed tragedies lie in the background of the ill-sorted relationship between Richard Savage and Samuel Johnson. *Irene: A Tragedy* and *The Tragedy of Sir Thomas Overbury* were indeed one of the few common denominators between Johnson and Savage. Otherwise the ratio between them was oddly proportioned. Savage's fascination for Johnson arose from his unquestionable possession of the very thing that Johnson lacked—the thing that young Samuel Johnson, like every young person, calls "Knowledge of Life." Savage had killed a man in a drunken brawl in a bawdy house. "Knowledge of Life was indeed his chief Attainment," Johnson says.[1]

But not just anyone "acquainted with all the Scenes of Debauchery"[2] could have so fascinated this serious and slightly prudish, twenty-nine-year-old married man. Savage's secondary attainments were equally irresistible. His origins were an impenetrable mystery: "I am, *nominally,* No-body's Son at all," he said.[3] Johnson's origins were painfully apparent: he was the son of a provincial tradesman. "In the taking off his hat and disposing it under his arm, and in his bow, [Savage] displayed as much grace as those actions were capable of."[4] Of this kind of grace Johnson was simply incapable. When Johnson met Savage in the last months of 1737 or the first months of 1738,[5] two of Savage's plays had already been produced on the stage of Drury Lane. The play that had brought Johnson to London in the first place had to wait eleven years to be produced on the same stage.

Most important of all, as "a Gentleman in Distress,"[6] Savage appealed simultaneously to two of Johnson's most powerful emotions: his instinct of what he called "Subordination" and his feelings of compassion. Johnson believed that "There is a reciprocal pleasure in governing and being governed"[7] and no one can doubt that the son of the

provincial bookseller sometimes enjoyed subordinating himself to the
legal heir of the second earl of Macclesfield and the natural son of the
fourth earl Rivers (as Johnson believed Savage to have been). But because Savage was "an *injured* Nobleman,"[8] Johnson's protective, paternal instincts were aroused, the feelings that required him many
years later to take up on his back a prostitute who had collapsed in the
street and carry her home to be nursed back to health. Savage's "Distress" included, but was by no means limited to, undernourishment. It
was, according to Dr. Edmund Bergler, *"self-chosen, self-provoked,*
[and] *self-perpetuated,"*[9] so Johnson could do little to alleviate it.

That *The Tragedy of Sir Thomas Overbury* was a failure was already
known to Savage, and presumably to Johnson as well, at the time of
their meeting. Even if Johnson had not read the play, which was published in 1724, he would soon have learned that Savage "had taken a
Resolution to write a second Tragedy upon the Story of Sir *Thomas
Overbury.*" Johnson himself may have been one of the friends who
blamed Savage for not choosing another subject. And he certainly
heard Savage assert "that it was not easy to find a better; and that he
thought it his Interest to extinguish the Memory of the first Tragedy,
which he could only do by writing one less defective upon the same
Story."[10]

With this judgment of *The Tragedy of Sir Thomas Overbury* no one
would quarrel today. It would not be easy to find a better subject for a
tragedy than the destruction of an attractive, thirty-two-year old
courtier-poet-diplomat, Sir Thomas Overbury, by a ruthless woman
who wanted to marry Overbury's protégé, Robert Ker, viscount
Rochester, and a favorite of James I. But neither would it be easy to
defend Savage's alterations of the plot. "To assist him in imposing a
pattern upon his chaotic materials," Clarence Tracy has said, Savage
"invented a character and a theme not found in the historical accounts:
Isabella, an orphan, ward of the Earl of Somerset, who falls in love
with Sir Thomas, is the character; and the theme is that of the Countess
of Somerset's own love for Sir Thomas."[11] In historical fact, Sir
Thomas Overbury died in the Tower on 15 September 1613. In October Lady Frances Howard, who had suborned the jailers to poison
Sir Thomas, was awarded a divorce from her husband, Robert Devereux, earl of Essex, on the ridiculous ground of his "incapability."
James I cooperated by elevating Ker to the earldom of Somerset in

November. And on the day after Christmas 1613 Lady Frances completed her defeat of Sir Thomas Overbury by marrying Somerset.

By moving back Ker's elevation to the earldom and his marriage to Lady Frances to the days before Sir Thomas was committed to the Tower, Savage loses much of the Jacobean hugger-mugger and all of the homosexual innuendoes of the historical sources. Savage imposes a pattern upon his chaotic materials, but the pattern imposed is the familiar love triangle. In Savage's play Lady Frances kills Sir Thomas for "slighted love."[12] In fact she killed him for more complex—and more interesting—reasons.

This initial error accounts for most of the subsequent defects in the play. Somerset's discovery of his wife's infidelity is accomplished through the comic device of an intercepted love letter. Lady Frances mistaking her husband for her lover in the dark of the Tower is also comic stuff. Nor do the allusions to *The Rape of the Lock* help to realize a tragic tone. Details such as these help to explain why Savage thought that "a total Alteration of the Plan"[13] was necessary. He knew that *The Tragedy of Sir Thomas Overbury* was a failed tragedy.

And although the evidence is not as clear, it appears that Johnson, at about the same time, may have begun to suspect that *Irene: A Tragedy* was a failed tragedy. Johnson started to work on his one play during the winter of 1736–37, while he "kept his academy" at Edial, near Lichfield. He borrowed a copy of Richard Knolles's *The Generall Historie of the Turkes* from Peter Garrick, eldest brother of his pupil David. He drew up a list of characters and a prose outline of a plot, and began to fill in the outline.[14] By March 1737, when three acts had been finished, he set out for London, in company with his pupil, "to try his fate with a tragedy."[15] Fate was not kind, however, and when next heard of Johnson is back in Lichfield trying to finish his tragedy. But it "was not executed with his rapidity of composition upon other occasions," Boswell tells us. It was "slowly and painfully elaborated," a bitter example, perhaps, of Johnson's principle that "a man may write at any time if he set himself *doggedly* to it."[16]

In the last months of 1737 Johnson returned to London to see whether he could make his way as a writer. The first step, of course, was to get *Irene* produced. He looked up Peter Garrick, now embarked upon a career as wine merchant, and read him the finished play at the Fountain Tavern in the Strand. Garrick in turn urged Charles Fleetwood, the impresario of Drury Lane, to have it produced. But fate again was unpropitious. "Mr. Fleetwood would not accept it, probably," Boswell supposed, "because it was not patronized by some man of high rank."[17] But Hawkins complained that the language of "this laboured tragedy" was "cold and philosophical."[18] Thus at the same time that he was becoming acquainted with Richard Savage, Johnson was encountering fears that *Irene: A Tragedy* was a failed tragedy.

The reasons for the failure of *Irene: A Tragedy* are more complex than they are in the case of *The Tragedy of Sir Thomas Overbury*. Ultimately they derive from Johnson's limited ability to create a character that is not himself. "No man," Macaulay said, "ever had so little talent for personation as Johnson."[19] And, as Macaulay noticed, almost all of Johnson's characters, whether "injur'd THALES" or a young Englishwoman interested in calendar reform or an Eskimo named Anningait, speak in one voice: Johnson's. Here is a gentle Ethiopian princess:

> Whether perfect happiness would be procured by perfect goodness, said Nekayah, this world will never afford an opportunity of deciding. But this, at least, may be maintained, that we do not always find visible happiness in proportion to visible virtue.[20]

In race, class, sex, occupation, and experience Nekayah is as different from Samuel Johnson as might be imagined. But her voice is that of the moral essayist:

> It has been the boast of some . . . moralists, [Johnson said], that . . . happiness is the unfailing consequence of virtue. But . . . we do not always suffer by our crimes; we are not always protected by our innocence.[21]

The same limitation is apparent in *Irene: A Tragedy*.

The story that Johnson fixed upon in *The Generall Historie of the Turkes* has all the fascination of the abomination. Muhammad II was the sultan of Turkey who finally won the city of Constantine for Islam in 1453 and put an end to the Byzantine empire. Johnson may have been attracted to him because he spoke five languages, wrote verse, and patronized the arts. But otherwise Muhammad was a perfect barbarian. One of his first acts upon succeeding to the throne was to order the murder of his two younger brothers, one of whom was an infant of eighteen months. During the first days of his occupation of Stamboul he entertained himself after dinner by watching Greek resistance leaders being tortured to death.[22]

Among the Greek prisoners rounded up for Muhammad's seraglio was "one *Irene* . . . of such incomparable beauty and rare perfection" that Muhammad fell slavishly in love with her. "*Mars* slept in *Venus* lap, and now the soldiers might go play," as Knolles put it. Muhammad the Conqueror was "at war with himself . . . Reason calling unto him for his honor, and his amorous affections stil suggesting unto him new delights." And his soldiers, instead of playing, began plotting to depose him. So to reestablish his command and to reassert his barbarianism, Muhammad decapitated the woman he loved before his assembled bassas and military commanders, and ordered a march on Belgrade.[23]

To Dryden these bleak horrors might have suggested another hero play: *Mahomet the Conqueror: or All for Empire*. To Johnson they suggested a morality play. In *Irene* the heroine dies because she embraces Islam (in the hope of mitigating the plight of her people) and because she is (falsely) accused of plotting to overthrow Muhammad. The moral is impeccable: apostasy does not pay; ends do not justify means. But the play reads like a series of versified *Ramblers*.[24] Like the death of Sir Thomas Overbury, the legend of Irene is another good story that is spoiled in the retelling.

In the fall of 1743, when Johnson was writing *An Account of the Life of Mr. Richard Savage,* his thoughts were dominated by the fact of the two failed tragedies. This can be confirmed in several ways, but most simply, perhaps, by focusing on the genre of *An Account of the Life of Mr. Richard Savage*. The title implies biography, but biography it does not seem to be. "The Business of the Biographer," Johnson said, "is . . . to display the minute Details of daily Life."[25] What he himself admired in biography was "The delicate features of the mind, the nice discriminations of character, and the minute peculiarities of conduct."[26] But *An Account of the Life of Mr. Richard Savage* is deficient in "minute Details" of Savage's daily life and "minute peculiarities" of his conduct. In a work of 180 octavo pages there is hardly a handful: Savage standing in the dark before his mother's house in Old Bond Street, hoping to catch sight of her as she crossed a room by candlelight; Savage peddling Steele's pamphlet from publisher to publisher until he could get enough to pay their reckoning in a petty tavern; Savage begging pen and ink from shop to shop to write down the speeches of *The Tragedy of Sir Thomas Overbury* that he was composing peripatetically.[27] And even in the few detailed scenes that Johnson described, Savage remains faceless and voiceless.

Johnson tells us that Savage's voice was "tremulous and mournful," but we never hear this voice in *An Account of the Life of Mr. Richard Savage*. The opportunities that Johnson had to give Savage a voice are simply thrown away. On the one occasion when Johnson quotes Savage's words, he throws them into indirect discourse as if to muffle the sound: Savage complained, Johnson writes, "with the utmost Vehemence of Indignation, 'That they [the subscribers to his retirement fund] had sent for a Taylor to measure him.' "[28] Johnson's practice in *An Account of the Life of Mr. Richard Savage* does not seem to conform to his theory of biography elaborated in *The Rambler* and *The Idler*. But if *An Account of the Life of Mr. Richard Savage* is not biography, what is it?

It seems too circumstantial to be a Theophrastan "character" and too particular to be a fable. Cyril Connolly "fraudulently" introduced it into his *Great English Short Novels* in 1953, but Johnson scorned historical fiction "filled with romantick adventures, and imaginary amours."[29] However blank his origins, Richard Savage is not a fictional character. The same objection probably overrules Matthew Hodgart's witty suggestion that *An Account of the Life of Mr. Richard Savage* is "a fairy-tale of the Male Cinderella with an unhappy ending."[30]

It ends, in fact, and begins like a moral essay:

> It has been observed in all Ages, that the Advantages of Nature or of Fortune have contributed very little to the Promotion of Happiness. . . .
>
> . . . Negligence and Irregularity, long continued, will make Knowledge useless, Wit ridiculous, and Genius contemptible.

The first review of *An Account of the Life of Mr. Richard Savage* called it an "improving treatise, on all the excellencies and defects of human nature,"[31] and it *can* be boiled down to a useful moral essay on self-deception:

> The Danger of this pleasing Intoxication must not be concealed; nor indeed can any one, after having observed the Life of *Savage,* need to be cautioned against it.[32]

In this view *An Account of the Life of Mr. Richard Savage* becomes a grotesquely overgrown *Rambler* with Richard Savage in the role of a Dicaculus, a Gulosulus, or a Nugaculus.

The weakness of this view is that it trivializes the admired Richard Savage. One of the most obvious rhetorical features of *An Account of the Life of Mr. Richard Savage,* its heavy reliance on indirect discourse, suggests not a novel, not a fairy tale, not a moral essay, but the scenario for a play, like the prose plot-outline that Johnson made for *Irene: A Tragedy.* Nor is Savage inconceivable as a tragic hero. He was certainly a hero to Johnson, who looked up to him "from a lower Station."[33] He is represented, in Johnson's account, to have accepted his superiority. Johnson quotes the letter in which Savage claimed for himself "that Presence of Mind, that serene Dignity in Misfortune, that constitutes the Character of a True Nobleman."[34] And Johnson affirms that it was "always Mr. Savage's Desire to be distinguished."[35]

Johnson also shows Savage to be plentifully supplied with the necessary hubris—"he always preserved a steady Confidence in his own Capacity, and believed nothing above his Reach"[36]—and suitably pursued by the avenging Furies of his mother's hatred, "aggravating his Misfortunes, and obstructing his Resource . . . with an implacable and restless Cruelty . . . from the first Hour of his Life to the last."[37] Johnson heavily underlines the ironies in Savage's downfall. About 1736 one of Savage's friends secured from Sir Robert Walpole the promise of a place or pension "not exceeding two hundred Pounds a Year." "Mr. *Savage* now concluded himself set at Ease for ever," Johnson says. But the promise was broken and instead of being "set at Ease for ever," Savage was reduced to sleeping "in Cellars, . . . upon a Bulk, or . . . among the Ashes of a Glass-house."[38] In 1738 when his friends were raising a subscription to enable him to retire into Wales, Savage easily represented to himself the delights of a cottage, "listening, without Intermission, to the Melody of the Nightingale." Johnson, who had just emigrated from the country, observes that "The Melody of the Nightingale" was "a very important Part of the Happiness of a Country Life" for Savage. But instead of a cottage, Savage found himself in jail in Bristol, whence he wrote to Johnson in January 1743: "I sing very freely in my Cage; sometimes indeed in the plaintive Notes of the Nightingale."[39]

In Johnson's account Savage's downfall is brought about, in the best Aristotelian fashion, "on account of some great error," or *hamartia.*[40] Savage's *hamartia* was self-deception, "this pleasing Intoxication" that Johnson the moralist warns against. Savage never suffered unpleasing thoughts "to sink into his Mind." He willfully turned away from "what he never wished to see, his real State."[41] Savage, therefore, failed the Augustan quest "to see things as they are."[42]

In Aristotelian terms, Savage's catastrophe involves irony but no *anagnorisis*, no change from ignorance to knowledge. He was "never made wiser by his sufferings," as Johnson saw. Savage never discovered what was happening to him, not even that he was involved in a catastrophe. In Freudian terms he is the very model of a masochistic parasite, the *Schnorrer*, a comic figure who consistently abuses anyone who tries to help him in order *"to achieve his unconscious masochistic aim–to be refused."*[43] He is, therefore, in Johnson's account, a failed tragic hero. He desired heroism but succeeded only in killing a man by mistake. Even his "appearing at the Head of a Tory Mob" turns out to be a fiction.[44] Johnson is forced to conclude that his hero is "absurd," an Augustan Don Quixote.[45] In the nineteenth century he would have been a novelist.

From Savage, Johnson turned his mind to a successful tragedy-hero. In the fall of 1743 when he was turning out *An Account of the Life of Mr. Richard Savage* under contract to Cave, he may already have been planning a new edition of Shakespeare. His next important published work, in any case, was *Miscellaneous Observations on the Tragedy of Macbeth*.

NOTES

1. Samuel Johnson, *An Account of the Life of Mr. Richard Savage* (1744), ed. G. Birkbeck Hill, *Lives of the English Poets,* 3 vols. (Oxford, 1905), 2:430 (hereafter cited as *Lives*). Emphasizing several differences between Savage and Johnson does not, of course, deny the similarities. A dozen of the latter are conveniently listed in James Boswell, *The Life of Samuel Johnson, LL.D.,* ed. G. Birkbeck Hill and L.F. Powell, 6 vols. (Oxford, 1934–50), 1:166n., 350n. (hereafter cited as *The Life*).

2. *Lives,* 2:390.

3. *The Poetical Works of Richard Savage,* ed. Clarence R. Tracy (Cambridge, 1962), p. 266.

4. Sir John Hawkins, *The Life of Samuel Johnson, LL.D.,* 2d ed. (London, 1787), p. 52 (hereafter cited as Hawkins).

5. The time and place of Johnson's meeting with Savage are unknown. Hawkins is vague (pp. 51–52) and Boswell follows Hawkins: Savage's "visits to St. John's Gate naturally brought Johnson and him together" (*The Life,* 1: 162). Since Savage's visits to St. John's Gate, where Edward Cave edited and published *The Gentleman's Magazine,* had begun in August 1733, while

Johnson's first piece in *The Gentleman's Magazine* did not appear until March 1738, there is nothing inherently improbable in William Cook's surmise that it was Savage who introduced Johnson to Cave ([William Cook], *The Life of Samuel Johnson, LL.D.*, London, 1786, p. 9). By the end of March 1738 Johnson knew Savage well enough to write commendatory verses for him (*The Gentleman's Magazine*, April 1738) and to cast him as a modern instance of Juvenal's Umbricius in *London: A Poem* (*The Life*, 1: 123, n. 3). Savage had been joking for years about retirement to Wales ([Richard Savage], *An Author To be Lett*, London, 1729, p. 10) and in "the beginning of the year 1738" his friends made the joke a reality by "a subscription for his support, in a place . . . far distant" (Hawkins, pp. 55–56, 86).

6. *Lives*, 2: 412.

7. *The Life*, 1:408.

8. *Lives*, 2:337 (italics added). Juvenal's Umbricius becomes "injur'd THALES" in *London: A Poem*, line 2. The epithet is wholly Johnson's; there is no equivalent for it in Juvenal, Satire III.

9. Edmund Bergler, "Samuel Johnson's 'Life of the poet Richard Savage'—A Paradigm for a Type," *American Imago* 4 (December 1947): 49.

10. *Lives*, 2:406.

11. Clarence R. Tracy, *The Artificial Bastard, A Biography of Richard Savage* (Cambridge, Mass., 1953), p. 50.

12. *The Works of Richard Savage, Esq.*, new ed., 2 vols. (London, 1777), 1:124.

13. *Lives*, 2:406.

14. *The Life*, 1:100. The draft of *Irene*, now in the British Museum, was first published in *The Poems of Samuel Johnson*, ed. D. Nichol Smith and Edward L. McAdam (Oxford, 1941), pp. 336–77.

15. *The Life*, 1:106, 102.

16. *The Life*, 1:107; *Boswell's Journal of a Tour to the Hebrides with Samuel Johnson, LL.D.*, ed. Frederick A. Pottle and Charles H. Bennett, new ed. (New York, 1961), p. 23.

17. *The Life*, 1:111.

18. Hawkins, p. 199.

19. Thomas Babington Macaulay, *Critical and Historical Essays Contributed to the Edinburgh Review*, ed. F. C. Montague, 3 vols. (New York and London, 1903), 1:394.

20. Johnson, *Prose and Poetry*, ed. Mona Wilson (Cambridge, Mass., 1957), p. 439.

21. *The Adventurer*, 29 December 1753.

22. Richard Knolles, *The Generall Historie of the Turkes*, 5th ed. (London, 1638), pp. 333, 337–38, 348.

23. Ibid., pp. 350, 352, 353.

24. The authoritative study of *Irene* is by Bertrand Bronson in *Johnson and Boswell: Three Essays* (Berkeley and Los Angeles, 1944), pp. 431–68. An essay by Marshall Waingrow in *From Sensibility to Romanticism: Essays Presented to Frederick A. Pottle*, ed. Frederick W. Hilles and Harold Bloom (New

York, 1965), pp. 79–92, explores the complexity and interest of Johnson's casuistry in *Irene*. But neither of these critics claim that the play produces "the particular tragic pleasure . . . coming from pity and fear," that Aristotle desiderates. "There is not a single passage that ever drew a tear" (*The Life,* 4:45).

25. *The Rambler,* 13 October 1750.

26. *Lives,* 2:116.

27. *Lives,* 2:329, 331–32, 338–39.

28. *Lives,* 2:429, 411.

29. *Great English Short Novels,* ed. Cyril Connolly (New York, 1953), pp. vii, ix–x; *The Life,* 1:165.

30. M. J. C. Hodgart, *Samuel Johnson and His Times* (London, 1962), p. 33.

31. *The Life,* 1:169.

32. *Lives,* 2:380.

33. *Lives,* 2:321.

34. *Lives,* 2:421.

35. *Lives,* 2:386.

36. *Lives,* 2:403.

37. *Lives,* 2:324.

38. *Lives,* 2:391, 398–99.

39. *Lives,* 2:410, 423.

40. In an article on the Freudian tendencies of *An Account of the Life of Mr. Richard Savage,* John A. Dussinger remarks in passing that "The basic structure . . . resembles a Greek tragedy" (*ELH* 37 [December 1970]:564).

41. *Lives,* 2:372, 380.

42. *The Life,* 1:339.

43. *American Imago* 4 (December 1947):54. Johnson was aware that Savage "rejected . . . Kindness" (*Lives,* 2:401), but it was Pope who saw that "nothing will relieve him" (Pope, *Correspondence,* ed. George Sherburn, 5 vols., 1956, 4:432–33).

44. *Lives,* 2:385; Tracy, *The Artificial Bastard,* pp. 123–24.

45. *Lives,* 2:425, 429.

JEROME J. McGANN

The Significance of Biographical Context: Two Poems by Lord Byron

The aesthetics and literary criticism of this century, in this country, have been dominated, for a variety of reasons and in many different ways, by the concept of the autonomy of literary works. As a consequence, theorists and critics have tended to ignore, or even reject, what is (nevertheless) recognized to be one of the most traditional methods of literary commentary: biographical interpretation. Even while its sometime usefulness and importance is allowed for, biographical criticism is generally regarded as an "extrinsic approach to the study of literature."[1] There are, of course, good reasons for being wary of biographical methods of interpretation, and we all respect these reasons as much, and perhaps as justifiably, as we respect anything which has exercised its authority upon us for a long period. At the same time, we are also well aware that certain kinds of poems exist which seem positively to require biographical or historical or otherwise "extrinsic" methods of reading.

Satire, of course, is always tied closely to historical and political circumstances. Because of this, the plain prose meaning of a satiric passage can escape a reader who is uninformed about its historical context. Yet there can be no question of appreciating the poetic force of such passages if the prose sense cannot be construed.

But satire is no special case, except in the sense that it represents a limit of our critical opacity. Some of the greatest lyric poems in the language, it seems to me, also demand historical or biographical contexts if they are to be adequately read. Since my subject is Byron, I would cite a poem like "On This Day I Complete My Thirty-Sixth Year," which is perhaps his finest lyric effort. The greatness of this poem is intimately related to its context. Indeed, little less than an awareness of Byron's entire career in literature, in love, and in politics will suffice if the poem is to be understood. "On This Day" is a "statement" poem, in many senses. Minimally, this is to say that its prose sense and its poetic meaning feed upon each other. The more one understands of the context of the poem, the more will the verse carry itself alive into the heart. To read "On This Day," even at a minimal level, you have to know where it was written, and by whom, and when.

Where, by whom, when: these seem simple enough questions to answer. But in fact they are extremely difficult and complicated. To answer the question "where," for example, you cannot simply say "Greece" and think this an adequate answer. For the "where" in Greece is a place occupied by a number of important persons who impinge upon this poem (like Loukas Chalandritsanos, for example: but there are many people invoked by this poem). Moreover, the "where" is importantly Greece because it is *not* England and *not* Italy, or any of the more specific places in England and Italy that were important for Byron in the past. These "wheres" are left behind, and are crucial for "On This Day" just because they *have* been left behind. The poem is very much aware of these other places.

The "who" of the poem is also a problem in specification. Of course, the elementary answer is "Byron." But *what* Byron? This person needs to be seen as clearly and as specifically as possible. The poem defines these specifics in the normal ways that poetry always makes its definitions. But the specifics must be recovered; nor will a mere encounter with the isolated poem permit such a recovery. In the end, to read the poem's own specifying acts, the reader must reinvest them into the poem.

And the "when"? No simple matter either. For in this case, as in the two above, the problem is not merely to lay out free empirical data. As we all know, there is no such thing as a pure empirical fact as such. But that is only to say that all "facts," to be understood even *as* facts, have to be grasped within the elaborate network of other facts. That network *is* reality, and the reconstruction of such a network is the act of interpretation.

When we read a great poem like the *Epistle to Dr. Arbuthnot* or *The Marriage of Heaven and Hell,* we naturally perform the sort of operations I have been describing. *Natura naturata.* Yet we rarely—if I am to judge by the theoretical writings to be seen today, in this country, in such abundance—perform these operations self-consciously. *Natura naturans.* Literary theory is literary criticism at its most self-reflexive stage. Our literary theory—following, in general, the legacy of the New Criticism—is extremely self-conscious in many ways. Still, except for some Marxist critics, literary theory and literary criticism today almost never turn self-consciously upon the sort of interpretative operations I have been speaking about. Our critical thinking on these matters ought to be seriously reconsidered. What is intrinsic or extrinsic to a literary work is much more problematic than we customarily take for granted, or are willing to admit. Furthermore, *how* so-called extrinsic matters find themselves metamorphosed into a poem's "mode of existence" is perhaps an even more difficult matter to sort out.

In this essay I want to propose a case where some of these issues present themselves with what seems to me a special clarity. The demonstration takes for its subject certain typical instances of a widespread kind of verse: occasional poetry. Through it I want to show how and why it is by no means the case that biographical interpretation must be regarded as an extrinsic approach to a work of art.

My subject will be two poems by Byron which contain certain things in common, but which also differ in important ways. One is a little-known work, never collected and only published many years after his death, and the other is a famous lyric published during his lifetime, but which was a trouble to critics, editors, and readers for decades. Neither poem has the stature of a work like "On This Day," but they are useful for demonstration purposes precisely because the poems are less complex as poetry.

The poem that begins "Go—triumph securely," untitled in Byron's holograph fair copy MS, was first published in 1844 in Jesse's *Life of George Brummell* as "To ——." The provenance of the Jesse text was not directly from Byron's own MS but from some copy, and most immediately from Brummell's copy (which does not seem to survive). The existence of the Brummell publication was not widely known, however, so that later editions of Byron never included the poem in the collected works. (Byron's own MS did not surface until quite recently.) As a result of these circumstances, a slightly different version of the poem was printed in 1967 as an unpublished piece. In this case the text was derived from a MS in neither Byron's nor Brummell's hand.[2] According to this MS, the poem was addressed to Lady Frances Wedderburn Webster, with whom Byron had a brief flirtation late in 1813. It turns out that this attribution (along with its implied dating of the poem) is not correct. But the reasons for the attribution are plausible since they involve certain direct statements by Byron himself. To understand these reasons we must turn to another poem by Byron, the famous "When We Two Parted."

This poem was first published in Byron's *Poems* (1816), where Byron dated it 1808. This dating subsequently caused critics and editors much trouble in trying to identify the person to whom the poem was addressed. The "mystery" was solved in 1928 by John Gore, who came into the possession of a packet of letters from Byron to Lady Anne Hardy. A recurrent subject of the letters, written in 1822–23, was Lady Frances Wedderburn Webster and her husband. Webster was an old acquaintance of Byron's, and Lady Frances an old flame. In one of the letters Byron told Lady Hardy that he had deliberately misdated "When We Two Parted" when he first published it, that its subject was actually Lady Frances, and that he had in fact removed the poem's "concluding" stanza when he published it. He then wrote out the stanza for Lady Hardy.[3]

The rough draft MS of "When We Two Parted," now in the Lovelace papers,[4] shows that the original penultimate stanza was removed from the MS. This fact was not of course known to Lady Hardy, but it corroborates what she understood from Byron's letters, and settles for us the dating and contextual circumstances of his poem.

Byron's brief, and apparently celibate, affair with Lady Frances occurred late in 1813 while he was visiting the Websters at their country home near Rotherham. It ended sentimentally, and with an aftermath of certain letters, when Byron left their house after his brief stay. But in 1815 Byron heard the widespread gossip in London about Lady Frances's affair with the Duke of Wellington in Paris. These rumors occasioned his poem, written in late 1815; and the memory of all these events was revived in 1822 when he was writing to Lady Hardy, who was at that time herself involved in the current marital troubles of the Websters. Webster and his wife finally separated in Paris, Webster pursued Lady Hardy across much of Europe (but in vain), and Byron was asked to intercede in the Websters' affairs and help reconcile them. He did try, but he failed. When Byron sent his unpublished stanza to Lady Hardy, then, he reminded her that he had long before prophesied a sad end for Lady Frances.

She, poor thing, has made a sad affair of it altogether. I had the melancholy
task of prophesying as much many years ago in some lines of which the
three or four first stanzas only were printed, and of course without names
or allusions and with a *false* date. I send you the concluding stanza which
never was printed with the others.[5]

This narrative relates to the uncollected poem "Go—triumph securely" because its penultimate stanza is an earlier version of the unpublished stanza from "When We Two Parted." The two poems are in
fact very alike in many ways. The subject of both is a lady who has
broken her marriage vow to become the poet's lover. In the case
of "When We Two Parted," the poet later discovers that she has been
false to him as well, and he prophesies a career of infidelity. "Go—
triumph securely" also makes such a prophecy, though the woman of
the poem has not yet specifically betrayed her poet-lover.

Furthermore, these two poems occupy important places in a sequence of love poems written between 1808 and 1816, all of which
deal with the problems of illicit and betrayed love. One of the earliest of
them, a lyric only recently published ("Again Beguiled, Again Betrayed"), records Byron's reactions to Susan Vaughan, a servant girl at
Newstead Abbey with whom he had a brief affair shortly after his
return to England in 1811.[6] He discovered her infidelity, however, sent
her away early in 1812, and wrote a few poems about his disillusion-
ment. "Again Beguiled, Again Betrayed" is particularly to be noted
here because "Go—triumph securely" echoes the poem at certain
points just as "When We Two Parted" deliberately recalls "Go—
triumph securely."[7]

A final piece of information that bears upon this skein of events
involves Mary Chaworth, one of the most legendary of Byron's lost
loves. When she decided to marry John Musters, Byron wrote a series
of poems about his disappointment, though none involved any notion
that she had betrayed him. Most of these poems date from 1808, the
"*false* date" Byron gave in 1816 to "When We Two Parted." But late in
1813 Mary's marriage was in trouble, largely because of the philander-
ing of her husband, and she began writing to Byron seeking a renewal
of their "old friendship." Their correspondence was taken up just as
Byron was going over in his mind (and in his letters to Lady Melbourne) the strange cross-currents of his love affairs with Lady
Caroline and Lady Frances especially. He was therefore troubled by

and suspicious of Mary's new overtures of friendship. Her letters, and the breakup of her marriage, were proving his early love ideal only too human, like the other women to whom he had attached himself romantically since 1808.[8] Thus, when Byron dated "When We Two Parted" 1808 in his *Poems,* the *"false* date" bore in it an important "truth" (as Byron saw it) about a general pattern of experience in his life up to that time. It was as if the poem were in some degree applicable to any number of women he had loved, including Mary Chaworth. Byron was to clinch this suggestion in "The Dream," where Mary Chaworth's history up to 1816 served as Byron's model for his generalized vision of the disasters of romantic love.[9]

"Go—triumph securely" deals with this history as well. Lady Hardy surmised that the poem was addressed to Lady Frances, and it could well have been. In fact, it was written about Lady Caroline Lamb. We know this because Byron sent its penultimate stanza in a letter to Lady Melbourne in September, 1812, when he wrote the poem and when his relations with Lady Caroline were beginning to be broken off. After their stormy last weeks together, which were the scandal of London society, Lady Caroline was sent away to Ireland with her husband William. Commenting on his affair with her in his letters to Lady Melbourne, Byron repeated in prose many of the things he set down in his poem "Go—triumph securely." For example:

> If she does not take some accursed step to precipitate her own inevitable fall (if not with me, with some less lucky successor) . . . all will be well. . . . However, if after all "it is decreed on high" that, like James the Fatalist, I *must* be hers, she shall be *mine* as long as it pleases her, & the circumstances under which she becomes so, will at least make me devote my life to the vain attempt of reconciling her to herself, wretched as it would render me, she should never know it.[10]

Some three years after these letters Byron wrote "When We Two Parted" and plundered "Go—triumph securely" for the stanza he was eventually to drop from the poem and later to send to Lady Hardy. The transferral of the lines was an easy one for Byron to make since he had convinced himself, by 1815, that "the woman once fallen forever must fall." Indeed, his experiences with illicit and betrayed love made him think of himself as a sort of profane prophet in such matters, so that when he wrote both "Go—triumph securely" in 1812 and "When We

Two Parted" in 1815, he foretold careers of betrayal for both Lady Caroline and Lady Frances.

The histories I have described are normally thought to be "extrinsic" to "the poem itself." But if we allow that a poem's subject matter is "intrinsic" to the poem, if we allow that poetry—at least some kinds of poetry—can deal with matters of historical fact, then I do not see how certain poems, like these by Byron, can be properly read as poetry apart from such materials. The historical contexts bear crucially upon poems like *The Hind and the Panther* and *The Dunciad,* and in certain kinds of lyrics we run up against similar contextual situations.

Of course one could read "Go—triumph securely" without knowing its biographical context, but the force of the poetic statement would in such a case be drastically altered, diminished, even perhaps misrepresented. One could approach poetry in relative ignorance of the science of metrics, or with an impoverished store of information about literary tradition, or with little knowledge of the formal devices of verse, stylistic conventions, and genre theory. But the more ignorant one is about these matters, the less accessible does the poem become to precise critical description. Such ignorance would positively forbid a sensitive reading of poems like *Hugh Selwyn Mauberly* or the *WasteLand.* Like all poems, these have literary contexts, and a critic must be able to distinguish and deal with those contexts.

The case is, it seems to me, exactly the same for a poem's subject matter. You cannot deal with that subject matter critically unless you are able to distinguish what it is as precisely as possible. The narrative I have given for the contexts of Byron's poems surely helps to elucidate the statements which the poems are making. For example, consider the first stanza of "Go—triumph securely." The vow is specifically Lady Caroline's marriage vow, and it is "treacherous" because—specifically—she betrayed it in her affair with Byron. For his part, Byron—as we saw in his letters to Lady Melbourne—determined to keep his illicit love vow to Lady Caroline even though he knew it was, for various reasons, wrong to do so ("too faithfully"). In their dishonorable circumstances, this faithfulness would be at least one point of honor that would be kept.

One could move through this poem with a similar contextual commentary that would clarify the poem's simple statement level of meaning, which is not always easy to grasp and which is occasionally quite beyond one's grasping without a knowledge of the circumstances with which the poem is explicitly dealing. The case of this Byron poem is of course particular and special, but it represents a situation we encounter quite frequently in reading poetry. A great deal of verse will simply escape one's comprehension at an elementary statement level unless certain contextual facts are clear to the reader. Critical comprehension depends upon an initial clarification of literary and historical allusions, tropological maneuvers, stylistic devices, and even—sometimes—biographical references. Describing these matters is an elementary part of the critical act, for without such clarity we cannot reasonably deal with larger questions of meaning and value.

These larger questions, in the case of "Go—triumph securely," become more available to us once we have elucidated what is being said. Byron's is a bold—not to say reckless—poem in the sense that it presumes to assert, on the basis of certain personal experiences, a melancholy prophecy about Lady Caroline's "career," and to generalize about "once fallen" women. The "frown" that he wears is the badge of his sorrow as he thinks of her "inevitable" future. Byron justifies his bold factive assertion about Lady Caroline by resorting to a shrewd stylistic maneuver in lines 13–16. Because these statements are made in the form of aphorism, or proverb, Byron has signalled his reader to understand and accept certain other facts about his poem's statements: first, that he has had a wide personal experience in such matters, and second, that his own experience has been confirmed in the larger context of the experience of men in general, whose wisdom has been stored in proverbial lore. Of these matters I shall have more to say shortly.

But Byron's boldness has another, more dependably inevitable result which also affects the meaning we get from the *poem* (and not from the *man* as he is represented to be speaking the poem). To speak out in this way is to put one's statements at the mercy of history, to say and to stand by what one believes to be the truth. As a matter of fact, Lady Caroline did not have the notorious career Byron prophesied for her. Indeed, she proved in the end a good deal more faithful to Byron than he did to her, and this subsequent history adds a moral irony to the poem that considerably enlarges and complicates its meaning.[11]

It might be objected that the subsequent histories of Lady Caroline and Byron have nothing to do with the poem itself. It was written in

September 1812, and that date fixes the limits of its permitted historical relevance—if indeed one grants to the poem the relevance of any sort of historical material. But just as the poem invokes, as part of its subject matter, Byron's and Lady Caroline's relations up to 1812, its sententious "prophecy" forces the reader to consider their future careers insofar as these relate to the issues raised by the poem. In this context, we recognize that some of the things Byron says in his poem are "not true" in *fact*.

Yet Byron's mistaken—perhaps self-deceived—remarks, while unjustified in history, are completely justified in his poem. What the verse locates for its reader—the condition upon which its moral force depends—is a network of personal and social relationships which are arranged around the person of Byron. "Go—triumph securely" is written about Lady Caroline by a man whose experienced attitudes have been determined not only by their particular stormy relations, but (a) by certain ideas (like "honour") which are shown to have a special importance for Byron, and (b) by his own series of past experiences in love with a number of other women. Unlike the presence of Byron and Lady Caroline in the poem, these other persons appear obliquely by virtue of a number of literary devices. One of these I have already called attention to. Another obvious one is allusion—specifically, allusion to a series of other poems and events having to do with Mary Chaworth and Susan Vaughan explicitly, and perhaps with other women as well, like Mrs. Constance Spencer Smith.[12] The poem itself makes these matters part of its subject.

As a result, Byron's mistaken prophecy, and his ignorance about the nature of his own (or someone else's) capacity for faithfulness, while wrong in fact, are completely understandable, and poetically true, in the context of his poem. When we read this work in the context of its specified subject matter we are being given a rich exposure to the effects which circumstance can have upon a person's life, and to the self-deceptions into which our experiences and habits of mind so often and so easily lead us. "Go—triumph securely" is a dramatic point of focus where we see, in a clarified way, the force which circumstance exerts upon the individual in relation to himself and others. The poem is, in the end, a sort of moral lesson in human behavior; it increases our abilities to understand man's life in the historical world.

That this is a specifically poetic effect and not merely the result of historical accident should be evident in the facts of the poem itself, which has invoked its historical materials. But the permanence of the poem's statements—its freedom from damage by historical change and accident—is even more graphically illustrated if we hypothesize for a moment a different future for Byron and Lady Caroline. As a clarifying poetic lesson in human morals and behavior, "Go— triumph securely" would not have been changed had Byron gone on to a life of exemplary and upright behavior, or had Lady Caroline actually been "false unto many as faithless to one." The materials of the poem would have altered, of course, but the poem *as a poetic document*—the poem as device for clarifying human behavior—would not have been damaged. However things would have turned out for Byron and Lady Caroline, the poem would still be a poem, would still be in general the sort of poem that it is, and would still succeed in doing what it now does so well (though its "meaning" would be slightly altered).

The point is that Byron, by the conventions of his poem, has agreed to let events over which he has no exclusive or direct control write the finish to his poem's materials. This means that his poem will have to have a "poetic meaning" or "self-coherence" that can accommodate the vagaries of time and fortune. The principal surface moral of the poem is obviously dependent upon some specific set of future historical determinants. But the more general (and also more specific) poetic moral involves our sympathetic understanding of the reality of these people caught in time and entangled in the webs of their own and each other's characters. It does not matter whether Byron proves right or wrong in his prophecy; whichever way, the people and their relations will remain sharply and unalterably portrayed for us through the poem, and will remain objects of our sympathy and even our admiration. For we admire people, however pathetic or mistaken or misguided, who go to meet their own lives, and who agree to abide and deal with what they partly suffer and partly themselves create.

We get a further insight into why these things should be true if we recall briefly "When We Two Parted." That poem, as we know, deals with a situation very like the one dramatized in "Go—triumph securely." Byron is the same—faithfully faithless as ever—but the lady has changed, both in person and in character. "When We Two Parted" originally prophesied that Lady Frances would "prove false unto many / As faithless to one," and as it turned out, in this case Byron hit somewhat nearer the truth of the facts. This, of course, was an immense pleasure to his vanity, so in 1823 he maneuvered to get the dropped stanza back into the poem. The poem works, however, with or without the stanza, and with or without the events of 1822–23 involving Byron, the Websters, and Lady Hardy.

Why doesn't it matter whether Byron's "prophecies" about Lady Caroline and Lady Frances turned out true or not? Because the prophecies are not prophetic in a religious but in an ethical sense. Look again at the statements made in the stanzas sent in Byron's letters to Lady Melbourne and Lady Hardy. Both passages, but especially the penultimate stanza of "Go—triumph securely," depend upon what rhetoricians call *sententiae,* that is, statements which carry the force of a proverb or an aphorism. The nature of such statements is not that they should be exclusively true but that they should be generally true. Proverbs are notoriously contradictory. Consider, for example:

Too many cooks spoil the broth.

Many hands make light work.

These two statements do not negate each other, as they might if we read them in a context of logical relations. The statements involve what we call "wisdom," and their particular force and applicability depend upon circumstances. The nature of their truth may be clarified if we recall two opposing statements of proverbial wisdom from the book of Proverbs.

Answer not a fool according to his folly, lest thou also be like unto him.

Answer a fool according to his folly, lest he be wise in his own conceit.
[26:4–5]

The book of Proverbs recurrently presents such contradictory advice, though rarely so graphically as in this case, where the two statements run right upon one another in the text. Why they are not ethical contradictions is explained in the conditional clauses: that is, one follows certain courses of action toward fools under certain particular circumstances.

Byron's sententious wisdom in his two poems is to be understood in terms of this general context of the meaning of certain kinds of statements. In the case of "Go—triumph securely," Byron has invoked a wise saying, but he has misapplied it because he has mistaken the circumstances. This "mistake" becomes an important item in the poem's general statement, which does not involve a poetic representation of proverbial wisdom as such, but which dramatizes a person in the act of invoking such wisdom under very particular conditions. Byron's poem is using proverbial wisdom in the way Shakespeare's plays often use such statements, or Chaucer's tales, or a poem like *The Owl and the Nightingale*.

The same situation holds in respect of a poem like "When We Two Parted." That poem's existence as a poetic statement is unaltered whether the dropped stanza is or is not included. The particular form and meaning of the poem are altered slightly by the presence or absence of the *sententiae* of the stanza, as they are by the time when (the circumstances under which) Byron thought about replacing the stanza. But the poem as poetic document allows for this alteration. We might reasonably say, of course, that "When We Two Parted" would be a "different poem" if the stanza were introduced into it, and of course in some sense this would be true because the stanza would alter slightly our perspective upon the form and meaning of the poem as a whole. Nevertheless, it is a nice question—and one which we do not always face up to—as to how much, and what kind, of a difference it makes. Are the two versions of "La Belle Dame Sans Merci" really "different poems"; and if they are, how different are they, and how are they different? These matters are important and interesting, but I must leave them undiscussed here because my immediate concern is not so much with problems of those sorts as with the general relevance of biographical and historical materials to the "mode of existence of a literary work of art."[13]

It is generally taken for granted that "extrinsic" material of the sort I have been discussing may be relevant to the study of poetry in the sense that it throws light upon the process of poetic composition or on the psychology of the creative artist.[14] But certain kinds of poems by certain kinds of poets (not all "egotistical" like Byron) seem to qualify the scope of the material we are to consider as "extrinsic" to the poem. To know the historical contexts of "Go— triumph securely" and "When We Two Parted" is not only to be provided with information that may bear upon the psychology of Byron-as-poet, it is also to possess essential information for deciphering and evaluating the characterological and contextual elements of the personal dramas recorded in these poems. Byron-the-poet is using Byron-the-man as the subject of his verse, and the employment involves a specific skein of biographical references without which we cannot properly understand the characters and situations invoked in the poems. If the critic does not understand and describe these matters when he interprets the poems, his reading will have altogether missed the fundamental situation with which the poems are dealing. Without knowing these matters he cannot really see what the poems are saying, and therefore cannot even begin to speak certainly of the meaning or value of the poems. And, in fact, Byron's most personal poetry has been almost totally neglected by modern literary critics, not, I believe, because it is unworthy of critical attention (though some of it is), but because our modern critical habits have made it virtually impossible for us to approach these poems in the proper way. We do not think that fine details of biographical history are necessary to the literary critic. Such matters, we say, are the biographer's province. I do not think we should agree to think that way.

One final point. I have spoken of these poems as they occupy a place in a series of love poems by Byron that stretches from 1808 to 1816. Critics disinclined to admit the poetic relevance of minute biographical particulars might then agree that, while the "myth" of Byron's love life is relevant to the poems, the specific details of the myth are not. Such a critic might, for example, say that "Go—triumph securely" and "When We Two Parted" would be properly (better?) read if we agreed to see the women dealt with in the poems as one woman, a sort of psychological projection from Byron's character. In some sense—a very particular one—this view contains an important critical truth, as I myself have tried to indicate in this essay. But in the end it would not be correct enough and would miss the essential *differences* which define the special character of the two poems. Lady Caroline and Lady Frances, and Byron's particular attitudes towards them, share certain things in common; but the differences are also marked in the poems and in the special characteristics of the two ladies dealt with by the poems. To miss or neglect these differences is to miss the particulars of the poetry. The poems invoke these differences, inasmuch as they were written to two very different people at two very different times. An accurate reading of the poems cannot fail to register such differences as well as the specific historical and psychological facts which define them, and which Byron has redefined for us.

EXAMPLES

I.

Go—triumph securely, that treacherous vow
Thou hast broken I keep but too faithfully now
Yet never again wilt thou be to my heart
What thou wert, what I fear for a moment thou art.

To see thee, to love thee—what heart could do more?   5
To love thee to lose thee twere vain to deplore,
Not a sigh shall escape from my breast thus beguiled,
I will bear like a man what I feel like a child.

Though a frown clouds my brow, yet it lowers not on thee,
Though my heart may be heavy, at least it is free—   10
But thou, with the pride of fresh conquest elate
Alas, even Envy shall feel for thy fate.

For the first step of error none e'er could recall
And the woman once fallen forever must fall,
Pursue to the last the career thus begun   15
And be false unto many as faithless to one.

And they who have loved thee shall leave thee to mourne,
And they who have hated shall laugh thee to scorn,
And he who adored thee now weeps to foretell
The pangs that will punish thy falsehood too well.   20
                    [the Combe Martin text]

II.   When We Two Parted

            1.
When we two parted
In silence and tears,
Half broken-hearted
To sever for years,
Pale grew thy cheek and cold,   5
Colder thy kiss;
Truly that hour foretold
Sorrow to this.

2.

The dew of the morning
Sunk chill on my brow—   10
It felt like the warning
Of what I feel now.
Thy vows are all broken,
And light is thy fame;
I hear thy name spoken,   15
And share in its shame.

3.

They name thee before me,
A knell to mine ear;
A shudder comes o'er me—
Why wert thou so dear?   20
They know not I knew thee,
Who knew thee too well:—
Long, long shall I rue thee,
Too deeply to tell.

4.

In secret we met—   25
In silence I grieve,
That thy heart could forget,
Thy spirit deceive.
If I should meet thee
After long years,   30
How should I greet thee!—
With silence and tears.
              [text from *Poems* (1816)]

(Deleted stanza, numbered 4 in the Lovelace MS but called the "concluding" stanza by Byron in his letter to Lady Hardy):

Then fare thee well, Fanny,
Now doubly undone,
To prove false unto many
As faithless to one.
Thou art past all recalling
Even would I recall,
For the woman once falling
Forever must fall.
                    [text from Gore]

Notes

1. The background for my remarks here is the widely circulated handbook on literary interpretation by René Wellek and Austin Warren, *Theory of Literature* (New York, 1959), in particular section 3 ("The Extrinsic Approach to the Study of Literature"). I am aware that a few subsequent critics, like E.D. Hirsch, have quarrelled with some of Wellek and Warren's formulations on these matters. But the objections raised by other writers have not dealt with the problem of biographical criticism in the way that I propose to do here.

2. *Life of George Brummell* (London, 1844), 1: 288; H. M. Combe Martin, "Byron Trouvaille?," *Notes and Queries* (Jan. 1967): 26. The MS uncovered by Combe Martin is in the hand of Lady Anne Hardy. Byron's holograph MS was recently acquired by the Stark Library, University of Texas. It has never been published. All three texts differ slightly from each other.

3. See John Gore, "A Byron Mystery Re-Solved," *Cornhill Magazine* 64 (1928): 39–53.

4. The Lovelace papers are currently owned by Lord Lytton, who has generously allowed me access to them. The rough draft MS has never been published. In his letter to Lady Hardy, Byron said the missing stanza was the last, but the MS shows that the stanza removed from the MS was originally penultimate.

5. For details of Byron's affairs with Lady Frances see Leslie A. Marchand, *Byron: A Biography* (New York, 1957), 1: 410–31 passim, 2: 537 n., 580–81, 3: 1045, 1055. The letter to Lady Hardy is in Gore, "A Byron Mystery," p. 52.

6. The poem was published by Doris Langley Moore, *The Great Byron Adventure* (New York, 1959), p. 13. For further details on Byron's relations with Susan Vaughan see George Paston and Peter Quennell, *To Lord Byron* (London, 1939), pp. 23–39; Doris Langley Moore, *Lord Byron: Accounts Rendered* (New York, 1974), pp. 165–76. Most of Byron's poems to Susan Vaughan have not yet been published.

7. Compare, e.g., lines 7–8 of "Go—triumph securely" with "Again beguiled! again betrayed! / In manhood as in youth" (lines 1–2). Compare also lines 1–2 of "Go—triumph securely" with this cancelled passage from "When We Two Parted": "Thy vow hath been broken / But mine is the same" (lines 13–14, from the rough draft MS).

8. For Byron's and Mary's renewed relationship see Paston and Quennell, *To Lord Byron,* pp. 162–76; Marchand, *Byron,* 1: 428–66 passim. Mary separated from her husband in 1814 but they were reconciled in 1817—a fact which may have inclined Byron, in 1823, to tell Lady Hardy the "truth" about "When We Two Parted" and remove the implication (created by the *"false date"*) that the poem dealt with Mary.

9. The important poems written about Mary in 1808 are "Farewell! If Ever Fondest Prayer" and "Well! Thou Art Happy." In "The Dream" see especially sections II, III, V, and VII.

10. *Byron's Letters and Journals,* ed. Leslie A. Marchand (London, 1973), 2: 195, 200.

11. For Lady Caroline's history see Elizabeth Jenkins, *Lady Caroline Lamb* (Boston, 1932).

12. For Mrs. Constance Spencer Smith see *Childe Harold,* canto 1, sts. 29–35, "To Florence," and "The Spell Is Broke, The Charm Is Flown." When Byron was discussing his relations with Lady Caroline in his letters to Lady Melbourne, he specifically recalled his affair with Mrs. Spencer Smith (see *Letters and Journals,* 2: 198).

13. The specific "meaning" of this poem, of any poem, depends upon the verbal units which we agree upon as making up its statement. Thus, we obviously receive a different complex of specific meanings in "When We Two Parted" depending upon whether we read the poem with or without its deleted stanza. But the definition of those specifics is made in the instant act of critical interpretation. My concern here is not with the particular meaning of "When We Two Parted" as such, but with the general poetic context in which meaning in this poem is allowed to occur.

14. These allowances are widespread and are particularly mentioned by Wellek and Warren.

VICTOR BROMBERT

Stendhal's Silken Prison

Stendhal's claustrophilia answers the deeper needs of "Beylisme"—a name Henri Beyle-Stendhal himself gave to a semi-tender, semi-ironic way of watching himself cultivate his sensibility, as well as to the art of masking it. From the start, young Beyle conceives of the solitary tower as a privileged place. Writing to his sister from Richmond, where he spent several weeks in "deepest solitude," he asks: "Don't you think that Gil Blas, in the Segovia tower, enjoyed very sweet mental pleasures?" (*Corr.,* 3: 117–18).[1] The tower is quite spontaneously associated with a literary reference and an intellectual satisfaction. That solitude should appear to the young man as propitious to spontaneity ("When I am alone, I laugh and cry over a trifle . . . " [*Corr.,* 4: 143])—such a commonplace can hardly surprise. More significant is the bond between "solitude aérienne" and the act of writing. The "quatrième étage" is for him the symbolic locus of poetic meditation. Or better still, the garret: "Le vrai métier de l'animal est d'écrire un roman dans un grenier" (*Corr.,* 9: 186).[2]

All his heroes, even those who at first think themselves committed to action, share a longing for enclosure. Octave de Malivert, at the beginning of *Armance,* feels an acute nostalgia for his "petite cellule" of the Ecole Polytechnique which offered him the "image of retreat and tranquillity in a monastery" (1: 32). He later observes that his "unique pleasure" comes from living in isolation, with no one having the right to talk to him (1: 34). Julien, long before his prison experience, values precious moments of lofty solitude. As for Fabrice, is not all of his brief career a preparation for withdrawal and claustration? The mediocrity of his battlefield companions, the betrayal of epic and lyric illusions nurtured by Tasso and Ariosto, the loss of blood which cures him of his fervor for war: the mock heroic mode in *La Chartreuse de Parme* stresses the inadequacy of all action.

This basic option for retreat and privacy has its risks. Not only do all of Stendhal's protagonists (and he himself) learn Julien's lesson that "difference engenders hatred"; they discover that solipsism is a cause of blindness. The young Henri Beyle observes: "I am too busy looking at myself to see others" (*Pensées. Filosofia Nova*, 1: 137). But can he in fact see himself clearly at such proximity? To his sister Pauline, he writes, " . . . one must enjoy oneself in solitude." (The French is stronger: "jouir de soi-même" [*Corr.*, 2: 240].) The same idea, only the tone is somewhat sharper, reappears in a letter to de Mareste: " . . . the only worthwhile thing in this world is the *self*" (*Corr.*, 5:107). For retreat and self-enclosure are the necessary conditions of creative self-observation. From adolescence on, Stendhal indulges in cryptic note-taking, diaries, discussions and dialogues with himself, analyses of his defects and qualities, clinical self-consultations. The scribbling mania leads to amusing extremes. Yet even the scribblings on his clothes—those coded jottings, similar to a prisoner's secret messages, on his cuffs, his belts, his suspenders—betray the need to see himself both as object and subject.

Such privacy extends to moral values and to moral judgments. Duchess Sanseverina needs to be alone with herself to assess her own actions. Her great quality, we are told, is that she knows how to be "honest with herself" ("de bonne foi avec elle-même" [2: 120]). Fabrice, exercising self-arrogated prerogatives of self-judgment, occasionally indulges in self-clemency ("I forgive myself my fright" [2: 179]). Julien locks himself up in his room to become his severest judge. Needless to say, this private tribunal or private stage does not help solve the mystery of personality. The eye cannot see itself. That is Stendhal's anguished conclusion in his autobiographic *Vie de Henry Brulard* (126). "What kind of man am I?"—this self-addressed question on the first page of *Souvenirs d'Egotisme* haunted him all his life. But where is one to find the answer? Certainly not in the self: "I do not know myself; and that is what distresses me, when I think of it sometimes at night" (*Souvenirs d'Egotisme*, 1394). Lucidity is a deception. The trouble is that not even the "others" can solve the riddle of the self. To the most elementary question—is he intelligent? is he good? is he brave?—no answer is forthcoming. Caught between the desire to reveal himself and the fear of being penetrated by another conscience, Stendhal can only complicate the illusive quest of the self. And the mask he learns to wear in order to camouflage his intimate being does not, of course, help him unveil himself in his own eyes.

The yearning for lucidity and self-knowledge does indeed coincide with the need to dissemble. The intruding glance is wished for and feared at the same time. Hence the importance of disguises and the fictional joys of the incognito. "I would wear a mask with pleasure, I would change name with delight" (*Souvenirs d'Egotisme,* 1415). In the curious text entitled "Privilèges du 10 avril 1840," he imagines that some superior decree endows him specifically with the ability to become *another:* "Twenty times a year, the grantee will be able to change himself into the being he wants." The basic urge behind the dream of metamorphosis is to remain impenetrable. Such fantasies of masquerades are obviously related to the fiction-making impulse. They also cast light on the theme of a privileged *locus* where personal freedom could prosper, hidden and unmolested.

The temptation to dissemble and disguise, to hide what counts most, is an early trait of Henri Beyle. It is, from the outset, bound up with the act of writing. He admonishes his sister: "Say nothing of all that to anyone[. . . .] Do give up the bad habit of reading to anyone the letters I write to you"—"Above all do not show this letter to anyone." To invoke youth's natural embarrassment, or *pudeur,* in the face of elders is not enough in this case. What is involved is a deliberate stance. In another letter to Pauline, à propos "fools" (that is, à propos the "others"), he advises: " . . . let's prevent them from glossing our behavior by hiding our actions" (*Corr.,* 1: 8, 19, 69). In fact, the letters to Pauline turn out, in large part, to be a didactic exercise, a correspondence course on the art of secretiveness. But to hide what? Henri Beyle would answer—and Stendhal the writer was to turn this into a major theme: the "superiority" of sensitive souls who are always hated by the common herd called society. "You must hide your superiority, and enjoy yourself alone, in your room, reading a book that entertains you" (*Corr.,* 2: 240). The dissembling intentionality could not be more explicitly linked to the notion of solitude and withdrawal. "One must become a hypocrite," he advises, long before conceiving of the figure of Julien Sorel.

Yet this "superiority" which asks to be hidden cannot be equated with banal arrogance: lies and silence are to protect a sensibility that, far from strength, is experienced by Stendhal as supreme vulnerability. "In all my life, I never talked of that which mattered to me; the least objection would have hurt me to the quick" (*Vie de Henry Brulard,* 165). In depth, it is the idea (or ideal) of happiness that wants to be concealed. Is that not literally the Duchess's advice to Mosca when she becomes aware that the Prince is intensely angered by the "sight" of happiness? "We must keep our love a secret." ("Il faut cacher nos amours" [2: 140]). These subterfuges of Beyliste lifesmanship are revealing of the bond between fervor, deception, and disguised freedom. "Is not lying the only recourse of slaves?" (*Vie de Henry Brulard,* 135).

Concealment of "happiness," but also happiness of concealment. "What is the use of going so far afield to seek happiness; it is right under my eyes" (2: 176). Fabrice's sense of discovery, during his secret stay in abbé Blanès's tower, is revealing in a number of ways: the tower foreshadows the prison; the joys of a panoramic view suggest a possible mastery over his past and his self; the satisfactions of the overview are inseparable from the comfort of invisibility. Fabrice has indeed found a "convenient place to see without being seen" (2: 174).[3] Still this is not enough; between the imaginary gendarmes and himself he places an improvised screen: "a tattered scrap of old linen which he nailed against the window and in which he made two holes for his eyes" (2: 176). It is hard to attribute such voyeuristic camouflage to practical caution. Stendhal makes a point of invoking the irrationality of "l'âme italienne." What is involved is a fundamental retractility. For Stendhal, as for his heroes, lucidity is conceivable only from within a shelter. Hence the recurrent image of the hidden seer: Armance "hidden in the attic of the castle, behind a blind" can observe all the details of Octave's departure (1: 125); the ladies of Königsberg, in *Le Rose et le Vert,* watch the movements of the "messieurs" in the street by means of special mirrors affixed to their windows, while they themselves remain invisible, protected by "blinding metallic sheets" (2: 1074–75).

Ideal joy, to be sure, is attained only when the seeing eye is seen. But such yearned-for enchantment is not devoid of deep apprehension. The emergence of another's glance is tolerable only from within a protective enclosure.[4] Prison ultimately provides revelations— including that of love. In the meantime, the fleeting lyric moment requires the protection of the night. Julien discovers the delights of "vague and sweet reverie" during the evening hours in the gardens of Vergy (1: 279). Lucien Leuwen responds to the harmony of "soirées enchanteresses" in the woods. Fabrice sheds tears of happiness, "protected by deep night and vast silence" (2: 166). Gilbert Durand has related these nocturnal delights, part of a larger motif of claustrophilia, to Armida's enchanted gardens.[5] The comparison with Tasso is not arbitrary. *La Gerusalemme liberata* is mentioned in the opening pages of

La Chartreuse de Parme. As for the dream of invisibility and of magic metamorphoses, it would seem grafted onto another Renaissance reference, Ariosto's *Orlando Furioso:* "I often think of Angelica's ring; it would give me supreme pleasure to change into a tall, blond German, and thus to walk in Paris" (*Souvenirs d'Egotisme,* 1416).

This desire to disappear and to seek refuge in another body is intimately associated, as the "Privilèges du 10 avril 1840" indicate, with the keenness of the glance. Once again a magic ring confers special powers. "When the grantee carries on him or on his finger, for two minutes, a ring he will have held for a moment in his mouth, he will become invulnerable." Such invulnerability can be achieved also through insertion into an alien body-fortress. "Twenty times a year the grantee will be able to change into the being he wants." Better still: "four times a year and for an unlimited period each time, the grantee will be able to occupy two bodies at once." The wish for invisibility is bound up with the wish for perspicacity. The *privilégié* is most sharp-sighted when he is not exposed to another's seeing eye. Invulnerable, he will ten times per year enjoy "an eagle's eyesight." He will be "lynx-eyed." Article 21 is more precise still: "A hundred times a year, he will be able to see what any person he wishes is doing." With one significant reservation: " . . . with total exception of the woman he loves most." In the last analysis, any extreme form of happiness in Stendhal calls for obscurity and silence.

Walls, masks, impersonations function not merely as protective screens; they insure existential freedom. Enclosure and constraint serve the sense of becoming and of discovery. An accepted necessity allows the cultivation of that form of spontaneity Stendhal calls *l'imprévu.* Such a devious quest of the authentic self evidently involves the dialectics of role playing and spontaneity (the *rôle* and the *naturel*). At the outset of his first night with Mme de Rênal, Julien reverts, we are told, to his "natural role." The oxymoron stresses the fundamental compatibility of the two apparently irreconcilable terms. Play acting, on first thought, appears as the contrary of naturalness. This in itself points to an important ambiguity of Julien's character: the more he allows himself to be inspired by "le rôle de Tartufe," the more clearly this indicates that he is not naturally a hypocrite. Yet a role can become second nature. By wearing a mask, by merely trying it out, one risks seeing it adhere to one's face. Hence the Stendhalian fear of the definitive role. Mosca, about to surrender to jealousy, recognizes the danger:

"once I have spoken the fatal word *jealousy,* my role is marked out forever" (2: 155). Dialectically, however, *rôle* and *naturel* are interlocked in Stendhal. To play at being is a way of seeking or inventing one's self.

The frequent surprises experienced by Stendhal's protagonists— surprises stemming from their own actions and reactions—are proof that they are not inhibited by a fixed image of the self. Fabrice's astonishment upon arriving in jail is typical: "Could I be one of these men of valor of whom antiquity has given some examples to the world? Am I a hero without suspecting it?" Thirty-five years earlier, Stendhal jotted down in a notebook entitled "Pensées de Paris" a remark that suggests how dear this thought was to him: "the true hero performs his beautiful deed without suspecting that it is beautiful."[6] The opposite of a role? Yet only a temporarily assumed role holds out the promise of a similar revelation.

Every actor knows it: freedom of movement comes when the part is well-learned. Stendhal is keenly sensitive to the interrelations between a fixed scenario and the joys of improvisation. He himself never spun his fictions more freely than on a pre-established canvas. His characters, too, affirm their freedom to the extent that they accept the rules of a game. Mosca's charm and efficiency on that stage called the court of Parma have much to do with his not being duped by his own part. Inversely the court ("where he played such a beautiful role" [2: 119]) is theatrical—in other words a *game*—only for those who, like Mosca, remain generously available for what truly matters. Carried by the game, they can also dominate it. Surely it is not by chance that the Duchess's favorite pastime is *commedia del'arte,* where the set outline of a plot allows for improvisation. Comedy within comedy: "I have played a part on stage for one hour, and for five hours in the princess' room" (2: 429). Another passage, rich with theatrical vocabulary, explicitly stresses the alliance between role-playing and spontaneity. Having "staged" ("mis en scène") and masterfully played in the "Audience de Congé" (chapter 14), the Duchess withdraws from action to consider what idea she ought to form about "the scene that has just taken place." Stendhal adds (we know already that her conduct is unpredictable even to herself): "She had acted at random, for her own immediate pleasure" (2: 256).

To freedom through constraint corresponds protection through silence. The author's devious intrusions, the dissemblings of his irony, are part of a general rhetoric of obliquity which shields the lyricism embodied by his heroes. "Fabrice had an Italian heart; I crave the reader's pardon for him" (2: 166). This typically Stendhalian strategy finds its echo and commentary in his autobiographical writings, which constantly refer to the poetry of the unsaid or the unsayable. "I have never been able to speak of that which I adored; such a discourse would have seemed to me a blasphemy" (*Henry Brulard,* 151). Hence the frequent conditional sentences in his novels, these hypothetical structures that allow for the treating of a fictional situation as though it were real, and to create ironically a fiction on fiction. Hence also the dream of a metalanguage, of a special private code, to say that which cannot be said: "I would like to be able to write in a sacred language." This wish expressed in *Promenades dans Rome* is significantly placed after the still more revealing wish to be understood only by "persons born for music" (1: 72).

Does this refusal-wish account for Stendhal's stylistic casualness, his apparent *disinvoltura?* The fear of verbal "blasphemy" is no doubt a form of withdrawal, modesty in the sense of the French word *pudeur.* The word does indeed come up in relation to his own sensibility and to his own writings: "mes compositions m'ont toujours inspiré la même pudeur que mes amours." (*Henry Brulard,* 151, 97). Such a rift between the sign and the referent does not, however, in Stendhal's case imply the priority of the spoken or the written word. "The subject outdoes the saying," he observes on a number of occasions, appropriating some lines attributed to François I:

Qui te pourra louer qu'en se taisant?
Car la parole est réprimée,
Quand le sujet surmonte le disant.

What Stendhal sings is his nostalgia for silence. "With those I loved too much, mute." The shadings of regret and self-reproach suggested by this cryptic notation are a negligible price to pay for a certain type of happiness. Stendhal not only values silence, he considers it the irreplaceable sign of bliss. His ideal salon is the one where he would not have to play the role of wit, where he could listen and even forget his own presence. Behind the apparent bluntness of a letter to his friend de Mareste one perceives deep-lying satisfactions he associates with having neither to shine nor even to talk: "Le soir, société très gaie, très *musiquante,* très *foutante,* où je suis admis volontiers et sans avoir besoin de parler et de briller." Writing *Vie de Henry Brulard,* he stumbles on this lovely formula: "I willingly lapse into the silence of *happiness*" ("le silence du *bonheur*" [248]). Passion and speech are, as it were, incompatible. Already in 1804, twenty years before writing his first novel, he remarks in *Filosofia Nova* (2: 123), "the more passionate one becomes, the more speech fails one."

A sacred language. It would seem that it is through fictions of prisons that the dream of silence and special mediation was to be fulfilled. In all his constructs, Stendhal surrenders to the taste for messages by special intercession: secret graphs, codes, special meanings conveyed by opera recitatives, indirect signals. Not to speak clearly can be a deliberate strategy. Thus Duchess Sanseverina makes use of a particularly ambiguous fable by La Fontaine to communicate her meanings to the Prince. But such indirections cannot be viewed as mere tactical devices, nor even as part of a larger "elliptical" mode.[7] They most often serve what is most precious in Stendhal's fictional world: intimacy at a distance. The prisoner's cell, locus of inaccessible love, is also the symbolic place where secret messages and long-range mediation achieve this exquisite and ideal intimacy.

It is the writing process itself which, in the last analysis, is situated by Stendhal in an ideally confined space. "What a lovely place, the Grande Chartreuse, to write a tragedy!" (*Journal,* 534). An almost dreamlike sequence, in one of his earliest texts, adumbrates the images of the "prison aérienne." The young Henri Beyle imagines a "delicious valley" rich in "contours"; each of the contours in this emblematic topography represents a given passion. This valley, enclosing all times and all countries, is perfectly horizontal. But here is the exception. At the center of the valley (the Farnese fortress in *La Chartreuse de Parma* will also stand at the center of a vast plain), there is the region of artists and philosophers: "They live in an immense tower construction situated exactly at the center of the valley." The recognizable motif of elevated enclosure does not, however, constitute the sole interest of this early text (1804). According to Stendhalian logic, these superior inhabitants of the tower are endowed with *perfect vision* as well as *invisibility.* "Leur vue est infiniment pénétrante"—" . . . rien n'arrête leurs regards . . . "—"Leur vue est parfaite." But also: "Cette tour est invisible à tous les yeux autres que ceux des savants et des philosophes."[8]

The most significant thematic structures of his mature work

affirm themselves in this juvenile vision. Not only is freedom conceived in ascensional and separatist terms (the different artists climb to "varying heights"), but the most fundamental freedom is clearly associated with the act of writing. And this act belongs properly to the privileged world of claustration. Thirty years later, not so very long before writing *La Chartreuse,* Stendhal jots down the following observations concerning the "animal named writer"—observations that might well serve as epigraph, or conclusion: "Have you ever seen, benevolent reader, a silkworm that has eaten its fill of mulberry leaves? The simile is undignified, but it is so apt. This ugly animal no longer wants to eat. It needs to climb and weave its silken prison."[9]

NOTES

This essay is part of a larger study on Stendhal to appear in The Romantic Prison, *which will be published by the Princeton University Press in 1978.*

1. The page references are to the Divan edition (Paris, 1927–37), 79 volumes. For the novels, the Pléiade edition (1968, 1972) has been used.

2. This image of the writer's elevated quarters occurs in various contexts. About *Promenades dans Rome:* " . . . que je serais heureux à un quatrième étage, en en faisant un pareil . . . " (*Corr.,* 8:347). In *Vie de Henry Brulard:* " . . . depuis quarante-six ans, mon idéal est de vivre à Paris, dans un quatrième étage, écrivant un drame ou un livre" (261).

3. Jean-Pierre Richard has beautiful developments on the Stendhalian glance dominating landscapes "nettoyés de toute incertitude," and the shadow that protects that glance (*Littérature et Sensation* [Seuil, 1954], pp. 33, 51). See also Jean Starobinski's remarkable pages on the need to hide and the pleasure of masquerades in "Stendhal pseudonyme," *L'Oeil vivant* (Paris, 1961), pp. 193–244.

4. The already mentioned passage in *Le Rose et le Vert* also stresses the delights of "being seen." But in that case, the one who knows himself to be seen does not see. In any case, the metallic sheets provide a separation. One should also recall the game of glances, in *Lucien Leuwen,* between the young lieutenant and Mme de Chasteller, who is protected by her blinds.

5. *Le Décor mythique de la Chartreuse de Parme* (Paris, 1961), p. 162.

6. *Pensées. Filosofia Nova,* 1: 153.

7. See Gérard Genette, "Stendhal," in *Figures II* (Paris, 1969), pp. 155–93; also, for an interesting analysis of the relation of language to silence, Shoshana Felman's discussion of *Armance* in *La "Folie" dans l'oeuvre romanesque de Stendhal* (Paris, 1971), pp. 176, 179, 200.

8. *Pensées. Filosofia Nova,* 1:261, 258–60.

9. *Souvenirs d'Egotisme,* 1472. Prison de *soie* can also be read as a pun on prison de *soi* (prison of self).

IAN GREGOR

Spaces: *To The Lighthouse*

I, I, I,–how we have lost the secret of saying that. [1]
Virginia Woolf

I

On Wednesday, 28 November 1928, a year after the publication of *To The Lighthouse,* Virginia Woolf wrote in her diary:

> Father's birthday. He would have been 96, 96, yes, today; and could have been 96, like other people one has known: but mercifully was not. His life would have entirely ended mine. What would have happened? No writing, no books;—inconceivable.
>
> I used to think of him and mother daily; but writing the *Lighthouse* laid them in my mind. And now he comes back sometimes, but differently. (I believe this to be true—that I was obsessed by them both, unhealthily; and writing of them was a necessary act.) He comes back now more as a contemporary. I must read him some day. I wonder if I can feel again, I hear his voice, I know this by heart?
>
> So the days pass and I ask myself sometimes whether one is not hypnotised, as a child by a silver globe, by life; and whether this is living. It's very quick, bright, exciting. But superficial perhaps. I should like to take the globe in my hands and feel it quietly, round, smooth, heavy, and so hold it, day after day. [2]

In this casual diary entry we have, loosely assembled, elements central to the novel itself—the autobiographical pressure, the consolations of art, the persistent attempt to image the notion of "Life." These elements, imaginatively recreated and controlled, go into shaping a novel generally considered to be Virginia Woolf's most successful single work. The ease with which the diary entry recalls concerns present in the novel indicates the centrality of the personal element in its making.

This element has, of course, been widely noted and usually in the way indicated by a comment once made by Dr. Leavis:

> The substance of this novel was provided directly by life. . . . We know enough about Leslie Stephen, the novelist's father, and his family to know there is a large measure of direct transcription . . . [and there] is a clear relation between this fact and the unique success of *To The Lighthouse*. [3]

There is a truth in that judgment, but it is an equivocal truth. I would like to suggest in this essay that the relation between "the fact" and "the success" was considerably less "clear" than Dr. Leavis claims and that, so far from working in favor of the novel, the element of autobiography eventually begins to work against it.

To reflect on the criticism the novel has received in the fifty years since it was written is to be struck quite forcibly by two things which, taken together, seem somewhat at odds with each other. The first thing is that we can say with some confidence that, of all of Virginia Woolf's novels, *To The Lighthouse* has made the most immediate appeal. It has been written about again and again with a warmth and affection absent from accounts of her other novels, however much they may have been admired. The reasons are not far to seek—the generous presence of Mrs. Ramsay suffusing the novel, the depth and variety of the family relationships, the poignant reflections on death and the passage of time, the sharp sense of place. These admiring and affectionate accounts do not, however, prevent us noticing another thing: namely, the plurality of interpretation of the novel's overall meaning.

What would seem useful is a reflection on the novel which would concern itself with the disjunction between the clarity and immediacy with which the fiction makes its appeal and the troubling interpretative questions it seems to raise. I would like to argue that such a reflection will make us aware that this situation is caused by a flaw within the form of the work, a flaw which is itself the result of the novelist's attempt to meet the changing demands of the fiction as it develops. We can characterize those demands by saying that they bring about a change in the involvement of the novelist with her work which she feels she cannot evade. The fiction brings her to a point where she needs to change the inflection of her voice in a way that makes us recognize the justice in her own critical observation, "I, I, I,—how we have lost the secret of saying that."

II

In "The Anatomy of Fiction" Virginia Woolf observed, with *Emma* in mind, "Between the sentences, apart from the story, a little space of some kind builds itself up."[4] This sense of space is central to Virginia Woolf's own practice as a novelist. Central aesthetically, in that it is expressive of the dramatic expression she seeks; central metaphysically, in that it is ineluctably expressive of the void, the horror of which is both the source and the substance of her creative energy. "Space," "absence," "void"—these words lie at the heart of her work, and to see them at work in *To The Lighthouse* is to see the imaginative movement of that novel as it gradually develops and takes shape.

Though we talk of *To The Lighthouse* as being a novel in three sections, it is really the first of these sections, "The Window," which makes the decisive impact on the reader. It is this section that constitutes the achievement of the novel, a section which has its own artistic completion, a perfectly accomplished "novella" posing awkward problems for the novel which contains it.

Towards the end of section nine in "The Window" there occurs a conversation between Lily Briscoe and William Bankes about the picture she is painting. The drift of the conversation could well have occurred in Virginia Woolf's book on Roger Fry, turning as it does on the general question about representational and nonrepresentational art.

> What did she wish to indicate by the triangular purple shape . . . ? It was Mrs. Ramsay reading to James, she said. She knew his objection—that no one could tell it for a human shape. But she had made no attempt at likeness.

The debate is a familiar one. Bankes recalls a favorite picture in his own possession, "cherry trees in blossom on the banks of the Kennet," and while going on to accept Lily's own very different interest in terms of masses, lights, shapes, insists on the question "what did she wish to make of it"? Lily's rejoinder is to grasp her brush ("she could not even see it herself, without a brush in her hand"), resume her position at the canvas, and try to find "her picture" among "hedges and houses and mothers and children." "It was a question, she remembered, how to connect this mass on the right hand with that on the left . . . bringing the line . . . breaking the vacancy. . . ." But then suddenly her whole mood changes and she is flooded with gratitude to Bankes for the experience they have shared. The point at issue is no longer the "attempt at likeness" or "the triangular purple shape," her "picture" is not on the canvas, but within her, in the intensity of her response to the scene. It is Bankes's recognition of this that draws them together in affectionate sympathy. Earlier, Lily has talked of "that passage from conception to work as dreadful as any down a dark passage for a child," and Bankes's gentle curiosity has enabled her to find comfort in his unobtrusive recognition of her as someone whose painting should be thought of not in terms of its "aims" but rather an expression of her deepest self. The conversation concludes in a mood of exhilaration— "that one could walk away down that long gallery not alone anymore but arm in arm with somebody." A discussion which begins with talk about aesthetic principles concludes with a release of shared feeling, and has no need of formal expression for Lily and Bankes to feel its impact. It is a feeling caught and held in the way Lily "nicked the catch of her paint-box to, more firmly than was necessary, and the nick seemed to surround in a circle for ever the paint-box, the lawn, Mr. Bankes, and that wild villain, Cam, dashing past."

The beautiful gradations of feeling from the painting to the person work in an opposite way at the dinner party, when Lily, looking at Mrs. Ramsay, feels that she is pitying William Bankes:

> He is not in the least pitiable. He has his work, Lily said to herself. She remembered, all of a sudden as if she had found a treasure, that she had her work. In a flash she saw her picture and thought, Yes, I shall put the tree further in the middle; then I shall avoid that awkward space.

"That awkward space" presenting itself here sharply as a technical problem has behind it the earlier scene with Bankes, so that now we feel Lily has only to recall their "work" for their mutual feeling to be recalled and affirmed—the awkwardness of the space made awkward no longer.

The most intense moments in the dinner party belong, of course, to Mrs. Ramsay, and it is during one of these that we feel the harmony between contingent detail and individual feeling given its richest expression. Mrs. Ramsay, as the dinner party draws to an end, feels the occasion has been a great success:

"Andrew," she said, "hold your plate lower, or I shall spill it." (The Boeuf en Daube was a perfect triumph) Here, she felt, putting the spoon down, was the still space that lies about the heart of things, where one could move or rest; could wait now (they were all helped) listening; could then, like a hawk which lapses suddenly from its high station, flaunt and sink on laughter easily, resting her whole weight upon what at the other end of the table her husband was saying about the square root of one thousand two hundred and fifty-three, which happened to be the number on his railway ticket.

"The still space that lies about the heart of things where one could move or rest" is created by the density of particulars which surround it, and within those particulars, the reader, like Mrs. Ramsay, is free to maneuver, take his bearings, and share in the serenity of her mood. If Mrs. Ramsay can feel "the still space," it is because the very mobility of her sensibility has created it for us, a mobility created by the intensity of her response to the detail of the world about her. This space is not to be identified with any particular, but nevertheless can only exist by the defining presence of those particulars—the conversation, the company, her husband, "the exquisite scent of olives and oil and juice from the great brown dish"—all blend, for Mrs. Ramsay, into an exquisite harmony. It is a harmony made imaginatively present for the reader too, so that in his memory of the dinner party, it is the detail which remains suffused by a glow of feeling which exists somewhere "between" the characters and the author, the author and the reader. This notion of a space between, present in the conversation with Lily and Bankes and then much more powerfully in distinctive moments during the dinner party, becomes the virtual substance of an extended scene between Mr. and Mrs. Ramsay, which brings the first section of the novel to a close.

The episode opens with the Ramsays absorbed in their reading, he with Scott's novel, she with a volume of poems. "They did not want to speak to each other. They had nothing to say, but something seemed, nevertheless to go from him to her." Scott's novel dominates Mr. Ramsay's attention, "the poor old crazed creature in Mucklebackit's cottage made him feel so vigorous, so relieved that he felt roused and triumphant." He forgets himself completely as the fiction proceeds. "Steenie's drowning . . . Mucklebackit's sorrow . . . the astonishing delight and vigour it gave him." It is not the tragic tale that Scott tells which moves him so much as the completeness with which the novelist has understood, mastered, and communicated what he has to say. Scott's triumphant form has given form to Mr. Ramsay's feelings, and his reaction is one of delight and gratitude. The response which Mrs. Ramsay is making to the poem is similar. "All the odds and ends of the day stuck to this magnet; her mind felt swept, felt clean. . . . And there it was, suddenly entire . . . the essence sucked out of life and held rounded here—the sonnet." Again it is the achieved form that liberates and gives shape to the inchoate feelings of the reader. In this heightened state of awareness, first Mrs. Ramsay and then her husband long to break the silence but find the appropriate idiom hard to find, hard because it will be too sharply self-revealing, too explicit a gesture of dependence. "Do say something, she thought, wishing only to hear his voice . . . say anything as if for help." He breaks the silence and she takes his reproving remark with gratitude. The emotional pendulum swings, "He wanted something—wanted the thing she always found it so difficult to give him; wanted her to tell him that she loved him." The silence deepens. "Then, knowing that he was watching her, instead of saying anything she turned, holding her stocking, and looked at him. And as she looked at him she began to smile, for though she had not said a word, he knew, of course he knew, that she loved him. He could not deny it." Nothing is said, but the communication is complete.

This scene is for me the finest in the novel and arguably one of the finest in Virginia Woolf's work as a whole, because it conveys with unerring precision and delicacy the depth of feelings without words, feelings which have behind them years of shared living. Virginia Woolf in these pages is giving us a sense of married love which could be set without loss beside certain of the best pages in *The Rainbow*. To put it like that, however, is to see how radically different in approach the two novelists are. Lawrence making his language keep pace with the kaleidoscope of feelings he describes; Virginia Woolf making us feel its inadequacy, its hurried improvisations, its grateful acceptance of silent gesture: " . . . for though she had not said a word, he knew, of course he knew, that she loved him." That is the dominant note sounded in the passage and it recalls her remark about *Emma*, "Between the sentences, apart from the story, a little space of some kind builds itself up." Again and again throughout this first section of the novel and culminating finely in the scene between the Ramsays, we feel that Virginia Woolf has created just such a space, which is not an absence or a vacancy, but something, as she rightly says, "built." That building is partly the novelist's, creating a suggestively defining set of particulars which give the scene its substance, but it is also the reader's. The plentitude of imaginative life so effortlessly present in "The Window" is testimony to Virginia Woolf's mastery of her form, so that like Mr. Ramsay reading Scott we too, in reading these pages, are liberated into a sense of "astonishing delight."

III

"Such were some of the parts, but how string them together" wonders Lily as she watches preparations being made for the eventual sail to the lighthouse. It was a thought shared by Virginia Woolf as she contemplated the final section of her novel. In her diary we find her writing:

> 5 September 1926. At this moment I'm casting about for an end. The problem is how to bring Lily and Mr. R. together and make a combination of interest at the end. I am feathering about with various ideas. The last chapter which I begin tomorrow is In The Boat: I had meant to end with R. climbing on to the rock. If so, what becomes of Lily and her picture? Should there be a final page about her and Carmichael looking at the picture and summing up R's character? In that case, I lose the intensity of the moment. If this intervenes between R. and the lighthouse, there's too much chop and change, I think. Could I do it in a parenthesis? So that one had the sense of reading the two things at the same time?[5]

It is interesting that the difficulty of "an end" should present itself in such unequivocally "technical" terms, interesting because it helps to confirm the impression that in the last section, in marked contrast to the first, there is a sense of strain, or calculated effect. Or, putting it another way, there is the air of "a problem" being posed and "a solution" being looked for.

In one way, problem and solution emerge clearly enough and lend themselves to description. The most obvious feature of the third section is its structure, consisting of contrasting meditations on Mr. Ramsay's sail to the lighthouse juxtaposed with those of Lily as she tries to complete her painting. "The end" being reached when a significant conjunction is established between the two. Behind both enterprises we have the continuing influence of Mrs. Ramsay, tacitly present in the whole idea of the voyage, overtly present in Lily's thoughts as she struggles with her picture. Both voyage and painting take up and try to complete "unfinished business" of ten years previously.

From gloomy beginnings the sail prospers. The children gradually lose their hostility to the trip and to their father, and when, at last, James wins spontaneous praise from Mr. Ramsay for his steering, we feel amends have been made for the thwarted trip of years ago. When Mr. Ramsay, far out at sea, looks back at the house and sees it as a "frail blue shape like the vapour of something which had burnt itself away," the unhealthy spirit of an irrecoverable past would seem to have been exorcised, Mrs. Ramsay's spirit has triumphed, and the way is clear for a renewal of the relationship between Mr. Ramsay and his children.

Just as the voyage begins with the travellers ill at ease and uncertain of its outcome, so does the painting of the picture. "Here was Lily, at forty four, wasting her time, unable to do a thing, standing there, playing at painting, playing at the one thing one did not play at, and it was all Mrs. Ramsay's fault. She was dead. The step where she used to sit was empty." Unlike Lily's first picture, Mrs. Ramsay is no longer its subject, instead of "the triangular purple shape" there are only "empty steps." It is an overwhelming sense of an inner emptiness that Lily calls upon Mrs. Ramsay to fill, to the point at which she cries her name aloud, demanding why life is so short, so inexplicable. Perhaps then "the space would fill; those empty flourishes would form into shape; if they shouted loud enough Mrs. Ramsay would return." Her cry is heard. "Some wave of white went over the window pane. The air must have stirred some flounce in the room. . . . Mrs. Ramsay—it was part of her perfect goodness—sat there quite simply, in the chair, flicked her needles to and fro, knitted her reddish-brown stocking, cast her shadow on the step. . . . And Mr. Ramsay? She wanted him." Mrs. Ramsay, absent from the party to the lighthouse, absent from the picture, has returned to animate them both, making the past part of the present. In their respective ways James and Lily come to realize that no thing is one thing; the lighthouse is a visionary gleam and also a tower stark and straight, barred with black and white; tables and chairs can be on a level with ordinary experience, they can also be miraculous. The voyage is made, the picture completed; life and art are held in equipoise.

This would seem to be the formal design and intention of the last section of the novel; the problem is that it remains like that. Even in such a bald description as I have tried to give, some of the difficulties that Virginia Woolf has had to face in this section can be suspected.

The first and most obvious is with the character of Mr. Ramsay himself. The whole treatment of the voyage, delicately conveyed as it is, is that of moral discovery, the children for the father, he for them. But this must, of necessity, involve the reader in a kind of knowledge about Mr. Ramsay which he does not possess. On the boat the children gaze at him, eager to do his bidding. "But he did not ask them anything. He sat and looked at the island and he might be thinking, We perished, each alone, or he might be thinking, I have reached it. I have found it; but he said nothing." That description of Mr. Ramsay is entirely appropriate to the way in which Mr. Ramsay has been presented in the first half of the novel, but here it comes across as an evasion. His silence is very different from the silences that punctuated the reading scene with his wife, different because the inarticulateness of that scene is accompanied at every point and felt through the sensibility of Mrs. Ramsay. That guiding presence has now been withdrawn. Clearly, however, Virginia Woolf requires us to take Mr. Ramsay's approving "Well done" to James as a moral climax, a transcending of his egoism. But for this to be imaginatively communicated it would require a greater insight, or more accurately a different kind of insight, into Mr. Ramsay's character than anything we have been previously given. We have a climax without a context, and so far as the reader is concerned, trust has to do the work of recognition.

If an inadequacy between climax and context is felt in Mr. Ramsay's gesture of approval, it is felt more acutely in the presentation of Lily Briscoe painting on the lawn, not least because it is here that Virginia Woolf seems to want the main stress of the section to fall.

In the first section we have seen how deeply interfused Lily's reactions to her painting are with her reactions to William Bankes, Mrs. Ramsay, and the family in general. In the present section, the picture is again central and the terms in which she thinks about it are familiar. "The question was of some relation between those masses. She had borne it in her mind all these years." She begins to paint " . . . lightly and swiftly pausing, striking, she scored her canvas with brown running nervous lines which had no sooner settled there than they enclosed (she felt it looming out at her) a space. . . . For what could be more formidable than that space?" So far as this section of the novel is concerned, "that space" is too formidable. Here Virginia Woolf has not discovered a way of describing the painting which will enable her to put it within a psychological or metaphysical context. The picture remains stubbornly a canvas on a frame, the problems it sets, aesthetic ones of mass and line, the space, a vacancy. In a remark like the following, where Lily is recalling Mrs. Ramsay looking out to sea, we detect Virginia Woolf seeking an intensity of meaning, and obtaining only an exclamatory tone:

> Is it a boat? Is it a cork? . . . Lily repeated, turning back, reluctantly to her canvas. Heaven be praised for it, the space remained, she thought, taking up her brush again.

The painting, the picture are being pressed into an imaginative service they cannot sustain. We can feel the same thing in the sharp interrogation and assertion of the passage in which, with the gnomically silent Mr. Carmichael, Lily feels that if they both "demanded an explanation, why was [life] so short, why was it so inexplicable, said it with violence . . . then . . . the space would fill; those empty flourishes would form into shape; if they shouted loud enough Mrs. Ramsay would return." The tone would seem to indicate the extravagance, the hopelessness of desire, but Mrs. Ramsay does "return." It is the theatricality—the "light stuff" behind the window, "the stroke of luck" causing "the odd-shaped triangular shadow" to fall across the step—which indicates how far the novelist's reach, at this stage, has exceeded her grasp.

In this last section of the novel Virginia Woolf has set up too rigid a structure, so that the impression it gives is that of a steely dialectic, between Mr. Ramsay's voyage to the lighthouse on the one hand and Lily painting her picture on the other. In consequence, everything becomes emblematic, every gesture representative and significant. The fluidity and particularity so characteristic of the first section yield here to the overriding pattern. Looking about her, Lily sees Mr. Ramsay stride past talking to himself, "and like everything else this strange morning the words became symbols, wrote themselves all over the grey-green walls."

In making the influence of the past so pervasive, the section comes over as an epilogue to a tale already told, an epilogue whose function it is to make plain, to interrogate, to qualify, but not to bring imaginative life and bring it more abundantly. So we find monologues which seem to break free from a controlling dramatic context in their bleak explicitness. "What is the meaning of life? That was all—a simple question; one that tended to close in with the years. The great revelation had never come. The great revelation perhaps never did come. Instead there were little daily miracles, illustrations, matches struck in the dark. . . . " It is not the assertive explicitness of this as such that is troubling, but rather the loss of imaginative pressure that has made it possible. The fiction fades, and Lily's voice becomes interchangeable with the author's. To see why this is happening, it is useful to look at the short middle section of the novel, which begins to pose the problem of whose voice is speaking.

Virginia Woolf was in no doubt about what she wished to do in the section titled "Time Passes" and under no illusion about the difficulty of doing it. "Here," she writes in her diary, "is the most difficult abstract piece of writing—I have to give an empty house, no people's characters, the passage of time, all eyeless and featureless with nothing to cling to. . . . "[6] She is to set about the creation of vacancy; the dense life so vividly recreated in "The Window" is to give way to its opposite, give way, in Donne's words to, "absence, darkness, death; things which are not."[7] It is a hazardous enterprise particularly for a novelist, raising a problem not only about content, but, more radically, about whose voice is to be heard by the reader. It cannot be that of any individual character and it cannot, in the nature of things, be that of an omniscient narrator. Virginia Woolf seeks to overcome the difficulty by employing not one voice but many.

There is the harshly factual:

> (Mr. Ramsay, stumbling along a passage one dark morning, stretched his arms out, but Mrs. Ramsay having died rather suddenly the night before, his arms, though stretched out, remained empty).

The gently elegiac:

> Loveliness and stillness clasped hands in the bedroom, and among the shrouded jugs and sheeted chairs, even the prying of the wind, and the soft nose of the clammy sea airs, rubbing, snuffling, iterating, and reiterating their questions—"Will you fade? Will you perish?"—scarcely disturbed the peace.

The apocalyptic:

> . . . gigantic chaos streaked with lightening could have been heard tumbling and tossing, as the winds and waves disported themselves like the

> amorphous bulks of leviathans whose brows are pierced by no light of
> reason and mounted one on top of another, and lunged and plunged in the
> darkness or the daylight . . . in idiot games, until it seemed as if the uni-
> verse were battling and tumbling, in brute confusion and wanton lust
> aimlessly by itself.

Certainly, passages like this come across as having no specific voice,
but in the way that pastiche has no "voice." If there is anonymity, it is
the anonymity of a ventriloquist where the manner of the performance
becomes its own end. The style which seeks to escape style becomes all
style.

With the reassembly of the house party we might imagine that the
authorial presence would be easier to modify. But the questions raised
by "Time Passes" are, even in terms of the narrative, too insistent to
allow the fiction simply to resume its course. In the final section, "The
Lighthouse," the author is under a dual obligation which could be
divisive. On the one hand there is the obligation to a specific narrative
history initiated in part one; on the other, there is the obligation to
questions raised in part two by "the passage of time, all eyeless and
featureless." No matter how we describe this difference, what seems
clear is that the first two sections of the novel are juxtaposed in a way
that makes the structural effort of the final section one of mediation.
Lily Briscoe as a friend of the Ramsay family will help to carry the
narrative forward; Lily Briscoe as a painter will enable the novelist to
enter her fiction with a new directness and allow free play to that question with which the last section begins: "What does it mean then, what
can it all mean?"

IV

Questions of "meaning" seem far away when we come across the first
mention of the novel in the diary on 14 May 1925:

> I'm now all on the strain with desire to stop journalism and get on *To The
> Lighthouse*. This is going to be fairly short; to have father's character done
> complete in it; and mother's and St. Ives; and childhood; and all the usual
> things I try to put in—life, death, etc. But the centre is father's character.[8]

The autobiographical emphasis is firm and unequivocal and though
we can observe marked shifts of emphasis, the intention becomes the
deed, and "father's character . . . mother's and St. Ives and childhood"

are the material that make up the opening section and give it its memorability. We can judge the degree of personal involvement present in this recreation when we recall Virginia Woolf's remark that she used "to think of father and mother daily" and that writing about them had laid their spirits to rest for her. Nevertheless, that involvement had become transfigured in the absorbed intentness of her recreation, and though Mrs. Ramsay was, according to Vanessa Bell, "an amazing portrait of mother," she was also for Virginia Woolf a person whose sensibility allowed the author to explore her created world completely. We are not surprised to find her noting in her diary during the writing of this part of the novel, "I live entirely in it, and come to the surface rather obscurely. . . ."9

The very completeness of Virginia Woolf's imaginative recreation of her parents carries within it, for her, its own skepticism so that she is driven on beyond it into asking what such recreation means, what value it possesses, what can turn "an absence" into "a presence."

"But the centre is father's character." It is here of course that the novel departs most markedly from the scenario of intentions, departs not simply in its detail, but in the nature of its concern. The process of writing has taken her out of a recreated past, however vivid, into the obscurity and uncertainty of the present. "The centre," if we can think of the resolution of the novel in this way, is not to be found in any object of her imagination, but in looking at the act of imagining itself.

The recollection of her parents, the mutability of life, the affirmation and the limitations of art—we can see all these elements at work in the novel, but what we also see is that every extension of the elements has created new difficulties, and it has created them because it has involved the author more and more directly until there is nothing to separate the novelist from the novel. The structure has been worn thin trying to hold together a fiction which is really completed with Mrs. Ramsay's death and a fiction about the artist which emerges out of the contemplation of that death. But for Virginia Woolf these two fictions must be one; they are the story of the writing of this novel. What makes them discordant is that her imagination can no longer make coherent what her experience has given her as fact. And when Lily draws a line "there, in the centre" of her canvas to complete her picture, Virginia Woolf must do the same for the novel; it is not a conclusion, it is a line drawn across a space, a mark indicating a break in a work in progress.

The closing of that final space, bringing the painting and the novel simultaneously to their completion, concludes a treatment of space which, throughout the novel, has provided a dramatic notation for the constantly shifting involvement of the author.

In "The Window" Virginia Woolf, in recreating her past, explored the resonance of the space between people, space which both extended and guarded the individual, where feelings could find wordless expression, where speech could become gesture. That she was able to do this so triumphantly is testimony to the confidence with which she knew and felt that vanished world in a way that allowed her to become a loving but impersonal mediator. In "Time Passes" she seeks to strip that world of all its detail, and in place of the life-enhancing space she creates the space of emptiness and decay, death and the void. Having to write in no voice, she tries to write in many, but we begin to hear only her own, as questions start to form themselves, meanings begin to be insisted upon. The multiple voices of "Time Passes" become a dramatized presence in "The Lighthouse." In Lily's voice we can hear the author's. Space is now no longer a metaphor, "lying about the heart of things," it is there on the canvas, an invitation and a challenge, and "what could be more formidable?" The difficulties of the painting ("the question was of some relation between those masses") and the difficulties of writing the novel ("how to create a combination of interest at the end?") become virtually interchangeable. Spaces which, at the beginning of the novel, were created by the richness of its texture, become, by the end, gaps in the texture itself. But such a texture, we have to go on to say, could only have been created by an imagination of such purity of intent that its every creation contained within it its own skepticism. And it is in the unflinching acting out of *that* struggle that we see the difficulty of saying "I" for Virginia Woolf was the more radical difficulty of finding the "I" she had to express. *To The Lighthouse* may not have been wholly successful in this, but it enabled her to see what was at issue in such a way that the rest of her fiction would echo with Lily's questions as she painted her canvas and contemplated its "formidable space."

NOTES

1. "Reading," *Collected Essays*, 2 vols. (London, 1966), 2: 29.

2. *A Writer's Diary* (London, 1953), p. 138.

3. "After *To The Lighthouse*," *Scrutiny* 10 no. 3 (January 1942): 207.

4. "The Anatomy of Fiction," *Collected Essays*, 2: 138.

5. *Diary*, p. 99.

6. Ibid., pp. 76–77.

7. "A Nocturnall upon S. Lucie's Day."

8. *Diary*, pp. 76–77.

9. Ibid., p. 85. It is interesting to note how close in feeling the novel is to the mood she describes in the memoir she wrote in 1939. "Until I was in my forties . . . the presence of my mother obsessed me. I could hear her voice, see her, imagine what she would do or say as I went about my day's doings. She was one of the invisible presences who after all play so important a part in every life. . . . Then one day walking round Tavistock Square I made up, as I sometimes make up my books, *To the Lighthouse;* in a great involuntary rush. . . . I wrote very quickly; and when it was written, I ceased to be obsessed by my mother. I no longer hear her voice; I do not see her." "A Sketch of the Past," printed in *Moments of Being* (London, 1976), pp. 80–81. The whole memoir is of considerable interest in describing the emotional background of the novel.

Bibliography of Writings and Editions by Maynard Mack

I. *Books*

A History of Scroll and Key, 1842–1942. Printed for the Society by Daniel B. Updike at the Merrymount Press, Boston, 1942. Revised edition printed for the Society by Michael F. Bixler and Halliday Lithograph Corporation, Somerville and West Hanover, Massachusetts, 1978.

Pope, *Essay on Man: The Twickenham Edition of Pope's Poetical Works,* Volume 3, Part 1. London: Methuen and Co., 1950. New Haven: Yale University Press, 1951.

Alexander Pope: An Essay on Man—The Manuscripts of the Morgan and Houghton Libraries. Privately printed for the Roxburgh Club, Oxford, 1962.

Essential Articles for the Study of Alexander Pope. New Haven: Archon Books, 1964. Revised and enlarged edition, 1968.

King Lear in Our Time. Berkeley: University of California Press, 1965. London: Methuen and Co., 1966.

Pope, *The Translations of Homer: The Twickenham Edition of Pope's Poetical Works.* Volumes 7–8 (the *Iliad*), Volumes 9–10 (the *Odyssey*). London: Methuen and Co., and New Haven: Yale University Press, 1967.

The Twickenham Edition of Pope's Poetical Works, Volume 11 *(Index).* London: Methuen and Co., and New Haven: Yale University Press, 1969.

The Garden and the City: Retirement and Politics in the Later Poetry of Pope, 1731–43. Toronto: University of Toronto Press, 1969.

"Collected in Himself": Essays Critical, Biographical, and Bibliographical on Alexander Pope. Newark: University of Delaware Press, 1978. Forthcoming.

II. *Essays and Articles*

"The First Printing of the Letters of Pope and Swift." *The Library (Transactions of the Bibliographical Society)* 19 (1939): 465–85.

"A Couplet in the Epistle to Dr. Arbuthnot." *Times Literary Supplement,* September 2, 1939, p. 515.

"Pope's Horatian Poems: Problems of Bibliography and Text." *Modern Philology* 41 (1943): 33–44.

"A Manuscript of Pope's Imitation of the First Ode of the Fourth Book of Horace." *Modern Language Notes* 40 (1945): 185–88.

"A Letter of Pope to Atterbury in the Tower." *Review of English Studies* 21 (1945): 117–25.

"On Reading Pope." *College English* 7 (1946): 263–73. Reprinted in the Golden Anniversary *College English* Sampler 22 (1960): 99–107.

"Gay Augustan." *Yale Library Gazette* 21 (1946): 6–10.

"New Developments at Yale." *The Newsletter of the College English Association* 9 (1947), No. 1 (with Louis L. Martz).

"Directed Studies." *Yale Alumni Magazine* (1949): 8–10.

" 'Wit and Poetry and Pope': Some Observations on His Imagery." In *Pope and His Contemporaries*, ed. Landa and Clifford (1949), pp. 20–40. Reprinted in *The Modern Critical Spectrum*, ed. G. J. and N. M. Goldberg (1962).

"The Muse of Satire." *Yale Review* 41 (1951–52): 80–92. Reprinted in *Studies in the Literature of the Augustan Age*, ed. Boys (1952); *Discussions of Alexander Pope*, ed. Blanchard (1960); *Satire: Theory and Practice*, ed. Allen and Stephens; *The Practice of Criticism*, ed. Zitner, Kissane, and Liberman (1965); *Satire: Modern Essays in Criticism*, ed. Paulson (1969); *Critics on Pope*, ed. O'Neill (1969); *La Satira*, ed. Brilli (1974).

"The World of Hamlet." *Yale Review* 41 (1951–52): 502–23. Reprinted in *Tragic Themes in Western Literature*, ed. Brooks (1955); *Modern Essays on Shakespeare*, ed. Dean (1956, 1966); *An Introduction to Literary Criticism*, ed. Danzinger and Johnson (1961); *Writing Prose*, ed. Kane and Peters (1959, 1964); *Discussions of Hamlet*, ed. Levenson (1960); *A Treasury of Shakespearean Criticism*, ed. Siegel (1962); *A Shakespeare Scrapbook*, ed. Eastman and Harrison (1963); *Hamlet*, ed. Hubler: *The Signet Classic Shakespeare* (1963); *A Grammar of Literary Criticism*, ed. Hall (1964); *Shakespeare: The Tragedies*, ed. Harbage (1964); *Reader's Encyclopedia of Shakespeare*, ed. Campbell (1965); *Hamlet*, ed. Bevington (1968); *Hamlet: A Casebook*, ed. Jump (1968); *An Introduction to Shakespeare*, ed. Friedberg (1969); *Introduction to Drama and Criticism*, ed. Hurtik and Yarber (1971); *Literature: An Introduction to Fiction, Poetry, and Drama*, ed. Kennedy (1976).

"Pope." In *Major British Writers*, ed. Harrison (1953), 1: 749–59. Reprinted in *Pope: A Collection of Critical Essays*, ed. Guerinot (1972).

"An Affair of the Heart." *The Freshman Magazine* 1957, Vol. 4 (1954), No. 5.

"The Quick and the Dead." *Progress and Survival*, pp. 54–63. Published in part in *The Present-Day Relevance of Eighteenth-Century Thought*, ed. McCutcheon (1956).

"Pope's Correspondence." *Philological Quarterly* 36 (1957): 389–99. Review article of Sherburn's edition of Pope's letters, 5 volumes (Oxford, 1956).

"Two Variant Copies of Pope's Works . . . Further Light on Some Problems of Authorship, Bibliography, and Text." *The Library (Transactions of the Bibliographical Society)* 12 (1957): 48–53.

"Some Annotations in the Second Earl of Oxford's Copies of Pope's *Epistle to Dr. Arbuthnot* and *Sober Advice from Horace*." *Review of English Studies*, 2d series, 8 (1957): 416–20.

"A Mirror for the Lamp." *PMLA* 83 (1958), no. 5, pt. 2: 45–71.

"Matthew Prior." *Sewanee Review* 68 (1960): 165–76. Review article of *The Literary Works of Matthew Prior*, ed. Wright and Spears, 2 volumes (Oxford, 1959).

"The Jacobean Shakespeare." In *Jacobean Theatre: Stratford upon Avon Studies* 1, ed. Harris and Brown (1960), pp. 10–41. Reprinted in *Othello*, ed. Kernan: *The Signet Classic Shakespeare* (1963); *Essays in Shakespearean Criticism*, ed. Calderwood and Toliver (1970).

"On Teaching Drama." Circulated in *Reports and Speeches of the Third Yale Conference*, April 1957. Published in *Essays on the Teaching of English*, ed. Noyes and Gordon (1960). Reprinted in part as "Julius Caesar" in *Modern Shakespearean Criticism*, ed. Kernan (1970).

"Engagement and Detachment in Shakespeare's Plays." In *Essays on Shakespeare and Elizabethan Drama in Honor of Hardin Craig*, ed. Hosley (1962), pp. 275–96.

" 'The Shadowy Cave': Some Speculations upon a Twickenham Grotto." In *Restoration and Eighteenth-Century Literature: Essays in Honor of Dugald McKillop*, ed. Camden (1963), pp. 69–88.

" 'We Came Crying Hither': An Essay on Some Characteristics of *King Lear*." *Yale Review* 54 (1964): 161–86. Collected in *Essays on Shakespeare*, ed. Chapman (1965); and, somewhat revised, in *King Lear in Our Time*.

"A Poet in His Landscape: Alexander Pope at Twickenham." In *From Sense to Sensibility: Essays in Honor of Frederick A. Pottle*, ed. Hilles and Bloom (1965), pp. 1–29.

"Secretum Iter: Some Uses of Retirement Literature in the Poetry of Pope." In *Aspects of the Eighteenth Century*, ed. Wasserman (1965).

"To See It Feelingly." *PMLA* 86 (1971): 363–74. Reprinted in *American Council of Learned Societies Newsletter* 22 (1971), and *Prospects for the 70's*, ed. Firestone and Shugrue (1973).

"*Antony and Cleopatra*: The Stillness and the Dance." In *Shakespeare's Art: Seven Essays*, ed. Crane (1973), pp. 79–113. Reprinted in part in *Antony and Cleopatra*, ed. Rose (1976).

"My Ordinary Occasions: A Letter from Pope." *The Scriblerian* 9 (1976–77): 1–8.

" 'They Have Actually Turned Me Out': Vanbrugh to Marlborough." *The Scriblerian* 9 (1976–77): 77–83.

"Pope's Books: A Biographical Survey with a Finding List." In *English Literature in the Age of Disguise*, ed. Novak (1977), pp. 209–305.

"Pope's 1717 Preface with a Transcription of the Manuscript Text." In *Augustan Worlds*, ed. Hilson, Jones, and Watson (1978), pp. 85–106.

III. *Reviews*

Geoffrey Tillotson, *On the Poetry of Pope*. In *Review of English Studies* 15 (1939): 231–33.

Cleanth Brooks, *Modern Poetry and the Tradition*; Louis MacNeice, *Modern Poetry*. In *Yale Review* 29 (1939–40): 398–402.

Emery Neff, *A Revolution in European Poetry, 1660–1900;* B. Ifor Evans, *Tradition and Romanticism;* Elizabeth Drew and John L. Sweeney, *Directions in Modern Poetry;* David Daiches, *Poetry and the Modern World.* In *Yale Review* 30 (1940–41): 608–11.

Rudolf Stamm, *Der Umstrittene Ruhm Alexander Popes.* In *MLN* 18 (1943): 242.

The Kenyon Critics, *Gerard Manley Hopkins.* In *Yale Review* 35 (1945–46): 539–42.

Mark Van Doren, *John Dryden.* In *Quarterly Review of Literature* 3 (1946): 83–86.

Texas Studies in English. In *Philological Quarterly* 25 (1946): 158–61.

Donald Stauffer, *The Nature of Poetry.* In *Yale Review* 36 (1946–47): 346–48.

Rosamund Tuve, *Elizabethan and Metaphysical Imagery;* C. Day Lewis, *The Poetic Image,* W. Y. Tindall, *Forces in Modern British Literature, 1885–1946;* F. C. Matthiessen, *The Achievement of T. S. Eliot.* In *Furioso* 3 (1948): 68–73.

Norman Ault, *New Light on Pope.* In *Philological Quarterly* 29 (1950): 289–91.

F. W. Bateson, *English Poetry.* In *Yale Review* 40 (1950–51): 338–40.

D. G. James, *The Life of Reason.* In *Review of English Studies,* new series, 2 (1951): 283–85.

Patrick Cruttwell, *The Shakespearean Moment and Its Place in the Poetry of the Eighteenth Century;* Derek Traversi, *Shakespeare: The Last Phase.* In *Yale Review* 45 (1955): 267–73.

A. R. Humphreys, *The Augustan World: Life and Letters in Eighteenth-Century England.* In *Modern Language Review* 51 (1956): 103–05.

G. B. Evans, *Shakespearean Prompt-Books of the Seventeenth Century,* Volume 1, Parts 1 and 2. In *The Book Collector* 9 (1960): 470–73.

E. R. Wasserman, *Pope's Epistle to Bathurst: A Critical Reading with an Edition of the Manuscripts.* In *MLN* 76 (1961): 869–75.

Irving Ribner, *Patterns in Shakespearean Tragedy.* In *Renaissance News* 19 (1961): 290–92.

Hans-Joachim Zimmermann, *Alexander Popes Noten zu Homer: Eine Manuscript und Quellenstudie.* In *Archiv* 206 (1969).

E. G. Bedford and R. J. Dilligan, *A Concordance to the Poems of Alexander Pope,* 2 volumes. In *The Eighteenth Century: A Current Bibliography for 1974—Philological Quarterly* 54 (1975): 1016–18.

IV. *Class Texts*

Fielding, *Joseph Andrews* (1948). Introduction reprinted as "Joseph Andrews and Pamela" in *Sonderdruck aus Henry Fielding* (1971).

English Masterpieces: Milton (1950). Revised and enlarged edition (1961).

English Masterpieces: Modern Poetry (1950). Revised and enlarged edition (1961). (With William Frost and Leonard F. Dean.)

English Masterpieces: The Augustans (1950). Revised and enlarged edition (1961).

English Masterpieces: Selected Prose (1951). (With William Frost.)

World Masterpieces, 2 volumes (1956). (With Bernard M. W. Knox, J. C. McGalliard, P. M. Pasinetti, H. E. Hugo, René Wellek, and Kenneth Douglas.) Revised and enlarged edition (1964). Third edition (1975).

Antony and Cleopatra: Pelican Shakespeare (1960).

Masterpieces of the Orient (1961). (With G. L. Anderson.)

An Introduction to the Short Story (1964). (With Robert Boynton.)

Henry IV, Part I: Signet Shakespeare (1965).

An Introduction to the Poem (1965). (With Robert Boynton.)

An Introduction to the Play (1969). (With Robert Boynton.)

Hamlet; Henry IV, Part I; Julius Caesar; Macbeth: Hayden Shakespeare (1973).

Sounds and Silences: Poems for Performing (1975). (With Robert Boynton.)

V. *Critical Series*

Twentieth Century Views. Englewood Cliffs, N.J.: Prentice-Hall, Inc., 1962–78. 135 volumes.

Twentieth Century Interpretations. Englewood Cliffs, N.J.: Prentice-Hall, Inc., 1965–75. 80 volumes.

Index

Absalom and Achitophel (Dryden), 300
Account of the Life of Mr. Richard Savage, An (Johnson), 341
"Adam's Curse" (Yeats), 144
Addison, Joseph, 237; audience for, 263–64; *Cato,* 309; *Paradise Lost* criticism by, 263–81
Aeneid (Virgil), 33, 35–36, 41, 47, 230, 271, 275
Aesop, 85
"Again Beguiled, Again Betrayed" (Byron), 351
Alchemist, The (Jonson), 291, 306
Alciphron (Berkeley), 235
Alexander the Great, 184, 257
Alington, Alice, 169–72
Allusion: in Congreve, 287–96; in eighteenth-century literature, 297–318; history of events in, 300–01; referential, 298–304; repetition and, 304–11
"Allusion to Horace, An" (Dryden), 104, 113
Ambiguity, 299
"Among School Children" (Yeats), 147
Amores (Ovid), 109, 113
Anaphora, 305
"Anatomy of Fiction, The" (Woolf), 377
Anne, Queen of England, 253
"Answer to Mathetes" (Wordsworth), 138
Anteros myth, 295–96
Anthropology, 329–30
Antithesis, 231
Antony and Cleopatra (Shakespeare), 181
Aphorisms, 309
Arbuthnot, Dr., 248–51
Archilochus, 104
Architecture, 301
Arendt, Hannah, 301
Areopagitica (Milton), 40
Ariosto, 43, 58, 368
Aristophanes, 178
Aristotle, 9, 12, 275, 343, 344; criticism of, 268, 271; *Rhetoric* of, 4, 231

Armance (Stendhal), 365
Ars Poetica (Horace), 198
Art: Expulsion theme in, 71, 83; as literary subject, 175–76; self-consciousness in, 176–77
"Artemisia to Chloe" (Rochester), 110
Arte of Poesie (Puttenham), 85, 86, 231
Artist, as hero, 175–76
Art of Sinking in Poetry, The (Steeves), 301–02
Astronomy, 330
As You Like It (Shakespeare), 179, 201–03
Athenae Oxoniensis (Wood), 213, 215
Audley, Sir Thomas, 169–72
Auerbach, Berthold, 299
Augustan literature: Eros in, 296; poetry in, 3, 4, 6, 27; satire in, 104
Augustine, Saint, 220, 321, 326, 327–29
Autobiography: author's fascination with past experience in, 319–32; definition of, 319–20; in eighteenth century, 319–36; literary attitude in, 320–21; memoirs distinct from, 323; playwrights and, 327; public interest in lives of authors of, 321–23; scientific critical methods in, 330–31; self-portraits distinct from, 321, 323–24; sudden concentration of writers of, 326–27; urge to achieve meaningful pattern in, 324–26
Autobiography (Franklin), 324, 327
Autobiography of Benvenuto Cellini, The, 321, 327

Bacon, Francis, 177
Barish, Jonas, 207
Baroque art, 71
Bartholomew Fair (Jonson), 206
Bastard, The (Savage), 10
Bate, W. J., 301
Baucis and Philemon (Swift), 240
Baudelaire, Charles, 230
Baxter, Richard, 238
Beardsley, Aubrey, 148
Beardsley, Mabel, 148–50

Beare, W., 198
"Beautiful Young Nymph going to Bed" (Swift), 114, 236
Beauty, 79
Beckett, Samuel, 257
Bee, The (periodical), 8, 9, 14
Beggar's Opera (Gay), 299
Bell, Vanessa, 387
"Belle Dame Sans Merci, La" (Keats), 358
Bergler, Edmund, 338
Berkeley, George, 8, 235
Bernard, Saint, 214
Bible, 38, 75, 80, 269, 270
Biographia Literaria (Coleridge), 137
Blake, William, 83
Blas, Gil, 365
Bloom, Harold, 307
Boccaccio, Giovanni, 176
Boleyn, Anne, 164
Borges, Jorge Luis, 301
Boswell, James, 7, 322, 323, 339
Bretonne, Restif de la, 326
Bridgeman, Sir Orlando, 215
Brooke-Rose, Christine, 308
Brower, Reuben, 298
Buckingham, Duke of, 117
Buffon, Comte de, 330
Bunyan, John, 321, 328
Burghley, William Cecil, Lord, 96–97
Burke, Edmund, 303
Burnet, Gilbert, 103, 115
Burns, Robert, 20
Burton, Robert, 104
Butler, Samuel, 8, 105, 231, 236, 238
Byron, George Gordon, Lord, 238, 257; "Go—triumph securely," 350–62; significance of biographical context in, 347–64

Cadenus and Vanessa (Swift), 229
Caesar, Julius, 323
Callot, Jacques, 108
Campbell, O. J., 205
Campion, Edmund, 232
Canterbury, Lord, 164
Cardano, Geronimo, 321
Carmina Burana, 232
Caroline, Queen of England, 242
Casanova, Giovanni Giacomo, 321
Cassirer, Ernst, 329, 330

Catholicism, 327
Cato, 308, 309
Cato (Addison), 309
Cavaliers, 105
Cave, Edward, 344
Cavendish, Margaret, 328
Celestina, 202
Cellini, Benvenuto, 321, 326, 327
Centuries of Meditations (Traherne), 214–15, 219–27
Cervantes, Miguel de, 177
Chalandritsanos, Loukas, 348
Chambers, R. W., 163, 196
Chapelain, 271
Characterization, 85
Charles I, King of England, 39
Charles II, King of England, 105, 106–11, 113–14, 117
Chartreuse de Parme, La (Stendhal), 369, 372–73
Chaucer, Geoffrey, 85, 90, 163, 175, 196, 231, 358
Chaworth, Mary, 351–52, 355
Chiasmus, 231
"Chinese Letters" (Goldsmith), 8
Cholmondeley, Mrs., 20
Christian Ethnics (Traherne), 215
Christian tradition: autobiography and, 327–28; Thomas More and, 171–72
Churchill, Charles, 11
Churchill, Winston, 257
Church of England, 216
Cibber, Theophilus, 267
Cicero, 3, 222
"Circus Animals' Desertion, The" (Yeats), 147
Cistellaria (Plautus), 198, 200–01
Citizen of the World, The (Goldsmith), 8, 13
Civil History of the Kingdom of Naples (Giannone), 300
Clarendon, Earl of, 300
Clarissa (Richardson), 310–11
Clark, Colin, 123, 132, 137
Classical literature: allusions to, 301; English dramatists and, 177, 178; poetry and, 231; Pope's use of, 309; Swift's poetry and, 243
Cleopatra, 257
Coleridge, Samuel Taylor, 125, 137, 138
Colet, John, 166

Collected Poems (Yeats), 143, 149
Collected Works (Goldsmith), 3
Collection (Dodsley), 11
Collins, William, 27–28
Comedy: author's agent device in, 207–10; development of, 284–85
Commedia dell'arte, 370
Comus (Milton), 40, 41
Confessions (Augustine), 326, 328–29
Confessions (Rousseau), 324, 326, 327–28, 331
Congreve, William, 116, 283–96, 303, 306–08
Conquest of Granada, The (Dryden), 208
Conscience, and Thomas More, 163–71
Cooper's Hill (Denham), 300
Cotton, Charles, 105
Country Wife, The (Wycherley), 114–15
Couplets, 231–33
Cowper, William, 20
Creation: *Paradise Lost* and, 51–69; Platonic idea of, 79
Critical Essays (Scott), 23–24
Critical History of the Old Testament (Simon), 300
Criticism, 268, 349
Critique upon Milton, The (Addison), 264
Croyden, Vicar of, 163–64
Crutwell, Patrick, 181

Dante Alighieri, 35, 45
Davenant, Sir William, 108
Da Vinci, Leonardo, 177
Davis, Herbert, 293
Decameron, The (Boccaccio), 176
Defence of Poesie (Sidney), 177, 188
De Mareste, 366, 371
Denham, Sir John, 300
Dennis, John, 265, 271
Descartes, René, 330
Description of a City Shower, A (Swift), 230
Description of the Morning, A (Swift), 230
Deserted Village, The (Goldsmith), 8, 17; dedication of, 21–22; literal reading of, 22–23; poetic conventions in, 26–28; poetic self within, 23–26; rhetorical structure of, 3–4, 6, 7; sentimental aspect of, 4; sexual theme of, 24–25; similarities between *The Traveller* and, 20–21

Dialogue of Comfort, A (More), 167, 170
Dialogues (Rousseau), 323, 327–28
Dialogues Concerning Heresies (More), 167
Dichtung und Wahrheit (Goethe), 325, 327, 331
Dingley, William, 264
"Disabled Debauchee" (Rochester), 107–08, 109, 110, 111, 112
Dobell, Bertram, 215
Doctor Faustus (Marlowe), 178
Dodsley, Robert, 11
Don Juan (Byron), 33, 238
Don Quixote (Cervantes), 176
Dorimant (Etherege), 208
"Double Vision of Michael Robartes, The" (Yeats), 152, 156–57, 158
Downs, Captain, 104
Dryden, John, 264, 274, 300, 310, 341; on comedy, 208, 210; couplet form of, 230, 231; as critic, 265, 267, 271, 272; Earl of Rochester and, 103–04, 113; eighteenth-century allusions and, 294, 302, 303–04
Du Bellay, Joachim, 179
Dunciad, The (Pope), 27, 242, 302, 353
Dyscolus (Menander), 198

East Coker (Eliot), 71
Edwards, Philip, 179
"Ego Dominus Tuus" (Yeats), 153, 154–55
Ehrenpreis, Irvin, 298
Elder Brother, The (Fletcher), 294
Elegiac couplets, 231
Elegy (Gray), 7, 23, 25
Eliot, T. S., 71, 230, 298, 300, 301, 353
Elizabeth I, Queen of England, 186
Elizabethan period: drama in, 177–79; Spenser on, 86, 87, 90–91
Eloquent I, The (Webber), 218
Emma (Austen), 377, 380
English Autobiography (Shumaker), 312–20
English comedy, 207
Enlightenment, 329, 332
Ennius, 302
Epicoene (Jonson), 206
Epidicus (Plautus), 199
Epilogue to the Satires (Pope), 299
Epistles (Horace), 235

Epistle to a Lady (Swift), 237
Epistle to Augustus (Pope), 242
Epistle to Bathurst (Pope), 304–05, 308
Epistle to Dr. Arbuthnot, An (Pope), 233, 242, 250, 255, 302, 304, 309, 348
Erasmus, Desiderius, 166, 167, 177
Eros myth, 295–96
Essay on the Origin of Languages (Rousseau), 302
Essays (Montaigne), 321
Essays on Wit (Addison), 264
Essex, Robert Devereux, Earl of, 338–39
Etherege, Sir George, 112, 115, 207–10, 287
Euripides, 175
Eversole, Richard, 3
Every Man in his Humor (Jonson), 204–06
"Expostulation and Reply" (Wordsworth), 124

Fables (Aesop), 85
Faerie Queene (Spenser), 33, 95, 134
Father image, 303–04
Felton, Dr., 270
Filosofia Nova (Stendhal), 372
Fischer, John Irwin, 250, 251, 255
"Fisherman, The" (Yeats), 152–53
Fleetwood, Charles, 339–40
Fletcher, John, 294
Fontenelle, 330
France, 16
Franklin, Benjamin, 320, 324, 327, 330
Fratricide, 303
French Revolution, 311
Freudian school, 303, 344
Friedman, Arthur, 3
Friend, The (Wordsworth), 139
Frogs, The (Aristophanes), 175
Frye, Northrop, 204, 284
Furniture of a Woman's Mind (Swift), 236
Fuseli, Henry, 311

Garden, The (Marvell), 231
Garden and the City, The (Mack), 5, 304
Garrick, David, 339–40
Garrick, Peter, 339–40
Gay, John, 248–51
Generall Historie of the Turkes (Knolles), 339–40
Genesis (Bible), 43, 71, 72
Geology, 330

Georgics (Virgil), 230
Giannone, Pietro, 300
Gibbon, Edward, 300, 320, 323, 325, 326, 327–28, 330, 332
Giffard, Mr., 103
Goethe, Johann Wolfgang von, 320, 325, 327, 331
Goldsmith, Henry, 8, 11–13, 16, 17, 18
Goldsmith, Oliver, 3–30; autobiographical reading of poetry of, 4–5, 6; dedication of poems of, 10–12, 19, 21–22; economic views of, 14; Johnson and, 18–19; literal reading of *Deserted Village,* 22–23; poetic self within *Deserted Village,* 23–26; presence in *The Traveller,* 12–18; reception to *The Traveller,* 19–20; rhetoric attacked by, 9–10; rhetorical structure in poems of, 3–4, 6, 7; self-dramatization of, 19; sources of information about, 7–9
Golias, 231
Gondibert (Davenant), 108
Gonne, Maud, 144, 150, 151, 152
Good, Thomas, 225
Gore, John, 350
Gosson, Stephen, 177
Gothic novels, 311
"Go—triumph securely" (Byron), 350–62
Gray, Thomas, 6–7, 23, 25, 27–28
Greek literature: Augustan poets and, 27; Congreve's knowledge of, 283; request for applause in comedy of, 198
Greene, Donald, 322
Greene, Robert, 177
Greene, Thomas, 97
Gregory, Lady, 145
Gregory, Robert, 143, 147, 149, 153, 158
Grosart, Alexander, 214–15
Grotesque, 306
Gulliver's Travels (Swift), 236, 246, 256
Gusdorf, George, 328
Gwynn, Nell, 107

Hamlet (Shakespeare), 200; allusion in, 287–90; Congreve's allusions to, 293; skepticism of theater in, 188–91
Handel, George Frideric, 299
Hanford, James Holly, 39–40
Harding, John, 257–58

Hardy, Lady Anne, 350
Hartman, Geoffrey, 123, 137, 303
Hawkins, Sir John, 340
Hazlitt, William, 287
Heautontinorumenos (Terence), 200
Hecyra (Terence), 200
Henrietta Maria, Queen of England, 117
Henry IV, Part I (Shakespeare), 185–86
Henry VIII, King of England, 166, 168, 170
Henry Brulard (Stendhal), 371, 372
Hero, artist as, 175–76
Heroic poetry, 271–72
Hesiod, 175
Hexameter, 231
Higham, Charles, 215
Hind and the Panther, The (Dryden), 300, 353
Historia Poetarum et Poematum (Leyser), 232
History of the Council of Trent (Sarpi), 300
History of the Rebellion (Clarendon), 300
Hodgart, Matthew, 342
Holland, Norman, 285
Homer, 97, 235, 270, 275; autobiographical aspects of works, 31, 32–33; Milton and, 43, 44, 47, 49–50, 270, 275; narrator's role in poetry of, 35–38
Homonyms, 239
Hopkins, Gerard Manley, 235
Hopkins, John, 266
Hopkins, Robert H., 4, 14–16, 18–19
Hopton, Susanna, 225
Horace, 175, 264; Congreve and, 292–94; Earl of Rochester and, 104, 106; on playwriting, 198; Swift's style and, 234, 235
Howard, Lady Francis, 338–40
Hudibras (Butler), 105
Hugh Selwyn Mauberley (Pound), 353
Humanism: conception of poets and poetry in, 179–82; Elizabethan drama and, 177–79
Humble Petition of Frances Harris, The (Swift), 239
Hume, Robert D., 245–46, 243, 247, 330
Huysmann (painter), 116

Idler, The, 342
Iliad (Homer), 32–33, 34, 35–36, 275

Imitation: in *Paradise Lost,* 51, 52; repetition and, 299
"Imperfect Enjoyment, The" (Rochester), 111–13
Impersonation, 85
Individualism, 328
"In Memory of Major Robert Gregory" (Yeats), 144–47, 149, 153, 158
In the Seven Woods (Yeats), 144
Irene: A Tragedy (Johnson), 337, 339, 340–41
Irony: comedy and, 284; repetition and, 299–300; sentimentalism and, 6; Swift's use of, 254
Irving, Washington, 4–5

Jaarsma, R. J., 4
Jacobean drama, 177
James I, King of England, 339
James, Henry, 5
Jefferson, Thomas, 257
Johnson, Lionel, 145, 158
Johnson, Maurice, 247, 251
Johnson, Samuel, 3, 308; conclusion to *The Traveller* and, 18–19, 27; *Irene: A Tragedy,* 337–46; *Life of Savage,* 10; on *Deserted Village,* 20–21; on Swift, 235
Johnston, Kenneth, 137, 138
Joinville, Jean de, 323
Jones, Gareth, 246–47, 250
Jonson, Ben, 104, 210, 291, 309; *The Alchemist,* 291, 306–08; author's agent device in, 204–07; as playwright, 176, 177, 178
Journal (Stendhal), 372
Journal of a Modern Lady (Swift), 236
Jowett, Benjamin, 226
Joyce, James, 195, 257
Julius Caesar (Shakespeare), 179

Kant, Immanuel, 332
Keats, John, 48, 268, 358
Keener, Frederick M., 19–20
Kierkegaard, Soren, 305
Ker, Robert, 338–39
King Lear (Shakespeare), 176, 289–91, 294
Knolles, Richard, 339–40
Knowles, Dom David, 165
Knox, Bernard, 204
Kyd, Thomas, 177

Lady's Dressing Room (Swift), 236
Lamb, Lady Caroline, 352, 359
Lamb, Charles, 285
Lamb, William, 352
Lamy, Bernard, 302
La Rochefoucauld, Duc François de, 247, 248, 251
Latimer, Hugh, 164
Latin verse, 231, 232
Lawrence, D. H., 380
Leavis, F. R., 376
Le Bossu, 271, 272
Leibnitz, Gottfried Wilhelm, Baron von, 330
Lemprière, John, 295
Leutze, Emanuel, 258
Levi-Strauss, Claude, 330
Leyser, Polycarp, 232
Libretti, operatic, 299
Lien Chi Altangi, 13
Life and Genuine Character of Dean Swift, The (Swift), 237, 247
Life of George Brummell (Jesse), 350
Life of More (Roper), 163, 165–66
Life of Savage (Johnson), 10
Lincoln, Abraham, 257
Lines Written near Richmond (Wordsworth), 129
Long couplet, 233
Longinus, 243, 271
Longhi, Pietro, 148
Louis IX, King of France, 323
Louis XIV, King of France, 106–11
"Love and Wine" (Rochester), 110
Love for Love (Congreve), 283–96
Lovelance papers, 350
Love's Labor's Lost (Shakespeare), 184–85
Love-war metaphor, 106–11
Lucan, 309
Lucilius, 104
Lucretius, 310
Luther, Martin, 163
Lycidas (Milton), 40
Lyrical Ballads (Wordsworth), 121, 125–33

Macaulay, Thomas Babington, 340
Macbeth (Shakespeare), 191–92
Macclesfield, Earl of, 338
MacFleknoe (Dryden), 302

Mack, Maynard, 5–6, 189, 297, 298–99, 304, 391–94
Mahomet the Conqueror: or All for Empire (Dryden), 341
Maine, Duchess du, 323
Mann, David, 308
Man of Mode, The (Etherege), 114–15, 207
Map, Walter, 231
Margoliouth, H. M., 225
Marks, Carol, 218
Marlowe, Christopher, 178
Marmontel, 326, 327
Marriage of Heaven and Hell (Blake), 348
Marston, John, 104
Martz, Louis L., 86, 214
Marvell, Andrew, 146, 231
Marxist criticism, 349
Mary, Queen of Scots, 71
Mary the Cook Maid's Letter to Dr. Sheridan (Swift), 239
Masaccio, 71
Masters, John, 351
Matthews, William, 328
Medieval literature, 175, 195
"Meditations" (Traherne), 213–28
Melbourne, Lady, 351, 352
Memoirs, 323
Memoirs (Joinville), 323
Memoirs (de Staal), 322–23
Memoirs of Jacques Casanova de Seingalt, 321–22, 327
Memoirs of My Life (Gibbon), 325, 327–28
Menaechmi (Plautus), 200–01
Menander, 178, 198
Meninas, Las (Velásquez), 176, 185
Mercator (Plautus), 199
Mesmer, Friedrich Anton, 332
Metaphor, 231, 308
Meter, 231
Methodists, 9
Meyer, Herman, 298
Michael (Wordsworth), 125
Michelangelo, 71, 177
Michael Robartes and the Dancer (Yeats), 143
Middle Ages, 231
Midsummer Night's Dream, A (Shakespeare), 155, 186–88, 200–01
Milton, John, 232, 300; analogy between

God's creation and, 52–53; attitudes toward creation of, 51–69; autobiographical projection into *Paradise Lost,* 31–32; cause of liberty in, 39–40; deliverance theme of, 40–50; Eve as model of creation for, 59–65; Expulsion theme of, 71–84; religious beliefs of, 38–39; role of narrator in, 35–38, 44, 49–50; satanic model in creation of, 54–57; sense of agency of, 57–59

Miscellaneous Observations on the Tragedy of Macbeth (Johnson), 344

Misères de la guerre (Callat), 108

Modest Proposal, A (Swift), 256

Molière, 197, 235

Montagu, 111

Montaigne, Michel Eyquem, 321, 323, 326

Montesquieu, Baron de la Brède et de, 330

More, Sir Thomas, 163–74

Morton, Cardinal, 167

Moses, 43

Muhammed II, Sultan of Turkey, 340–41

"Muse of Satire, The" (Mack), 5–6

My Secret Life (Harris), 322

Mystery cycles, 177

Nashe, Thomas, 98

New Comedy: request for applause in, 198; romance theme in, 204

New Criticism, 349

New Science (Vico), 300

Newton, Sir Isaac, 258

Nietzsche, Friedrich Wilhelm, 302

Nightmare, The (Fuseli), 311

Obscenity, 105, 106

Ode on Intimations of Immortality (Wordsworth), 130

"Ode to a Nightingale" (Keats), 48

Ode to the Athenian Society (Swift), 229

Odyssey (Homer), 47; *Paradise Lost* and, 47, 49–50; narrator's role in, 35–38, 44; presence of Homer in, 32–33

Ong, Walter, 98–99, 100

On Poetry: A Rapsody (Swift), 229, 238, 242

On Temple's Illness (Swift), 229

"On This Day I Complete My Thirty-Sixth Year" (Byron), 347

Operatic libretti, 299

Orlando Furioso (Ariosto), 368

Overbury, Sir Thomas, 338–39

Ovid, 109, 113, 164, 231

Owl and the Nightingale, The, 358

Painting, 71

Palladian architecture, 301

Panegyric, A (Swift), 232

Paradise Lost (Milton), 300; Addison's commentaries on, 263–81; analogy between God's and Milton's creation in, 52–53; attitudes toward creation in, 51–69; autobiographical projection into, 31–32, 39; deliverance theme in, 40–50; dialogue with omniscience in, 31–50; Eve as model of creation in, 59–65; expulsion theme in, 71–84; fiction in, 273–74; narrator's role in, 35–38, 44, 49–50; popularity of, 266; satanic model in creation in, 54–57; sense of agency in, 57–59; structure of imitation in, 51–52

Paradise Regain'd (Milton), 33, 40

Parody, 229

Parricide, 303

Parsons, Robert, 115

Partridge, John, 257

Pastoral Dialogue (Swift), 239

Patronage system, 180–81, 182

Pensées, Filosofia Nova (Stendhal), 366

Pericles (Shakespeare), 179

Personification, 85

Perspective, 209

Peter, Saint, 169

Petrarch, 108, 176, 177

Petronius, 148

Phaedrus (Plato), 294–95

"Phases of the Moon, The" (Yeats), 152, 153–56

Philosophy of the Enlightenment (Cassirer), 329

Pindar, 305

Plato, 79, 294–95

Plautus, 178, 198, 199, 200–01, 202

Play-within-a-play, 176, 182–84; *1 Henry IV,* 185–86; *Hamlet,* 189–91; *Love's Labor's Lost,* 184–86; *Macbeth,*

Play-within-a-play (*continued*)
191–92; *The Tempest*, 191–95
Pleasure of the Imagination, The (Addison), 264, 265
Poems of Felicity (Traherne), 221
Poetical Works of Thomas Traherne, The, 215
Poetics of Quotation in the European Novel (Meyer), 298
Polite Conversation (Swift), 235
Political satire, 11
Political science, 330
Political writings, 311
Pollexfen, George, 145, 158
Pope, Alexander, 104, 117, 230, 231, 235, 301, 348; allusion in, 297, 298–99, 302–05, 339; biographical information reflected in writings of, 5–6, 19–20, 255; Goldsmith and, 8, 14, 27; repetition in, 304–05, 308–09; Swift and, 233–34, 242, 247, 248–51
Postelthwayt, Malachy, 14
"Poverty" (Traherne), 221
Prelude, The (Wordsworth), 33, 123, 124–28, 130, 131, 132, 136, 137, 138, 139
"Prayer on Going into My House, A" (Yeats), 153
Preaching, 9
Pre-Romanticism, 6
Price, Martin, 236
Primitivism, 305
Principles of Literary Criticism (Richards), 298
Prior, Sir James, 4
"Privilêges du 10 avril 1840" (Stendhal), 367
Procrustes, 3
Prodigal Father parable, 303
Progress, 301
Progress of Love, The (Swift), 240
Progress of Marriage, The (Swift), 240
Progress of Poesy, The (Gray), 27–28
Promenades dans Rome (Stendhal), 371
Prosopopoia, or Mother Hubberds Tale (Spenser), 85–102
Protestants, 38, 327
Proverbs (Bible), 357
Proverbs, 306, 308–09
Psalm 72, 171
Psalm 107, 73–76

Psalm 111, 76
Pseudo-aphorisms, 306, 308
Public Ledger, The, 8
Puritans, 105, 106, 177
Puttenham, George, 85, 86, 231

Quintana, Ricardo, 3
Quintilian, 3, 9

Rabelais, François, 177
Racine, Jean, 235
Rainbow, The (Lawrence), 380
"Ramble in St. James's Park, A" (Rochester), 112–13
Rambler, The, 341, 342
Rape of the Lock, The (Pope), 339
Rawson, Claude, 230
Recurrence, 299–300
Reflux, 306
Religio Laici (Dryden), 300
Renaissance: artistic self-consciousness in, 176; drama in, 176, 194, 195; Expulsion theme in, 71; individualism in, 328; perspectives of scenery in, 209; repetition in, 298
Repetition, 298, 304–11
Responsibilities (Yeats), 143, 144, 150, 152
Restoration, 209
Reveries (Rousseau), 330–31
Rey, Marc-Michel, 326
Reynolds, E. E., 163
Reynolds, Sir Joshua, 20, 21, 22
Rhetoric: allusion and, 305–06; Goldsmith's attack on, 9–10; in Goldsmith's *Deserted Village*, 3–4, 6, 7; sentimentalism and, 6
Rhetoric (Aristotle), 4, 231
Rhyme, 231
Rick, Richard, 167
Richards, I. A., 298
Richard III (More), 166
Richard III (Shakespeare), 178–79
Richardson, Samuel, 310–11
Righter, Anne, 191
River, Earl of, 338
Rochester, John Wilmot, Earl of, 103–21, 208
Rochester, Dowager Lady, 117, 118
Rochester, Lady, 116
Roland, Madame, 326

Roman Catholicism, 327

Romance, 202, 204

Roman comedy: authorial intervention in, 200–01; prologues in, 199–200; request for applause in, 197, 198–99

Roman Forgeries (Traherne), 215

Roman literature, 283

Romant (Chaucer), 85

Romantic comedy, 284–85

Romantic Paradox (Clark), 132

Romantics, 296, 311

Romant of the Rose, 85

Roper, Margaret, 163–64, 168, 169–72

Roper, William, 163, 165

Roscommon, Wentworth Dillon, 232, 265

Rose et le Vert, Le (Stendhal), 368

Rousseau, Jean-Jacques, 302; autobiography of, 320, 323, 324, 326, 327–28, 332; on historic truth, 30–31

Ruines of Time, The (Spenser), 91

Said, Edward W., 246–47, 258

Salgado, Gamini, 293

Salmasius, 39

Samson Agonistes (Milton), 40

Sarpi, Paolo, 300

Satire: Augustan mode of, 104; comedy and, 284; Earl of Rochester and, 103–21; historical and political circumstances and, 347; romance and, 204; travesty as device in, 105–06

Satire (Horace), 234

"Satyr against Reason and Mankind" (Rochester), 110

Savage, Richard, 10, 12, 337–46

Savile, Henry, 114

Scarronides (Cotton), 105

"Scepter Lampoon, The" (Rochester), 106–11

Schakel, Peter, 256

Schmeller, Andreas, 231

Schoeck, R. J., 165

Schoenmann, Lilli, 331

Scott, John, 23–24

Scouten, Arthur H., 245–46, 247, 253

Scriblerians, 300, 301–02

Seasonable Advice (Swift), 258

Second Defense of the English People (Milton), 39–40

"Second Prologue to the 'Empress of Morocco' " (Rochester), 109

Secularization, 328–29

Segal, Erich, 199

Select Meditations (Traherne), 216–19, 223–24

Self-portraits, 321, 323–24

Sentimentalism, 6

Sentimental Journey, A (Sterne), 302–04

Shakespeare, William, 146, 155, 175–96, 276, 302; allusion in, 287–91, 292–93; authorial intervention in plays of, 200–01; comic agents in *The Tempest,* 203–05; conception of poetry in *Sonnets,* 179–82; irony used by, 155; play-within-the-play device used by, 182–95

Shapiro, Karl, 292

Shapiro, Michael, 207

Shelley, Percy Bysshe, 105, 215

"Shepherd and Goatherd" (Yeats), 145, 146

Short couplet, 231–33

Shumaker, Wayne, 319–20, 329

Sidney, Sir Philip, 95, 177, 178, 179, 186, 188

Simon, Richard, 300

Sistine Chapel, 71

Slepian, Barry, 253–55

Smith, Constance Spencer, 355

Socrates, 294–95

"Solitude" (Traherne), 221

Somers, Lord, 269

Sonnets (Shakespeare), 179–82

Sororicide, 303

Souvenirs d'Egotisme (Stendhal), 366–67, 368

Spanish Friar, The (Dryden), 274–75

Spectator (Addison), 237, 263–81

Spenser, Edmund, 31, 33, 58, 85–102, 134, 179

Staal Delaunay, Madame de, 322–23

Steeves, Edna Leske, 301–02

Steele, Richard, 210, 341

Stendhal, 365–72

Stendhal, Pauline, 365, 366, 367

Sterne, Laurence, 302–04

Stevens, Wallace, 195

Storm, Leo F., 4

Structuralism, 330

Suetonius, 33

Summers Last Will and Testament (Nash), 98

Swift, Jonathan, 113, 300, 330; affective response to, 256–57; antecedents to short couplets of, 231–33; biographical information in, 255–56; experiments with varied verse forms by, 239–41; inventoried objects and words in, 235–39; multiplication of identities in *Verses* of, 247–48; personal identity questions in, 245–62; Pope's imitation of, 233–34; rhetoric and poems of, 229–44

Synge, John, 145, 158

Tale of a Tub (Butler), 231, 256, 302

Taming of the Shrew, The (Shakespeare), 182–84, 185

Tasso, Torquato, 31, 58, 368

Tempest, The (Shakespeare), 192–95, 203–05, 289–90

Temple, Sir William, 229, 255

Terence, 178, 198, 200–01, 205

Thackeray, William Makepeace, 5

Theocritus, 294

Third Satire of the Second Book (Horace), 292–94

Thomson, James, 215

"Thought from Propertius, A" (Yeats), 150

"Timon" (Rochester), 109

Timon of Athens (Shakespeare), 179

To Congreve (Swift), 229

To His Coy Mistress (Marvell), 231

Tonson, Jacob (the elder), 266, 269

"To the Cuckoo" (Wordsworth), 127

To The Lighthouse (Woolf), 375–89

Tower, The (Yeats), 143, 147

Tracy, Clarence, 338

Tragedy of Sir Thomas Overbury (Savage), 337, 338–39, 341

Traherne, Thomas, 213–28; autobiographical passages in, 213, 219–23; biographical data on, 213–14; discovery of manuscript of, 214–15; friends identified in works of, 224–25; intimacy with deity by, 225–26

Traherne, Philip, 221, 225

Traherne, Philip, 221

Traveller, The (Goldsmith), 4–7, 10–20, 26; examination of Goldsmith's presence in, 12–18; Johnson and conclusion to, 18–19; reception of, 19–20; similarities between *The Deserted Village* and, 20–21

Travesty in satire, 105–06

Trinummus (Plautus), 198

Tristram Shandy (Sterne), 298, 299, 302

Troilus and Cressida (Shakespeare), 181

Truculentus (Plautus), 202

Truth, in autobiography, 330–31

Turpio, Lucius Ambivius, 200

Twenty-Third Idyl (Theocritus), 294

Uphaus, Robert W., 246–47

"Upon a Bee Entomb'd in Amber" (Dingley), 264

"Upon a Dying Lady (Yeats), 148–50, 153

Utopia (More), 166, 167

Vagantes, 231

Vanbrugh, Sir John, 116

Van Voris, W. H., 289–90, 294

Vaughan, Henry, 214–15

Vaughan, Susan, 351, 355

Ventriloquism, 306

Verb metaphor, 308

Verses on the Death of Dr. Swift (Swift), 229, 241, 245–62

Verses Wrote in a Lady's Ivory Table Book (Swift), 234, 235, 243

Vicar of Wakefield, The (Goldsmith), 5

Vico, Giovanni Battista, 300, 302, 305

Vie de Henry Brulard (Stendahl), 366, 368

Virgil, 97, 175, 230, 264; allusion in literature and, 302, 310; autobiographical information in writings of, 31; "I sing" beginning of, 33, 58; Milton and, 41, 43, 47, 49, 270; narrator's role of, 35, 36

Vision, A (Yeats), 145, 147, 153

Visionary allusions of Romantics, 311

Visionary poetry of Wordsworth, 123–41

Volpone (Jonson), 178, 206

Voltaire, François Marie, 330

W. H. (Shakespeare's patron), 180

Wade, Gladys, 225

Wain, John, 287

Waingrow, Marshall, 249, 251

Walpole, Robert, 253
War-love metaphor, 106–11
Wasteland, The (Eliot), 353
Waugh, Evelyn, 118
Way of the World, The (Congreve), 283–85, 306–08
Webber, Joan, 218–19
Webster, Francis Wedderburn, 349–50, 356, 359
Wellington, Duke of, 350
"When We Two Parted" (Byron), 350–62
Whigs, 27
Whiteheall, Robert, 117
Whitshed, Lord Chief Justice, 258
Wilde Swans at Coole, The (Yeats), 143–60
William III, King of England, 308
Williams, Aubrey, 27
Wilmot, Lord, 117, 118

Wood, Anthony, 213, 215
Woolf, Virginia, 303, 375–89
Wordsworth, Dorothy, 129, 134
Wordsworth, William, 20, 33, 123–41, 149
"World of *Hamlet,* The" (Mack), 189
Wright, Thomas, 231
Wycherley, William, 112, 114–15, 287

"Yarrow Unvisited" (Wordsworth), 127
Yeats, William Butler, 257; conception of poetic form by, 147–49; life and art in *The Wild Swans at Coole,* 143–60; struggles of artist reflected, 152–56; use of self in poems of, 147, 149–52

Zeugma, 231, 305
Zoology, 330